CQ Guide to Current American Government

2007 FALL

CQ Guide to Current American Government

2 0 0 7   F A L L

CQ PRESS

A Division of Congressional Quarterly Inc. Washington, D.C.

SELECTIONS FROM *CQ WEEKLY*

Congressional Quarterly Inc.

Congressional Quarterly Inc., a publishing and information services company, is the recognized national leader in political journalism. CQ Inc. serves clients in the fields of business, government, news and education with complete, timely and nonpartisan information on Congress, politics and national issues. CQ Press is a division of Congressional Quarterly Inc. The Library Reference imprint of CQ Press publishes this work and hundreds of others on the institutions, processes and policies of government to serve the needs of librarians, researchers, students, scholars and interested citizens. Other titles include *Guide to the Presidency, Guide to Congress, Guide to the U.S. Supreme Court, Guide to U.S. Elections* and *Politics in America.* CQ Press's American Government A to Z series is a reference collection that provides essential information about the U.S. Constitution, Congress, the presidency, the Supreme Court and the electoral process. *Congress and the Nation,* a record of government for each presidential term, is published every four years. CQ Press also publishes *CQ Researcher,* a weekly print periodical and online reference resource covering today's most debated social and political issues. Visit www.cqpress.com to learn more about these and other publications of CQ Press.

CQ Press
1255 22nd Street, NW, Suite 400
Washington, DC 20037

Phone: 202-729-1900; toll-free, 1-866-4CQ-PRESS (1-866-427-7737)

Web: www.cqpress.com

Cover photo credits: CQ/Scott J. Ferrell (Rep. Charles Rangel and Atlanta mayor Shirley Franklin; House Speaker Nancy Pelosi); U.S. Department of Defense (USS *John C. Stennis*)
Cover design: Auburn Associates, Inc.

♾ The paper used in this publication exceeds the requirements of the American National Standard for Information Sciences—Permanence of Paper for Printed Library Materials, ANSI Z39.48-1992.

Printed and bound in the United States of America
11 10 09 08 07   1 2 3 4 5

ISBN 978-0-87289-365-8
ISSN 0196-612-X

Contents

Introduction

Guide to Current American Government is a collection of articles from *CQ Weekly,* a trusted source for in-depth, nonpartisan reporting on and analyses of congressional action, presidential activities, policy debates and other news and developments in Washington, D.C. *CQ Weekly* broadened its editorial focus in January 2005 to cover the intersection of government and commerce more closely. The articles, several of which reflect this expanded focus, have been selected to complement introductory American government texts with up-to-date examinations of current issues and controversies. They are divided into four sections: Foundations of American Government, Political Participation, Government Institutions, and Politics and Public Policy.

Foundations of American Government. This section discusses issues and events that involve interpretation of the U.S. Constitution, foundational principles such as federalism and democracy, and political ideologies and political culture in the United States. In this edition of the *Guide,* the first article profiles Gerald Ford and his role as successor to President Richard Nixon in the aftermath of Watergate. The articles that follow assess innovative antipoverty programs that cities and states have undertaken in partnership with the private sector, the growth in size and influence of the conservative Federalist Society, and efforts by local governments to take the lead in urban initiatives that were once the province of state and federal government.

Political Participation. The articles in this section examine current issues in electoral and party politics, voting behavior and public opinion. Selected for this edition are articles that consider the Democrats' return to lead-ership in both houses of Congress in the 2006 midterm elections. Also discussed are the AFL-CIO's attempts to regain lost membership and to reassert its political influence now that Democrats are back in power, comedian Al Franken's bid for a Senate seat in Minnesota in 2008, and the new Democratic majority's plans to alleviate the "middle-class squeeze."

Government Institutions. This section sheds light on the inner workings of Congress, the presidency and the federal courts. Included here are articles that focus on new Speaker of the House Nancy Pelosi, the attempts by Democrats to stop President Bush's plan to increase troop levels in Iraq, the credibility of Attorney General Alberto Gonzales following the firings of eight U.S. attorneys in 2006, and the president's increased reliance on executive rule-making authority. Also appearing in this section are articles that explore the push for tort reform by business lobbies, the growing inclination of the Supreme Court to take the side of school administrators in cases pertaining to students' free speech rights, and the wisdom of placing term limits on Supreme Court justices.

Politics and Public Policy. The articles in this section profile major policy issues on the national agenda. This edition features articles that investigate the growing application of death sentencing at the federal level, the emerging influence of centrist Democrats, opposing perspectives on President Bush's strategy toward Iran, the changing tactics of gun control advocates in the aftermath of the Virginia Tech shootings, and evidence of inadequate care by the Department of Veteran Affairs for troops returning from Iraq and Afghanistan.

Foundations of American Government

This section covers current issues in American politics that involve the core principles of democracy: individual rights and liberties, the role of government, the limits of federalism, and American political ideologies and political culture. These foundations frame the attitudes, interests and institutions that dictate political choices and outcomes.

The first article in this section explores the remarkable life and career of Gerald Ford, who died on December 26, 2006, at age ninety-three. Ford was a politically moderate man who became the first president in American history to be sworn in without having been elected to the presidency or vice presidency. He is best remembered for his leadership and the unifying role he played during one of the nation's greatest institutional crises, Watergate and its aftermath. Ford's pardon of Nixon, which came on the heels of his ascension to the presidency, provoked considerable controversy at the time, but his mutually respectful relationship with Congress helped smooth the rough edges of the struggle over presidential privilege that had embroiled the executive and legislative branches of government leading up to Nixon's resignation.

Poverty is an issue that has long been overlooked by the federal government on a comprehensive level, but one that briefly attained national prominence in the months following Hurricane Katrina. As the vividness of the hurricane's destruction has faded from the national consciousness, however, the prospects for a grand discussion on poverty have all but disappeared, leaving the conversation to state and local governments, think tanks and policy organizations. The second article details the antipoverty programs that some cities are developing with the hope that these initiatives can later be implemented at the national level.

The third article examines the growing influence of the Federalist Society, a twenty-five-year old organization made up of 40,000 conservative and libertarian lawyers, judges and academics. The Federalist Society does not officially take positions on legislation or nominees—it generally focuses on core ideas instead of specific positions—but its members most certainly do. Less than one percent of lawyers nationwide belong to the organization, but more than one-third of President Bush's circuit court nominees are members, a testament to the society's rapidly emerging role in American politics and policy. This article discusses critics' fear that the Federalist Society seeks to wage "ideological war" against orthodox liberalism.

The last article examines the role that municipal governments play in the crafting of urban initiatives and other public policy. Seizing on the opportunity that the new Democratic majority in Congress represents, the mayors of traditionally Democratic urban areas are asking Washington to not only fund a variety of local initiatives but also to follow the lead of local governments in matters once considered the province of federal or state government. Some experts believe that this could lead to a paradigm shift in the relationship between Congress and local government, which would imply fundamental changes in federal urban policy.

The President That Congress Created

Unique in history, Gerald R. Ford drew on hill friendships to refocus a nation in crisis

Gerald R. Ford Library

President Ford on a train in the Soviet Union enroute to talks with Leonid Brezhnev in November 1974.

From *CQ Weekly,* January 1, 2007.

Gerald Ford frequently said his life's ambition was to be Speaker of the House of Representatives. But because he lived in interesting times, Ford, who died in December 2006 at the age of 93, well surpassed that goal.

He was the country's first appointed president, initially named to replace Spiro T. Agnew as vice president when Agnew resigned amid scandal in 1973. Ten months later, he assumed the presidency when Richard Nixon left office in disgrace on Aug. 9, 1974.

Ford's significance was often overlooked amid all the wreckage of Watergate. He was a good-natured antidote to the Nixon administration, helping to reassure ordinary citizens and a Washington officialdom that had been shaken by the scandal. The 38th president of the United States had spent nearly a quarter-century in Congress — longer than any other president in history, including Lyndon B. Johnson. Ford served nine of those years as House minority leader.

As much as he fought with the Democratic majorities in Congress during his 30 months as president — making frequent use of the veto to block their initiatives — Ford also tried to use his old congressional ties to smooth the relationship between the White House and Capitol Hill, which had suffered greatly under Nixon, even before Watergate. When Ford took office, he reserved several

THE FRESHMAN: In his office at 321 Cannon in January 1949, when he began his quarter-century representing the Grand Rapids area of Michigan in the House.

firm him as vice president in 1973 after Agnew resigned — a process that wasn't spelled out in any great detail in the 25th Amendment and had never been tested. They also made it easier for the government to recover from Watergate.

"He was always a 'congressman's congressman.' That always stood him in good stead with the rest of the members," said Robert H. Michel of Illinois, one of Ford's successors as House Republican leader, who held the job from 1981 to 1994. "He never forgot that Congress was a very important part of the process, and that's because he had served here for so long."

Ford, who represented the counties surrounding Grand Rapids, Mich., his home since toddlerhood, also was a reminder of an earlier time in politics, before partisan differences turned personal and bitter. In his memoir, "A Time to Heal," Ford recalled the backslapping conversation he had with Thomas P. "Tip" O'Neill Jr. of Massachusetts, who was then the House majority leader, as Ford was about to become president. "Christ, Jerry, isn't this a wonderful country?" O'Neill told Ford. "Here we can talk like this and you and I can be friends, and 18 months from now I'll be going around the country kicking your ass in."

O'Neill wasn't the only Democrat who felt warmly toward him, even though Ford was as partisan as anyone in politics; during his last year in Congress, he voted in support of Nixon's positions more often than all but one other Republican. And Democrats weren't shy about taking him on after he became president, resisting his economic plans and fighting his efforts to help Vietnamese refugees as Saigon fell in 1975. But Ford was just too affable and well-liked to have any real enemies.

"He was a person who respected the opinions of others," said Republican Rep. Ralph Regula of Ohio, who

hours each week for private time with members of Congress who wanted to see him. He even went to the Hill to testify about his decision to pardon Nixon — something that would be unthinkable today, given the arm's-length treatment President Bush and his advisers have given Congress when lawmakers try to investigate their actions.

Ford had the bad fortune to become president at a time when Congress was chipping away at the powers of the presidency. That experience shaped the perspective of two of his chiefs of staff, Dick Cheney and Donald H. Rumsfeld, who in recent years have led the Bush administration's fight to swing the balance of power back to the executive branch. The post-Watergate era also changed Ford's own view of Congress, and he bristled at his former colleagues' attempts to take a more active role in foreign affairs.

But those tensions never led him to shut out his former associates. In fact, lawmakers and historians believe Ford's friendships on the Hill made it easier for Congress to con-

came to Congress in 1973, the year Ford was elevated from House minority leader to vice president. "You never heard Jerry say a mean word about anybody."

In hindsight, Ford's presidency also marked another milestone: He came to power just as the Republican Party was starting to swing toward Ronald Reagan's brand of conservatism, the unapologetic devotion to ideology that inspires most of the party's leaders today. Ford was one of the last of the old-guard, pragmatic Republicans to hold power, and he barely survived a primary challenge from Reagan in 1976, which helped set the stage for Reagan's landslide victory four years later.

Ford always considered himself a fiscal conservative, but he was no ideological firebrand. In Congress, he said he was a "moderate in domestic affairs" and a "dyed-in-the-wool internationalist in foreign affairs." And his own choice for vice president after he moved into the White House, Gov. Nelson A. Rockefeller of New York, was an icon of the moderate wing of the GOP — the wing that has nearly disappeared in recent years.

Presidential historian Fred I. Greenstein said Ford "reflected a certain kind of Republican ethos from an earlier time" that endures in a handful of moderates, such as Maine Republican Sens. Olympia J. Snowe and Susan Collins, who represent an endangered minority in their party.

OFF TO CONGRESS

Gerald Rudolph Ford Jr. was given the name of the Michigan paint salesman who adopted him as a young boy after marrying his mother, Dorothy. She had moved to Michigan in 1916 after divorcing her abusive first husband, Leslie Lynch King, after whom Ford had originally been named when he was born in Omaha in 1913. (He is the only person besides Bill Clinton, who was born William Jefferson Blythe III, to use a fundamentally different name as president than the one he was given at birth.)

A University of Michigan football hero and a Yale-educated lawyer, Ford served in the Navy during World War II, after which he returned to Grand Rapids and became prominent in an organization of young Republicans trying to clean out the remnants of an old county political machine. The congressman who represented the area at the time, Bartel J. "Barney" Jonkman, was an isolationist Republican whom Ford considered a

holdover from the old machine. In 1948, Ford told his cohorts that someone ought to mount a challenge. "If you feel that strongly," his friends replied, "why don't you run yourself?"

Ford did — and because Congress was still in session and Jonkman had to stay holed up in Washington, he "had an open field" to campaign throughout the district without any competition, he wrote in his memoir. Ford swept Jonkman out with 62 percent of the vote in the primary, then coasted into Congress at age 36 with 61 percent of the vote in the general election, against Democrat Fred J. Barr. He never got less than 60 percent of the vote in any of his dozen races for re-election.

By his own account, Ford spent a lot of time on the House floor, listening to speeches and learning parliamentary procedures. That's how he met Nixon, who was then a second-term congressman from southern California. Ford also won a seat on the Appropriations Committee, eventually becoming the top Republican on the Defense Subcommittee and, later, the senior Republican on the full panel.

Like all of his House Republican colleagues, Ford kept hoping for GOP gains in the elections. Democrats had controlled both houses of Congress almost continuously since Franklin D. Roosevelt was first elected president, in 1932 — the exceptions being 1947-48, during the Truman administration, and 1953-54, after Dwight D. Eisenhower's 1952 landslide. After the midterm election in 1962, when Republicans gained only two seats in the House, several younger party members decided it was time for new blood in the GOP leadership. In January 1963, they persuaded Ford to run for chairman of the House Republican Conference against the incumbent, 67-year-old Charles Hoeven of Iowa, a World War I veteran who had been in the House for two decades. Ford made the race and edged out Hoeven. One of the "Young Turks" who helped launch Ford's career in the leadership was a 30-year-old freshman Republican from Illinois named Don Rumsfeld.

Two years later, in 1965, the same group decided it was time to challenge the top Republican in the House, Minority Leader Charles Halleck of Indiana, who had been in Congress since 1935. Once again, the insurgents drafted Ford to run, and once again the race was close. But in the end, Ford defeated Halleck, 73-67, in a secret ballot.

Ford always believed he owed his victory in the minority leader race to the votes of the Kansas delegation — a

AP Images

THE DRIVER: As House minority leader Ford earned a reputation as a gentle dealmaker. Here, Ford argues in Congress on April 20, 1965, that a merchant ship shortage is hampering the U.S. war effort in Vietnam.

pawn in the hands of the White House, and 50 percent of the members are puppets who dance when the president pulls the strings," he said in a 1966 speech. He also appeared with Senate Minority Leader Everett M. Dirksen in weekly televised news conferences that Capitol reporters nicknamed "The Ev and Jerry Show."

"Jerry could give a good, rip-roaring speech on the floor on behalf of our principles when he had to," Michel recalled. "I was always proud to say I came up under Jerry Ford's leadership. He was a good model to emulate, and it always served me well."

In his voting record, Ford lived up to his self-description as a fiscal conservative. He voted against the creation of Medicare in 1965 and against three minimum wage increases. He voted for funding cuts to Great Society programs and opposed President John F. Kennedy's 1963 tax cut. Although liberal Democrats later criticized his civil rights record, he did vote for the Civil Rights Act of 1964 and the Voting Rights Act of 1965.

Ford and Johnson never got along well; it is Johnson, in fact, who is credited with one of the most famous put-downs of Ford's intellect — that he appeared to have played too much football without a helmet. But even after his House colleague Nixon won the presidency in 1968, Ford chafed at the stiff-arm treatment Congress received from the White House. Nixon aides, led by chief of staff H.R. Haldeman and domestic policy adviser John Ehrlichman, kept congressional Republicans at a distance. "We would have liked to be helpful, and we were frozen out," Michel recalled.

Ford had been mentioned as a possible running mate for Nixon in 1968, and he was mystified when the No. 2 spot on the ticket went instead to Agnew, who had

bloc he won with the support of a congressman from the western part of the state named Bob Dole. A decade later, Ford picked Dole, a freshman senator, to be his 1976 vice presidential running mate. That campaign boosted Dole's national name recognition and helped pave the way for his nomination for the top of the GOP ticket in 1996.

As minority leader, Ford earned a reputation as a gentle dealmaker — not a calculating strategist like Lyndon B. Johnson but someone who relied on personal appeal to win help from his colleagues. "He looks at you with a sad look in his eye, as if to say, 'Pal, I need you,' " Rep. Edward J. Derwinski, a Chicago-area Republican, said at the time. "Sometimes you go along just because it's to help an old pal."

But Ford was capable of delivering biting political speeches, especially against Johnson's Great Society programs, most of which he opposed. "Congress is now a

The Shortest Tenures

Ten of the 43 presidents served less than one term. The four with shorter tenures than Gerald R. Ford all died in office, as did John F. Kennedy. The rest were vice presidents who ascended to the top job; among them, only Ford was nominated by his party to seek election in his own right.

John Tyler	1,428 days
Andrew Johnson	1,419 days
Chester A. Arthur	1,261 days
John F. Kennedy	1,036 days
Millard Fillmore	968 days
Gerald R. Ford	895 days
Warren G. Harding	881 days
Zachary Taylor	492 days
James A. Garfield	199 days
William Henry Harrison	31 days

SOURCE: CQ / Lindsay Mangum

been an obscure Maryland county executive just a few years earlier. When Nixon first floated Agnew's name at a meeting during the nominating convention in Miami Beach, Ford "let out a loud horse laugh," his longtime congressional chief of staff, Robert T. Hartmann, wrote in a memoir, "Palace Politics."

Ford said his real wish was to become Speaker, anyway. But he watched in frustration as his best chance at achieving that goal slipped away in 1972, when Nixon carried 49 states in his landslide re-election but Republicans managed to gain only 12 seats in the House — leaving the Democrats with a 51-seat margin. Ford and his wife, Betty, agreed that he would run for one last term in 1974 and then announce his retirement from Congress.

UNEXPECTED OPPORTUNITY

Then, in October 1973, the vice presidency opened up. Agnew, who had gotten caught up in a bribery scandal, was forced to resign after pleading no contest to a charge of tax evasion for not reporting the income. Nixon needed to fill the post quickly, without a bruising confirmation battle in Congress, and he asked each Republican in Congress to suggest three names. Michel and other GOP leaders said Ford was their choice.

"I wrote back and told him my three suggestions were, No. 1, Jerry Ford; No. 2, Jerry Ford; and No. 3, Jerry Ford," Regula recalled. "He was the ideal choice.

He had experience in the Congress. He looked the part. He had established himself as a Republican leader. And he had a real knack for working across the aisle."

Ford was far from everyone's first choice. Among all Republican leaders, he finished far back in the pack, behind Rockefeller and Reagan, followed by Treasury Secretary John B. Connally. Nixon himself preferred Connally, a former Texas governor who had become a Republican only in 1973; Nixon intended to endorse him for president in 1976. But Democratic leaders told Nixon that Connally would have too much trouble getting confirmed by Congress. Ford, they said, would have a much easier time. And, as Nixon wrote later, they were the ones who would have to approve the nomination.

So on Oct. 12, 1973, at a ceremony in the East Room of the White House, Nixon made it official. "He is a man who, if the responsibilities of the great office I hold should fall upon him, as has been the case with eight vice presidents in our history, we could all say the leadership of America is in good hands," the president said of Ford.

That was no minor consideration. Congress was in the thick of hearings about the Watergate scandal, and Nixon was increasingly looking like a target. Already, talk of impeachment or resignation was in the air. So when the Senate Rules Committee and House Judiciary Committee began Ford's confirmation hearings in November 1973 (both chambers, under the 25th Amendment's arrangement for unelected vice presidents, had a vote on confirmation), lawmakers questioned him not just as a vice presidential candidate but as a possible president.

How did he feel about executive privilege, they asked, given that Nixon was fighting at the time to withhold the Watergate tapes from Congress? Ford said that no president had "unlimited" executive privilege, and that when there were documents that could prove a president's guilt or innocence of criminal behavior, "they should be made available." But he also insisted, "I don't think Congress, or the public generally, has any right to all personal and confidential conversations and documents of the president."

Ford answered questions about his personal finances, separation of powers, foreign affairs and the independence of the Watergate prosecutor. He stressed that his 25 years in Congress would be his greatest asset as vice president because his experience would enable him to serve as "a ready conciliator and calm communicator between the White House and Capitol Hill." That was "the greatest single need of our country today," he said, because much of the nation was "beginning to worry about our national government becoming seriously weakened by partisan division."

Ford briefly encountered objections from liberal Democrats on the House Judiciary Committee, among them John Conyers Jr. of Michigan, who didn't think a president who faced possible impeachment should be able to nominate a potential successor. Others simply voted against Ford because they objected to his politics. "I said, 'Jerry Ford is a nice man, but his views are opposed to those of the people in my district,' " recalled Democratic former Rep. Robert F. Drinan of Massachusetts, who served on the Judiciary Committee during the hearings.

But Democratic leaders reasoned that Nixon had a right to choose someone who shared his political views. On Nov. 27, the Senate approved the nomination, 92-3, and on Dec. 6, the House did as well, 387-35. Rep. George E. Danielson, D-Calif., told Ford, "I'm thinking you're going to be president within a year."

It took less time than that. On Aug. 9, 1974, Nixon resigned in the face of certain impeachment in the House and removal from office by the Senate. Ford, the affable "congressman's congressman" who was installed as vice president by his former colleagues, was sworn in as the first president in American history who hadn't been elected by the public.

GERALD RUDOLPH FORD JR.

Born: July 14, 1913, in Omaha

Died: Dec. 26, 2006, in Rancho Mirage, California

Family: Married Elizabeth "Betty" Bloomer Warren on Oct. 15, 1948; sons Michael Gerald, John Gardner and Steven Meigs; daughter Susan Elizabeth

Religion: Episcopalian

Education: U. of Michigan, B.A. 1935; Yale U., L.L.B. 1941

Military Service: Navy, 1942-46 (discharged as lieutenant commander); Naval reserve, 1946-63

House: Elected in 1948 with 61 percent of the vote in Michigan's 5th District (Grand Rapids area); re-elected 12 times with at least 60 percent; chairman of the GOP Conference, 1963-64; minority leader, 1965-73

Vice President: Nominated by President Richard Nixon to succeed Spiro T. Agnew, Oct. 12, 1973; confirmed by the Senate, 92-3, Nov. 27; confirmed by the House, 387-35 (Ford voting "present"), and sworn in as the 40th vice president, Dec. 6

President: Inaugurated the 38th president upon Nixon's resignation, Aug. 9, 1974; defeated by Jimmy Carter for election as president on Nov. 2, 1976, taking 48 percent of the popular vote and 240 electoral votes

THE BIGGEST CHALLENGE

At first, Ford, still accustomed to a congressional-size office, was determined to be his own chief of staff. But he soon became overwhelmed and decided he had to delegate the job. In September, he brought in Rumsfeld, his former congressional colleague and a member of his transition team, to run the show.

Rumsfeld, in turn, hired as his chief deputy a longtime aide named Dick Cheney — a "bright young political scientist," Ford recalled in his memoirs, who could easily fill in for Rumsfeld if he had to. In November 1975, Ford moved Rumsfeld over to become Defense secretary after firing James R. Schlesinger, who had clashed with others in the administration and had criticized members of Congress for wanting to hold down defense spending. Cheney became White House chief of staff.

Despite the unusual circumstances surrounding how he got the job, Ford began his presidency with high approval ratings. But they plummeted less than a month later after Ford announced the one decision that most Americans still remember about his presidency: On Sept. 8, 1974, he granted "a full, free and absolute pardon onto Richard Nixon for all offenses against the United States" in the Watergate cover-up.

Immediately, many Americans — and many of his former colleagues in Congress as well — wondered whether Ford had cut a deal in advance with Nixon. Not so, Ford insisted. He just couldn't do his job if he had to spend several hours every day dealing with questions about how a criminal prosecution of Nixon might proceed — one that could take at least two years to reach a conclusion, maybe as many as six. "I had to get the

A Brief but Busy Term in the White House

Gerald R. Ford was president for only two and a half years, but he faced some formidable domestic and international challenges: The former Michigan congressman had to deal with fallout from Watergate, a turbulent economy and the fall of South Vietnam.

Nixon pardon

The decision, which Ford said was in the best interest of the country, would shadow his presidency and doom his 1976 campaign.

Whip Inflation Now

Ford's initial response to the troubled economy, the WIN buttons, became an emblem of his economic approach. He and Congress cut taxes and tried to control spending — for instance, he refused to bail out New York from its fiscal crisis in 1975.

Vietnam withdrawal

South Vietnam collapsed and the last U.S. personnel were withdrawn from Saigon in 1975.

Mayaguez incident

Ford sent Marines to rescue a merchant ship that had been seized by Cambodian forces. (*Left*, Ford meets with the National Security Council.)

Assassination attempts

Squeaky Fromme and Sara Jane Moore both pointed guns at Ford, but neither succeeded, and both went to prison for life. (*Above*, Ford is rushed to safety after an attempt on his life.)

Gerald R. Ford Library

monkey off my back," he wrote. But he didn't tell any of his former running buddies at the Capitol what he planned to do until the day of the announcement. He was afraid the news would leak.

Today, some of Ford's House colleagues say he did the right thing by pardoning Nixon. In the current environment of around-the-clock coverage of political scandals, they say, it's easy to imagine how a prolonged Nixon trial could have been even worse. With Nixon pardoned, the country could move on. "I thought it was absolutely the right decision," said Regula, who believes Ford's action was a "profile in courage."

But at the time, Congress bombarded Ford with questions about whether there was a quid pro quo. So he decided to prove that he had nothing to hide. On Oct. 17, 1974, he returned to Capitol Hill to testify about the pardon before the House Judiciary Subcommittee on Criminal Justice. No other sitting president is believed to have given such formal testimony to Congress.

"I want to assure you, members of this subcommittee, members of Congress and the American people, there was no deal, period, under no circumstances," Ford testified. Most of his staff opposed his decision to testify, he later wrote, but he decided it was the only way to put the issue to rest.

Even so, the new president made a point of telling the House members at the beginning of his testimony that he still believed in executive privilege, that he was testifying voluntarily and that his appearance on the Hill should not be seen as setting a precedent for any of his successors.

SQUEEZED FROM ALL SIDES

It wasn't Ford's only battle with Congress over the powers of the presidency. Even though he still had many friends on the Hill, Congress in general was hostile to his policies. Democrats held strong majorities in both the Senate and the House, and their numbers swelled after the 1974 election. The Watergate backlash helped Democrats gain 43 seats in the House, for a total of 291, and four in the Senate, for a total of 61.

Those were the numbers Ford had to face as Congress, in the wake of Vietnam, followed by Watergate, moved even more assertively to tighten its authority over the executive branch. The year before Ford became president, Congress pushed into law the War Powers Act, which requires the president to inform Congress when he committed troops overseas and required him to obtain congressional authorization

THE LEADER: House Minority Leader Gerald Ford is saluted by President and Mrs. Johnson, Senate Majority Leader Mike Mansfield and Speaker of the House John McCormack.

to keep troops in battle longer than 60 days. (Ford had voted against the bill.)

In 1974, Congress passed a law that created the annual budget resolutions lawmakers now use to set spending levels. Congress also restricted the president's ability to impound funds, requiring congressional approval to terminate programs and introducing procedures that would allow lawmakers to require the president to release funds. Extending its oversight of national security, the Senate in 1976 created a permanent intelligence committee to keep watch on the CIA and other intelligence agencies. The action followed a 15-month investigation of intelligence operations by a committee headed by Democratic Sen. Frank Church of Idaho, which revealed a history of abuses, including buggings and assassination attempts.

These experiences — together with long-running foreign policy battles, such as Congress' insistence on maintaining an arms embargo on Turkey over Ford's opposition — influenced the outlook of Ford advisers

when they rose to power themselves. Nearly three decades later, in December 2005, Cheney was the vice president and, in a meeting with reporters, cited the war powers resolution and the impoundment law as two examples of the congressional actions he believed had weakened the powers of the presidency during the 1970s.

Ford's view of Congress also changed significantly during his time as president. It had become "too fragmented" to solve serious problems, he wrote, because it spent too much time responding to special interest groups. Moreover, he wrote, "Congress was determined to get its oar deeply into the conduct of foreign affairs. This not only undermined the Chief Executive's ability to act, but also eroded the separation of powers concept in the Constitution."

Still, Ford never gave up on his colleagues. He "understood the Congress as an institution that involves give and take, bargaining and negotiation," and "his regard for the Congress led him to treat it with respect," said Roger B. Porter, who served as executive

AP Images

THE 38TH PRESIDENT: Taking the oath of office from Chief Justice Warren E. Burger in the East Room of the White House on Aug. 9, 1974.

secretary for the Economic Policy Board during the Ford administration and is now a professor of government and business at Harvard University's John F. Kennedy School of Government.

Ford did, however, make frequent use of one of the only tools he had to shape policy: the veto. He vetoed 17 bills in 1975 and 20 in 1976. But he wasn't just saying no to everything Congress did. Porter argues that many of Ford's vetoes were "designed to bring people back to the negotiating table rather than simply to kill a piece of legislation."

For example, after he vetoed a short-term tax cut extension in 1975 because it wasn't accompanied by spending cuts, Congress sent it back with a promise to do so should the tax cuts be extended again. Ford signed that version.

That September, Ford was the target of two assassination attempts in California. In the first, he escaped injury inSacramento when Lynette "Squeaky" Fromme's gun misfired — and once again 16 days later, when a bystander deflected Sara Jane Moore's aim in San Francisco.

Unfortunately for Ford, the Democratic Congress wasn't his only challenge. Conservatives in his party were angry at him for choosing Rockefeller as his vice president, as well as for offering amnesty to Americans who left the country to avoid military service in Vietnam and for signing the 1975 Helsinki accords, which were widely seen as a recognition of the Soviet Union's right to dominate Eastern Europe.

Popular culture was also unkind to Ford. His public stumbles, including instances in which he fell down the steps of Air Force One and ate a tamale with the shuck still on, were repeatedly lampooned, most notably on "Saturday Night Live."

Shortly before Thanksgiving in 1975, Reagan, who had just finished eight years as California's governor, announced that he intended to challenge Ford for the Republican presidential nomination in the coming year. Reagan ran a stronger race than Ford ever expected, and it was one of the reasons Ford eased Rockefeller out of the No. 2 slot. The race was undecided until the third night of the Republican convention in Kansas City, Mo., in August 1976, when Ford won 1,187 delegates to Reagan's 1,070.

Today, many conservatives see Reagan's 1976 challenge as the trial run that allowed him to remake the Republican Party in the 1980s. But Ford, who considered himself a conservative, thought the firebrand ideas of Reagan and his supporters would doom the party. "I recognized that these right-wingers would always be on my back," Ford wrote in his memoir. "I had to call the shots as I saw them from the nation's point of view, and I knew from my own experience that trying to satisfy these zealots would doom any general election hopes in 1976."

Wounded by the Nixon pardon and the Reagan challenge, Ford entered the fall election more than 20 percentage points behind the Democratic nominee, former Gov. Jimmy Carter of Georgia. He tried to close the gap by debating Carter, and by the end of the campaign he

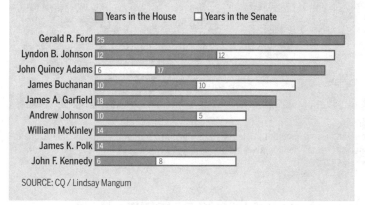

The Longest Hill Pedigrees

In addition to being the only person elevated to national office by Congress — not by the public and the Electoral College — Gerald R. Ford edged out three others for the distinction of having spent more time as a member of Congress than any other president. (Except for John Quincy Adams, all the presidents who served in both chambers were House members first.)

■ Years in the House   □ Years in the Senate

	House	Senate
Gerald R. Ford	25	
Lyndon B. Johnson	12	12
John Quincy Adams	6	17
James Buchanan	10	10
James A. Garfield	18	
Andrew Johnson	10	5
William McKinley	14	
James K. Polk	14	
John F. Kennedy	6	8

SOURCE: CQ / Lindsay Mangum

was gaining rapidly. But on Election Day, he fell short, taking 48 percent of the popular vote. In the Electoral College, Carter's 297-240 victory was the closest presidential contest in 60 years.

"Jerry is a nice man, and a poor man. I feel for him," said Drinan. "We put him out there, and then he was wiped out."

THE AFTERMATH

Four years later, Reagan seriously considered tapping Ford as his own running mate, but the two could not agree on the parameters of a power-sharing arrangement. And in his three decades of retirement, Ford was better known for the celebrity golf tournaments he attended than for the kind of political activism that other modern ex-presidents, notably Carter, have embraced. But Ford didn't stay completely on the sidelines. He became a voice of moderation, urging his party to build a broad base and realize that "you can't win a presidential election just relying on the hard-core right wing of the party."

He announced that he and Betty both favored abortion rights, a marked departure from the anti-abortion sentiment that dominates the modern Republican Party. He joined the advisory board of the Republican Unity Coalition, an organization of gay and straight Republicans that aimed to make homosexuality a "non-issue" for the GOP.

And in 1998, he spoke out against the impeachment of President Bill Clinton, putting himself at odds with most of the Republicans in Congress at the time. Ford said a drawn-out impeachment and Senate trial would be a "terrible waste of time," and proposed in a New York Times op-ed piece that Clinton should simply come to the House floor and face a public rebuke for making false statements about his affair with former White House intern Monica Lewinsky.

Ford also teamed up with his former rival Carter to co-chair the National Commission on Federal Election Reform, which recommended a series of changes to address the voting problems that were exposed in the 2000 presidential election. The recommendations inspired many of the provisions that became law in 2002.

In recent years, Ford steered a careful, middle-of-the-road course in all of his comments on current events. In a 2001 speech to the National Press Club, he applauded George W. Bush for moving ahead with his tax cut plan rather than trimming back his agenda after his disputed election in 2000.

"This is a potentially historic realignment," Ford said of the Bush tax cuts. But he also said that if the tax cuts resulted in deficits, "they ought to correct it, the sooner the better."

In the same speech, Ford urged House Speaker J. Dennis Hastert, R-Ill. to reach out to Democrats to win their help in passing major bills. "You can't ignore the opposition when you have only a 10- or 11-vote margin," because there will always be defections on major votes, Ford said. "If I were the Speaker, I would be very kind and gentle and hopefully get cooperation from the other side."

That's not the way politics works these days, but it was a perfect illustration of the calming influence Ford tried to assert as he struggled to hold the country together during one of the worst political crises in its history. In 2003, Regula recalled, Ford put his skills to good use in a speech at the University of Akron. Ford's mes-

THE EMPLOYER: Both of his chiefs of staff went on to even more prominent posts. In 1975, Ford promoted his first top aide, Donald H. Rumsfeld, at left with Ford, to his first run as Defense secretary. He then elevated a mid-level adviser, Dick Cheney, shown with another Ford administration official at the White House in 1976.

sage, Regula said, was, "Get involved. Don't give up on your system of government. It works." It's the standard message any politician would say in a speech at a college campus. But it was Ford, as much as anyone else, who had earned the right to say it.

FOR FURTHER READING

Ford's House record, 1973 CQ Weekly, p. 2759; confirmation as vice president, 1973 Almanac, p. 1060; Nixon resignation and Ford pardon, 1974 Almanac, p. 867; War Powers Act (PL93-148), 1973 Almanac, p. 905; impoundment curbs (PL 93-344), 1974 Almanac, p. 145; intelligence oversight, 1976 Almanac, p. 294; election overhaul law (PL 107-252), 2002 Almanac, p. 14-3.

New Perspectives on Poverty

Cities and social organizations are addressing the hardest aspects of helping America's poor with surprising success

In the immediate aftermath of Hurricane Katrina in 2005, poverty seemed prominent on the national agenda. Images of thousands of poor people trapped and desperate in the flooded streets and rooftops of New Orleans, of people dying from neglect in an American city became a national embarrassment. Political leaders at all levels promised to address, in President Bush's words at the time, "the deep, persistent poverty" that the storm and flood had revealed. But the poignancy and promises did not last. The refugees of New Orleans were bundled off to other cities and Washington's attention shifted to the flaws of the nation's emergency-management system and the rebuilding of Louisiana's levees. "The urgent trumped the important," said Rep. Phil English, a Pennsylvania Republican who has worked on poverty issues for years.

Such political amnesia has happened before. A decade ago, when Congress overhauled the federal welfare system to limit benefits and require recipients to find jobs, many lawmakers and anti-poverty advocates hoped that it would clear the way for a national dialogue on how to lift people out of poverty. The discussion never took place: Poverty slid off the agenda, and another national election is about to come and go with the poor, at best, a peripheral issue.

From *CQ Weekly,*
October 23, 2006.

It's Expensive to Be Poor

An analysis of demographic data by the Brookings Institution found that those making less than $30,000 a year pay more on average for loans, are less likely to have a savings account and are likelier to shop at smaller grocery stores, which often have higher prices.

	Annual Income		
	Below $30,000	$30,000 to $59,999	$60,000 to $89,999
Have a savings account	35%	53%	68%
Expected interest on $5K auto loan	$1,256	$1,155	$969
Average rate on home loan	6.9%	6.5%	6.0%
Large grocery stores per 100,000 people*	1.4	3.2	4.0

SOURCE: Matthew Fellowes, Brookings Institution
* At least 10,000 square feet, based on median neighborhood income

The question at this point is whether anyone cares — and, as important, whether anyone has new ideas for addressing a problem that the political establishment in Washington often seems to have given up on.

The answer to both those questions is yes. A few years after Katrina and a decade after the last overhaul of the nation's welfare laws, the debate over poverty is alive and vigorous, though mostly outside official Washington. The conversations are taking place in policy think tanks and organizations, as well as in local and state governments that are considering and even implementing programs that have the potential to work at a micro level where large-scale federal efforts have not. The discussions range across a broad policy landscape and are often deeply pragmatic, taking into account the financial and bureaucratic limits of government action and the various problems of economics, education, location and culture that keep people poor. Many of the ideas are worth watching because they could fairly be scaled up to the national level.

Cities and states, where officials are directly confronted with the problems of poverty in a way that Congress is not, have in particular become "leading thinkers and doers" on this issue in recent years, said Matt Fellowes, a scholar at the Brookings Institution in Washington.

Big cities such as San Francisco and smaller ones such as Kalamazoo, Mich., are organizing partnerships with private companies, foundations and even low-income communities themselves to address some of these issues, such as finding ways to lower the high cost of being poor — basics, such as food, and loans cost more in low-income neighborhoods — and helping poor families save more of the money they earn.

In September 2006, the city of San Francisco announced a deal with local banks and credit unions to help low-income families open accounts and enter the financial mainstream.

Days before that announcement, on the other side of the country, New York Mayor Michael Bloomberg proposed a set of new ideas for helping poor families in his city stay on track, on the job and in school. Among the ideas: cash payments, funded with private dollars, that would reward healthy, productive behavior.

In Washington, the U.S. Conference of Mayors has formed a task force on poverty to get local and national policy makers thinking in new ways about poverty — and pressing the 2008 presidential candidates to address the issue.

A core group of lawmakers in Congress, along with aides and researchers, are thinking hard about how to address the "asset gap" between the poor and everyone else — helping low-income families save for retirement or homes, pay for college education, or start small businesses.

Meanwhile, at think tanks and universities in Washington, New York and elsewhere, researchers are working on proposals for getting single men — who were largely left out of the debate over welfare 10 years ago — into the labor force, where they can play a constructive role lifting families out of poverty.

Others are looking at ways to strengthen early-childhood programs and better equip schools to help children get out of poverty. Proposals include incentives to states to better align their high school graduation requirements with the skills students will need for college and work, and targeted grants to improve the quality of teaching and raise teacher pay in schools in high-poverty areas.

BETTER SHOPPING: Community activist Mattie Jordan-Woods
got a full-service grocery built in the poor Northside section of
Kalamazoo. 'What it will do is start the movement of business to
the neighborhood,' said Jordan-Woods, joined here by produce
manager Allen Hawkins.

Fellowes points out that recent efforts by mayors in
big cities, such as New York, Philadelphia and Los
Angeles, to seize control of their failing school systems
are very much grounded in the hope that improved
schools can reduce poverty.

"What we're seeing is people saying, 'OK, we
reformed welfare. Now what do we do about poverty?'
They're not the same thing," said Ray Boshara, who is
working on asset creation proposals at the New America
Foundation, a social policy institute in Washington.

It's all very much a scattered work in progress — "little straws in the wind," as one expert, Robert Greenstein
of the Center on Budget and Policy Priorities, put it.
Fellowes said people are often working on different facets
of the problem around the country, without a real connection to the bigger picture.

What is lacking, he and others say, is the political leadership that could put all the pieces together into a broader,
coherent plan — one that squares with fiscal and political
realities at a time when budgets are tight and politicians
are leery of anything that looks like the big-government
solutions of the past.

"You're seeing innovation all over the place," said
Boshara. "No one has synthesized it. Somebody who can
package this innovation in a coherent way, frame it in the
right way, can do a lot to move the agenda forward."

THE HIGH COST OF BEING POOR

Poverty has been among the most intractable of national
problems. The federal government has been addressing it
in varying degrees for nearly three-quarters of a century.
Although there have been successes, such as Social
Security, and failures, such as Model Cities, there has been
no lasting decline in the nation's poverty rate for more than
a generation.

Economists say a whole range of social, economic and
political conditions contribute to keeping people in
poverty, and it has been clear that traditional government
programs such as President Lyndon B. Johnson's War on
Poverty were not enough themselves to end poverty.

By the time Congress moved to overhaul the welfare
system, that program was widely discredited. Critics said
welfare's open-ended cash assistance discouraged work,
marriage and the self-reliance that poor families need to
climb out of poverty. It also has become clear in the years
since the 1996 welfare law that simply moving off public assistance and into work, although it may have raised
the incomes of poor people, was not in itself enough to
leave poverty behind.

In fact, the keys to stability and long-term success for
families are many: good child care and transportation;
job skills; bank accounts and other means of savings;
home ownership; good health care. Housing patterns
that isolate low-income families in neighborhoods far
from jobs and basic services are also a big problem.

A major reason why many of the efforts under way in
cities and elsewhere are so promising is that they avoid
old-style government approaches and address many different angles of the poverty problem.

The challenges are tough, but at bottom, there's nothing mysterious about them. And the approaches that
cities and others are trying are often simple, even

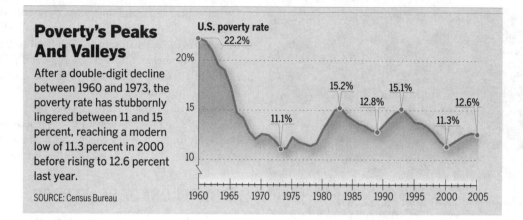

Poverty's Peaks And Valleys

After a double-digit decline between 1960 and 1973, the poverty rate has stubbornly lingered between 11 and 15 percent, reaching a modern low of 11.3 percent in 2000 before rising to 12.6 percent last year.

SOURCE: Census Bureau

U.S. poverty rate
22.2%
20%
15.2%
15.1%
12.8%
15
12.6%
11.1%
11.3%
10

1960 1965 1970 1975 1980 1985 1990 1995 2000 2005

obvious, and tightly focused — and they don't involve a big new government bureaucracy.

In Kalamazoo, a city of 75,000 in southwestern Michigan, community activists and city officials stitched together a public-private partnership to get a full-service grocery store for one low-income neighborhood on the edge of downtown, a place called Northside, which most local businesses had fled years before.

It's a Felpausch Food Center — nothing too fancy, part of a family-owned chain in the area — and it may seem a small and prosaic thing. But many of the families struggling to get by in Northside have no cars, and they had been paying $20 for a round-trip cab ride to grocery stores across town. Or they were paying inflated prices for milk and other staples at corner convenience stores.

Those were holes in their budgets that were draining away money week after week, money they could not afford to lose.

Initiatives such as Kalamazoo's are an example of addressing the "other side of the ledger" for poor families, as Fellowes at Brookings puts it. The focus is not just raising the incomes of poor families but also finding ways to reduce the higher costs they pay because they are either too poor or too isolated to get access to stores and services that middle-class people take for granted.

San Francisco's banking initiative is rooted in the same idea. The city teamed up with local banks and credit unions to offer low-cost "starter accounts" to poor families, with no minimum balances. There are "second chance" accounts, too, for people who have had problems in the past with bounced checks and overdrafts.

The ultimate aim is getting them away from payday

lenders and check-cashing businesses that charge high fees and triple-digit interest rates, allowing families to save more of the money they earn.

Besides earning some community good will for participating in the program, banks improve their ratings with federal regulators, which score them in part based on how much they lend in underprivileged neighborhoods. The government looks at such things when banks ask for approval for mergers or other kinds of expansions.

In the San Francisco area, an estimated 50,000 people have no bank accounts, and the city hopes to reach at least 10,000 of them.

"These are folks who are already working very hard for, in many cases, very little money," said David Augustine, a spokesman for the city treasurer's office. "This is something that will improve their bottom line."

It's significant, too, that San Francisco and Kalamazoo undertook their initiatives without creating a new government agency.

The state of Michigan contributed money to the Kalamazoo project, with nudging from the Republican Speaker of the state House at the time. The project got $400,000 in federal money, thanks to the local congressman, Republican Fred Upton. The city matched that with $400,000 from a federal community development block grant.

Private foundations and citizens contributed, too. The city government created a "renaissance zone" around the development, to remain tax-free for 12 years, and it guaranteed a $2 million mortgage on the property.

And there was another benefit to Northside from that grocery store: The jobs it provides are valuable first-work experiences for local young people, said Mattie Jordan-Woods, the long-time Northside resident and community activist who led the effort.

"Long term, what it will do is start the movement of business to the neighborhood," Jordan-Woods said.

That movement is already happening: Where there once were blighted buildings around the grocery, now there is a variety store and a pizza parlor. A bank has moved in nearby. There's a child care center and a community meeting place, run by a community development organization led by Jordan-Woods.

It was good for Kalamazoo as a whole, too, said the town's mayor, Hannah McKinney, who is also an economics professor at Kalamazoo College. Nearly a third of the city's population lives below the official poverty line — more than double the national poverty rate — and that's a huge drag on a community that is itself struggling economically, hard hit in recent years by the loss of manufacturing jobs.

Paper mills, important to the local economy, have closed. Other businesses packed up and left, too. Between the 1990 and 2000 censuses, Kalamazoo lost more than 3,000 residents.

To regain its footing and prosper, the city needs healthy families, neighborhoods that work, McKinney said. "People are a key economic resource, and we can't let vast numbers of our populace not be productive. We can't just wall them up and turn our backs."

THE RIGHT CHEMISTRY

The specific problem that San Francisco is going after with its banking initiative — the higher costs that poor families wind up paying for financial services — is one that's been getting particular attention around the country in recent years. Based on surveys of consumer expenditures by the Federal Reserve that Fellowes has analyzed, more than 4 million low-income households nationwide pay higher interest rates for home loans than better-off families do.

Anti-poverty advocates contend that "predatory lenders" are fleecing the poor.

New York state and New York City are going after the problem by subsidizing "banking development districts" to encourage banks to open in under-served areas.

States are also addressing the issue with regulation. Georgia, for example, essentially banned payday lending by capping the annual percentage rate at 16 percent for loans of $3,000 or less. Rates for the cash advances from payday lenders can reach into the triple digits.

Other states are trying to crack down on unscrupulous mortgage lenders who go after poor families with high-interest loans and bad agreements that strip away the equity they have built up in their homes.

It's also an issue to which Congress could easily lend its clout, Fellowes said. In fact, three Democrats in the House, Barney Frank of Massachusetts and Melvin Watt and Brad Miller of North Carolina, have introduced legislation modeled on North Carolina's predatory lending law.

The trouble is that the issue so far has been defined in Washington as part of the Democratic or liberal agenda, Fellowes said. The legislation has no Republican cosponsors, and it has gone nowhere.

Likewise, Democratic Sen. Edward M. Kennedy of Massachusetts has introduced a bill aimed at reducing child poverty in the United States by half in 10 years — funding the initiative with a special 1 percent tax on the wealthy. That bill also has no Republican cosponsors.

In fact, addressing poverty in a big way takes a difficult bipartisan alchemy, a blending of Democratic and Republican philosophies that's a rarity in Congress these days.

Yet there are areas where lawmakers in Washington have demonstrated that it can be done: The earned-income tax credit, for example, which reduces or eliminates taxes for working families with children, is an idea embraced by both parties as an effective anti-poverty tool.

Researchers at such places as Brookings and the New York-based social policy think tank MDRC — it was started as the Manpower Demonstration Research Corporation — are talking about expanding the credit to other low-income workers. A former Republican congressional aide who helped write the 1996 welfare law, Ronald Haskins at Brookings, is one of the big advocates of that idea.

The particular target is single men. The argument now is that helping get more such men into the labor force would improve the lot of poor families — and help decrease the crime and out-of-wedlock births that are holding poor communities back.

There is also a bipartisan group in Congress, called the "savings and ownership caucus," that has had considerable success finding common ground on strategies to help low-income families build up assets such as retirement savings.

Edwards' Efforts For the Poor

Former Sen. John Edwards is the only politician of any prominence really making an issue of poverty these days. He built his brief 2004 presidential campaign around a concern for the poor and the eroding middle class, and after returning home to North Carolina, he founded a think tank in Chapel Hill to focus on the issue — the Center for Poverty, Work and Opportunity.

Poverty is a very difficult issue politically for his party, and Democrats and anti-poverty advocates are watching Edwards closely. Whether he can generate public support for a new campaign to end poverty, or build a viable presidential campaign around the issue in 2008, will indicate to political Washington whether there's any future in focusing so intensely on the poor.

Democrats were the party of the New Deal, the Great Society and the "war on poverty" of the 1960s, but they are ever mindful today of the risk of looking like the big-government Robin Hoods that their Republican critics have made them out to be. Focusing on the middle class is a safer bet politically.

"One of the things that's refreshing about Edwards is that he uses the 'P word' — he talks about poverty," said Sandy Schram, a professor of social policy at BrynMawr College and an expert on welfare and the poor. " 'Poverty' among Democrats is almost as verboten as 'liberal.' "

Finding the right way to talk about the issue is critical, and it calls for rhetorical balance. Nothing will happen unless the middle class goes along, so any initiatives must speak to their values, aspirations and even self-interest.

At the same time, any meaningful campaign against poverty is going to have to tackle the kind of concentrated poverty that Hurricane Katrina revealed last year in New Orleans, which can seem far removed, even alien, to middle-class America.

Edwards — who during his single Senate term was affiliated with the centrist New Democrats, which include such moderates as Evan Bayh of Indiana and Mary L. Landrieu of Louisiana — says any proposal must fit within the paradigm of the 1996 welfare overhaul, which put new emphasis on work and personal responsibility.

"I don't think this will work unless the solutions embrace the values that most Americans care about," he said last month.

This is how he put it in a policy address on the issue this past summer in Washington: "We need to restore the dream that is America. But we also need to do it in a way that all Americans will be proud of. Not just by giving handouts to the poor, or pumping money into a broken government program. But by finding ways to help everyone who works hard and makes smart choices get ahead."

He has proposed, for example, creating a million temporary "stepping stone" jobs — such as working for non-profits, building parks or helping to keep neighborhoods clean — that he said would help people improve their lives in the short-term and get valuable work experience that will help them over the long haul.

Framing the Issues

Democratic leaders bristle at any suggestion that their party is gun-shy on the issue of poverty. They point to their support for proposals to raise the minimum wage and expand the availability of affordable housing. At a forum last September on Capitol Hill sponsored by House Democrats, titled "Economic Security for All Americans," they did talk in populist terms about the poor and the widening gap between the "haves" and "have-nots" in America.

House Democratic leader Nancy Pelosi of California said her driving concern is that so many children — nearly one in five last year — live in poverty.

But others, such as Schram, say it's hardly a secret that Democrats — and Republicans, for that matter — are far

Income is what people need to get by, those lawmakers say. Assets — a bank-account nest egg, a home, a small business — are what get people ahead, put them solidly in the middle class.

A panel discussion on the subject in September 2006 on Capitol Hill featured two of the most conserva- tive members of the Senate, Republicans Rick Santorum of Pennsylvania and Jeff Sessions of Alabama, along side Rep. Patrick J. Kennedy, a Rhode Island Democrat and the son of Sen. Kennedy. Other members of the savings and ownership caucus include Democratic Sen. Charles E. Schumer of New York, who this year is the

more comfortable talking to middle-class concerns. And indeed, the six-point list of legislative priorities that House Democrats laid out in this Congress, which they called "Six for 06," includes only two proposals specifically focused on the poor: raising the minimum wage and expanding Pell Grants to help students from low-income families pay for their college education.

Some Democrats and poverty experts stress the need to unite the interests of the middle class and the poor — something they say is both good policy and good politics.

Elizabeth Warren, a law professor at Harvard University who spoke last March at one of the seminars Edwards has organized, says that programs designed to help low-income families, but which are open to everyone, are ultimately stronger and more enduring than those focused only on the poor. She gives as an example offering a college education to any student willing to do public service after graduation to pay off the debt. The goal should be strengthening the middle class and opening it, giving the poor opportunities to move up, she said.

"If our policies are aimed at squeezing a few more dollars from those that have to give to the poor, then the middle class and the rich are united," she said. "They lock arms to resist."

That kind of talk makes some Democrats and anti-poverty activists nervous. They worry that the poor would get lost in the shuffle — or worse, that such a framing would too easily become a dodge for politicians to avoid addressing the needs of the poor. Ronald Walters, a political scientist at the University of Maryland, says that, for example, it's fine to open the door to college, but many low-income families are not equipped to walk through without more help. "You need a dedicated poverty program, and this is the third rail," Walters said. "No one wants to touch it."

Edwards' message is often quite broad. In 2004 he spoke about the "two Americas": one for families who have everything they need and one for everybody else. He emphasizes now his support for stronger labor laws to make it easier for

unions to organize, particularly for low-paid service work — a change that he says will give working families the clout to negotiate for better pay and benefits. He has also proposed paying the first year of college tuition for any student at a public college who stays out of trouble and agrees to take a part-time job.

But at the same time, Edwards has proposed an initiative that the middle class might see as threatening: He wants to hand out 1 million housing vouchers to low-income families to integrate neighborhoods economically, and allow poor families to find housing closer to jobs and schools. That's something middle-class suburbanites might very well resist, although Edwards does balance it with proposals for overhauling the bureaucracy at the Department of Housing and Urban Development, which he says would help pay for the vouchers.

'Transformational Message'

He also relies to a great degree on a moral argument to make his case, speaking to notions of fair play and justice. It's a scandal that a country as rich as the United States should have such persistent, systemic poverty, he says. What's more, no one who is working and playing by the rules should be living in poverty.

"I believe we'll find out once again that poor people are just like everyone," he said this past June at the National Press Club in Washington. "They want to work, they want to do right by their children, and given the chance, they will work their hearts out."

Edwards said the poverty issue alone is not enough to base a presidential campaign on, but it could be a part of a "large transformational message" for the nation. And he said he is confident that Americans want to help end poverty — and that the disaster of Hurricane Katrina brought home in a way that still resonates how much poverty is out there.

"It troubles people," he said. "Katrina brought it in a very real way into people's living rooms."

head of his party's Senate campaign committee, and Phil English, the Republican congressman from Pennsylvania.

The ideas circulating among the group have bipartisan appeal because they join government action with a reliance on markets and investment.

Among them is something called a KIDS account. Every child at birth would get a savings account, with $500 from the federal government to start it off. Children in families with incomes below the national median would get up to $1,000 each.

Thereafter, the government would match deposits for

low- and moderate-income families, and at the age of 18, a child could use the money to pay for postsecondary education, put it toward a house, or keep it socked away for retirement. At 30, he would have to start paying back the initial $500 deposit, which would go into new accounts for children.

Private givers, such as companies, could contribute to individual KIDS accounts, and the government would match that money, too.

The goal of such ideas, English said, is "empowering people of limited means without creating a new bureaucracy or a handout." Giving low-income families a sense that they have a stake in the economy, something to work for, could change the culture of poverty, he said. The program, he said, would increase the likelihood that low-income families "will become people who help pull the wagon, rather than sit in it."

That's something conservatives as well as liberals can support, he said.

A 'NICE LITTLE STEPCHILD'

Then why haven't ideas like KIDS accounts become reality? Someone in the audience at the September 2006 panel discussion on asset creation put that question to the lawmakers in attendance, and their answer begins to address the broader issue of why so little is happening on poverty at the federal level.

First, as Santorum pointed out that day, there has been no strong constituency and no groundswell of support to push such proposals forward. Until there is, Santorum said, "we're going to be considered the nice little stepchild."

Second, there always seem to be more immediately pressing issues getting in the way. After Katrina, all the problems that had subsumed the issue of poverty before that disaster came rushing back quickly: the war in Iraq, national security, high gasoline prices.

And politically, addressing poverty is difficult for both parties. Reach much beyond proposals such as KIDS accounts, and the bipartisan comity begins to break down, Santorum said.

On the Republican side, conservatives resist new programs because they fear new government entitlements. Democrats are wary of appearing to be big-government spendthrifts.

For both sides, it's a safer bet politically to focus on the middle class, and indeed, the issue of poverty generally scores low on voters' list of concerns.

"People don't believe it has much potency politically," said John Edwards, a former Democratic senator from North Carolina and his party's vice presidential candidate in 2004.

About a year after Hurricane Katrina, Edwards tried to call public attention back to poverty, which he has made his signature issue. In a June speech at the National Press Club in Washington, he issued a shoot-for-the-moon challenge to the nation — end poverty in 30 years. (Edwards' quest, p. 18)

"Poverty is the great moral issue of our time," Edwards said. "We have an obligation to do something about it. Not just alleviate some of the symptoms. Not just find ways to help some of the people. But end it."

By then, Edwards was a lonely voice on the national stage. He received some polite news coverage, but there was no resounding "amen" from the political establishment in Washington.

Across town that day, the Senate was debating the Iraq War and Democratic proposals advocating the withdrawal of U.S. troops.

And yet it was just a few months later that city leaders in New York and San Francisco rolled out their anti-poverty programs. In both cases, they framed the initiatives in terms that spoke to pragmatic economic concerns, as well as higher aspirations for their communities — and provided evidence that it is possible to bridge ideological divides and interest groups to get something done on poverty.

BUSINESS DECISIONS

In San Francisco, the treasurer's office argued that helping low-income people get bank accounts was not just the right thing to do, it made good business sense for banks to expand their customer base by helping people into the financial mainstream.

In New York, Bloomberg presented his poverty initiatives as vital for his city's economic future. His proposals, partly based on the work of a 32-member blue ribbon commission, include a tax credit to help low-income New Yorkers pay for child care and a plan to seek private-sector money to pay for what Bloomberg calls "conditional cash payments" to reward families for making sound decisions.

The payments, Bloomberg said last September, would be designed "to encourage parents and young people to engage in healthy behavior, and to stay in school, stay at work, and stay on track to rise out of poverty."

"Unlocking the tremendous potential of people with more dreams than dollars is the key to our whole city's prosperity," he said.

Bloomberg is a former Democrat whose moderate politics sometimes cause conservatives to question his new Republican credentials. But his anti-poverty ideas were praised by none other than Newt Gingrich, the defiantly conservative former House Speaker who was a key driver of the 1996 welfare overhaul. Gingrich, in a radio commentary on American Public Media's "Marketplace," singled out for particular praise the mayor's proposal to reward poor families with cash for healthy behavior and smart choices.

In so doing, Gingrich made his own pitch for a national commitment to the issue of poverty — and neatly summed up the central challenge for the activists, researchers and local leaders who have kept their focus on the poor even as the rest of the country moved on to other things.

Welfare caseloads have declined dramatically over the past decade, "but we didn't end poverty in America," Gingrich said.

"Now," he said, "the question is how to help those still left out of the American dream."

Mayor McKinney in Kalamazoo is using the same kind of economic arguments as is Bloomberg, and there are signs that the community is building a long-term consensus around addressing poverty.

An anonymous group of private donors has agreed to pay to send graduates of Kalamazoo public schools to any public university or community college in the state — an initiative called "the Kalamazoo Promise." The group will pay 100 percent of the tuition for kids who have attended local schools from kindergarten through high school.

Meanwhile, the Chamber of Commerce has joined city officials and local activists — with whom it once clashed over a campaign to raise the local minimum wage — to form something called the Poverty Reduction Initiative. The aim is to get a wide range of public and private groups in the same room to discuss ways they can collaborate to reduce poverty locally.

It's only begun, but it's now coordinating an initiative involving 10 different groups to provide employment services, job training and housing assistance for low-income families.

"I think we're creating a grass-roots level movement to put poverty back on the national agenda," McKinney said. "But I think we're doing it in a less ideological, more pragmatic way."

"These are Americans," she said. "The American dream is being lost at the local level. And we have to work together to restore it."

FOR FURTHER READING

1996 welfare law (PL 104-193), 1996 Almanac, p. 6-3; Edwards campaign, 2004 Almanac, p. 18-3.

Federalist Pipeline Fuels Movement on the Right

As conservative group grows in size and influence; liberals say it's time for the left to play catch-up

LEADING FROM THE RIGHT: Eugene B. Meyer, left, and Leonard A. Leo head the organization, which was started by a handful of young conservatives 25 years ago and now numbers 40,000.

From *CQ Weekly*, December 11, 2006.

About 800 of Washington's legal elite gathered at the Capitol Hilton in early December 2006 for an invitation-only event, a rare moment of candid public commentary from not one but two sitting Supreme Court Justices.

In the latest of a series of such public appearances, Antonin Scalia and Stephen G. Breyer had a polite but often pointed exchange about the role of the courts and the meaning of the Constitution, fundamental questions that often divide the two and have been the subject of books by each.

Seats were doled out evenly among the two sponsoring organizations, the relatively young and liberal American Constitution Society and its better-known and much more conservative counterpart, the Federalist Society.

The Federalist Society has become a favorite target of liberals, who have described it as a cultish group in which membership and knowledge of the "secret handshake" provide guaranteed access to the levers of political and judicial power. This was particularly true during the confirmation process for the two most recent Supreme Court justices, Samuel A. Alito Jr., who most definitely was a member, and Chief Justice John G. Roberts Jr., whose Federalist status a decade ago became practically the only controversy associated with his nomination to the court.

But as the gathering at the Hilton and others like it have shown, there is a growing sense on the left that it is time to move beyond

A debating format has been favored since the first Federalist conference in 1982, and events today attract the biggest names from the political and legal communities. Its programs draw crowds on college campuses and at lawyers' division meetings; those events drive membership and loyalty, which has valuable long-term payoff.

The group has also fed what its executive vice president, Leonard A. Leo, calls the "pipeline," a pathway from law school student membership to the lawyers' chapters and from there to bigger and better things.

This survival and growth has given conservatives hope that their movement is alive and well, even as Democrats are taking control of Congress and the policies of a Republican president were repudiated by the voters in the midterm election. The dif-

CQ / Scott J.Ferrell

EXAMPLE FOR LIBERALS: Federalist chief Meyer, left, with Lisa Brown of the American Constitution Society, cosponsored a forum on constitutional interpretation last week with Breyer, right, and Scalia.

talk of secret handshakes and toward direct engagement with the 25-year-old Federalist Society, which now counts 40,000 conservative and libertarian lawyers, judges, academics and law students nationwide among its members.

In fact, as that membership continues to grow and penetrate the legal establishment, the left has answered with its own group based on a strikingly similar model. Lisa Brown, the executive director of the ACS, acknowledges that her side has some serious catching up to do. The Federalists' liberal counterpart is "in part a recognition of the effectiveness of the model they built," she said, "both in terms of generating ideas and the means of implementing them."

The Federalists pride themselves on being an organization focused on the exchange of ideas, a place where the right's various factions can come together, hash out differences, debate, network and engage with opponents. The group does not lobby or take political positions on legislation or nominees — although, of course, its members do.

ference between "movement conservatives" and party-line Republicans is becoming increasingly clear; for many Federalists, the November losses are all but irrelevant. Eugene B. Meyer, the society's longtime president, points out that the organization's growth continued apace despite political transitions and setbacks over the last quarter-century — the departure of Ronald Reagan and the elections of Bill Clinton, to name two.

"For our members,"Meyer said in an interview, "the very fact that what they are interested in is ideas, the given fact of an election, even one that was an extraordinary sweep . . . wouldn't much impact what we do."

Consistent growth is a sign, Federalists believe, that their movement can continue prospering at the grass roots: in law offices, classrooms and courtrooms across the country. The care and feeding of young conservative minds, they contend, will lead to a broader network of lawyers and leaders who later come to public service and put those principles into practice.

"They generate ideas; they encourage smart thinking; they educate," said the outgoing chairman of the

Republican National Committee, Ken Mehlman, himself a Federalist. "They are a critically important part of Right America."

BUILDING THE PIPELINE

The original Federalists were a group of friends who met as undergraduates at Yale and then came to Washington to join the Reagan Revolution. After dispersing to law schools around the country, they acted to turn their campus club into an intellectual dynamo. A sort of cognitive dissonance drove their decision. "There was no student organization that seemed interested in Reagan's legal ideas," recalled Lee Liberman Otis, one of the founders, "and this seemed a little odd given that he had just won the presidency."

Timing was definitely on their side: When they had to decide whom to recruit as the faculty sponsor for one of their first chapters, they chose a professor at the University of Chicago named Antonin Scalia. He accepted; four years later, he was on the Supreme Court.

Some of the founders wound up in the Reagan Justice Department under Attorney General Edwin Meese III. He and several others from the Reagan old guard remain forces in Federalist circles, but a younger generation allied with the current administration has also stepped to the fore. Along with Mehlman, Attorney General Alberto R. Gonzales and his predecessor, John Ashcroft, are both friends of the society.

The largest membership section today is practicing lawyers, which makes sense given the decades of law students who have graduated from law school chapters. Leo was hired in 1991 in part to oversee the development of "practice groups" in the growing lawyers' division. These groups are organized by area of legal practice, and officers coordinate loosely with the national office on programming. They provide a prime opportunity for professional and social networking.

The society operates under a genuine concept of local control: law school and lawyers' chapters possessing independent authority over programming. "There's a lot of federalism in the Federalist Society,"quips Meyer. The national office in Washington, with a paid staff of 21, offers financial support, advice and general direction — but not much more. The group's publications are only now taking on the more polished look of an organization

with tens of thousands of members. Funding comes from individual donors in the "Madison Club," corporate benefactors and such expected conservative outlets as the Scaife Foundation, the Koch Foundation and, until its recent closure, the John M. Olin Foundation.

The society functions as a kind of perpetual law school campus with branches scattered across the country. Even though the group is growing, part of its impact is not in membership per se or outright recruitment — on which it's never spent much more than 10 percent of its budget — but in facilitating dialogue and building the pipeline.

And that conduit's ability to deliver some high-octane people into positions of power has not been lost on the legal left.

"For 50 years, we had a set idea of what 'mainstream' judges were, what kind of forward progress was necessary to bring minorities and women and others into the political system," Sen. Hillary Rodham Clinton said in an interview. "There didn't need to be an outside organization because there was an inside seat that many people had, on the courts, in the government, in law firms and elsewhere."

But conservatives — namely the Federalist Society — have unmade that consensus, "and they deliberately set out to do so," the New York Democrat said. "I think you have to respect that."

CONSPIRACY THEORIES

Liberals may respect the society, but they are deeply concerned. The decidedly conservative tenor of Bush judicial nominees has Democrats worrying aloud about the Federalists' influence in the judicial branch.

"Fewer than 1 percent of lawyers across America are members of this Federalist Society. Yet over one-third of President Bush's circuit court nominees are members of the Federalist Society,"Richard J. Durbin of Illinois, the Senate Democratic whip, claimed during the debate on the nomination of Priscilla Owen for the 5th U.S. Circuit Court of Appeals. "If you do not have a Federalist Society secret handshake, then, frankly, you may not even have a chance to be considered seriously by the Bush White House."

Of course there is no such handshake, but the absence of mystery goes well beyond that. Meetings are almost entirely open to the public, and membership is only a point and click away at the society's Web site. Anyone can join; a student membership is $5 and a "general" membership is $50. There is no form requiring declarations of party affiliation or ideology.

Erwin Chemerinsky, a Duke University law professor and a liberal who often argues before the Supreme Court, cautions that the Federalists' openness to debate does not mean the group lacks an agenda. "Just look at their mission statement," he says.

Indeed, the statement does declare a kind of ideological war, asserting that law schools and the legal profession are dominated by an "orthodox liberal ideology which advocates a centralized and uniform society" and calling for a "reordering" of priorities in the legal system "to place a premium on individual liberty, traditional values, and the rule of law."

Ralph G. Neas, president of the liberal advocacy group People for the American Way, agrees that the willingness to debate serves as no cover for ideology or the shrewd implantation of a political agenda. "It's not a debating society, it's a very sophisticated political-legal network that knew exactly from 1982 on where they wanted to go and where they wanted the country to go," he said.

At the same time, personal connections can lead to a different view. Democratic Rep. Howard L. Berman of California, a social friend of Federalist head Meyer, recalls how he once invited an anti-Bush ally of the Federalist Society who is a Heritage Foundation expert to testify at a hearing — ruffling the feathers of some of his liberal colleagues. "Obviously, I disagree with their conception of constitutional law," Berman said of the society. "But you can challenge them, you can argue with them. They love to engage."

More than a few law school deans say the same thing, even those holding sway over liberal bastions such as Harvard and Columbia — where a card-carrying Federalist, David M. Schizer, recently became dean. Introducing a leading conservative judge at a conference last year, Dean Elena Kagan of Harvard declared, "I love the Federalist Society, but you are not my people."

The line got a laugh, but Kagan was serious. "These are highly committed, intelligent, hard-working, active students who make the Harvard community better, just the like the American Constitution Society makes the Harvard community better," she said.

CORE IDEAS, NOT POSITIONS

As the mission statement suggests, the Federalists are held together by several core ideas. But in many cases, fault lines can be found in the specifics. The professed belief in "limited government," for example, remains a unifier, though it means one thing to social conservatives and quite another to libertarians.

Federalists also tend to agree on the role of the judge as a participant in the democratic process. Slogans such as "no legislating from the bench" imagine broad judicial deference to the laws written by state legislatures and Congress, though libertarians will also use the term "majoritarian" to characterize what they see as a wrong-headed, inherent trust in the decisions of majorities, which can sometimes be wrong — even unconstitutionally wrong.

And Federalists are generally united on methods of constitutional interpretation, with the notion of "original intent" having entered the popular vocabulary as a response to the "living Constitution" espoused by Chief Justice Earl Warren and later given voice by Justice William J. Brennan Jr. Conservatives including Scalia, however, have continued to refine the concept of original intent, and no forum has been more important in this process than the Federalist Society. At his appearance last week with Breyer, for example, Scalia was quick to disclaim a philosophy of original "intent" in favor of original "understanding." The first focuses on a law's authors, the second on its readers. This matter is by no means settled among those on the right, however.

Indeed, society members vehemently disagree on any number of specific issues. To be a Federalist does not mean one is laissez-faire or protectionist, anti-abortion or

❝They generate ideas. They encourage smart thinking. They educate. . . . They are a critically important part of Right America.❞

— Republican Party Chairman Ken Mehlman

in favor of reproductive rights; factions exist on both sides of these issues and many others. Libertarians clash with social conservatives over free-speech issues, trade policy, Iraq, civil liberties and the interpretation of the Constitution's church-and-state clause. The factions were at heated odds, for example, in last year's national debate over whether to continue the feeding tube for the brain-damaged Florida woman Terri Schiavo. Another big fissure is over budget policy, with the Bush administration drawing a constant stream of fire from many in the Federalist ranks who view themselves as more fiscally conservative than the president.

There are broad unifying factors as well, of course — one clear example being the 2005 Supreme Court decision, in *Kelo v. City of New London*, upholding a municipality's use of its "eminent domain" powers to further private development in an economically depressed neighborhood. Among Federalists, there was something here for everyone to hate: Libertarians were outraged at what they viewed as the encroaching hand of an all-powerful state, while social conservatives derided an activist court telling communities how to organize themselves: Today eminent domain, tomorrow gay marriage, and so on down the slippery slope.

Another unifying episode was Bush's failed effort in 2005 to put Harriet Miers, who was then the White House counsel, on the Supreme Court. Ripples of discontent quickly spread across the conservative airwaves and blogosphere as soon as the president proposed her as the successor to Sandra Day O'Connor. The Federalist Society took no position on the nomination, in keeping with its policy as a 501(C)(3) nonprofit group. But its members and boosters were among the quickest to enter the fracas — and the most prominent.

Robert H. Bork, a former federal appeals court judge whose outspoken conservatism doomed his own chances for the high court two decades ago, was characteristically blunt. "It's a slap in the face to the conservatives that have been building a legal movement," he said on CNN. Though Bork, a national co-chairman of the Federalists, does not speak for the organization, his views were representative of many in the rank and file.

Other media-savvy Federalist allies such as John Fund of The Wall Street Journal and William Kristol of The Weekly Standard joined in. Leo, who was then on leave from the Society to advise the White House on judicial nominations, found himself in a tight spot. "There's no

question that people made their assessment and felt this was not consistent with conservative legal principles that had been articulated over the years," he said. "Individuals in the movement are not always going to embrace what the political power base does."

Leo stayed on as an administration adviser, however, through the nomination and confirmation of Alito after Bush gave up on Miers. In the end, Fund told the society's national student convention this fall, "it was the finest hour of the Federalist Society . . . because Samuel Alito now sits on the Supreme Court."

THE PULL OF POLITICS

Although the electoral and legislative challenges facing the Republican Party loom large, there's no sign that movement conservatives, like so many of those in the Federalist Society, are ready to give up the game. Their project has been on the upswing for a generation, and the current Bush administration — despite its disappointments for many in the movement — has resulted not only in the seating of many conservative judges but also in an increased prominence of conservative ideas.

Nowhere has this been clearer than in foreign policy, in which the concept of pre-emptive war has been backed up by theories of national sovereignty and constitutional interpretation incubated in Federalist circles. And nothing has set conservatives more on fire, nor served to unify their many factions, so much as the perceived creeping specter of international law, one of the society's declared current areas of focus.

"We felt that international law was for the left today what constitutional law was for them 35 years ago," Leo said, "the empty vessel into which they would pour all sorts of concepts that they couldn't get through the political process."

But constitutional law remains central to the battle over the role of the courts and the separation of powers. In the run-up to the invasion of Iraq, Bush began asserting not only the United States' absolute right to launch a pre-emptive strike but also a wide-reaching executive authority that he says is granted in Article II of the Constitution. Reflecting another legal concept now being pushed hard in conservative circles, Bush has also asserted co-equal authority, along with the courts, to interpret the meaning of newly minted laws, which he does through the statements he often issues when signing legislation.

For years, the Federalist Society has been home to vigorous debate over these very issues. Still, there is no single society view on the matter. The infamous "torture memo," arguing for broad presidential war powers, was drafted by a junior Justice Department official, John C. Yoo, who has won the Federalist Society's top award for legal scholarship. Yet longtime Federalist booster Richard Epstein co-wrote a legal brief in the Supreme Court case *Hamdan v. Rumsfeld* arguing against many of Yoo's ideas. Epstein's side carried the day in the court — and prompted a subsequent overhaul of the treatment of military detainees — but in the new debating chamber of the right, the conversation is by no means over.

Some among the Federalist legion express frustration over this recourse to debate in the face of electoral or legal defeat. The pull of politics is strong, but Meyer stands by the Federalist formula, and the group will strongly resist taking positions on specific issues. "Lots of people meet each other in our organization and are enthusiastic about ideas — and these develop in practice," he said. "But it will not be something that the organization does."

FOR FURTHER READING

Detainee rules (PL 109-366), 2006 CQ Weekly, p. 2624; presidential power, 2006 CQ Weekly, p. 2858; Supreme Court, 2005 Almanac, pp. 14-3, 14-7; Schiavo, 2005 Almanac, p. 14-16; Kelo case, 2005 Almanac, p. 14–12.

Cities Hit the Hill with New, Stronger Position

They took the lead on key issues as Washington stalled; now mayors want a bigger say in where federal dollars go

CQ / Scott J. Ferrell

Making Contact: Rangel, the new chairman of House Ways and Means, greets Atlanta Mayor Shirley Franklin at a 2005 summit meeting of mayors on ways to stop the traffic in illegal guns.

It's been a long while since the nation's mayors have looked to Washington with so much optimism. As many of them see it, their dealings with the federal government during the Bush administration have been mostly about fighting budget cuts in urban programs such as housing and community development. With Congress back in the hands of Democrats, a party more closely aligned with urban interests than the Republicans, they expect a friendlier relationship and more money for traditional city programs.

But times have changed as well as party control, and in the 12 years since Democrats were last in power, the very nature of urban America — as well as how it is governed — has been shifting.

Powerful demographic and economic forces — immigration, the globalizing economy, a new wave of interest in old-style urban neighborhoods — are reshaping city cores and adjacent suburbs around the nation, and also blurring distinctions between urban and suburban issues. There are more people living in poverty in suburbs now than in cities, for example.

At the same time, local officials have been moving to solve their own problems and have been aggressively staking claims to a wider range of issues they consider important and neglected by Washington — such as poverty or environmental policy. In some areas, cities and

From *CQ Weekly*, February 5, 2007.

adjacent suburbs have begun forming alliances to address common interests and problems.

Some mayors and urban policy experts say that all of these changes argue for a new paradigm in the relationship between Washington and local government, even a fundamental rethinking of federal urban policy. Indeed, the very assertiveness of cities may alter the dynamic between local government and Congress.

Cities are still looking for money, but more than ever, they are coming to Washington pushing their own ideas on public policy.

They want Congress to support local initiatives and, more than that, to follow their lead on a range of issues, including some once thought of primarily as the province of federal or state government: poverty, housing finance, even alternative energy and global warming.

The U.S. Conference of Mayors, in a 10-point plan delivered to Congress in January 2007, proposed, for example, a $4 billion "energy and environment block grant" program to support an array of local initiatives aimed at reducing greenhouse gases and encouraging the development of alternative energy sources.

If Congress wants to address such issues, "make us a partner," urges Dannel Malloy, the Democratic mayor of Stamford, Conn. "Many cities have taken the last 12 years to reinvent themselves, reinvent how they do business," he said. "We're ready."

REASONS FOR OPTIMISM

Some urban policy experts argue that federal policy is stuck 20 or 30 years in the past, when center cities had lost their economic purpose and urban and suburban areas were worlds apart. Neither of those things are broadly true today. The new realities have implications for federal policy in such areas as transportation, economic development, and housing, said Bruce Katz, director of the Metropolitan Policy Program at the Brookings Institution in Washington.

For one thing, with many cities coming back into their own in the new economy, Washington ought to be thinking about helping them play to their strengths, rather than trying to restore federal funding, Katz said.

"In the near term," he wrote in a January 2007 op-ed, "the challenge is not the lack of funding in many cases, but the absence of imagination and perspective."

That conversation, at best, has only begun, and forging a consensus about what a federal urban policy ought to

look like, even among cities themselves, is going to be difficult. They're a diverse bunch, with different needs, attitudes and circumstances. Some are booming while others are still struggling.

Everyone is also very busy trying to deal with local issues and address their own individual needs. "As a mayor, when I think about national politics, I don't think about cohesive policy," said Chris Doherty, the Democratic mayor of Scranton, Pa. "I think I have to get what I can get and move on. Because that's what the big cities are doing."

And though Democrats may be friendlier toward cities than Republicans were, they are quick to remind them that budgets are tight. Competition for money and attention in the new Congress will be fierce, and Democrats also must

> **"The challenge is not the lack of funding in many cases, but the absence of imagination and perspective."**
>
> — Bruce Katz, Brookings Institution

be concerned with the care and feeding of rural and "exurban" voters who helped them in last fall's election.

But for all that, there is indeed good reason for cities to be optimistic that a Democratic Congress will be more receptive to their priorities and ideas. House Speaker Nancy Pelosi represents the city of San Francisco and was raised in Baltimore, where her father and brother were mayors. A delegation from the Conference of Mayors was the first outside group she met with after she took the Speaker's gavel in January 2007.

There's also Charles B. Rangel, the new chairman of the House Ways and Means Committee and a native of Harlem, and Barney Frank, the chairman of the Financial Services Committee, whose House district includes dense Boston suburbs and urban areas south of the city.

Frank's committee has jurisdiction over Community Development Block Grants, which President Bush has been trying to cut, and Frank wants to put more money into them — a big priority for cities.

He also has jurisdiction over another big Bush target, the Hope VI housing initiative, designed to help revitalize failed public housing. Frank said he and other lawmakers want to put more money into the program and refine it to ensure that it's doing the best job of preserving existing housing and breaking up concentrated poverty by distributing affordable housing throughout cities.

He's interested, too, in getting more federal money to help cities reclaim polluted "brownfields" industrial land for redevelopment.

Pelosi, for her part, met privately with mayors in January 2007 at the Capitol and chose the annual Conference of Mayors meeting in Washington as her venue to offer her morning-after critique of Bush's State of the Union address. Her office volunteered that the choice underscored her commitment to cities.

She thanked cities prominently for their ideas on alternative energy and global warming and said she had appointed a former mayor of Kansas City, Mo., Democratic Rep. Emanuel Cleaver II, as the liaison between cities and a special congressional task force on global warming. "We will be following your lead," Pelosi said.

NEW REALITIES, NEW STRENGTHS

According to city officials and analysts such as Katz, many of the best ideas for dealing with a range of issues have been coming from the local level, while Washington has been gridlocked and while congressional allies of cities have had to put a lot of energy into just preserving existing urban programs. Some of the initiatives could be scaled up to work nationwide and many deserve federal support, they say.

New ideas for fighting poverty, for example, are being tried in New York City, San Francisco and other areas. Cities such as Seattle and Austin have their own initiatives for reducing energy use and cutting greenhouse gases from cars and local power plants.

City officials are talking up those ideas prominently in Washington and elsewhere. "The green agenda is now being laid by cities," said Bart Peterson, the Democratic mayor of Indianapolis and president of the National League of Cities, another group lobbying for cities and towns.

At a recent meeting of the league in San Diego, Peterson and other cities' officials called for federal, state and local collaboration on energy efficiency, as well as transportation and crime. Cities want a prominent voice, too, in ongoing debates about overhauling federal immigration and telecommunication laws.

City officials also are far more plugged in than Washington is to the forces that have been reshaping metropolitan areas, analysts said. Lines have blurred between suburban and urban, with many older suburbs outside cities such as Cleveland, Chicago and Washington now sharing many of the same issues as cities — traffic congestion, an aging infrastructure, poverty and crime.

That's something suburbs and cities are coming to realize. The suburbs around Cleveland, for example, have their own association, called the First Suburbs Consortium, and have collaborated with the city on initiatives to fight predatory lending and encourage the rehabilitation of old housing. Those sorts of partnerships hold the potential to remake political coalitions.

"The dichotomies that split America for decades are long gone," said Robert Puentes, another fellow at the Brookings Institution.

At the same time, Katz argues that the density of metropolitan areas, their diversity, cultural life, and proximity to universities and medical research centers have made them more attractive in a knowledge-based globalized economy — with the potential to become even more powerful engines for the national economy.

Katz said that Washington needs to be thinking about urban policy in more holistic ways that connect urban cores to surrounding areas — and invest in them in ways that enhance their strong points.

The federal government, for example, could coordinate grants for transportation, environmental remediation and homeland security to help cities reconnect to isolated waterfronts and encourage the sort of vibrant, pedestrian-friendly downtowns that the new "innovation economy" values, he said.

Getting all the players in Washington and back home to step back and think in such sweeping ways is a very big order, but city leaders say they do see a new opening for a fresh conversation with the federal government if they can take advantage of it. The change in mood was palpable at the recent meeting of the Conference of Mayors, Malloy said.

It was, he said, "like a depression has lifted."

FOR FURTHER READING

Frank's agenda, 2006 CQ Weekly, p. 2996; cities and poverty, p. 2802; mayors and gun crime, p. 1294.

Political Participation

Political participation is the lifeblood of U.S. democracy. This section is devoted to the groups and individuals who help choose the country's leaders and set its course. The articles in this section examine the results and larger significance of the 2006 midterm elections and highlight prospects for change in the 110th Congress, including a restoration of congressional oversight, attention to middle-class concerns and a renewed pro-labor agenda. The fifth article also previews the Senate campaign shaping up in Minnesota in advance of the 2008 election.

In what was widely perceived as a repudiation of President Bush's handling of the war in Iraq, Democrats mounted a sweeping comeback in the 2006 midterm elections, taking control of both houses of Congress for the first time in twelve years. The first article in this section examines how Democrats gained the majority by wooing moderate and independent voters, and how they plan to maintain their advantage in Congress by exercising their oversight capacity on a new strategy for Iraq and a host of other issues. The next two articles analyze the election results for each house of Congress. In addition to growing public opposition to the war, a rash of corruption scandals contributed to dissatisfaction with the ruling party. Caught in the middle of this were a number of moderate Republican House members who had often voted against Bush's policies but were victims of the Democratic groundswell. The Democratic victory in the fight for control of the Senate was the biggest surprise in the 2006 elections. What seemed like an insurmountable deficit in the polls only a few months earlier was erased by the tide of anti-Republican and anti-incumbent sentiment, giving the Democrats control of the Senate by a slim margin.

The AFL-CIO views the Democratic majority in Congress as an opportunity to redirect national attention to labor issues. The organization maintains its traditional political goals, such as increasing the minimum wage and putting a freeze on new trade agreements, but its current focus is an overhaul of the corporate bankruptcy code. The fourth article in this section explains how the group is striving to protect its workers as struggling companies shed worker benefits to stay in business. Furthermore, the union, which recently lost millions of members following the defection of the Teamsters and the Service Employees International Union, needs to prove to workers that it is still able to deliver results.

The next article contemplates liberal comedian Al Franken's entrance into the race for incumbent Republican Norm Coleman's Minnesota Senate seat in 2008. Historically, Minnesota has been a reliably Democratic state in presidential elections, but Republicans have made inroads in the state in recent years. Franken's candidacy will likely make for a high-profile and serious campaign.

With rising medical costs, college tuition rates, working hours, mortgage payments and participation in 401(k) retirement plans, many Americans are caught in the "middle-class squeeze." The last article explains that the Democrats' campaign promises to address the economic problems of the middle class might be downsized as both parties gear up for the race for the White House in 2008 and President Bush continues to wield his veto pen.

A Hill Full of Hard Looks

An unprecedented focus on the Iraq War, from why to what now, will top the agenda of new chairmen

CQ / Scott J. Ferrell

Giving Notice: "We need to re-establish the legislative branch of government," said Reid, center, with Sens. Charles E. Schumer of New York, left, and Richard J. Durbin of Illinois.

From *CQ Weekly,* November 13, 2006.

Following his re-election two years ago, President Bush claimed the confidence of the American people in his Iraq War policy. The voters, he said repeatedly, were the ones who hold him accountable. And they returned him to office.

In recent months, Bush used a similar argument to explain why he had not dismissed Donald H. Rumsfeld, the abrasive defense secretary who came to symbolize the botched planning for the war. The final responsibility for the war "rests with me," Bush said at an Oct. 25 news conference. He called Rumsfeld a "smart, tough, capable administrator" and saw no need for radical changes: "I believe that the military strategy we have is going to work."

Last week, the voters had another chance to deliver their verdict on the war, and on Bush's accountability. This time, it was a full-throated vote of no confidence. Democrats easily swept into power in the House, picking up at least 28 seats and ending a dozen years of Republican control, and won an even more uphill battle to gain control of the Senate. Within hours, Rumsfeld was on his way out. And Bush faces a Congress that could force a much deeper accounting for the war's blunders — along with a lengthy list of other controversies that Democrats have been waiting to investigate for six years.

The return of congressional oversight, the check on the executive branch that was mostly pushed to the sidelines under one-party government, will be the most immediate and visible change when the new Congress convenes next year. Simply by taking the reins of congressional committees, Democrats have the potential to reverse years of decline in oversight and explore the performance of the executive branch in ways that haven't been attempted for most of the Bush presidency.

They may be able to achieve some legislative accomplishments. Bush suggested he might be able to find common ground with Democrats on raising the minimum wage, and maybe even the broad rewrite of immigration policy that Republicans were unable to agree on.

But that is not where the new Democratic majority will have its biggest impact. Like a car that suddenly roars to life after sitting idle in the driveway all winter, the congressional oversight machine will be the most startling feature of the new Congress simply because it's there at all.

Democratic chairmen will look at waste, fraud and abuse in contracting — in the rebuilding of Iraq, in the reconstruction of the hurricane-devastated Gulf Coast, and in the Department of Homeland Security. They won't be able to end wasteful practices, but they might put a dent in the abuse simply by holding it up to public scrutiny.

They'll probe the administration's ties to K Street lobbyists, a ripe subject given that exit polls showed that voters' top concern in this election was corruption. They'll look at how the administration is running the Medicare prescription drug benefit and what is being done to address climate change, where there might be holes in the regulation of food and drug safety — all with the goal of changing policies through oversight.

They will explore how well the 2004 overhaul of intelligence agencies has worked and they'll press the FBI to fix problems such as the shortage of Arabic translators and its inability to design a workable computer system to sift through intelligence reports.

In Their Sights

Iraq
Military strategy, strain on the Army, contracting abuses, prewar intelligence

War on terrorism
Treatment of detainees, warrantless surveillance program, FBI troubles

Afghanistan
Instability, resurgence of Taliban

Katrina
Waste and fraud in reconstruction

Department of Homeland Security
Waste, fraud and abuse

Corruption
White House ties to lobbyists

Medicare
Implementation of the prescription drug benefit

Energy
Vice president's 2001 policy task force

Health care
Drug and medical-device safety

Environment
Climate change, use of science research

And nowhere will the oversight efforts be more crucial than the administration's basic goals in Iraq and its conduct of the war, the issue that the next House Speaker, California Democrat Nancy Pelosi, calls the single clearest demand for change that emerged from the election. Rumsfeld's departure, long demanded by Democrats, could be just the first of a series of changes yielding to the public pressure that essentially fired the Republican majority in Congress. (Pelosi's agenda, p. 72)

"We know that 'stay the course' is not working, has not made our country safer, has not honored our commitment to our troops and has not brought stability to the region," Pelosi said the day after her party won the House. "We must not continue on this catastrophic path."

Oversight efforts may be intended more to expose the failures in the administration's strategy than to push it toward a new one. As often as Democrats have called for a "new direction" on Iraq, they will probably be wary of taking the lead on a direction that could backfire — just as the Republicans quickly learned the risks of trying to dictate too much policy from Capitol Hill when they took control of Congress in 1995. There are political and practical limits on what the new majority can do. They can't issue subpoenas to investigate everything that might interest the Democratic base; that's the cartoon stereotype of a revenge-hungry party that they're trying to shed.

But they have several other avenues for oversight: hearings, phone calls, confirmation hearings, document requests, studies, even asking the simple questions they believe the Republicans never asked. All of that can be done without having to compromise with the administration or congressional Republicans at all.

"We need to re-establish the legislative branch of Congress," said Senate Minority Leader Harry Reid of Nevada, who will become the new majority leader next year. "We need to have the Constitution and its checks and balances and its separate and equal branches. We

Swing Voters Change Course

When Republicans surged to control of Congress in the elections of 1994, they declared a "conservative revolution," aimed at toppling liberal New Deal and Great Society policies that had undergirded Democratic dominance of Capitol Hill for six decades.

Now, 12 years later, the Democrats who terminated that Republican reign by sweeping control of the House and the Senate placed no such grand ideological label on their election-year rhetoric, neither during the nationwide campaign nor in their leaders' statements in the immediate aftermath of their electoral triumph.

Far from flying a banner of a Liberal Restoration, the Democrats succeeded this year in what's better described as the Push-back of the Pragmatists. They won their majorities by proving they can play in the middle of the political spectrum and the middle of the country.

If nothing else, they have successfully — if perhaps only temporarily — re-engineered the nation's electoral paradigm by laying bare the tired and trite distinctions between Republican "red" and Democratic "blue." This election turned, as will the next one in 2008, on self-described independent voters who predominate in "swing" districts and states. Last week, they turned away from President Bush and his GOP allies in Congress, in search of something else.

The beneficiaries of that turn this year are the Democrats. The question for both parties now is, what do these independent and generally moderate voters want from their government in Washington? The party that answers that question best will have a leg up on the 2008 election for president and future control of Congress.

Shades of Purple

Of the six states in which the Democrats unseated Republican Senate incumbents, four were carried by President Bush at the top of the GOP ticket just two years ago with margins ranging from 2 percentage points in Ohio to 20 points in Montana.

Although two of those states are traditional Midwestern partisan battlegrounds — Ohio and Missouri — both had been trending Republican in recent years. The other two, Virginia and Montana, could only be described as bedrock Republican territory.

On the House side, voters in 19 of the 28 districts where the Democrats had confirmed takeaways at the end of Election Week had, just two years ago, favored Bush over Democratic presidential challenger John Kerry. Those districts — many of them regarded as securely Republican entering this midterm campaign year — were strung from eastern New Hampshire to the Central Valley of California, and included seats in upstate New York, the South, the interior Midwest and the fast-growing Mountain West state of Arizona.

Most of those districts have substantial rural territory. Others are mainly in suburbs and exurbs. What both groupings have in common is that Democrats had been lagging behind Republicans.

The numbers do not include a number of near-misses for Democrats in districts that are usually strongly Republican turf. Among these are the nine seats for which the vote count was too close to call at week's end, plus one in Texas for which a December runoff between a Republican and a Democrat will decide the result.

The Democrats scored most of their victories by pursuing centrist postures and successfully dodging the "liberal label" applied by Republicans that so often has been fatal to Democratic aspirations.

Republicans faced a challenging political environment caused by dissent over the war in Iraq and plummeted approval ratings for Bush and the Congress they controlled. Many of their candidates danced awkwardly between distancing themselves from Bush and the party leadership and staying loyal enough to avoid alienating their conservative Republican base voters. About three dozen of them stumbled in that dance.

The new "bluer" political map provides both parties with their directions for the 2008 campaign. Republicans must ponder whether this year's election was a blip or one that would force them to rethink the strategy developed by Bush adviser Karl Rove of focusing primarily on turnout among the Republican base. It was a plan that worked in 2002 and 2004 but failed to meet the party's needs in the chaotic election of 2006.

Democrats, who showed this year that many places thought to be deeply Republican red are really "purple," will be probing to see how many of these and other previously hostile regions their party can put in play in 2008. But they will do so with the knowledge that many districts the Democrats won are already at the top of the Republicans' target list for the next round.

The Democrats during the midterm campaign did not hesitate to pummel Bush and the Republican leadership in Congress, whom they blamed for the intractable U.S. military commitment to Iraq, a "middle-class squeeze" in the economy, and failures of management epitomized by the Bush administration's response to the calamity that Hurricane Katrina wreaked in August 2005.

But the Democrats did not have to tone down this critique this year because it appealed not only to their base of liberal activists but also to politically unaffiliated swing voters.

According to exit polling conducted by Edison Media Research and Mitofsky International for a combine of broadcast and cable television networks, Democratic candidates were favored by 57 percent of respondents who said they were not affiliated with either major party and who made up 26 percent of voters. The Republicans were favored by 39 percent of independents, which pollsters said was a 9 percentage-point drop for the Republicans from the 2002 elections.

The Democrats dominated among self-described moderates, who made up just less than half of the respondents. The 60 percent to 38 percent Democratic edge among those voters amounted to a 7 percentage-point drop-off for the GOP from 2002. Many of these voters found the Republican message more compelling in 2002 and 2004, especially its emphasis on national security and fighting terrorism in the wake of Sept. 11. The loss of faith in the GOP among many swing voters in the two years since Bush was re-elected — spurred largely by Iraq, Katrina and a series of damaging corruption scandals — contributed to the steep declines in job approval ratings for Bush and the GOP-controlled Congress.

Democrats held big advantages over Republicans, according to exit polling, on most of the big issues that voters said were important to them. On the overriding issue of the war in Iraq, 35 percent of the respondents said the subject was extremely important, and Democrats led among them by 60 percent to 39 percent for the Republicans. On the economy, 39 percent said it was extremely important — and those voters broke 59 percent to 39 percent for the Democrats. And among the 41 percent who said corruption and scandals in government were extremely important, Democrats led 59 percent to 39 percent.

To win the Senate, the Democrats had to overcome significant disadvantages. There were more Democratic than Republican seats up this year (18 to 15); 12 of the 15 Republicans seats in play were in states carried by Bush over Democrat John Kerry just two years ago; and of the eight GOP seats the Democrats managed to seriously contest, six were in states that in 2004 were colored Republican red.

All of the victorious Democratic candidates energized their base voters by criticizing the Iraq War and other unpopular aspects of the Bush administration, playing up ethical lapses by congressional Republicans and accusing the GOP of extreme partisanship that had caused policy gridlock. But among them,

only Ohio's Sherrod Brown had a legislative record that gave Republicans ammunition to try to brand him as too liberal, and he managed to deflect that effort by focusing on populist themes such as the impact of foreign trade deals on American jobs. Bob Casey in neighboring Pennsylvania gained note for some conservative positions on social issues, notably abortion.

Messages Aimed at the Mainstream

Among those who picked up Democratic House seats, a few candidates could be defined as liberal activists. The best example was the huge come-from-behind upset by Democratic social worker Carol Shea-Porter over two-term Republican Rep. Jeb Bradley in eastern New Hampshire's 1st District, which was fueled by voter outrage over the war in Iraq.

But most of the members of the instantly historic Democratic Class of 2006 presented decidedly mainstream images to voters in the politically competitive districts where they ran.

Take, for example, the first two Democrats in the state-alphabetical listing of new members: Arizona's Harry E. Mitchell and Gabrielle Giffords, both of whom used the state Senate as their springboards. Mitchell, who won an upset over Republican Rep. J.D. Hayworth in the suburban Phoenix 5th District, says he plans to work in a bipartisan fashion with Republicans. Giffords, who won the southeastern 8th District seat left open by retiring GOP moderate Jim Kolbe, calls herself a consensus-builder.

Then there are Midwestern newcomers such as Brad Ellsworth, a county sheriff who ended the long hold of conservative Republican John Hostettler in southwestern Indiana by talking tough on crime and playing up his socially conservative views; and former pharmaceutical chemist Nancy Boyda, the upset winner over Republican Jim Ryun in Kansas' 2nd District, who calls for a bipartisan commission to deal with problems in the nation's health care system.

As with most big swing elections, the new majority party won some seats that will be hard to hold. This is particularly the case in House districts the Democrats won predominantly because of serious scandals involving the seats' previous Republican occupants, Bob Ney of Ohio, Mark Foley of Florida and Tom DeLay of Texas.

But the Democrats' gains this year also open a window of opportunity for the party to broaden its national political base. The agendas that incoming House Speaker Nancy Pelosi of California and Senate Majority Leader Harry Reid of Nevada pursue — and whether their approach is one of conciliation or retaliation — will go a long way toward determining if 2008 is another Democratic success or a comeback by Republicans chanting "we told you so."

have not had a legislative branch of government for six years."

SEEKING ALTERNATIVES

Rumsfeld's abrupt dismissal the day after the election was widely seen as a pre-emptive move to take some of the bite out of the new majority's oversight efforts on Iraq. Most senior Democrats said that Rumsfeld's departure would not be enough without a substantive change in the administration's Iraq policies. "I don't care who the secretary of Defense is. The final decision-maker is the president," said Carl Levin of Michigan, who will become the new chairman of the Senate Armed Services Committee.

Reid's first proposal to Bush that day was to call a bipartisan summit on Iraq, with congressional leaders, committee chairmen and ranking members all hashing out alternative strategies with the president. The move was framed as a peacemaking gesture after the electoral rout, but it also suggested a Democratic majority that is reluctant to take ownership of a specific new Iraq strategy — a note of caution that is also apparent in the vagueness of its initial oversight plans.

"They don't want to be saddled with this. This is the president's war," said James Dobbins, director of the RAND Corporation's International Security and Defense Policy Center. "I think the Democrats will be leery of doing much more than asking probing questions."

Of the likely new chairmen, only Joseph R. Biden Jr. of Delaware, who would take over the Senate Foreign Relations Committee, has shown signs of trying to advance a specific plan for Iraq. Biden, who probably will run for president in 2008, is calling for a federation government in Iraq that would create three autonomous regions for the warring Shiites, Sunnis and Kurds.

Biden says he wants to hold "a serious, full-blown week or more of hearings on what alternatives are to the present policy." He could use those hearings to push the administration to consider his plan, though other foreign policy experts from both parties think it would be impractical, as the sectarian groups aren't easy to divide geographically.

Levin is another strong Democratic voice on Iraq, but his oversight plans are more vague. Together with Jack Reed of Rhode Island, Levin sponsored a non-binding resolution earlier this year that called for a phased withdrawal of troops to begin by the end of the year, but with no specific timetable or deadline. Levin says he'll try to round up support from Republicans for a similar, non-binding resolution — giving it the kind of bipartisan cover it didn't have before.

Those who will chair the defense and foreign policy committees in the House, however, have committed to little other than hearings to expose what they consider the mismanagement of the war effort.

Tom Lantos of California, who's in line to become the next chairman of the House International Relations Committee, says he'll hold hearings within the first three months on planning failures such as the lack of enough forces to secure weapons caches in Iraq, as well as waste and fraud in the reconstruction effort.

"Obviously, the Republican Congress has failed miserably in its oversight of the war," said Lantos, a veteran investigator who probed the abuse of the Section 8 housing voucher program in the late 1980s. "We will demand accountability and change."

Ike Skelton of Missouri, a defense hawk who probably will become the new chairman of the House Armed Services Committee, would focus mainly on the strain the war is placing on the armed forces. "Forty percent of Army and National Guard equipment is in Iraq and Afghanistan. You can't train this way," he said.

Skelton plans to examine the assistance the military provides to U.S. soldiers and their families, including the chronic shortages of body armor for troops in Iraq, the adequacy of their training and the health care they receive. He also has called for hearings into a report by the Special Inspector General for Iraq Reconstruction that found thousands of U.S.-made weapons bought for Iraqi security forces are missing.

CAUTIOUS STRATEGY

That kind of systematic examination of the planning errors and oversight weaknesses in Iraq may be enough as a starting point, some prominent Democrats argue, because the immediate problems in the war effort are as important to address as the need for a long-term strategy.

"If we can't understand in detail how we went wrong and why, then we might lack confidence in our ability to effectively implement even a broad change of course," said retired General Wesley K. Clark, former supreme allied commander of NATO, who ran for president in 2004 and is considered a possible contender in 2008.

But there may not be much more the new Congress can do on its own, even under Democratic majorities. Realistically, it can't use one of its ultimate oversight tools — the power of the purse — to reduce funding for the war. Pelosi says that is not an option while U.S. troops are still overseas.

Even in the Vietnam War, when Congress eventually did cut off funds for combat operations, it didn't do so until after the 1973 peace agreement had been signed and U.S. troops had been withdrawn.

"They're not prepared to withhold funds. They're not prepared to require a new authorization," said Lee Feinstein, a senior fellow at the Council on Foreign Relations. "They're going to be very careful about what they'll do."

Some Democrats also are conscious that an aggressive effort to withdraw troops too early could cause the United States to lose its leverage to demand more progress from the Iraqi government in stabilizing the country. And given that the party has only recently regained some public trust on national security, some Democrats don't want to jeopardize those gains by pushing for a quick pullout.

Democrats should "look carefully at the history of the Vietnam War and not take over the war policy in a way that puts the onus on them for a withdrawal," said Will Marshall, president of the Progressive Policy Institute, a centrist think tank affiliated with the Democratic Leadership Council. "The Democrats of that era won an argument about Vietnam and lost a bigger battle over which party could better handle national security."

They could use the confirmation hearings for Rumsfeld's replacement to push for a less open-ended approach to the war. Robert M. Gates, Bush's choice to become the new defense secretary, has a reputation as more of a foreign policy realist than a neoconservative. In 2004, the former CIA director co-chaired a Council on Foreign Relations task force on Iran that recommended the United States deal with the regime rather than trying to overthrow it or waiting for it to fail — a blunt challenge to the Bush administration's policies.

But even though confirmation hearings can be a useful vehicle for oversight, Gates' hearings may be only a limited opportunity for Democrats. They're expected to take place during the lame-duck session of the out going Congress, before the Democrats assume control. That gives them less time, and therefore less leverage, to hold up the nomination if they're not satisfied with Gates' ideas on new Iraq strategies.

The best hope for both Bush and the new Democratic majority could be the upcoming report by the Iraq Study Group, a bipartisan panel headed by James A. Baker III — who served as secretary of state under Bush's father — and former Rep. Lee H. Hamilton, who also co-chaired the respected Sept. 11 commission.

Given that Bush's Iraq strategy has been scolded by the voters but Democrats may not want to commit to their own, the Baker-Hamilton report, expected as soon as December, could be an escape valve that gives both sides ideas to adopt. It doesn't hurt that Gates was a member of the group.

"It could be that any course corrections that are going to be made might be made by the time the new Congress convenes," said Dobbins of the RAND Corporation.

A WORLD OF QUESTIONS

The search for a new strategy in Iraq will be the most urgent oversight topic in the new Congress, but hardly the only one. Democrats who have been cooling their heels for years, eager to investigate topics they believe the Republican majority neglected, are already drawing up lists of hearings and probes to conduct now that they have the power to do it.

John D. Dingell of Michigan, a longtime master of oversight who will return to his old perch as chairman of the House Energy and Commerce Committee, has a lengthy and wide-ranging agenda he wants to pursue. He wants to hold hearings on drug and medical device safety, the implementation of the Medicare prescription drug program, Medicaid waivers, the consolidation of media ownership, online child pornography and climate change.

He's also interested in nuclear security at the Department of Energy, port security and the overall effectiveness of such agencies as the Environmental Protection Agency and the Food and Drug Administration.

"Our oversight will be fair, vigorous and focus on the business of Congress rather than politics," said Dingell. "This will not be political oversight. This will be oversight the way it should be done."

Patrick J. Leahy of Vermont, who will take the helm of the Senate Judiciary Committee, plans to press the administration for more details on the National Security Agency's surveillance program and its treatment of detainees.

Leahy also says he'll put a major focus on the FBI, including hearings on why the agency has been unable to modernize its computer system — which he calls "a train wreck in slow motion" — and how it plans to address its shortage of Arabic translators, which led to a backlog of untranslated recordings before the Sept. 11 attacks.

Leahy intends to grill the FBI on why it hasn't made more progress in its probe of the 2001 anthrax attacks. That's no academic matter to him, since his name was on one of the two anthrax-filled letters that was headed to

> ❝Our oversight will be fair, vigorous, and focus on the business of Congress. . . . This will be oversight the way it should be done.❞
>
> — Rep. John D. Dingell, D-Mich.

the Capitol — and because "one of the people who opened the letter that I was supposed to get died."

"I will not play gotcha. I don't believe in that," said Leahy. "But I have a reputation for doing oversight over Democratic administrations, and I'm going to do oversight over this one. So many mistakes have been made, so many have been swept under the rug that we've got to do something about it."

John D. Rockefeller IV of West Virginia, the incoming chairman of the Senate Select Intelligence Committee, is calling for a 10-year plan to fight terrorism around the world. Like Leahy, he wants to examine the FBI's missteps. He also wants to look at the implementation of the 2004 intelligence overhaul and proposes an "agency by agency review" of the intelligence community, focusing on how information is collected and what is being done about the lack of language skills.

And Rockefeller wants to finish some unfinished business: the committee's probe of how the Bush adminis-

tration used intelligence before the start of the Iraq War, an investigation that has dragged on for years, stalled by partisan infighting.

Lantos, in addition to examining the failures in Iraq, wants to look at the resurgence of the Taliban in Afghanistan and develop a plan for stabilizing the country. He also plans to look at the administration's refusal to open direct talks with North Korea and Iran; the role of Iran and its proxies in the Middle East; ways to secure loose nuclear materials around the world; the global AIDS crisis; and policies for reducing global warming.

MISTER INVESTIGATION

Of course, Henry A. Waxman of California, whose jurisdiction as chairman of the House Government Reform Committee is potentially the broadest of all, has his gavel ready. He has been one of the Republicans' favorite bogeymen; they tried to rally GOP voters by portraying him as a partisan, subpoena-spitting machine who would harass Bush full-time if Democrats won control of the House.

Waxman is doing his best not to play into the stereotype. He talks about his oversight agenda only in general terms — that he would focus on waste, fraud, and abuse and "make sure the government's money is spent wisely." He says such an agenda should win bipartisan support and that Republicans will have a say in it.

He talks about how burdensome and time-consuming subpoenas can be for administration officials, and how Congress can get results in other ways — sometimes just by asking the right questions. Mostly, he vows not to repeat the excesses he believes Republicans engaged in during the last four years of Bill Clinton's presidency, when Rep. Dan Burton of Indiana, who was chairman of the Government Reform panel at the time, issued more than 1,000 subpoenas to the Clinton administration and the Democratic Party.

"Our jurisdiction knows no bounds. We can investigate anything," Waxman said at a September panel discussion on congressional oversight. "But I think we need to approach it with balance and without duplication of effort."

Still, Waxman's priorities are well known from his past work. He has called for greater scrutiny of contracting abuses in Iraq and in the rebuilding of the Gulf Coast after Hurricane Katrina. He has sponsored legislation to set up a special commission, modeled after the Sept. 11 commission, to investigate abuses of detainees at Abu Ghraib and Guantánamo Bay. And he has specifically cited subjects like the Medicare prescription drug benefit and border security as targets for greater oversight.

In a report in January on areas where Congress has not done enough oversight, Waxman included Vice President Dick Cheney's 2001 energy task force.

SETTING PRIORITIES

The new Democratic leaders plan to have a hand in the oversight efforts, too. Reid says he'll expect reports from the committees every two weeks on their oversight activities. Pelosi says she'll let the committees and the Democratic caucus decide what investigations to pursue, but the incoming chairmen say she'll be the one who sets priorities and settles jurisdictional conflicts.

Democrats are practically elbowing each other out of the way to establish a new "Truman committee" like the post-World War II panel headed by Sen. Harry S Truman that investigated wartime profiteering. It has been a popular proposal among Democratic lawmakers and candidates this year, and several of the future chairmen have talked about launching similar investigations of contracting abuses in Iraq.

"It's likely that this is the largest amount of waste, fraud and abuse in the history of this country," said Byron L. Dorgan of North Dakota, chairman of the Senate Democratic Policy Committee. "And it's happened right under the nose of this Congress."

Democrats have promised to make sure that the Iraq inspector general's office, which has uncovered numerous problems in the reconstruction effort, doesn't go out of business next October as planned. Pelosi has said that "extending the tenure of the inspector general will be a priority for the new Congress."

Dorgan has held a series of unofficial hearings through the policy committee to highlight the lack of official oversight of contractors in Iraq. Ignored as a partisan exercise at first, the hearings recently have drawn a scattering of media coverage for prying out some revelations about Iraq even without the subpoena power and other investigative tools the official committees have.

One September hearing, for example, featured testimony from a former employee of Halliburton Co. — the

CQ / Scott J. Ferrell

QUESTION TIME: Democrats have six years of questions stored up for the Bush administration. Michigan Rep. John D. Dingell is a tough interrogator who returns to the helm of the Energy and Commerce Committee.

largest U.S. contractor in Iraq — who charged that the company inflated the number of troops its recreational facilities served so it could ask for more money.

A July hearing explored reports that another contractor, Parsons Inc., completed only 20 out of 142 health clinics it was supposed to build under a $200 million contract.

And at another September hearing, retired Army Maj. Gen. John Batiste, who headed the 1st Infantry Division in Iraq, accused Rumsfeld of incompetent leadership that allowed the insurgency to take hold. He would have said the same thing to any congressional committee that asked for his views, he said, but none of them did.

"Right now, we have no oversight, really," said James A. Thurber, director of the Center for Congressional and Presidential Studies at American University, who co-hosted the panel discussion on congressional oversight in September.

"There's very little follow-up on inspector general reports from the Department of Defense and the Department of Homeland Security and other departments that have had problems. There's a backlog of issues to address."

AVOIDING EXCESS

With so many potential targets, however, Democratic leaders and outside advisers are trying to rein in any temptation by the new committee chairmen to subpoena any-thing that moves — or to use the next two years to seek revenge for all of their frustrations over the last six years.

Pelosi has tried to set the tone, shooting down any talk of impeaching Bush — a prospect that had been dis-cussed quite openly by John Conyers Jr. of Michigan, who will become the new chairman of the House Judiciary Committee.

Now, Conyers says his oversight agenda would steer clear of impeachment, in the interest of pragmatism. That's a striking difference coming from the man who released a 350-page report in August on the administra-tion's actions called "Constitution in Crisis."

"I have said, and I say again, that impeachment is off the table," Pelosi said the morning after the election. "This election was about the future . . . not about the Republicans."

That's certainly the tone the new chairmen are trying to set, at least in their public comments. "The business of oversight, when it's done right, is to find out if the laws are being properly implemented, if money is being properly spent, if any laws need to be changed," said Dingell.

With some topics, there will be hot debates about whether to investigate. Pelosi has expressed an interest in re-examining the failures of prewar intelligence that sug-gested Iraq had weapons of mass destruction, but she hasn't committed to such a probe — and other promi-nent Democrats say it would be a mistake to start by reopening that subject.

"I sure hope we don't start with any of that," said Biden. "We have time to go back and get a more accu-rate record for history. We don't have a lot of time to try to save us and Iraq."

Congress has plenty of other oversight tools besides impeachment and subpoenas, and the new majority can make a significant difference even if, as several Demo-cratic leaders and future chairmen suggest, it simply returns to routine oversight.

For starters, Congress has the power to deny or sig-nificantly reduce funds to departments and agencies that don't perform well, or don't cooperate with lawmakers. It can perform oversight when it authorizes or reautho-rizes programs. The confirmation process for presidential nominees can be a form of oversight, if lawmakers ask tough questions and are willing to vote against nominees that don't answer to their satisfaction.

Hearings by committees and subcommittees are a well-known form of routine oversight, but even letters, phone calls and e-mail exchanges with administration officials can make clear what Congress expects of them. Studies by congressional staff, reports by the Govern-mental Accountability Office, and audits and investiga-tions by the inspectors general all can help Congress keep tabs on the executive branch — as long as lawmakers pay attention to them.

"Oversight needs to be balanced and fair," said Scott Lilly, a senior fellow at the Center for American Progress and a former Democratic staff member on the House Appropriations Committee. "It needs to be relatively free of obvious political considerations, and it needs to be done with as much bipartisan cooperation as possible. And it needs to be directed at improving the operation of the government, not headline grabbing."

FINDING ABUSES

Not all oversight disappeared over the last six years. Thomas M. Davis III of Virginia, the outgoing chairman of the House Government Reform Committee, teamed up with Waxman on some investigations, including a July report that found $34.3 billion in Department of Homeland Security contracts that were plagued by waste, overcharges or mismanagement. The two also released a highly publicized report in September that found 485 contacts between the White House and dis-graced lobbyist Jack Abramoff.

Senate Finance Committee Chairman Charles E. Grassley of Iowa regularly fires off letters to administra-tion officials about the implementation of health pro-grams and recently pressed the FBI to explain the apparent lack of progress in the investigation of the 2001 anthrax attacks. Sen. John McCain of Arizona has won praise for his work investigating the Air Force's costly 2004 plan to lease refueling tankers from Boeing.

And Rep. Christopher Shays of Connecticut has con-ducted numerous oversight hearings as chairman of the Government Reform subcommittee on national security, holding several hearings on the Iraq War and diving into such subjects as government secrecy and protections for national security whistleblowers.

Overall, though, there has been a clear decline. Peter Stockton, who worked for Dingell as an investigator on the House Energy and Commerce subcommittee on oversight and investigations, said the situation has gotten so bad that one congressional committee — which he declined to name — recently sent a Freedom of Information Act (FOIA) request to an agency it was overseeing.

The staff members apparently were unaware that a congressional committee doesn't have to write a FOIA letter, said Stockton, now a senior investigator at the Project on Government Oversight. It can simply demand the information.

"We were just stunned," he said. "If you're a congressional committee, you write a demand letter. 'We want it Friday, close of business.' "

It's unclear how much cooperation Democrats will get from an administration determined to preserve as much presidential authority as possible and that has often been reluctant to share information with Congress.

Bush has used his signing statements, for example, to reject congressional demands for consultation and information. Rumsfeld refused to disclose many documents to the Senate about the Boeing tanker deal. Justice Department officials repeatedly dodged questions in hearings about the NSA surveillance program, even as they asked Congress to authorize it.

Last month, Waxman released the results of records he and Davis compiled on administration officials' travel on private jets at taxpayer expense. Of the 15 departments and agencies asked for their records, one didn't bother to provide any: the Department of Homeland Security, whose poor record of responding to congressional requests has made it notorious on Capitol Hill.

Last year, the Department of Defense hung on to supporting documents in the most recent round of base closings until Susan Collins of Maine, the chairwoman of the Senate Homeland Security and Governmental Affairs Committee, issued a subpoena, one of the rare

Republican committee chiefs to do so. And in January, two Department of Labor officials walked out on a Senate Appropriations subcommittee hearing after the chairman, Arlen Specter of Pennsylvania, asked them to stay to answer additional questions.

When Congress encounters such obvious slights from the administration, Lilly said, Democrats need to crack down. "That has been the major failing of the Republicans that have attempted oversight," said Lilly. "If the administration says, 'That's not knowable' or 'We don't have to tell you that' . . . then there have to be consequences for that."

It can start by using Congress' power of the purse, Lilly said. If Cheney refuses to disclose records from his energy task force, "the undisclosed location he spends so much time in is paid for by the taxpayers and funded by appropriations that are passed by the Congress," said Lilly. "So you can start by taking that away."

That may be an extreme scenario, but even on routine matters, oversight experts will be watching the new majority to see if it can reverse a long decline in Congress' basic institutional knowledge of how to watch the executive branch.

"It doesn't take Houdini to figure out how to do it," said Stockton. "You don't rush into things. You take the time to learn the issues, where the sources are. Your relationship with the press is important. If you have a good hearing and nobody knows about it, it's not going to have much of an impact."

These days, Stockton's group runs training sessions for congressional staff members on oversight skills. The latest session, on Oct. 20, drew "a whale of a turnout," he said.

"Everyone seemed to be interested in how you frame questions, how do you put on a hearing and so forth." In the coming months, his sessions could become a booming business as Congress tries to relearn what oversight is about.

Voter Discontent Fuels Democrats' Day

More than a few seats rearranged at the ballot box

Nationwide dissatisfaction with the Bush administration and local disgust with the scandal-plagued Republican-controlled Congress propelled House Democrats on Nov. 7 to their biggest gains since the Seventies.

In ending a dozen years of GOP control and wresting a House majority from the Republicans for the first time since 1954, Democrats were poised to make a net gain of at least 28 House seats — and possibly more, pending the results of many close races where final vote tallies were pending. It was the party's biggest electoral gain since the Watergate era.

Buoyed by a strong showing among political independents, the Democrats easily surpassed the threshold of 15 seats they needed to clinch a majority. They were guaranteed to exceed the 26-seat net gain their party made in 1982, the first midterm election in the presidential tenure of Ronald Reagan.

Should every outstanding House race break in favor of the party that is currently leading — and if the parties split a pair of December runoff elections inLouisiana and Texas, as is expected — the 110th Congress will feature 232 Democrats and 203 Republicans, a precise partisan mirror image of the Congress that convened two years ago. Barring any partisan turnovers in the 110th Congress, the GOP will need to match the net gain of 15 seats in 2008 that was required of the Democrats this year.

From *CQ Weekly*, November 13, 2006.

The Democrats did that — and then some. They defeated a minimum of 20 House Republicans and also wrested away eight other districts that GOP incumbents had left open to resign, retire or seek other office.

The Democrats registered seat gains across the nation — particularly in the Northeast and in the Ohio River Valley. They began Election Day with a bang, unseating four Republican incumbents in Indiana and Kentucky, the first states to report results. On the West Coast, the party cheered the defeat of California Rep. Richard W. Pombo, chairman of the Resources Committee.

The Democratic upswing even spread to reliably Republican-leaning states such as Kansas, where Rep. Jim Ryun was defeated by Democrat Nancy Boyda — two days after President Bush campaigned for Ryun in Topeka.

"From sea to shining sea, the American people voted for change," said California Rep. Nancy Pelosi, who stands to become House Speaker when Congress convenes Jan. 3.

Pending a final vote count in one Georgia district, the Democrats retained every one of the seats they defended — a task neither party had accomplished in nearly 70 years.

Rep. Thomas M. Reynolds of New York, the chairman of the National Republican Congressional Committee (NRCC), said some of his members failed to prepare themselves to run in a turbulent political environment where low public approval ratings of the Congress and disenchantment with the Bush administration hampered many Republicans.

Those members, he said, did not "localize" the contests and draw sharp enough issue contrasts with their Democratic rivals, who tended to "nationalize" the election by linking Republicans to Bush.

"Unprepared members were swallowed up by the sour national environment," Reynolds said Nov. 8.

THE HOUSE

110th Congress		109th Congress	
Republicans	195	Republicans	229
Democrats	229	Democrats	201
Undecided	9	Independent	1
Pending runoffs	2	Vacancies *	4

* Three were Republican-held; one was Democratic-held

DEMOCRATS

Net gain as of Nov. 10	28
Freshman	40
Incumbents re-elected	188
Incumbents defeated **	1

REPUBLICANS

Net loss as of Nov. 10	28
Freshman	12
Incumbents re-elected	182
Incumbents defeated **	21

** One from each party was in primary

OPPOSITION TO THE WAR

More to the point, the election results yielded significant evidence that voters repudiated Bush — and, by extension, his House Republican allies — for their handling of the unpopular Iraq War.

A CNN exit poll found that 56 percent of respondents disapproved of the Iraq War — and they preferred a Democratic member of Congress to a Republican member of Congress by a margin of 80 percent to 18 percent. An exit survey conducted by Democratic pollster Douglas E. Schoen found that a 22 percent plurality of voters identified the Iraq War as the most important issue in their vote for Congress — and 82 percent of those voters backed a Democrat.

"I know there's a lot of speculation on what the election means for the battle we're waging in Iraq," Bush said Nov. 8. "I recognize that many Americans voted last night to register their displeasure with the lack of progress being made there."

Enough New Blue For a Majority

Even with an unusually large group of nine races still too close to call, a review of where the parties took seats, held seats and lost seats amply demonstrates where the Democrats made the inroads they needed to win the House after a dozen years in the minority. While so far not a single Democratic incumbent has been declared the loser, the party did particularly well in the Northeast, where it now holds 23 of 29 seats in New York and 11 of 19 in Pennsylvania — and is poised to control 20 or 21 of the 22 seats in New England. Democrats also continue to dominate coastal districts but picked up at least nine seats in the Midwest, all of them covering rural territory. The core of Republican strength continues to be in the South and Southwest and in many rural areas.

Two More House Elections Coming

No matter the outcome of the recounts and legal challenges that are still keeping nine contests in limbo, it will take two more elections — runoffs in Louisiana and Texas — to complete the roster of House members for the 110th Congress.

On Dec. 9, voters in and around New Orleans will choose among two Democrats: the incumbent William J. Jefferson, who is seeking a ninth term, and state Rep. Karen Carter. They finished atop 11 others last week in one of Louisiana's unique all-party congressional primaries, the rules for which require a second round if no one wins an absolute majority the first time. Jefferson, who won his last term in the overwhelmingly Democratic district two years ago with 79 percent of the vote, took 30 percent, a reflection of how much he has been politically weakened by the federal bribery investigation of which he is at the center. Carter, who has the backing of the state Democratic Party, says the cloud of suspicion has eviscerated the congressman's ability to effectively represent a district devastated last year by Hurricane Katrina.

Later in the month — officials will set a date after completing their Nov. 7 canvass — voters will return to the polls in South Texas' recently reconfigured 23rd District, which takes in much of San Antonio and also hugs the Rio Grande River. In that race, Democrats have a chance, if not a sturdy one, of augmenting their new majority. Republican Henry Bonilla took 49 percent of the overall vote in his bid for an eighth term — falling just short of the majority necessary to win the election outright. He will face Democratic former Rep. Ciro D. Rodriguez, who cinched a spot in the runoff with 20 percent. Bonilla has the edge, in part because his war chest is as brimming as the challenger's is starved. But the cumulative vote for the six Democratic candidates matched Bonilla's vote percentage.

The unusual blanket primary was required by the federal courts, which redrew the boundaries of five South Texas districts to comply with a Supreme Court decision that partially invalidated the 2003 Republican-drawn congressional map on the grounds that it unconstitutionally weakened Hispanic voting rights in Bonilla's district.

Nowhere was this more evident than in New Hampshire's eastern 1st District, which takes in Dover and Manchester. Two-term incumbent Jeb Bradley was upset by Democrat Carol Shea-Porter, a little-known liberal activist whose underfunded campaign concentrated heavily on her opposition to the war. Shea-Porter's win almost certainly was the biggest surprise of the 2006 election.

Her win also typified the Democrats' resounding success in the northeastern United States, a historically "Yankee Republican" region that has shifted decidedly to the Democrats in recent years — a partisan counterweight to the Republican political realignment in the South.

In New Hampshire's western 2nd District, which includes Concord and Nashua, moderate six-term Rep. Charles Bass was defeated by Democratic lawyer Paul W. Hodes, whom Bass trounced by 20 percentage points two years ago. The victories by Hodes and Shea-Porter delivered both of New Hampshire's House seats to the Democrats for the first time since 1912.

In New York, Democrats defeated two Republican incumbents, nearly knocked off three others — including Reynolds — and also won the seat of retiring moderate GOP Rep. Sherwood L. Boehlert. The GOP will hold just six of 29 House seats inNew York next year.

The Democrats also unseated four House Republicans from Pennsylvania: Curt Weldon and Michael G. Fitzpatrick in suburban Philadelphia; Don Sherwood, who fell to political scientist Chris Carney in northeastern Pennsylvania; and Melissa A. Hart, who was upset by Jason Altmire, a former hospital association executive and congressional aide, in a culturally conservative district near Pittsburgh.

GLOOM FOR GOP MODERATES

Republican moderates bore a disproportionate brunt of the losses on Election Day.

Many GOP centrists represent districts that were politically competitive or even lean Democratic in politically neutral years, and Democrats pounced on them in an election year that trended strongly to their party — even though many of the Republican moderates had voting habits that were frequently at odds with the Bush administration.

Rep. Jim Leach, a 30-year House veteran and one of the GOP's most prominent and widely respected moderates, was shockingly defeated by Democratic college professor David Loebsack in a Democratic-leaning district in southeastern Iowa that nonetheless had re-elected Leach by handsome margins in most of his previous 15 elections.

Leach in 2002 voted against the resolution that authorized the president to wage military operations in Iraq — part of a contrarian voting record that made him the least conservative Republican in the House. But Loebsack argued that Leach's party affiliation was a detriment to the Democratic-leaning district.

Other prominent Republican moderates who lost Nov. 7 included Nancy L. Johnson, a senior member of the Ways and Means panel who was trounced by Democratic state Sen. Chris Murphy in Connecticut's northwestern 5th District, which includes Danbury, New Britain and most of Waterbury; and Pennsylvania's Fitzpatrick, who lost to lawyer Patrick Murphy, one of a handful of Democratic veterans of the Iraq War who were victorious on Election Day. In eastern Connecticut's 2nd District, Rep. Rob Simmons was narrowly trailing Democratic former Rep. Joe Courtney in a race still too close to call.

SCANDALS TAKE TOLL

The Republicans would have limited their losses had some GOP incumbents not been buffeted by personal scandals separate from the unfavorable national political environment.

A top Democratic prize in the Nov. 7 election was the suburban Houston district long represented by former Majority Leader Tom DeLay — the veteran political infighter whose aggressive efforts to ensure a "permanent" Republican majority caused ethics problems that ultimately led to his resignation from the House in June.

Democratic former Rep. Nick Lampson, a 2004 casualty of a DeLay-engineered redistricting map, fended off Houston city councilwoman Shelley Sekula Gibbs, who was forced to wage a write-in campaign after DeLay decided to renounce the GOP nomination. (At the same time, Sekula Gibbs did win a separate special election to serve the final two months of DeLay's unexpired term).

The GOP also surrendered the rock-ribbed northeastern Pennsylvania district of Sherwood, who was felled by Carney in no small part because of the incumbent's admission last year of an affair with a young woman (whose allegations of physical abuse the congressman vigorously denied).

Democrat Zack Space, an elected municipal attorney, won a seat in a landslide in the culturally conservative eastern Ohio district recently vacated by six-term Republican Bob Ney.

Ney had recently pleaded guilty to federal corruption charges that stemmed from an investigation into his ties to former lobbyist Jack Abramoff. Republicans were badly hurt by the fact that their preferred candidate, state Sen. Joy Padgett, was asked by Ney to run in his stead (and the fact that the disgraced congressman did not immediately resign his seat following his guilty plea). That enraged GOP leaders and allowed Space and his Democratic surrogates to continuously link Padgett to the embattled Ney. Padgett won just 38 percent of the vote — an embarrassing showing in a district that Bush dominated just two years ago.

In Florida's south-central 16th District, encompassing Port St. Lucie and parts of Port Charlotte and Wellington, Democratic businessman Tim Mahoney edged Republican state Rep. Joe Negron to win the seat that Republican Mark Foley resigned in September after disclosures that he sent inappropriate electronic messages to teenage boys who had served as House pages. Foley's name appeared on the ballot, though votes cast for him were automatically awarded to Negron.

All four districts comfortably backed President Bush's re-election in 2004.

"We also lost several seats by self-inflicted wounds," Reynolds said. "We had a number of reliable Republican seats where the member had a problem. And either they could not straighten it out with their constituents, or they left it to the candidate succeeding them to deal with it."

Illinois Rep. Rahm Emanuel, Reynolds' counterpart at the Democratic Congressional Campaign Committee (DCCC), said, "Every district that had an issue related to the professional conduct of that [Republican] member switched and became Democratic."

"That was eight seats — half of the 15 that you needed," he said.

PLAYING THE FIELD

Republicans entered Tuesday in a deep defensive crouch: On Election Day, more than 50 GOP-held districts featured highly competitive races, a playing field much larger than in previous election cycles.

Of the $83.6 million that the NRCC reported in "independent expenditures" — funds that the parties expend on television ads and mail pieces without consulting their preferred candidates — $80 million, or 96 percent, was spent in districts defended by Republicans.

Decline of the 'Kerry Republicans'

As Democrats plotted how to pick up the 15 seats they needed to win back the House, their eyes turned early on to the 18 districts that preferred John Kerry for president in 2004 while simultaneously electing a Republican to the House. Democratic strategists bet that well-funded and seasoned candidates could win those seats in an anti-GOP political environment. The strategy paid off Nov. 7: Democrats took both "Kerry Republican" seats that were left open and beat seven of the GOP incumbents — and are still hopeful of prevailing in two more especially close challenges that may go to recounts.

DISTRICTS	KERRY'S 2004 MARGIN (percentage points)	GOP INCUMBENT	MEMBER 2004 MARGIN (percentage points)	2006 RESULT (percentage points)
Iowa 2	11.5	Jim Leach	20	Lost by 3
Connecticut 2	9.7	Rob Simmons	8	Trailing by 0.1
Delaware AL	7.6	Michael N. Castle	39	Won by 18
Iowa 1	6.5	Jim Nussle	12	Democrat won open seat by 12
Pennsylvania 7	6.3	Curt Weldon	18	Lost by 13
Connecticut 4	6.1	Christopher Shays	5	Won by 3
Illinois 10	5.5	Mark Steven Kirk	28	Won by 7
New Hampshire 2	5.1	Charles Bass	20	Lost by 7
Pennsylvania 8	3.4	Michael G. Fitzpatrick	12	Lost by 1
Pennsylvania 6	3.3	Jim Gerlach	2	Won by 1
New Mexico 1	3.3	Heather A. Wilson	9	Leading by 1
Colorado 7	3.2	Bob Beauprez	12	Democrat won open seat by 13
Washington 8	2.6	Dave Reichert	5	Leading by 2
New York 25	2.5	James T. Walsh	90	Won by 2
Kentucky 3	2.0	Anne M. Northup	22	Lost by 2
Florida 22	1.8	E. Clay Shaw Jr.	27	Lost by 4
Connecticut 5	0.4	Nancy L. Johnson	22	Lost by 12
Pennsylvania 15	0.2	Charlie Dent	19	Won by 9

spent in districts defended by Republicans.

The NRCC was forced to spend money in unlikely venues such as the Kansas district won by Boyda and an open Idaho district that the GOP barely held despite the fact that Bush took nearly 70 percent of the vote there two years ago.

"If we're going to be a national party, we have to be able to compete everywhere," Democratic National Committee Chairman Howard Dean said Nov. 8. "And last night we did compete everywhere. That's very, very important. Can we do better? Yes. But this is a huge step forward — and, frankly, one I didn't expect."

DCCC chief Emanuel said his team early on recognized the importance of fielding top-flight challengers, in the expectation that they would be well-positioned to win in the campaign's home stretch.

"What you couldn't see a year out, but which became

apparent three months out, was we were going to have an expanded field with expanded opportunities for Democrats," Emanuel said Nov. 8.

As a case in point, Emanuel pointed to the victory of Arizona state Sen. Harry Mitchell over six-term Republican Rep. J.D. Hayworth in a politically competitive district that takes in Scottsdale and Tempe. Democratic strategists recruited Mitchell as a much stronger challenger than the hapless foe Hayworth crushed by more than 20 percentage points in 2004.

By contrast, the Republicans failed to put many Democratic-held seats in play. Just five districts now held by Democrats were considered to be highly competitive, and the party appeared to retain them all.

Democrats retained the at-large Vermont seat that liberal Independent Rep. Bernard Sanders gave up to wage his successful Senate campaign. Freshman Rep.

Melissa Bean of Chicago's northwestern suburbs and exurbs and five-term Iowa Rep. Leonard L. Boswell of Des Moines defeated strong GOP challengers.

It is still unclear whether Democratic Rep. John Barrow will be re-elected, though he held a narrow lead in his eastern Georgia district over a seasoned Republican challenger, former Rep. Max Burns. The other close race in Georgia finally fell in favor of incumbent Democrat Jim Marshall, who beat former Rep. Mac Collins.

Several House Democrats whom party strategists expected might face highly competitive contests wound up winning handily. They included Rep. Chet Edwards, who trounced Republican Van Taylor, a businessman and Iraq War veteran, in a strongly conservative district in central Texas that includes Bush's ranch in Crawford.

An unusually large number of races remained too close to call at week's end. As of Nov. 9, there were nine contests — not including the runoffs next month in Louisiana and Texas — for which the final vote was too close to call.

Excepting Barrow's Georgia seat, the GOP is the incumbent party in each of those districts. Republican incumbents in uncalled races are Robin Hayes of North Carolina; Heather A. Wilson of New Mexico; Jean Schmidt and Deborah Pryce of Ohio; Dave Reichert of Washington; Barbara Cubin of Wyoming; and Simmons of Connecticut. All except Simmons have nominal leads in the balloting. The Republicans also have a tiny lead for the open Florida seat held by Katherine Harris, who ran unsuccessfully for Senate.

Hunger for Change Key to Democrats' Hat Trick

Long-shot capture of Senate relied on nation's anger

Going into this campaign season, Democrats seeking to retake control of the Senate were looking at a seemingly impossible task. They needed a net gain of six seats to reach the magic number of 51, and to get there, they had to do three things:

- Win six of eight at-risk Republican seats.
- Hold all three of their open seats.
- Defend all 15 of their incumbents, including four who appeared highly vulnerable to GOP takeover.

Such an achievement was almost inconceivable several months ago, before Republicans across the country were brought low by the unpopularity of the Bush administration and its war in Iraq, along with a series of scandals that called to question the judgment of the party's leadership and stirred up an already nascent anti-Republican, anti-incumbent mood.

Campaigning largely on dissatisfaction with the president, Congress and the world at large, Democrats pulled the hat trick, eking out a one-seat margin of control. It's the first time since 1986

From *CQ Weekly*, November 13, 2006.

that Democrats have won control of the Senate via the ballot box (their short-lived majority for part of 2001 and all of 2002 came from the post-election defection of Vermont Republican James M. Jeffords). Their new majority is technically 50 Democrats and one independent: Vermont's Bernard Sanders, who won his Senate seat as an independent but has always caucused with Democrats during 16 years in the House. (Connecticut's Joseph I. Lieberman lost the Democratic primary this summer and won the general election on his own ballot line, but he says he remains a loyal member of the party and should be counted in their ranks.)

Still, the impending coup hung in the balance for two days after the first election results came in. Razor-thin margins in the Virginia and Montana contests raised the specter of recounts that could have stretched the final determination for months. But the Republican incumbents conceded Nov. 9.

And although Virginia and Montana were the nail-biters, Democratic takeovers in Missouri, Ohio, Pennsylvania and Rhode Island were no less vital. Each win came on the back of a strategy by New York Sen. Charles E. Schumer, chairman of the Democratic Senatorial Campaign Committee, to nationalize the issues and ask voters: Do you want more of the same?

"The message of this election came down to one word: change," Schumer said Wednesday at a rally in Washington.

CRUISE CUT SHORT

In Virginia, George Allen's fall from grace after one term has mirrored the party's struggle nationwide. Allen was a popular one-term governor before his election to the Senate in 2000, and just months ago was touted as a top presidential contender for 2008. Initially, he was expected to cruise through a re-election race against his upstart opponent, former Navy Secretary Jim Webb. But

THE SENATE

	110th Congress		109th Congress
Republicans	49	Republicans	55
Democrats	50	Democrats	44
Independent	1	Independent	1

REPUBLICANS

Net loss	6
Freshman	1
Incumbents re-elected	8
Incumbents defeated	6

DEMOCRATS

Net gain	6
Freshmen*	9
Incumbents re-elected	15
Incumbents defeated	0

* Includes Independent, who will caucus with Democrats

having come under fire for comments some deemed racially insensitive, Allen found himself trailing Webb by more than 7,000 votes out of 2.4 million cast. With Webb's lead confirmed after all votes were counted two days after the election, Allen announced Nov. 9 that he would step aside to prevent adding "more rancor" to the process.

"The people of Virginia, who I always call the owners of the government, have spoken — and I respect their decision," he said.

Rancor was at a premium in the race, which was one of the bloodiest of the year. Allen ultimately appeared to be undone by the combination of his own inopportune comments and disapproval of Congress' job; Webb took serious flak for allegedly misogynistic comments he made earlier in his career, but appeared to ride the wave of overall discontent into Congress.

Earlier in the day, another nasty battle, in Montana between scandal-plagued incumbent Republican Conrad Burns and the Democratic president of the state Senate, Jon Tester, ended when the incumbent declared that his campaign "fought the good fight, and we came up just a bit short." Final vote counts indicate that Tester, an organic farmer in addition to his legislative duties, led Burns by fewer than 3,000 out of 404,000 cast.

Burns, who has represented Montana in the Senate since 1989, was the senator most endangered by his ties to convicted lobbyist Jack Abramoff, the central figure in a sweeping influence-peddling scandal. Democrats hammered Burns on what they said were his questionable ethics, and were aided by Burns' own proclivity for colorful statements that brought a rain of bad press, including jokes about employing an illegal Guatemalan immigrant. Among their other turns of phrases, Democrats said Burns' legacy was one of "embarrassment, corruption and 'ka-ching.' "

Declaring victory, Tester called for a different kind of government. "It is absolutely, critically important that we change the direction of the country," he said, and called for a bipartisan approach to solving national problems.

Where the Action Was

The Republican loss of six seats last week nearly matched the last time the party lost control of the Senate in an election — 20 years ago, when seven incumbents were ousted. As was the case in 1986, the Republicans who were defeated this time were a relatively junior bunch: Their average senatorial service was a decade, and none of them chaired a standing committee (although between them they had chaired a dozen subcommittees). Perhaps one of the reasons for this year's Democratic success was the relative paucity of Senate contests in the South, where the GOP held on to its single open seat while losing a seat in Virginia. Still, Republicans next year will hold all but five of the region's 26 seats.

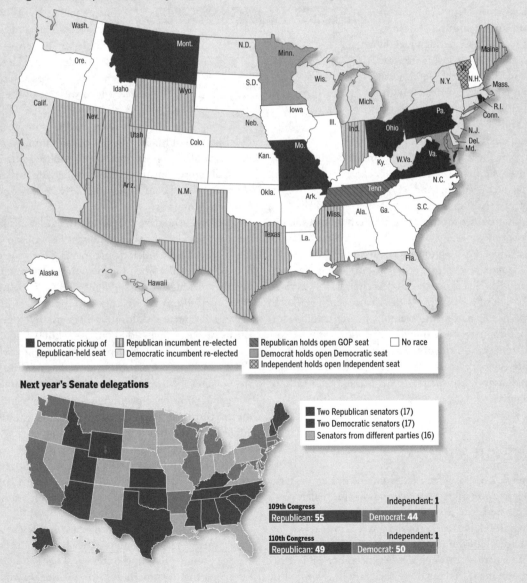

■ Democratic pickup of Republican-held seat
▦ Republican incumbent re-elected
▢ Democratic incumbent re-elected
▨ Republican holds open GOP seat
■ Democrat holds open Democratic seat
▧ Independent holds open Independent seat
□ No race

Next year's Senate delegations

■ Two Republican senators (17)
■ Two Democratic senators (17)
■ Senators from different parties (16)

109th Congress
Republican: 55 | Democrat: 44 | Independent: 1

110th Congress
Republican: 49 | Democrat: 50 | Independent: 1

"It really is time to put politics aside. . . . Now is the time to roll up our sleeves and get some things done," he said.

FOUR BIG ONES

Among the other Democratic takeovers — Claire McCaskill's defeat of Sen. Jim Talent in Missouri; Rep. Sherrod Brown's victory over Sen. Mike DeWine in Ohio; Bob Casey's ouster of Sen. Rick Santorum in Pennsylvania; and Sheldon Whitehouse's defeat of Sen. Lincoln Chafee in Rhode Island — the national mood played into Democrats' hands.

Voters "all over America tonight have said, 'We want change,'" said the party's floor leader in the Senate, Harry Reid of Nevada. "All over America they've come to the conclusion, as we did some time ago, that a one-party town just simply does not work."

• **Missouri.** Talent, who has represented Missouri for one term, acknowledged as much when speaking with supporters as he conceded to McCaskill, the state auditor, early the morning after Election Day. Talent said his defeat "was not for any lack of support or work or vigor anywhere around this state. . . . The headwind was just very, very strong this year."

Speaking to her supporters, McCaskill declared her victory a rejection of the mud-slinging tactics that had marked the tight race, and declared her election the voters' call for a different course. "The great state of Missouri has spoken!" she said. "Tonight we have heard the great voice of Missourians, and they have said, 'We want change.'"

• **Ohio.** In Ohio, where Republicans had begun pulling their money weeks ahead of the election based on DeWine's falling poll numbers, Brown's victory represents a significant pickup for the Democrats. Brown, who represented northeastern Ohio during seven terms in the House, ran a campaign focused largely on jobs and opposing policies he said were outsourcing U.S. jobs. He won the race with 56 percent of the vote. "In the middle of America, the middle class won," Brown told his supporters.

• **Pennsylvania.** Casey, Pennsylvania's state treasurer, was slightly favored for almost his entire campaign against Santorum, a two-term senator who had come under fire for his conservative social stances even before his Republican brethren were brought low by poor approval ratings for the president, a worsening situation in Iraq and a spate of scandals. Although Santorum had held the seat since the so-called Republican revolution of 1994, Casey easily outpolled him, 59 percent to 41 percent.

• **Rhode Island.** Whitehouse's victory over Chafee, a well-known moderate whose opposition to the war in Iraq and stances on social issues made him palatable to voters in the "blue" state of Rhode Island, hinged largely on a bloody primary contest between Chafee and conservative Republican Steve Laffey, the mayor of Cranston.

The primary challenge, which culminated Sept. 12 in Chafee's victory with 54 percent of the vote, split the moderate and conservative wings of the Republican Party. Moderates argued that Chafee was the only Republican liberal enough to hold on to a Senate seat in such a Democratic state. Conservatives who supported Laffey, including the anti-tax organization Club for Growth, argued that Chafee's moderate viewpoint made him just as bad as a Democrat.

But after Chafee cleared the primary — with no small amount of help from the Bush White House and top Senate Republicans — Democrats had an easier time tying him to the unpopular president. Whitehouse argued that Chafee's election would bolster the GOP ranks in the Senate and help them maintain the majority. He won the contest 53 percent to 47 percent.

NOT A ROUT

Republicans did manage to claim a few important Senate victories. They held on to Tennessee's open Senate seat when Republican Bob Corker, the former mayor of Chattanooga, defeated Democratic Rep. Harold E. Ford Jr. in the highly competitive race to succeed Bill Frist, the GOP majority leader, who said when he first won his seat in 1994 that he would stay only two terms. Ford was seeking to become the first African-American from the South to ever win a Senate election. (There was an appointed black senator during Reconstruction.)

It was a high-stakes race: Ford spent $10.6 million and Corker $14 million during the election cycle. Corker won the contest 51 percent to 48 percent after a raucous round of mud-slinging ads from the GOP candidate and the national party that branded Ford a "playboy." One ad financed by the Republican National Committee, which opponents argued was racially motivated, featured a white woman winking at the camera and asking Ford to "call me." Corker disowned the ad but its impact reverberated throughout the mid-South state.

Republicans also held on to their Arizona Senate seat, with incumbent Jon Kyl defeating Democrat Jim Pederson in a race that Kyl was favored to win. In the days just before the election, the DSCC dropped $1 million for advertisements in the Phoenix and Tucson media markets for the race, which Schumer had called "the sleeper" of the 2006 election cycle.

Pederson's largely self-funded campaign, however, was hampered by late-breaking allegations that he laundered donations designated for state races through other state parties to circumvent campaign finance regulations. Kyl won the race with 53 percent of the vote, compared with 44 percent for Pederson.

HOLDING THEIR OWN

One factor that aided Democrats was their ability to retain control of the seats they already held, including four states that had been considered particularly vulnerable: New Jersey, Maryland, Nebraska and Washington.

New Jersey Sen. Robert Menendez declared victory Tuesday night with 53 percent of the vote against a vig-orous challenge by Thomas H. Kean Jr., son of a popu-lar two-term governor.

Menendez's win gives him his first full term after being appointed to the seat in January by Democrat Jon Corzine, the previous occupant, who took over the gov-ernor's mansion, despite Republicans' allegations that Menendez was a corrupt urban "boss."

In the contest for the open Senate seat in Maryland, where Democrat Paul S. Sarbanes is retiring after five terms, 10-term Democratic Rep. Benjamin L. Cardin defeated Republican Lt. Gov. Michael Steele, 54 percent to 44 percent. Steele, the first African-American elected to statewide office in Maryland, had won the support of sev-eral top black Democratic officials who crossed party lines to publicly back him. Their support, however, was not enough to catapult Steele in a heavily Democratic state.

Nebraska Democrat Ben Nelson defeated self-funded Republican Pete Ricketts, the former Ameritrade CEO, to win a second term with 64 percent of the vote. Washington's Maria Cantwell, who won her 2000 race with 49 percent of the vote, managed to hold on to her seat against businessman Mike McGavick with 57 per-cent of the vote.

Democrats also held their seat in Minnesota, where Amy Klobuchar beat GOP Rep. Mark Kennedy for the seat that Democrat Mark Dayton gave up. In Michigan, first-term Sen. Debbie Stabenow fought off Oakland County Sheriff Mike Bouchard. Democrat Bill Nelson eas-

Senators Up for Re-Election in 2008

DEMOCRATS (12)	REPUBLICANS (21)	
Max Baucus of Montana	**Lamar Alexander** of Tennessee	**Lindsey Graham** of South Carolina
Joseph R. Biden Jr. of Delaware	**Wayne Allard** of Colorado	**Chuck Hagel** of Nebraska
Richard J. Durbin of Illinois	**Saxby Chambliss** of Georgia	**James M. Inhofe** of Oklahoma
Tom Harkin of Iowa	**Thad Cochran** of Mississippi	**Mitch McConnell** of Kentucky
Tim Johnson of South Dakota	**Norm Coleman** of Minnesota	**Pat Roberts** of Kansas
John Kerry of Massachusetts	**Susan Collins** of Maine	**Jeff Sessions** of Alabama
Mary L. Landrieu of Louisiana	**John Cornyn** of Texas	**Gordon H. Smith** of Oregon
Frank R. Lautenberg of New Jersey	**Larry E. Craig** of Idaho	**Ted Stevens** of Alaska
Carl Levin of Michigan	**Elizabeth Dole** of North Carolina	**John E. Sununu** of New Hampshire
Mark Pryor of Arkansas	**Pete V. Domenici** of New Mexico	**John W. Warner** of Virginia
Jack Reed of Rhode Island	**Michael B. Enzi** of Wyoming	
John D. Rockefeller IV of West Virginia		

ily won a second term representing Florida despite a well-publicized challenge from GOP Rep. Katherine Harris.

And in the intensely watched race in Connecticut, Lieberman — the 2000 Democratic nominee for vice president — won his independent bid for a fourth term, which he launched after losing the Democratic primary Aug. 8 to anti-war candidate Ned Lamont. Lieberman defeated Lamont and Republican Alan Schlesinger in a race that state officials said drew record turnout.

Vermont's Senate race likewise was considered effectively a retention for Democrats as Sanders, who always caucused with the party in the House, handily won the seat left open by fellow independent Jeffords, who did likewise in the Senate

The other 17 senators on the ballot — 10 Democrats and seven Republicans — all safely won re-election, among them such GOP stalwarts as Indiana's Richard G. Lugar and Utah's Orrin G. Hatch, and such Democratic icons as Edward M. Kennedy of Massachusetts and Robert C. Byrd of West Virginia.

Such a high share of the Senate races may not go as quietly in 2008, when the Democrats will work hard to expand their new majority by contesting many of the 21 GOP-held seats while defending only a dozen. Five of the 21 Republican senators facing re-election in two years won in 2002 by fewer than 10 percentage points, while only three of the Democratic candidates won by such tight margins.

AFL-CIO Writes a New Chapter for Workers

AFL-CIO president John Sweeney and House Speaker Nancy Pelosi.

In its IOU for the 110th Congress, Big Labor has an overhaul of the bankruptcy code at the top of the list

From *CQ Weekly*, December 4, 2006.

Big Labor claims big credit for putting Democrats back in charge on Capitol Hill. Union members, said AFL-CIO President John Sweeney the day after the election, "drove a wave that elected a pro-working families majority." Now labor is demanding legislative results in return.

"We'll be holding them accountable," the group's top lobbyist, Bill Samuel, said in an interview.

The question is, for what? The AFL-CIO, which represents 53 unions and 10 million workers, wants to raise the minimum wage, make it easier for workers to organize unions and put a freeze on new trade agreements.

None of that is new to labor's agenda. And at least as far as the minimum wage goes, the incoming Democratic leadership is on board, allowing labor to check that one off.

What is surprising is the item at the top of Samuel's list: an overhaul of the corporate bankruptcy code. Big manufacturers, where most union members are employed, are struggling in the global marketplace, facing bankruptcy and shedding worker benefits as they reorganize to stay alive. In an acceptance of this economic reality, the labor group is investing labor's resources and new political clout in the an effort to make sure that workers get a bigger piece of the post-bankruptcy pie.

"Everyone believes that corporate bankruptcy is broken," Samuel said. "More companies are declaring bankruptcy and the first thing they eliminate is union bargaining and retiree pensions and health benefits." Corporate executives, he complained, end up with million-dollar payouts for this restructuring work and their workers get little or nothing.

Already Samuel has assembled a team of bankruptcy lawyers, who are drafting legislative language, and he's shopping ideas on the Hill and trolling for sponsors.

Samuel oversees a team of 10 in-house lobbyists in the AFL-CIO's 16th Street headquarters. The industrial gray granite building is just down the street from the more posh offices of the U.S. Chamber of Commerce and across Lafayette Park from the White House, where Samuel worked for Vice President Al Gore. Samuel's office is less than half as large as a typical corporate lobbyist of his stature. It holds just his desk, a small round table and a few bookshelves. Other than dated drawings from his now-college-age children, there is no art.

In some ways, the modest room mirrors his legislative agenda. Rather than charging ahead with a progressive plan to mandate retirement security or ensure universal health care, the AFl-CIO mostly is trying to preserve what workers have already achieved.

But the push on corporate bankruptcy may be more ambitious than it seems on the surface. It's a difficult issue for labor to take on because it involves the intricacies of financial reorganization and an appreciation for the pressures of international commerce. And companies with armies of lobbyists will be certain to want their say in the bill.

Elizabeth Warren, a Harvard Law School professor who specializes in bankruptcy law, says the labor movement is "smart" for taking on an issue that might seem out of its bailiwick. "When a company files for bankruptcy, someone in that group will walk away with a lot fewer assets," said Warren. "Lately, it's been the employees. This is about the labor unions pushing back."

It was tough enough for Congress to overhaul personal bankruptcy rules in 2005, with the backing of big banks and credit card companies. Corporate bankruptcy is such a thicket that Congress hasn't attempted to revamp Chapter 11, which governs corporate reorganizations since 1978.

Samuel has well-positioned allies on Capitol Hill. Vermont Democrat Patrick J. Leahy will be chairman of the Senate Judiciary Committee, which oversees bankruptcy legislation. Leahy co-sponsored a bill in early 2006 to restrict the ability of corporate chief executives to strip their companies of worker benefits while extracting large payouts for themselves. The effort went nowhere, but Leahy was backed by Richard J. Durbin of Illinois, who will be Democratic whip, and by Michigan's two Democratic senators, Carl Levin and Debbie Stabenow.

Asked about the AFL-CIO's new initiative, Leahy expressed interest in opening up the corporate bankruptcy code.

"It defies common decency and fairness when employees are left holding the bag for the failure of a mismanaged company while the top executives reap extravagant windfalls," Leahy said in an e-mailed statement. He added that he wants to find a bipartisan approach "to ensure the bankruptcy law requires greater scrutiny in corporate reorganization plans to protect and recognize the important contributions of loyal employees."

DUMPING PENSIONS

Sixty-five large companies have shed their pension plans in bankruptcy reorganizations since 1980 — 42 in the past six years, according to data analyzed by Lynn LoPucki, a law professor at UCLA.

These are major companies that employ or contract with hundreds of thousands of workers. UAL Corp., parent of United Airlines, saved itself $4 billion when it convinced a bankruptcy court last year that it could not survive if it had to pay pensions to its retirees. Meanwhile, 400 executives awarded themselves 8 percent of the post-bankrupt company, worth an estimated $115 million. The top eight UAL executives also granted themselves a combined $3.5 million in annual salaries, plus bonuses. Chief Executive Officer Glenn Tilton kept his $4.5 million in pension benefits and took a $3 million signing bonus.

Also dumping pension plans in 2005 were Arizona-based US Airways Group Inc. and Ohio-based bicyclemaker Huffy Corp.

Retirees from those companies still receive a pension when they turn 65, paid by the federal Pension Benefits

Guaranty Corporation (PBGC). But the amounts will be less than they expected because of congressionally mandated ceilings on PBGC-paid retirement benefits. And the PBGC doesn't guarantee health care coverage that employees might have been promised for their retirement.

A big concern is whether the Detroit-based automakers will be next to dump their employee benefits.

WHY THE AFL-CIO

One problem the union may have is making the case that an overhaul is necessary in the first place. UCLA's LoPucki said there are already laws in place to prevent companies from raiding workers' pensions in bankruptcy court, but those laws are not being enforced by judges.

"They don't want to deny a company anything that they want because future companies won't come to their court," LoPucki said.

Regardless, the issue makes for good politics for the AFL-CIO itself, which lost 3 million members last year when the International Brotherhood of Teamsters and the Service Employees International Union defected. Taking on corporate bankruptcies shows union members that the umbrella union is working to deliver concrete results to its members. A minimum wage increase, for example, may be viewed as nice, but most union workers earn well above the $7.25 an hour that a raise is likely to yield. Universal health care is a lofty goal, but most union workers are already covered.

The big financial threat to workers and retirees at heavily unionized industries now is that the manufacturing companies that employ them are struggling. And it's happening at a time when many of those employees are approaching retirement age. Union membership is

Items on AFL-CIO's To-Do List For Congress

- Raise the federal minimum wage to $7.25 an hour.
- Pass the Employee Free Choice Act (S 842, HR 1696), which would amend the National Labor Relations Act to make it easier for workers to form unions.
- Allow the Medicare program to negotiate prescription drug prices directly with drug companies.
- Create incentives for companies that provide domestic jobs instead of setting up off-shore operations.
- Restore money for college loans that was reduced recent years.

highest among workers age 45 to 64 — that group accounts for 16.5 percent of all union members, according to the most recent Labor Department statistics. Their pensions and retiree health care benefits are more valuable to them than their current wages.

The focus on corporate bankruptcy may also provide a way for the AFL-CIO to remake its public image away from being totally focused on opposing international trade. Samuel, for one, lamented that "we can't seem to get away" from the "protectionist" brand.

That's not to say that the group is not still pushing a controversial trade agenda. Its policy, which calls for a freeze on new free-trade agreements, cleaves the Democratic Party, separating those who are uncomfortable with globalization from the centrists who adhere to a broader economic approach favored by the party's high-tech corporate allies.

But trying to sell bankruptcy law overhaul as a way to protect helpless workers against greedy executives carries populist appeal that most Democrats and many Republicans may share. And it might be a natural bookend to last year's passage of a sweeping overhaul of personal bankruptcy law, which consumer groups criticized as excessively punitive.

Already, though, the contours of the debate are coming clear. Corporations can be expected to argue against the pension protections by saying that such measures would hurt existing jobs.

Hugh Ray, head of the bankruptcy practice at the Houston law firm of Andrews Kurth, dismissed the idea as "populist politics" that ignores real-world practical concerns. "They want to take away the right of companies to dump their old-time pensions, which is a heinous thing to do," he said. "The inability to do that would lead to liquidation of the company and the loss of the remaining jobs."

Ray pointed out that General Motors' pension and retiree health care obligations saddle it with huge embedded costs. "It's a $1,500 hickey on every car," he said. "It's eating them alive."

He predicted that Congress is more likely to pass a law "that lets them get off the hook on health care rather than legislation that says they can't get off the hook."

Harvard's Warren agreed that the problem facing labor's initiative is difficult. "It poses a Gordian Knot for

labor," she said. "They want these businesses to survive. No one benefits if the company folds. But they don't want the businesses to survive solely on the backs of the workers who gave up their retirements."

FOR FURTHER READING:

Personal bankruptcy overhaul (PL 109-8), 2005 Almanac, p. 3-3; beackground on pensions and PBGC, 2006 CQ Weekly, p. 2178 and 2005 CQ Weekly, p. 2624; Leahy's bill is S 2556.

Franken Bid Another Test of Minnesota's 'Blueness'

AP / Adam Hammer

CAMPAIGNING: Franken campaigning in Albert Lea the weekend before the election for Tim Walz, the Democrat who defeated Republican Gil Gutknecht.

From *CQ Weekly*,
February 5, 2007.

Comedian's non-standard résumé fits recent election history, but GOP sees state as ripe for a color change

It will take a while yet to determine exactly where the challenge to Norm Coleman ranks among the Democrats' bids for expanding their narrow Senate majority next year. But the Minnesota contest is already grabbing outsized attention for a nascent 2008 Senate race, thanks to the celebrity surrounding the increasingly certain candidacy of comedian Al Franken.

Franken's first foray into politics was "covering" the 1988 presidential primaries for NBC's "Saturday Night Live" — "I'm standing here with a three-meter dish on my head" — and he would be a first-time candidate for public office. But for the past two years he has been combining his comic talent and his liberal views as the star host on the Air America radio network; he is expected to formally launch his candidacy in his swan-song appearance on the air, scheduled for Feb. 14.

Comedic performers win federal elections about once a decade: Fred Grandy of TV's "Love Boat" won a House seat in Iowa in 1986, and fellow Republican Sonny Bono took a California seat in 1994. So in that sense Franken's timing may be right on. Still, in most states the idea of sending a funnyman to Congress is a non-starter.

The '08 Senate Campaign: An Early Line

Because the Republicans now hold 49 seats, they could guarantee control of the Senate next year by taking just two seats away from the Democrats — not a very tall order at all, by historical standards. But the task is made more difficult by the peculiarities of the political calendar: Of the 33 Senate seats to be filled on Nov. 4, 2008, the Republicans are defending 21, the Democrats only a dozen. Beyond that, at least at this relatively early stage, the Republicans are genuinely in danger of losing a half-dozen seats, whereas only two of the Democrats' seats appear genuinely vulnerable to partisan takeover.

THE MOST VULNERABLE REPUBLICAN SEATS

 COLORADO: The only open Senate seat in the nation so far, because incumbent **Wayne Allard** (left) is retiring after two terms, is also the Democrats' clearest shot so far at a pickup. The party scored major gains in the state in 2004 and 2006 and is likely to nominate **Rep. Mark Udall,** who's been prepping for this race since shortly after arriving in the House in 1999.

 MAINE: Susan Collins has been a popular GOP moderate for a decade, but the state's been trending more Democratic. The challenger will likely be **Rep. Tom Allen,** who since 1997 has had a solid hold on the seat covering the state's populous southwest corner.

 MINNESOTA: Even without the celebrity factor of **Al Franken**'s looming candidacy, Democrats in this "light blue" state certainly would target the relatively moderate **Norm Coleman,** who's seeking a second term.

 NEW HAMPSHIRE: John E. Sununu won his seat by just 4 percentage points in his 2002 Senate race debut, and Democrats are trying to stoke momentum from their huge state gains in 2006, when they took over both House seats and the state legislature. A big field is already forming.

 NORTH CAROLINA: The state has a tradition of Senate seat turnovers and close races, and Democrats view one-termer **Elizabeth Dole** as vulnerable. They aspire to recruit popular **Gov. Michael F. Easley,** but so far he's demurred.

 OREGON: Democrats have a slight edge in the state but must overcome the high approval ratings of **Gordon H. Smith** (left) throughout his two terms and a reputation for independence, which was underscored by his recent turn against the Iraq War. Talk of a challenger centers on **Rep. Earl Blumenauer** of Portland.

THE MOST VULNERABLE DEMOCRATIC SEATS

 SOUTH DAKOTA: Tim Johnson (left), who won his second term by just 524 votes in 2002, has long been viewed as vulnerable in this solid "red" state — especially if popular GOP **Gov. Michael Rounds** decides to run. Johnson's long recovery from his December brain hemorrhage has put this contest on unofficial hold.

 LOUISIANA: After two razor-thin wins, **Mary L. Landrieu** has pushed up her ratings with her efforts to draw federal aid to recover from Hurricane Katrina in 2005. But that legendary storm also drove tens of thousands of voters to leave New Orleans, the base of her political support. The GOP field appears wide open.

This is Minnesota, though, where Franken's biography will hardly be the most unusual. There, a series of establishment politicians such as Hubert H. Humphrey and Walter F. Mondale have been succeeded by a series of iconoclasts: Rudy Boschwitz, the eccentric plywood magnate, who served two terms in the Senate; peripatetic college professor Paul Wellstone, who took that Senate seat in 1990 and held it until his death just before the 2002 election; and Jesse Ventura, the professional wrestler, who won a term as governor.

Coleman, who succeeded Wellstone, isn't exactly cut from traditional political cloth either, especially for a Republican. A native of Brooklyn who still has a thick New York accent, he entered political office in 1993 by winning the mayoralty of St. Paul, as a Democrat. That came after a time as a Vietnam War protester and rock group roadie.

In fact, if Franken is elected to the Senate it may well be attributable at least as much to his oddball résumé as to his Democratic affiliation. That is because Minnesota, which was one of the most reliably Democratic states during the heyday of Humphrey and Mondale, has become much more "light blue" in recent times. Three of the previous five senators were Republicans, and three of its eight House seats are now GOP-held. So is the governor's mansion, and Ventura was the last independent in the nation to secure a governorship, in 1998.

The Republicans' choice of Minneapolis-St. Paul to host their 2008 presidential nominating convention underscores the GOP view that the state has the potential to trend its way, just as the Democrats hoped to emphasize their newfound success in the Rocky Mountain West by picking Denver as their convention city.

NOT QUITE NATIVE

Many Americans still think of Minnesota as the bluest of the Democratic states, and there is some evidence for it: Democrats have carried it in the past eight presidential contests, their longest streak in any state — because Minnesota favored Mondale when no other state did against Ronald Reagan in 1984. Humphrey's name is on the main terminal of the Twin Cities' airport, the bubble-domed stadium in downtown Minneapolis and a public policy institute at the University of Minnesota.

While President Bush lost the state twice, however, he did so by just 2 percentage points in 2000 and 3 points in 2004. Even in the midst of last year's anti-Republican tide, Republican Gov. Tim Pawlenty staved off a serious

Democratic challenge and won a second term.

Republicans have steadily made inroads among voters in the fast-growing Twin Cities suburbs. That has supplemented a Republican base in rural areas, where issues such as abortion and gun control turned voters against the Democrats, said Wy Spano, director of the Center for Advocacy and Political Leadership at the University of Minnesota-Duluth.

From 1995 through 2000, the state was represented in the Senate by Wellstone, perhaps the most liberal senator at the time, and Republican Rod Grams, one of its staunch conservatives.

Franken has serious potential strengths as a candidate: passion, populism, national prominence and fundraising abilities. He already has garnered gratitude after founding his Midwest Values PAC and doling out $1.1 million to Democratic campaigns during the 2006 cycle.

Yet Franken does not have a lock on the nomination. Other possible candidates include Susan Gaertner, whose résumé as the prosecutor for St. Paul parallels that of Amy Klobuchar, who vaulted from being the county prosecutor in Minneapolis to the Senate last year.

Franken has gibed that he would be the only New York-born Jewish candidate in the race who actually grew up in Minnesota: His family moved to the state when he was very young, and he attended high school in the Minneapolis suburb of St. Louis Park. But the would-be challenger is a longtime New York City resident who purchased a home in Minneapolis in 2005 after he started considering the 2008 race against Coleman.

His humor is often barbed, and Republicans haven't waited for him to get in the race before throwing his words in his face. The National Republican Senatorial Committee issued a news release last week lambasting comments Franken made in 1988 about the nation's "debt addiction," with a headline reading: "Franken details crack addiction and debases President Reagan at the same time."

TARGETING COLEMAN

Even without Franken, Democrats would have Coleman high on their target list of incumbent senators next year. Part of it is personal. Many Democrats still resent him for switching to the GOP in 1996, a move he attributed largely to his opposition to abortion. Democrats also remember that he won his seat by just 2 points over Mondale, who was recruited as a stand-in after Wellstone's death.

Democrats also hope to maintain momentum they built upon the public's anti-Republican mood last year, when Klobuchar ended up with a 20-point victory in what had been a tossup race against GOP Rep. Mark Kennedy for the seat left open by Democrat Mark Dayton's retirement. In addition, Democrat Tim Walz ousted six-term Republican Gil Gutknecht from a House seat that stretches along the state's border with Iowa. And big gains gave Democrats complete control in the state legislature.

Republican strategists say they are confident Coleman can withstand any challenge, and he had already banked $1.8 million for the race as of the end of last year. And the timing of the GOP convention, which opens on Labor Day, could be a publicity boon for the senator — if his party has at least partially recovered its public standing from its 2006 debacle. But Coleman might find himself pressed to distance himself from the party if its public approval ratings remain low, or if the GOP nominates a presidential ticket too conservative for Minnesotans' tastes.

Coleman's past as a Democrat could be an asset if, as is likely, he campaigns as a political moderate during his re-election campaign. In the past two years he stood with his party on 77 percent of the votes that pitted most Democrats against most Republicans; only five GOP senators had lower party unity scores.

Democrats describe him as a political chameleon. They point out that Coleman — who could hardly be described as media shy — made numerous TV appearances promoting Bush's agenda during his first two years in office, which coincided with the president's campaign for a second term. And, in fact, in those years Coleman's party unity score was 91 percent.

FOR FURTHER READING

Last year's Senate elections, p. 48.

Small Steps for Big Problems of the Middle Class

Voters responded when
Democrats vowed to take on
middle-class problems, but with
government split and budgets
tight, grand goals yield quickly to
baby steps

When Carolyn B. Maloney was pregnant with her first child in the early 1980s, she was sure she was going to be fired. She was working as a staff aide in the New York Legislature, which at the time had no maternity leave policy at all.

"I was told, 'There is no leave. People just leave,' " Maloney said. The human resources director suggested she go on disability. She refused. Having a child is a joyous occasion, she said, not a disability.

Times have changed since then, but the incident gave Maloney a personal understanding of one of the many pressures the middle class faces today: the struggle to balance growing workloads and family needs. Now an eight-term Democratic member of the House representing the east side of Manhattan and parts of Queens, she is one of those leading a drive to expand the Family and Medical Leave Act. Last week, she introduced a bill that would require employers to allow their workers 24 hours of unpaid leave a year for school activities such as parent-teacher conferences. It would also create pilot programs to help states provide paid family leave and to provide paid family leave to federal workers.

From *CQ Weekly*,
March 12, 2007.

❝❝I was told, 'There is no leave. People just leave.'❞❞

— Rep. Carolyn B. Maloney, D-N.Y.

CQ / Scott J. Ferrell

She would love to do more. In an ideal world, Maloney would like a national right to paid family leave — an idea also being promoted by Democratic senator and presidential candidate Christopher J. Dodd of Connecticut — since the dozen weeks workers are allowed under the Family and Medical Leave Act are unpaid, and many can't afford to take it. But it's not an ideal world. "We have an $8 trillion debt," Maloney said. "It comes down to, how are we going to pay for it?"

It's the kind of dilemma that Democrats are confronting all over Capitol Hill, on a range of issues that spans much of their domestic agenda, as they try to find ways to address the middle-class squeeze that so many of their candidates talked about in their campaigns last year. Iraq and corruption may have topped the list of public concerns that swept the Democrats into power, but voters also expressed anxiety about rising costs, stagnant or unstable incomes, and the competing demands of work and family.

"Everywhere I went, people responded to this," said freshman Democratic Sen. Jim Webb of Virginia, who was identified mainly with his opposition to the Iraq War but also spoke often to middle-class economic anxieties last fall. "It basically goes to the American sense of fairness."

And yet, the prescriptions Democrats are pursuing — for the next two years, at least — aren't exactly the second coming of the Great Society. There are plenty of reasons for that. There's no money, as Maloney points out. The Democrats just got into power, and they don't want to overplay their hand with the public. President Bush is still in the White House with a veto pen, and he and the Democrats don't agree on much. And with the next presidential election only a year and a half away — and good odds of winning back the White House — the Democrats have an incentive not to try to solve every problem now.

Instead, the new majority is focusing on bite-sized, narrowly targeted measures designed to address one part of a larger problem, or to provide a first step that may lead to more ambitious initiatives down the road — if the Democrats come out of the 2008 elections with a stronger hand.

"It's not going to be a period of big legislative results, but it is going to be a period of increasing debate," said Jacob S. Hacker, a professor of political science at Yale University and author of "The Great Risk Shift," which argues that economic statistics don't capture the pressures most families face. "That debate," he said, "will set the stage for what might happen in two years if Democrats pick up seats in the Senate and maybe even win the White House, which does not seem so improbable."

That's why business groups are following the emerging debates closely, knowing that even incremental changes in laws such as the Family and Medical Leave Act, which was enacted 14 years ago, could force them to adjust to new federal requirements even as they wrestle with existing ones. The proposals should be seen as "the preliminary lay of the land for the next Congress with a different occupant in the White House," said G. Roger King, a partner in the Jones Day international law firm who specializes in labor and employment law. "You have to follow it closely, and you have to worry about it."

COMPETING PRESSURES

The term "middle-class squeeze" is vague enough to sweep up almost any domestic issue a politician wants to talk about, and some do just that. For example, the chairman of the House Education and Labor Committee, Democrat George Miller of California, includes on his "Strengthening America's Middle Class" agenda the upcoming reauthorization of the 2002 education policy overhaul known as No Child Left Behind, which is largely aimed at boosting achievement among low-income children. Many Democrats cite their effort to increase the minimum wage as a likely achievement for the middle class this year, even though it is, by definition, aimed at workers in low-wage jobs.

Still, there is a general agreement on the basic elements of the "squeeze," based on the issues that have come up most often at recent congressional hearings and in numerous reports generated by public policy think tanks.

Americans are struggling with rising medical care costs, and they're paying more out of pocket to cover those expenses, if they have health insurance at all. Since 2000, such insurance premiums have risen more than four times as fast as wages, and many employers are shifting those costs to their workers. In 2003, one out of every five Americans paid more than 10 percent of their income for health care, a sharp increase over the last decade.

They're concerned about layoffs and the steep drops in income when people who lose their jobs have to take lower-paying ones. In testimony before the House Ways and Means Committee in January, Hacker said income instability is rising at about the same rate for American workers regardless of how much education they have. An average

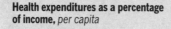

Health Care Costs' Continued Rise

Health care costs have been rising faster than income for years, increasing the burden on middle-income as well as low-income families.

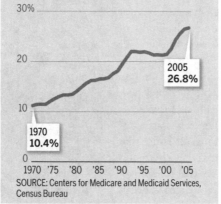

Health expenditures as a percentage of income, *per capita*

2005
26.8%

1970
10.4%

SOURCE: Centers for Medicare and Medicaid Services, Census Bureau

worker, he said, is now two-and-a-half times as likely to see his income drop by 50 percent or more as a typical worker 30 years ago.

They're putting in hours and facing more crises in tending to their children's needs and, in many cases, the care of elderly parents. Nearly seven out of 10 mothers of school-age children work outside the home now; less than half did in 1975. Nearly one in four households are caring for elderly relatives, and more still are expected to do so in the future. In 2002, a survey by the Families and Work Institute found that 45 percent of workers said work and family responsibilities conflicted "a lot" or "some." In 1977, only 34 percent felt that way.

And retirement pressures are on the rise as more employers offer their workers 401(k) plans, which carry more risk for the workers if the markets perform poorly, as opposed to traditional pension plans. Three in 10 workers aren't saving for retirement at all, and many of those who are saving expect retirement benefits that are increasingly being cut back, according to the Employee Benefit Research Institute.

Democrats themselves define the middle-class squeeze as the twin pressures of declining middle-class incomes — real median household income dropped between 2000 and 2005 — and the rising costs of things such as health care, energy, and college tuition. As this happens, Americans are taking on record amounts of debt. Since 2001, they've had more household debt than disposable income every year.

TAKING THE FIRST STEP

That's a full plate of issues, and each one is so big in scope that Congress probably could do little more than pick away at it under the best of political circumstances. With divided government, a lame-duck president and a presidential election next year that will give both parties

Flexibility Scheduling

Lots of groups would be thrilled to see Congress consider broad measures to help make workplaces more family-friendly, reducing one of the biggest pressures of the "middle-class squeeze." There is one, however, that would be just as happy if it didn't do anything. At least, not yet.

Workplace Flexibility 2010, an organization based at the Georgetown University Law Center and funded by the Alfred P. Sloan Foundation, has spent the past three years gathering research and holding briefings for Capitol Hill staff members on the problems workers face in balancing their jobs and their lives. Now, the group wants to start reaching out to the stakeholders — employers, workers, women's groups, social conservatives, and practically anyone else who cares — to try to develop a national policy everyone can support.

The whole idea, though, is that the effort will take time. Specifically, it's supposed to take until 2010.

"Our goal, very clearly, is not . . . to try to draft a piece of legislation today," said Chai Feldblum, a Georgetown law professor who serves as the group's co-director. "We actually want to develop a policy approach that is acceptable to employers and employees. That's a huge thing. It's not the way Washington typically works."

Her approach sets the group apart from other work-and-family organizations that are expected to support a bill by Democratic Sen. Edward M. Kennedy of Massachusetts that would require employers with 15 or more workers to provide at least seven days of paid sick leave each year. Some hope the bill, if it gets through Congress, will open the door to other legislative efforts, such as paid family leave.

Feldblum's group, however, is taking its cues from a Tony Blair initiative that got employers and employees in Great Britain together on a mutually acceptable way to balance their needs. The result was a law that allows British workers with children under age 6 to ask for flexible working arrangements such as part-time hours, flextime, hours averaged over a year, job sharing, or working from home.

If it's at all possible to accommodate the request, the employer is supposed to do so; if not, the business reason has to be explained in writing. The whole process is governed by clearly defined application procedures, and the employee is urged to give a little in the negotiations too. Last year, the law was expanded to cover workers who have to care for adults such as spouses, partners, or relatives.

Charting Its Own Course

Feldblum's group isn't necessarily trying to duplicate the British solution. (The right to ask for flexible work arrangements, she points out, isn't the same as the right to have them.) But it is trying to duplicate the approach, which she hopes would lead to honest discussions between employers and employees.

"I've been in Washington 25 years. I've always played it the way the game is always played, which is, I draft something based on what my constituents want and then go negotiate with the other side," Feldblum said. "This is truly different."

Whether it succeeds remains to be seen — but at the very least, Feldblum hopes the dialogue will encourage more members of Congress, as well as national and state political leaders, to talk about the work-life strains Americans face. "We need to deal with workplace policy as a nation," she said. "It's definitely not happening enough, which is why we exist."

> **"We actually want to develop a policy approach that is acceptable to employers and employees. . . . It's not the way Washington typically works."**
>
> — Georgetown law professor Chai Feldblum

an incentive to keep potent issues alive, these aren't the best of conditions. "That's the difficulty. It's so huge that you pretty much have to take it on one bite at a time," said Webb.

When Republican Pat Roberts first ran for the Senate in 1996, he came face to face with one of the most intractable pressures on middle-class and working-class parents: the rising cost of child care. As he knocked on doors in Dodge City, a town of 25,000 people in southwestern Kansas, he asked a single mother with two children what he could do to make her life better.

"Mister, it's your world. I'm just living in it," the woman told Roberts. Taken aback, he tried again. Surely there's something I can do, he said. "She said, 'Yes, you can find some opportunity to put my kids here in a day care center that I can afford so I can get the kind of restaurant hours I used to have. Then I wouldn't have to apply for welfare.' "

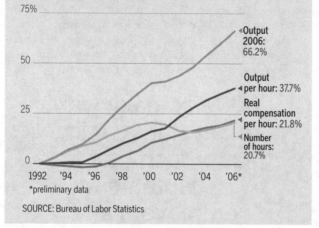

Efficiency, Wages & Hours All Up

Though Americans are more productive than in the past, and wages have increased, so has the number of hours worked, a source of stress. This chart shows output, wages and hours as a percentage of 1992 levels.

Percent change in productivity since 1992

Output 2006: 66.2%

Output per hour: 37.7%

Real compensation per hour: 21.8%

Number of hours: 20.7%

1992 '94 '96 '98 '00 '02 '04 '06*
*preliminary data

SOURCE: Bureau of Labor Statistics

modest measure aimed at reducing 401(k) fees that can eat away at workers' savings.

"I think doing the piecemeal approach satisfies a particular itch, which is to do something now," said Christian E. Weller, a senior economist at the Center for American Progress, a liberal think tank that provides policy ideas to Democrats. "To take on issues like health care and energy will require a larger national debate, but also longer-term congressional negotiations."

So Roberts has been trying, for 10 years, to pass a modest bill to provide grants to help small businesses provide child care for their workers. This year, he may finally achieve his goal: His measure was added by voice vote as an amendment to the Senate minimum wage bill. But until now, he said, his legislation has never gotten much support because other lawmakers preferred to push for more ambitious child-care proposals that never passed.

"It's such a meager first step," Roberts said. Rather than holding out for the ideal approach, he said, "it's much easier if you just take a first step and then build on it."

So rather than trying to overhaul the entire health care system, Congress is focusing on lowering the cost of Medicare prescription drugs and reauthorizing federal help for uninsured children. Rather than requiring employers to pay wages to workers taking family leave, Congress is more likely to consider a bill, to be introduced in the Senate this week, that would require a minimum number of paid sick leave days, since four out of 10 workers don't even have those.

And rather than trying to revive traditional pension plans or provide 401(k)s for people who don't have them — much less overhaul Social Security right before a presidential election — Congress will probably start with a

That larger national debate is already beginning, thanks to the early start of the 2008 presidential campaigns. Among Democrats, Sen. Hillary Rodham Clinton of New York has talked about expanding the Family and Medical Leave Act and has scolded employers for not raising wages to keep pace with productivity. Sen. Barack Obama of Illinois is campaigning on plans to reduce college costs, encourage savings, set up individual retirement accounts for workers who aren't covered by 401(k) plans at work, and require a minimum number of paid sick days.

Even former Sen. John Edwards of North Carolina, who has staked out his ground in the race by focusing on poverty, talked up ideas for helping the middle class at a series of house parties in New Hampshire last month. He wants to rewrite the tax code to give better tax benefits to middle class families, provide incentives to help them save money, and tackle the debt problem by imposing tougher regulations on credit card companies and mortgage lenders.

And all three have promised to offer plans to provide health insurance to everyone. Edwards outlined an ambitious proposal last month, and Clinton and Obama are set to follow. On the Republican side, former Massachusetts Gov. Mitt Romney is sure to be quizzed about his state's law that requires all state residents to buy health insurance — though his campaign says he's not going to try to do the same thing nationally.

In the meantime, lawmakers are counting the small victories when they can get them. Democratic Sen. Carl Levin of Michigan, who chairs Homeland Security's Permanent Subcommittee on Investigations, held a hearing on credit card penalties last week that could lead to legislation. He's not sure what to do about the excessive penalties yet, he says; such a bill is "months away."

But just by holding the hearing, he may already have helped one consumer. Wesley Wannemacher, who testified at the hearing about how he ended up with $7,500 in interest and penalties over six years as he struggled to pay off a $3,200 credit card balance, was told by Chase Bank USA — shortly before he testified — that they were letting him off the hook. "It shows you the power of oversight," Levin said. But how to help other debt-ridden middle-class families who use other banks and don't happen to be testifying before Congress? "That takes legislation," he said.

WORRIES OVER WELL-BEING

With 47 million uninsured Americans, a shrinking group of employers who provide health coverage, and six out of 10 Americans worrying that they won't be able to afford the cost of health insurance over the next few years, the health issue is far too large to be tackled in a comprehensive way in this Congress.

President Bush has proposed moving away from the employer-based health care system by offering standard tax deductions for the cost of health insurance, regardless of who offers it. But his ideas have received little interest among congressional Democrats, who think middle-class workers could be hurt as health care costs rise and the deductions don't.

Instead, the Democrats' main health care initiatives are the House-passed bill to require the government to negotiate Medicare prescription drug prices — which Bush has threatened to veto — and the upcoming reauthorization of the State Children's Health Insurance Program (SCHIP), which could get hung up by a fight with the administration over whether states should be allowed to cover parents.

Given the problems in getting those two small steps through the system, anything broader that might tackle medical costs is out of the question. That's why experts are looking to the presidential campaigns to drum up support, maybe even a public mandate, for larger changes. "There comes a point where you have to realize the importance of leadership from the White House," said Jeanne M. Lambrew, an associate professor in the department of health policy at The George Washington University and a former health policy adviser to President Bill Clinton.

Of the Democratic presidential aspirants, Edwards was the first to propose a plan to provide universal coverage, which would require businesses to buy insurance plans for their workers, provide subsidies, create purchasing pools — and then require all Americans to have health insurance.

Romney, however, isn't about to try to take the Massachusetts health care overhaul national. "He's never said he thinks that's a fit for the federal government," said spokesman Kevin Madden.

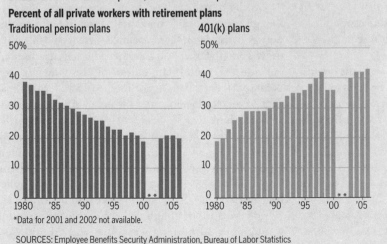

The Shifting Nature of Retirement Plans

The rise of defined-contribution plans, such as 401(k)s, since the 1980s has exposed workers to more risk in their retirement incomes than they had under defined-benefit plans, or traditional pensions.

Percent of all private workers with retirement plans

Traditional pension plans | 401(k) plans

*Data for 2001 and 2002 not available.

SOURCES: Employee Benefits Security Administration, Bureau of Labor Statistics

"He thinks states are in the best position to do innovative stuff for health care, using market forces."

In the meantime, Democrats will try to find other tweaks Congress can make to the current system that might slow the explosion of health costs. They're working on proposals to make generic drugs more widely available — another step to bring down the cost of prescription drugs — though the pharmaceutical industry will probably oppose those efforts.

In addition, Senate Finance Committee Chairman Max Baucus has said he'd like to try again to improve health information technology, an effort that stalled last year. The Montana Democrat also wants to spend more on comparative effectiveness research, which tries to produce a better sense of which drugs and surgeries work well and which don't.

BALANCING WORK AND LIFE

Family policy expert Jody Heymann is quoted frequently about how few countries are left in the world that don't guarantee paid leave for new mothers. She always used to recite the same list: Lesotho, Liberia, Swaziland, Papua New Guinea and the United States. This year, she had to shorten her list; it turns out Lesotho has paid maternity leave now.

Getting the United States off that short list by instituting paid family leave appears to be too heavy a lift for Congress this year. Rather than tackling a proposal that could require employers to offer weeks of paid leave, Democratic Sen. Edward M. Kennedy of Massachusetts is expected to introduce a bill this week that would take a smaller step on a different issue: requiring employers to offer seven paid sick days annually.

Meanwhile, Dodd, one of the sponsors of the original Family and Medical Leave Act, has said he plans to introduce a bill requiring businesses to offer paid family leave, a longtime goal of liberal Democrats. He'd call for six weeks of leave, to be funded jointly by employers, workers and the federal government. He'll even have a prominent co-sponsor: Republican Ted Stevens of Alaska, a longtime advocate of women's rights who gives his own staff 12 weeks of paid maternity leave.

But a sick leave bill may be all Kennedy can manage, given the concerns business leaders have raised about even going that far. Some are still unhappy about how the original family leave law has been implemented — they complain about workers taking the leave in short bursts, often with little or no notice — and they don't want new leave requirements.

"Our position is that, before you start talking about other kinds of leave, you really need to fix the Family and Medical Leave Act so it works for all employers and employees," said Michael P. Aitken, director of governmental affairs at the Society for Human Resource Management.

Still, supporters of the Kennedy bill hope it will lead to other expansions of national leave policies. "We are well past due for some changes that would help workers bring balance to their lives," said Debra L. Ness, president of the National Partnership for Women and Families.

Some Democrats are also trying to help middle-class families with a package of tax cuts. Sen. Charles E. Schumer of New York, the vice chairman of the party caucus and a member of the Finance Committee, joined several freshman Democrats in introducing a package last month that would double the child tax credit, expand the dependent care tax credit to cover more child care expenses, and offer tax relief for people caring for elderly parents who don't live with them.

"Right now, the majority of families are headed by two working parents," said Anne Kim, director of the Middle Class Project at Third Way, a centrist policy and strategy group that helped design the tax cut package. "How many of our government policies are geared toward them? They're not. They're geared toward single earners."

On that much, at least, some conservatives agree — though they wouldn't necessarily reach the same solutions. Current labor laws "assumed there would be a full-time, working father and a mother who stayed at home," said John C. Goodman, author of "Leaving Women Behind: Modern Families, Outdated Laws," and president of the National Center for Policy Analysis, a conservative think tank.

Rather than mandating leave policies or imposing other requirements, Goodman — who has tried to interest Bush's advisers in the issue — recommends giving employers more flexibility to offer health care and other benefits to employees who don't work 40 hours a week. "You'd see a lot of couples where both of the parents would work 30 hours a week," he said. "Employers would find a way to deal with that."

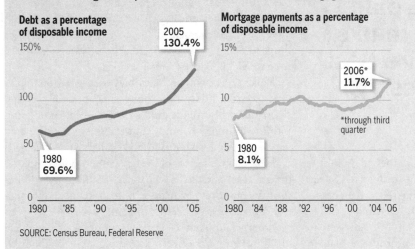

Growth of Consumer Debt, Mortgage Burdens

Consumer debt carried by Americans has exceeded their disposable income every year since 2001. Home mortgages add to the burden, especially because soaring house prices have increased the size of mortgages.

Debt as a percentage of disposable income

2005 **130.4%**

1980 **69.6%**

Mortgage payments as a percentage of disposable income

2006* **11.7%**

*through third quarter

1980 **8.1%**

SOURCE: Census Bureau, Federal Reserve

INCOME SECURITY

Hanging over many U.S. workers, including office workers, is the threat of losing their jobs and paychecks. In December about 200 Maytag workers in Newton, Iowa, worked their last shifts at a plant that once employed 2,600. Over time, that number had dwindled down to less than 1,000. And that was before the latest round of layoffs.

"When 2,000 jobs go away from Maytag in the middle of Iowa, those jobs aren't coming back," said Democrat Jim McDermott of Washington, chairman of the House Ways and Means subcommittee on income security and family support.

McDermott and Schumer are working together on a bill to provide "wage insurance" to people who lose a job and have to take one at lower pay. There's no guarantee it will advance very far, particularly since some labor groups — who clearly share the concern about layoffs — think such a program would just subsidize low-wage jobs rather than promoting better ones.

But McDermott thinks it's time to at least look into the idea. "We're going to have to pay a lot more attention to the safety net," he said. "I'm thinking about the one piece that I have."

There's already a small wage insurance provision in the Trade Adjustment Assistance program which is supposed to assist people who lose their jobs because of trade. But critics say the program hasn't helped very many people. At a hearing before the Joint Economic Committee two weeks ago, Lael Brainard, vice president and director of the Global Economy and Development program at the Brookings Institution, testified that only 64 percent of people who participated in the program found jobs between 2001 and 2004, and their average wages were 20 percent lower than at their old jobs.

Besides, Brainard says, lots of people lose their jobs for reasons that have nothing to do with trade. She wants to expand wage insurance to cover all workers who are permanently displaced from jobs they have had for at least two years. She estimated that a program that would cover half the income loss, up to $10,000, for two years would cost roughly $3.5 billion a year.

But labor groups say they don't want to see subsidies going to low-wage jobs and possibly drawing funds away from other economic security programs. Webb, a member of the Joint Economic Committee, wasn't crazy about the idea either. "It seems to be a more compensatory situation where you're trying to make up for something bad that has happened, rather than trying to come up with a good trade policy that would create fairness," he said.

Another idea under consideration would be a tax code overhaul called "income averaging," a proposal promoted by Lily L. Batchelder, an assistant professor of law and public policy at New York University, who also testified at the Joint Economic Committee hearing.

The idea is to use the tax code to smooth out large income reductions. People who had to take lower-paying jobs could carry back personal deductions to previous years, getting a refund for those years, and average out their income over two years if their earnings are low enough to qualify for the earned income tax credit.

"Romney won't try to take the Massachusetts health care plan national; he thinks such issues are best left to states."

RETIREMENT

The "big idea" in Democratic circles these days for the retirement safety net has nothing to do with Social Security. It isn't even about returning to the days of traditional pensions. It's a national 401(k) plan.

Gene Sperling, a former economic adviser to President Clinton, has been promoting the plan in recent years to anyone who will listen — a "universal 401(k)" to help people who can't get retirement plans through their jobs, with a two-to-one federal match for the first $2,000 in savings by low-income families and a one-to-one match for middle-income families. It's aimed at a huge gap in the retirement system: Nearly half of American workers don't have any retirement plan through their employers.

At the moment, congressional Democrats don't seem to be biting on the idea. Instead, they're more likely to try to address a narrower issue in the retirement system: 401(k) fees that can eat away at a family's savings.

The issue, explored last week at a House Education and Labor Committee hearing, is whether workers are being charged too much for things such as investment management, financial advice, recordkeeping, and customer services.

"People underestimate the importance of lowering 401(k) fees," said Weller of the Center for American Progress. "Fees can have a huge impact on the overall accumulation of savings."

It works like this, according to the Government Accountability Office: A worker who leaves $20,000 in a 401(k) account for 20 years and is charged 0.5 percent in fees will see that balance grow to $70,500 at the end, assuming a 7 percent return on the investment. If that same worker is charged 1.5 percent in fees, that balance drops to $58,400 at the end of the 20 years — a loss of roughly $12,000 in potential savings.

Miller says he will probably propose legislation to prevent excessive 401(k) fees, though it's not clear yet what shape that will take. "I didn't have that in mind going into the hearing," he said, "but the GAO says the only way we can deal with it is to make a legislative change."

Most likely, the goal of the legislation would simply be greater disclosure of the fees, since the Employee Retirement Income Security Act doesn't require much information on them now. Better information from the plan sponsors would allow the Department of Labor to regulate 401(k) plans more effectively, according to Barbara D. Bovbjerg, the GAO analyst who testified at the hearing.

Others concede that even though most people aren't aware of the fees, simply knowing more about them won't do much to reduce them. But it's a start, they say. "Congress is in the first stages of identifying the problem," said Weller, but "the solution is clear: more disclosure and increased competition to lower the fees."

It's not exactly on the scale of a Social Security overhaul, but that may be how this Congress strengthens the retirement piece and other areas of the middle-class squeeze: a few dollars at a time.

FOR FURTHER READING

Maloney's bill is HR 1369; Schumer's bill is S614; minimum wage increase (HR 2), p. 747; student loan debate, p. 711; SCHIP reauthorization, 2007 CQ Weekly, p. 639; Medicare prescription drug bill, p. 183; Family and Medical Leave Act (PL103-3), 2003 Almanac, p. 389.

Government Institutions

The articles in this section shed light on the workings of the major institutions of American government, focusing in turn on Congress, the presidency, and the federal judiciary.

The first article on Congress focuses on Nancy Pelosi, the Speaker of the House of the 110th Congress. While Pelosi has been a reliably liberal vote on most issues, she has successfully forged alliances with conservatives within her party—the so-called Blue Dog Democrats. Pelosi's preference of pragmatism over ideology has helped foster more unity among House Democrats than at any time in the last fifty years.

The dust had barely settled after the watershed midterm elections that gave the Democrats control of Congress when President Bush proposed a troop "surge" to quell the mounting violence in Iraq. The second article in this section looks at the challenges congressional Democrats face as they attempt to stop the president's plan.

The third article examines congressional attempts to counter the widening crisis of foreclosures brought on by the practice of subprime lending. The debate in Congress over solutions has intensified as the pace of foreclosures threatens the U.S. economy as a whole.

The last article in this section examines the issues surrounding President Bush's embattled attorney general, Alberto Gonzales. The firing of eight U.S. attorneys in 2006 and credibility issues have led many Democrats and Republicans on Capitol Hill to question Gonzalez's ability to lead the Justice Department effectively.

In the aftermath of his party's resounding defeat in November 2006, President Bush has been relying increasingly on the often-overlooked but potent policy lever of his executive rule-making authority. The article on the executive branch considers the use of this tool in the context of

president's second term and waning influence. It provides a historical context for this method of circumventing congressional oversight, focusing on the years of the Reagan White House through the current administration.

The first article on the judiciary examines the question of punitive damages as they relate to the larger question of tort reform. Business lobbies are pressing for tort reform at the legislative and judicial levels, but the author argues that juries and judges in state court systems—not corporate wrongdoers—should determine civil damages.

Throughout the country, school administrators are showing a willingness to punish students for speaking out on controversial issues, leading to court challenges that seek to uphold students' First Amendment rights. In its seminal decision on students' free speech rights, *Tinker v. Des Moines Independent Community School District* (1969), the Court determined that the constitutional rights of students should not change once they enter the schoolyard. The second article discusses the Supreme Court's increasing tendency to apply a more narrow interpretation of the precedent, often taking the side of school administrators. The author looks at this question in light of a recently heard case out of Alaska.

The third article on the judiciary examines the issue of term limits for Supreme Court justices. Some observers speculate that Chief Justice William H. Rehnquist misled Justice Sandra Day O'Connor about his own retirement plans to effectively force her to leave her position. If true, this would not be the first time that a justice has used retirement for political purposes, bringing into question whether term limits should be instituted to prevent similar political calculations from entering the august body's judicial mission.

Woman of the House Brings a Sense of Power

Pelosi's pragmatism to be fully tested in Speaker's chair

CQ / Scott J. Ferrell

MADAM SPEAKER: Political pragmatism rather than ideology helped Pelosi unify House Democrats; now she needs consensus victories to keep them in power.

From *CQ Weekly*, November 13, 2006.

When Nancy Pelosi was elected the leader of the Democratic party in the House in late 2002, the job seemed unenviable. Her party was virtually powerless in a Congress dominated by a popular president and a conservative agenda. Pelosi's predecessor, in fact, Missourian Richard A. Gephardt, had quit after failing for the fourth election to regain the majority. In another two years, Democrats would lose even more seats. Most of what President Bush wanted, House Republicans passed, sometimes without a single Democratic vote.

Democrats' irrelevance seemed reinforced by their new leader. Pelosi was on the left wing of her party, a longtime member of the Progressive Caucus and representing the heart of San Francisco, one of the most liberal cities in the country. Indeed, Republicans used Pelosi as a symbol to stir up their conservative voters: Watch out, they warned, or this West Coast liberal will become the next Speaker of the House.

Pelosi did continue to vote as a liberal on most issues. But her leadership approach over the past four years, as she sought to unify her party in the face of Republican dominance in the House, has been more pragmatic than ideological. Indeed, Pelosi's practice of reaching out to conservatives in her own party and trying to find consensus issues and positions will most likely continue when she becomes Speaker this winter with a relatively narrow governing majority.

"The GOP are saying that the House will become the high-taxing liberal institution of old. There ain't no way that's going to happen," said Texas Democrat Charles Stenholm, who led the conservative Blue Dog faction of the party in the House before losing his seat in the 2004 election because of redistricting. "She's going to want to get something done," Stenholm said, "and with 37 Blue Dogs, Pelosi's not going to be a wild-eyed liberal."

Stenholm didn't support Pelosi when she ran for party leader in 2002 because he feared her liberalism. But after working with her for two years in the Capitol and then observing her for another two from a downtown Washington law firm, where he is a policy adviser, Stenholm says he is impressed with how Pelosi listens to conservative Democrats and refuses to cater to left-wing extremists. "She proved me," he said.

Pelosi's agenda for her first weeks as Speaker is revealing, focused as it is on relatively non-controversial initiatives such as raising the minimum wage, cutting student loan interest rates and reimposing fiscal discipline — things that most Democrats, and even some Republicans, can agree on. Her to-do list lacks the hard partisan edge of the conservative "Contract with America" that Newt Gingrich and his victorious Republican colleagues set out to pass after the 1994 elections and that included limits on product liability lawsuits, a cut in capital gains taxes, a line-item veto and tougher prison sentences.

Gingrich's approach, passed on through GOP leaders such as Tom DeLay of Texas, who would become House majority leader before leaving Congress, and Speaker J. Dennis Hastert of Illinois, was to stake out positions and proceed no matter what the other party thought or did.

NANCY PATRICIA PELOSI

Hometown: San Francisco

Born: March 26, 1940, in Baltimore, the daughter of Annunciata and Thomas D. D'Alesandro Jr., a Democratic House member from Maryland (1939-47) and mayor of Baltimore (1947-59)

Family: Husband, Paul F. Pelosi; daughters Nancy Corrine, Christine, Jacqueline and Alexandra; son Paul Jr.

Religion: Roman Catholic

Education: Trinity College (Washington), A.B. 1962

Profession: Public relations consultant

Early political posts: Chair, California Democratic Party, 1981-83; chair, 1984 Democratic convention host committee; finance chair, Democratic Senatorial Campaign Committee, 1985-86

House history: First elected with 63 percent in June 1987 special election in what is now California's 8th District (most of San Francisco); re-elected to 10th full term last week with 81 percent

Rise in power career: Appropriations Committee, 1991-2003 (top Democrat, Foreign Operations Subcommittee, 1997-2001); Select Intelligence Committee, 1993-2003 (top Democrat, 2001-03); elected minority whip, 118-95, over Steny H. Hoyer of Maryland in October 2001; elected minority leader, 177-29, over Harold E. Ford Jr. of Tennessee in November 2002; unopposed for re-election as party leader in 2004

Hastert would consider only major legislation that a majority of his caucus — a "majority of the majority" — would support.

Pelosi seems more willing to negotiate — with conservatives in her party and, presumably, Republicans.

In her first full news conference after the election, Pelosi said Americans "spoke out for a return to civility in the capitol in Washington and how Congress conducts its work." Democrats, she said, "pledge stability and bipartisanship in the conduct of the work here. And we pledge partnerships with the Republicans in Congress and with the president, and not partisanship."

There are limits to her pragmatism; she has deeply held beliefs on issues such as abortion and AIDS funding. And some Democrats will want to pay Republicans back for what has been their essentially one-party rule of the House. But for Pelosi, who learned politics from her father when he was serving in Congress and as mayor of Baltimore, winning is paramount and more important than scoring ideological points.

And winning, in Pelosi's book, means party unity and party discipline. Once she charts a course for her party, she demands allegiance in achieving it and will punish those who cross her. She has already moved to impose more control on committee chairmen than they have been accustomed to under recent Speakers.

As a power broker and party disciplinarian, in fact, Pelosi is more like Tom DeLay than either of them would probably admit.

"Your sense of watching her in closed meetings of Democrats is that she's more the Baltimore machine pol

A Quieter Hand At Senate's Helm

Nancy Pelosi will command most of the attention when the 110th Congress convenes and Democrats begin to exercise their first working majority in more than a decade. But to get anything done, the party will rely even more on the talents of incoming Senate Majority Leader Harry Reid — a taciturn and sometimes dour man who does his best work out of the limelight.

Armed with a one-vote majority and a thorough knowledge of Senate rules, the 66-year-old native Nevadan will try to push Democratic priorities through a chamber filled with excitable liberals and Republicans still bitter over their Election Day rout and deeply suspicious of efforts to dismantle their agenda. Reid's tactical savvy and his ability to count votes will be critical, since every roll call vote that comes up short will be heralded as a failure of the new Democratic Congress.

"He's going to need to reach across ideological lines in his own party, and he'll have to be able to talk to Republicans," said Eric Herzik, a University of Nevada political science professor and long-time Reid observer. "He's better behind the scenes than out front."

Indeed, Reid is not a polished speaker, and at times seems he seems genuinely awkward in the spotlight. Despite a long public career, he has only in recent years been willing to talk about his background. Reid often begins introspective speeches speaking *sotto voce* about being born poor in the tiny mining town of Searchlight, Nev. His mother washed clothes for a living and his father was an alcoholic who committed suicide. Political profiles invariably mention his days as an amateur boxer, signaling that even in his august years, Reid has the pugnacity of a middleweight fighter.

But Reid was not destined for a boxer's life. The future senator wanted out of Searchlight and applied himself in high school, becoming student body president. A history teacher, Donal O'Callaghan, who was also the local Democratic chairman, took an interest in young Reid and helped arrange a college scholarship at Utah State University. He also helped Reid get a job as a Capitol Police officer while he studied law at George Washington University.

Reid returned to Henderson and, at age 28, won election to the Nevada Assembly. When O'Callaghan was elected governor in 1970, Reid was elected the youngest lieutenant governor in state history. The mold was set, and after an unsuccessful Senate run against Paul Laxalt in 1974, Reid won a House seat representing Las Vegas in 1982. Four years later, his second attempt at winning a senate seat proved successful when he narrowly defeated Republican Rep. Jim Santini with a hair more than 50 percent of the vote.

Along with Pelosi, Reid will be the public face of the party in charge, a position that will invite more scrutiny into his politics, his personal life and his controversial finances and family connections. Earlier this year, he had to amend his financial disclosure statement with the Senate after revelations emerged that he had profited from lucrative land deal in Nevada.

Reid's most daunting task will be managing expectations and egos. In the rows behind him in the Senate chamber, seven Democrats will squirm with presidential ambition, hoping to stand out from the pack. And after Pelosi's "100 hours" of legislation roars out of the House in January, Reid will have to temper the excitement and negotiate with Republican Leader Mitch McConnell of Kentucky over what has a chance of passing.

than a West Coast liberal," said a former Democratic aide. "She has a good intuitive sense of power and an extremely acute sense of how to use it."

REACHING OUT

After Pelosi took the reins of the House Democrats in 2002, her first move was to shed the image of a San Francisco liberal. She quit the Progressive Caucus, an organization of more than 50 mostly liberal House members founded in 1991.

Then Pelosi reached out to moderates and conservatives within the party in an effort to unify and strengthen their opposition to Republicans. She picked a conservative South Carolinian, John M. Spratt Jr., to be assistant to the leader. She brought John Tanner of Tennessee, who founded the conservative Blue Dog coalition, into leadership meetings.

"This time for new direction has given us an opportunity, a chance to prove to the American people that we can work with the Republicans," Reid said Nov. 9. "They've set a very bad example in not working with us. We're not following in that example."

Practicing From the Minority

Being a scrapper, a wily parliamentarian and a behind-the-scenes operator has served Reid well in his two years as minority leader.

Reid, who previously was Democratic whip for six years under Tom Daschle, lined up the votes for the top spot within hours of the former floor leader's defeat in South Dakota in 2004. He quickly put colleagues on notice that

CQ / Scott J. Ferrell

REID'S RISE: He will need to work with the GOP to advance Pelosi's agenda.

Shortly before the Nov. 7 election, Reid told McConnell in a phone call, that he would convene "real" conference committees to write the final draft of bills. Both parties will participate and they will be open to the public, he has said. Republicans often conducted conferences behind closed door and excluded Democrats.

Reid priorities for the 110th Congress will be cutting health care costs, promoting alternative energy sources such as wind and solar power, making college tuition more affordable, and strengthening the pension system.

Though he will promote bedrock Democratic values, Reid, more than many in his caucus, understands the need to consult with conservatives in order to deliver results. No stranger to working across the aisle, Reid, a practicing

he would be a stickler for following the chamber's rules and that he would not operate in an ad hoc fashion. Reid is more likely than current Republican Majority Leader Bill Frist to let Senate committees work their will, rather than bypassing the panels to bring his own priorities directly to the floor.

"The night I learned I was going to be minority leader, I called up all of the members of my caucus and said, 'There will be no more task forces," Reid said. "All of our work will be done through committees."

Mormon, already votes with Republicans in favor of restrictions on abortion. Last year, he voted with a majority of Democrats against a majority of Republicans only 92 percent of the time — a party unity score that didn't even place him in the top 10 among Senate Democrats.

But observers warn that Reid's independence and outward pragmatism belies a steely determination.

"He likes to say he'd rather dance than fight, but a lot of people have gotten bruised dancing with him," Herzik said. "Tread lightly taking him on."

To keep Democrats united, she would call upon defense-district hawks such as Ike Skelton of Missouri to speak against Republican bills in caucus meetings.

On occasion, Pelosi has challenged the liberal wing of her party. This year, for example, she blocked a move by John Conyers Jr. of Michigan to seek the impeachment of President Bush.

Activists in her San Francisco district complain that she is not liberal enough. Code Pink, an anti-war group,

has picketed her meetings, complaining that she has voted for bills to fund the Iraq War. The gay community fumes that Pelosi has not spoken up for same-sex marriage.

The result has been that Pelosi has accomplished what her predecessors could not: House Democrats have been more unified than at any time in the past 50 years. Last year, the average Democrat voted with the party's position 88 percent of the time on votes where a majority of

Democrats opposed a majority of Republicans. That unity approached the 90 percent achieved by the historically better disciplined Republicans.

Pelosi's party discipline record was helped by outside forces. The 2002 and 2004 elections reduced the number of Democrats, especially Southern conservatives, that she would have to accommodate.

Meanwhile, the Republican practice of excluding Democrats from the drafting of major legislation and not letting them offer amendments or alternatives helped to galvanize Pelosi's troops.

"If you gave them a chance to participate more and offer alternatives, I think she would have a much harder time holding all of the Democrats together," said former Republican Rep. Robert S. Walker of Pennsylvania in an interview over the summer.

Still, no small part of the answer to Pelosi's success stems from the political education she received in her childhood. Her father, Thomas J. D'Alesandro Jr., was a New Deal member of the House when she was born in 1940, and after serving four terms he went on to become mayor of Baltimore for 12 years. Her oldest brother would later become mayor too.

Pelosi, the last of six children and the only daughter, slept with a stack of Congressional Records underneath her bed. Constituents regularly visited her family's brick row house in Baltimore's Little Italy. She was tutored in the art of the political machine; her father had young Nancy write down the things he had done for people in the "favor file," favors that could be called in later.

"Our whole lives were politics," Pelosi told the California press when she first ran for Congress in a 1987 special election. She won.

But before that she married her college sweetheart and moved back to his hometown of San Francisco. Paul Pelosi became a wealthy investor, and the future House Speaker soon used their spacious home for hosting Democratic fundraisers. While rearing five children, she rose through the California state party ranks and was a candidate to head the National Democratic party in 1985.

Pelosi continued to be an exceptional fundraiser when she arrived in Washington. She shared the largess with party colleagues, which helped to engineer her rise on the Hill.

ENFORCING DISCIPLINE

Pelosi saves her most ruthless side for within the Democratic family. Getting everyone on the same page is important, but it is effective only if you can keep them there. Pelosi does.

Pelosi holds rank-and-file Democrats accountable for their votes and demands an explanation when they cannot vote with the party. She threatened to remove New York Rep. Edolphus Towns from his seat on the Energy and Commerce Committee after he sided with Republicans on a free-trade pact and then failed to show up for an important vote.

In the Social Security debate, Pelosi forced House Democrats to take a hard stand against Bush's proposal for private investment accounts. Several Southern Democrats embraced the White House plan and were keen to make a bipartisan deal; other Democrats wanted to fix the program by raising payroll taxes on the rich. But Pelosi maintained that the best strategy was simply to oppose the White House proposal, and she forbade Democrats from offering alternatives that Republicans could attack.

The caucus obeyed Pelosi for five months, by which time Bush's initiative was faltering. It was liberal Robert Wexler of Florida who eventually crossed Pelosi and introduced a Social Security bill that raised payroll taxes for the wealthy.

Pelosi telephoned Wexler to express her displeasure, and her press office quickly told the media that Wexler's bill was not the Democratic party position. Wexler found only one Democrat willing to sign on to his legislation, and with Pelosi and most Democrats disavowing it, Republicans were unable to make the tax increase an issue. By the summer of 2005, Bush abandoned his Social Security drive altogether.

In the elbowing for leadership roles, Pelosi has a long memory. After she bested Rep. Harold Ford Jr. of Tennessee for the party leadership, she effectively isolated him. She still doesn't get along with Maryland's Steny Hoyer, whom she defeated in a hard-fought race for Democratic whip in 2001. Shelley Berkley of Nevada, who voted for Hoyer in that race five years ago, appears to be losing out for a seat on the powerful Ways and Means Committee.

Pelosi uses the levers of committee assignments to

Pelosi's Agenda at a Glance

Nancy Pelosi has been careful not to overreach with the agenda that she says House Democrats will follow in their first 100 legislative hours in power — about five weeks — this winter. Most are popular items. Party leaders have a broader, long-term legislative agenda they will try to enact, much of it proposals the Republican majority has ignored for years.

The 100-hour agenda includes a package of House rules changes that include pay-as-you-go budgeting and legislation that would:
- Increase the minimum wage.
- Cut the interest rate on student loans by half.
- Allow the government to negotiate with drug companies for lower prices for Medicare patients.
- End tax breaks for oil companies.
- Broaden the types of stem cell research allowed with federal funding.

The Democratic agenda, which party leaders have been revising and adding to over the past year, also includes:
- A new plan for the Iraq War that would require Iraqis to take responsibility for their country and begin a phased reduction of U.S. forces. Special Forces would be increased, however. Democrats emphasize the need to refurbish both active-duty and reserve military forces, as well as helping first-responders such as police and firefighters.
- An end to tax breaks that critics say reward companies for moving jobs overseas.
- Making college tuition payments deductible from taxes, permanently, and expanding Pell Grants for low-income students.
- Encouraging the development of energy-efficient technologies and alternatives to imported oil, such as biofuels.
- Enactment of pension legislation designed to protect employees' financial security.
- Expansion of personal savings incentives.

their maximum, creating new rules and riding roughshod over the seniority system.

When rising star Chaka Fattah of Philadelphia was in line to become ranking member of the House Administration Committee, which controls coveted room assignments, Pelosi told Fattah he would have to give up his Appropriations seat to take it.

But then Pelosi tried to appoint her loyalist John Larson of Connecticut to the seat instead, even though he sits on the exclusive Ways and Means Committee. Only after critics pointed out the double standard did Pelosi relent.

Pelosi consolidated her power further when she restricted membership on the Financial Services Committee, where members easily raise millions for the Democratic Party from Wall Street. As of last year, any new member that Pelosi appoints to Financial Services may not sit on any other "A" committees, such as Appropriations or Ways and Means.

THE COMING SCRUTINY

For the past four years, Pelosi has successfully balanced her leadership pragmatism, her program of reaching out to conservatives, with her liberalism. As Speaker, though, her every action will get a lot more attention than when she was waging a guerrilla campaign as minority leader.

Her voting record still wins almost perfect scores from the liberal groups, such as Americans for Democratic Action, the National Abortion and Reproductive Rights Action League and the AFL-CIO.

The advisers Pelosi counts on most are liberals too: Californians George Miller and Anna G. Eshoo, David R. Obey of Wisconsin, Rosa DeLauro of Connecticut and Frank Pallone Jr. of New Jersey. An exception is Rep. John P. Murtha, a powerful Defense appropriator, whose support of Pelosi was critical in winning her party posts. And it was Miller who told Pelosi to pick Spratt as the conservative to bring into the leadership structure, even though Spratt had been a Hoyer supporter. Miller had worked closely with Spratt when they were regional whips under Gephardt and vouched for him.

Some conservatives and Midwesterners complain that Pelosi does not really care enough about what they think because her inner circle is small and almost entirely liberal.

Stenholm points out that as much as Pelosi has reached out to the Blue Dogs, she won't pay much attention to the Democrats' tiny anti-abortion caucus. "I will be the first one to say that it is going to be absolutely imperative as Speaker of the House that she brings in the Blue Dogs," said Stenholm, now an agricultural lobbyist.

Her challenge will be to balance this inner liberalism with the practicalities of governing in the House, and finding enough issues that everyone can agree on to make a difference.

"There will be a lot of midnight oil burned in Congress in finding policies that all Democrats can support," predicted Stenholm.

Waging War on the Surge

An unpopular plan to send more
U.S. troops to Iraq leaves Congress
weighing the hard questions of
how and when to wrest war-
making power from the president

Edward M. Kennedy could barely restrain himself. A few hours before President Bush announced to the nation that he was sending 21,500 more troops to Iraq — digging even more deeply into a war that has lost the support of most Americans — the liberal icon insisted that the Senate should push back as quickly as possible by passing his bill to make Bush ask Congress for permission first.

"I would think it would be a matter of days," not weeks, Kennedy told reporters. "I'm going to get it in a timely way." In case anyone missed the urgency, the Massachusetts senator laid it on the line: "This is the overarching issue of our time."

On the other side of the Capitol, Rep. Dennis J. Kucinich of Ohio, the longtime Iraq War opponent who is making his second run for the White House, handed out copies of his proposal to cut off all funding for the war — not just for the extra troops — and spend $7 billion to bring the troops home. "If you're opposing 20,000 troops, you ought to oppose 140,000," he said as he buttonholed colleagues in the Speaker's lobby outside the House chamber during a vote. "We need to end the war, not fund it."

From *CQ Weekly,*
January 15, 2007.

Highlights of the President's Plan

President Bush's new strategy for Iraq to quell violence over the next 12 to 18 months includes more U.S. troops in some areas, more reconstruction aid, a set of requirements for Iraq's government to meet and a greater regional approach. Bush also has pledged to consult more often with congressional leaders and senior lawmakers. Following are the major points of his plan:

WHAT THE UNITED STATES WILL DO
Military
- The plan is to put five more combat brigades, or about 17,500 troops, into Baghdad beginning Jan. 15. These troops will work alongside Iraqi units and be embedded in their formations. Their mission will be to rid Baghdad neighborhoods of insurgents and terrorists and to train Iraqi security forces to continue such protection after U.S. troops leave. Bush said the added troops would better ensure that insurgents do not return once they have been cleared out of a neighborhood.
- Another 4,000 Marines would be sent to bolster U.S. forces in Anbar province, a mostly Sunni region. They will work with Iraqi and tribal forces to fight al Qaeda terrorists who have made the province a stronghold.
- Bush says the additional forces will cost $5.6 billion, which will be added to his fiscal 2007 supplemental spending request in February. Earlier estimates had put that supplemental request at $160 billion.

Reconstruction
- The plan would provide about $1.2 billion for reconstruction, immediate civilian needs and other projects to improve the daily lives of Iraqis. The money also will be part of the supplemental spending request.
- The reconstruction request will include $414 million to double the number of provincial teams made up of military and civilian experts to help Iraqis make the transition to self-reliance.
- The United States will put a coordinator in Baghdad to oversee how economic assistance will be spent, and commanders will have greater flexibility in using the money.

Regional strategy
- The United States will work to stop the flow of weapons and training assistance from Iran and Syria that is helping insurgents and terrorists in Iraq.

- An added carrier strike group was deployed to the region recently, and the U.S. military will send Patriot air defense systems there.
- U.S. officials will work to help Iraq and Turkey resolve border problems.

WHAT IRAQ HAS PROMISED
- The Iraqi government has committed to providing $10 billion for reconstruction.
- Three Iraqi army brigades will be shifted to Baghdad by the end of February, bringing the number of Iraqi brigades in the capital to 18.
- New rules of engagement will give Iraqi commanders greater control of their forces and the ability to crack down on all militias regardless of their religious sects.
- Iraq will be responsible for securing all of its provinces by November.
- The government will pass legislation allowing oil revenues to be shared with all citizens.
- Provincial elections will be held later this year in an effort to give more power to local leaders.

WHAT BUSH PROMISED CONGRESS
- In his televised address last week, the president said he would form "a new, bipartisan working group" with Congress "that will help us come together across party lines to win the war on terror." Among the group's missions that Bush envisions:
  - Increasing the size of the Army and Marine Corps.
  - Figuring out a way to persuade talented U.S. civilians to go overseas and "help build democratic institutions in communities and nations recovering from war and tyranny."

Even Sen. John Kerry of Massachusetts, the 2004 Democratic presidential nominee who was famous for his caution about opposing the war, threw his support behind the Kennedy approach. "It's not enough just to say, 'We don't support this,' then have the president roll right over us and do it anyway," Kerry told reporters. "Congress has to stand up and be counted on this."

And yet, getting Congress to "stand up and be counted" on a substantive response to the troop "surge" Bush proposed Jan. 10 is more difficult than the newly empowered Democrats ever would have imagined.

Barely two weeks into their new jobs, House Speaker Nancy Pelosi of California and Senate Majority Leader Harry Reid of Nevada were confronted with a political challenge so grave it would test the skills of far more experienced congressional leaders. In proposing to send even more American men and women into such an unpopular war, Bush was essentially daring Congress to stop him. To do so, Democratic leaders would have to force a confrontation that would reopen the decades-old constitutional struggle — never fully settled — over how much power Congress has to limit the president's ability to wage war.

They may be prepared to do it. Many Democrats would be ready for a confrontation, and they hear plenty of Republicans blasting Bush's plans with such a fervor that they sound ready for it, too. But it's one thing to agree that lawmakers oppose the surge. It's another to get Democrats and Republicans together to take the far more momentous next step of taking away the president's power to order it.

Should Congress deny Bush the funds he would need to increase the U.S. forces in Iraq? Should it give him the money, but with a slew of conditions and strings attached? Should it limit the number of troops? Cut off the funding for the war completely? Or simply issue a politically devastating vote of no confidence, with lawmakers from both parties joining in, and hope that's enough to get Bush to back down?

For now, Congress is going to start with the last option. This week, Senate Democrats are expected to introduce a non-binding resolution that would outline the Bush proposal and allow senators to cast a symbolic vote for or against it. The vote, which party leaders hope to turn into a bipartisan rejection of the plan, would take place the week of Jan. 22 and would be followed by a similar referendum in the House.

Some Democrats are hoping, in perhaps a bit of wishful thinking, that a strong bipartisan vote for the Senate resolution could force Bush to reconsider the surge and eliminate the need for Congress to take any further action. "It would seem to me, if there is a bipartisan resolution saying, 'We don't support this escalation of the war,' that the president's going to have to take note of that," Reid said. "I think that's the beginning of the end, as far as I'm concerned."

If it's not, though, it will take weeks — maybe months — before Congress decides what else it's prepared to do to actually stop the surge.

This is the war that is opposed by six out of 10 Americans, has taken the lives of more than 3,000 U.S. soldiers and has wounded nearly 23,000 others, has almost single-handedly destroyed Bush's support among the public, and is one of the main reasons his party lost control of Congress in November. It has lost Bush the support of former allies in his own party, and many of them aren't buying his argument that a stepped-up U.S. presence is the way to bring the escalating sectarian violence under control. Neither is the public, apparently: A Washington Post-ABC News poll taken the day of Bush's speech found that 61 percent oppose the idea, with 52 percent saying they strongly opposed it.

When a war is this unpopular, it wouldn't seem so hard for Congress to force the president to wind it down. But the political reality, even now, is that nothing can happen in Congress until Democratic leaders can get their diverse rank-and-file to decide exactly how they want to do that. And in the Senate, they won't be able to do anything until they can get at least some Republicans on board.

For all of the opposition to Bush's plan, the prospect of curbing the president's war-making powers is too sobering to make that an easy sell — and not just to Republicans, but to centrist Democrats as well.

"There is one commander in chief," said Sen. Ben Nelson of Nebraska, one of the many Democrats from Republican-leaning states who aren't ready to force a confrontation with Bush just yet.

Even Republican Sen. John W. Warner of Virginia, whose recent criticisms of the Iraq situation make him one of the Democrats' best hopes for an ally, isn't anxious for Congress to try to limit Bush's ability to deploy troops. "In an ongoing operation," said Warner, "you've got to defer to the commander in chief."

TESTING THE NEW LEADERSHIP

Pelosi and Reid owe their jobs, in no small part, to the voters who rejected Bush's leadership of the war. And they've called, many times, for Bush to begin to withdraw troops from Iraq, concentrating on training and counterterrorism rather than combat.

They fumed on the afternoon of the speech as Bush called them to the White House to tell them formally what they and everyone else had already heard informally: that he was sending more troops to help Iraqi forces secure neighborhoods from violence. In return, he said, the Iraqi government has promised to meet specific goals such as taking over security in all of the country's provinces by November.

"It is clear that we need to change our strategy in Iraq," Bush said in his prime-time address. He called the continuing violence "unacceptable," and declared that "where mistakes have been made, the responsibility rests with me." But the new plan, he said, reflects the consensus of leaders of both parties that "failure in Iraq would be a disaster for the United States."

Democrats consider Bush's plan an escalation, and some worry that he might broaden the conflict to the borderlands of Iran and Syria. In his speech, Bush said U.S. forces would "interrupt the flow of support from Iran and Syria" for terrorists in Iraq, and a day later they raided an Iranian diplomatic office in northern Iraq, arresting six Iranian officials.

Senior House and Senate Democrats were said to be considering a resolution that would require Bush to seek authorization before taking military action against Iran or Syria.

To Pelosi and Reid, Bush's proposal for a surge in forces was as if he had not been listening — not to the voters who put the Democrats in power, and not to the bipartisan Iraq Study Group headed by former Secretary of State James A. Baker III and former Democratic Rep. Lee H. Hamilton of Indiana, which called for the beginning of a withdrawal of U.S. troops and stepped-up diplomatic efforts in the region. "Last night, the president — in choosing escalation — ignored the will of the people, the advice of the Baker-Hamilton Commission, and the guidance of his top generals," Reid said in a floor speech the day after Bush's address. "In choosing to escalate the war, the president stands alone."

And yet, neither Democratic leader was in a rush to pull the plug. Their plan, for the moment, is to let a series of congressional hearings pick Bush's plan apart while they try to build support for some concrete response — perhaps restricting the funding for the war, perhaps capping the number of new troops, perhaps setting a host of conditions for the funding.

That way, they believe the ground could be set for a move against the troop increase when Congress takes up Bush's next request for a supplemental spending bill to fund the war, which could be weeks away. It would also increase the odds that whatever action they take against Bush would look reasoned and bipartisan, they believe, rather than just a knee-jerk Democratic response intended to embarrass a Republican president.

That plan isn't likely to quiet the Democrats in both chambers who are agitating for a faster move against the surge, and possibly against the war itself.

"Congress must use its main power — the power of the purse — to put an end to our involvement in this disastrous war," Democratic Sen. Russ Feingold of Wisconsin declared at a Senate Foreign Relations Committee hearing the day after Bush's speech, as Secretary of State Condoleezza Rice, who was testifying in behalf of the president's plan, listened in stony silence. "And I'm not talking here only about the surge or escalation. It is time to use the power of the purse to bring our troops out of Iraq."

But as a practical matter, Reid and Pelosi may not be able to move any faster. Whatever response they choose, it can't be acceptable just to Democrats. Reid, for example, has only a 51-vote majority in the Senate. And that counts Independent Joseph I. Lieberman of Connecticut, who showered Bush with praise for his proposal and isn't likely to support a congressional counterstrike under any circumstances.

To overcome the likely filibuster, Reid would need 60 votes — which means finding Republicans who won't just talk about their reservations about Bush's strategy, but are willing to force him to back off.

The leaders' caution, however, was enough to make some anti-war groups needle the Democrats with blunt reminders of why they were elected in the first place.

The day after Bush's speech, a new coalition called Americans Against Escalation in Iraq — including liberal political groups such as MoveOn.org Political Action and Campaign for America's Future, as well as the

Service Employees International Union — announced a nationwide campaign of rallies and advertising to pressure Congress to bring a quick end to the war, including a march on Washington on Jan. 27.

"This Congress was elected with a very clear mission: to lead this nation out of its disastrous occupation of Iraq," said Eli Pariser, executive director of MoveOn.org Political Action. "It is Congress' moral obligation to act, and to act soon."

Former Democratic Rep. Tom Andrews, now national director of Win Without War, said it was time for Congress to "step up and put an end to this madness — and not simply with non-binding words and phrases."

CONSIDERING OPTIONS

Technically, Congress has no shortage of tools to change Bush's Iraq strategy, if it chooses to use them. It can prohibit the use of funds for a surge in troops. It can cap the number of troops the president can send to Iraq. It can set limits or conditions on the missions of the troops. It can even stop funding the Iraq War altogether.

All of these are similar to options that have been used by Congress in past wars, according to a paper by the Center for American Progress, a liberal think tank, compiled to coach lawmakers on the possible ways they might respond to Bush. *(Congress, p. 85)*

"They have done this in the past. They can do it if they want," said Lawrence J. Korb, a senior fellow at the center. "And it really is up to them to take the lead. They are a coequal branch of government."

Politically, however, many of these steps can't be taken easily, even with a conflict as unpopular as the Iraq War. And there are technical issues that could make even a simple goal — stopping the surge — more difficult than it might seem.

Cutting off the funding for the war altogether, as Kucinich wants to do, would raise the prospect of the one charge that still terrifies many Democrats: that they would be choking off support for U.S. troops while they're engaged in combat.

Over and over, House and Senate Democrats, particularly the ones from red states and districts, have insisted they won't be part of any confrontation with Bush that

CQ / Scott J. Ferrell

BEARING THE BRUNT: Rice arrived at the Senate Foreign Relations Committee prepared to close the sale on Bush's plan. Instead, she got a dose of senatorial disbelief. "I think this speech . . . represents the most dangerous foreign policy blunder in this country since Vietnam," Nebraska's Chuck Hagel told her.

undercuts the troops. "I don't think there are a lot of Democrats who feel that withholding funds to men and women who are in harm's way is ever a good idea," newly elected Sen. Claire McCaskill of Missouri said after Senate Democrats discussed options at a luncheon the day before Bush's speech.

Even Kennedy's idea, which would simply require the president to get congressional authorization to send in more troops, raises fears among some centrist Democrats that it would open them up to the same charge. "It's very dangerous," said freshman Rep. Jason Altmire of Pennsylvania. "We have a lot of troops over there — 140,000, whatever the number is. We can't do anything at the congressional level that would pull the rug out from under them."

Senate Republican leaders are fully aware of the Democrats' vulnerability, which is why they might try to put them on the spot by forcing them to vote on an immediate withdrawal of U.S. forces. And Senate Minority Leader Mitch McConnell of Kentucky essentially dared the Democrats to deny Bush the funds for a troop

Occupational Hazards

The "surge" in U.S. forces that President Bush plans for the months ahead will bring the total troop level to just above the 150,000 soldiers and Marines in the country at the conclusion of the 2003 U.S. invasion. In between, troop levels have varied as the insurgency ebbed and flowed and as Iraq held national elections. Extended tours of duty and faster turnarounds at home have stretched U.S. forces.

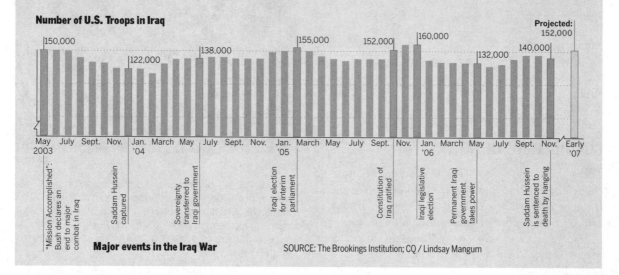

Number of U.S. Troops in Iraq

150,000 122,000 138,000 155,000 152,000 160,000 132,000 140,000 Projected: 152,000

May 2003 · July · Sept. · Nov. · Jan. '04 · March · May · July · Sept. · Nov. · Jan. '05 · March · May · July · Sept. · Nov. · Jan. '06 · March · May · July · Sept. · Nov. · Early '07

Major events in the Iraq War

"Mission Accomplished": Bush declares an end to major combat in Iraq

Saddam Hussein captured

Sovereignty transferred to Iraqi government

Iraqi election for interim parliament

Constitution of Iraq ratified

Iraqi legislative election

Permanent Iraqi government takes power

Saddam Hussein is sentenced to death by hanging

SOURCE: The Brookings Institution; CQ / Lindsay Mangum

---

increase. "I would just encourage my Democrat friends to be honest about what they want," McConnell said.

There are technical limits to Kennedy's idea, too. As Kennedy himself acknowledged, Bush can start the surge long before Congress can lift a finger to stop it, simply by extending deployments of troops who are already in the region and would otherwise be leaving. All his bill would do, Kennedy said, is cap the number of troops at whatever level existed at the time the legislation passed.

Pelosi, meanwhile, is considering options for blocking the troop increase in the supplemental spending bill, but she has not publicly advocated doing that. Bush said the additional troops would cost $5.6 billion.

Even then, though, Democratic skeptics don't think it would be easy to tell how to draw the line between old troops and new. "I'm sure he'll structure the supplemental in such a way that you won't be able to distinguish easily between the surge and the current operations," Altmire said.

As House Appropriations Committee Chairman David R. Obey of Wisconsin put it: "You know, if you've

got a shirt that's 90 percent cotton and 10 percent polyester, it's pretty hard to separate the fibers. That's pretty much what you're looking at with this supplemental."

Another option being considered by John P. Murtha of Pennsylvania, chairman of the House Defense Appropriations Subcommittee, would be to provide the funds for more troops only in exchange for meeting certain benchmarks, such as specific readiness levels in the armed forces. That plan has a good chance of winning Pelosi's backing, given that Murtha is a longtime friend who has continued to consult with her closely since he lost his race for House majority leader.

"There's no question we have the capability" to write conditions into the supplemental, said Murtha. "He's got to sign that, or there won't be any funding."

To buy time to work through those issues and consider other alternatives, Democratic leaders are relying on a kind of "death by hearings" strategy — building the case for congressional action against the surge through an onslaught of committee and subcommittee hearings that would expose the flaws they see in Bush's new plan.

Congress a Reluctant Tactician

During past disagreements with the White House over military commitments abroad, Congress has at times tried to impose limits on the number of troops that could be deployed or, in cases where the public opposed the operation, limits on the amount that could be spent to support combat activities. But direct intervention is rare. Following are several of the higher-profile cases:

Vietnam War. Congress took its first action to limit the war in June 1970 when it adopted the Cooper-Church amendment to a foreign military sales bill which prohibited any further military incursions into Cambodia. The debate ultimately led to passage of the 1973 War Powers Resolution that limited a president's ability to wage war without a congressional declaration. In June 1973, shortly after the last U.S. troops left Vietnam pursuant to the Paris peace agreement, Congress cleared a supplemental spending bill that barred any further U.S. military operations in Indochina. In December 1974, in a foreign aid bill, Congress limited the number of U.S. personnel who could be in Vietnam to 4,000 after six months and 3,000 after one year.

Lebanon Peacekeeping. Congress had misgivings about President Ronald Reagan's commitment of Marines to a multinational peacekeeping force in Lebanon, and in June 1983 it passed legislation requiring the president to seek Congressional authority for any "substantial" increase in the U.S. commitment. In September, Congress on its own authorized Reagan to keep the troops in Lebanon for another 18 months. But after the bombing of a Marine barracks in Beirut in October, the House considered a resolution requiring a faster withdrawal. The resolution was defeated, 153-274.

NATO Country Deployments. Congress in 1984 wanted to put a ceiling on the number of U.S. troops stationed in Europe as a way to pressure NATO allies into paying more

of the cost of keeping them there. Reagan went along, but he balked at an amendment to withdraw 30,000 troops a year from Europe for three years unless the allies increased their own defense spending. Reagan won: The Senate tabled the amendment, 55-41.

Somalia Peacekeeping. The deaths of 18 U.S. Army Rangers in Somalia in 1993 chilled Congress on the peacekeeping mission there that had begun under President George Bush and was continued by President Bill Clinton. Congressional leaders and Clinton jointly agreed that U.S. participation in the U.N. mission would end in March 1994, but the U.S. deaths touched off a furor in the House, which on Nov. 9 voted 224-203 in favor of withdrawing forces by Jan. 31, then voted 226-201 to return to the later deadline that the House, the Senate and Clinton had agreed to.

Troops in Bosnia. In June 1997, the House narrowly rejected a proposal to force the withdrawal of U.S. peacekeeping troops from Bosnia by the end of that year. The House had opposed the mission since late 1995, when Clinton promised up to 20,000 as part of a broader 60,000-soldier NATO mission to help enforce a peace agreement ending that country's brutal civil war. Similar Senate efforts to block the troop deployment collapsed after a peace accord was reached in Dayton, Ohio. Even so, the House adopted, by a 3-1 margin, a non-binding resolution repudiating Clinton's troop pledge and came within a few votes of passing a bill that would have denied funds for the mission.

House Armed Services Committee Chairman Ike Skelton of Missouri, for example, announced a series of hearings that would look at "the likely impact of the president's Iraq policy on security in Iraq and on America's military posture," as well as military readiness and strategic risk. It's unlikely that the topics were chosen randomly, since Skelton and other senior Democrats believe the Iraq War has stretched the military and hurt the readiness and training of the armed forces.

Democrat George Miller of California, chairman of the House Education and Labor Committee and a close ally of Pelosi, compared the approach to the way his party rallied opposition to Bush's Social Security overhaul plan in 2005 by methodically highlighting all of the dangers they saw in it, leading to its collapse without a single vote. "It wouldn't be the first time they put a proposal out there and it just fell apart," said Miller.

The hearings by the committee chairmen, Miller said, are "going to play an important role in pulling this apart.

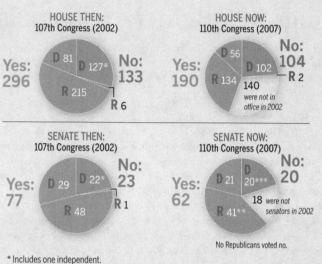

The Vote for the War, Three Elections Later

The majorities that voted in October 2002 for the law (PL 107-243) authorizing the Iraq War were both lopsided and bipartisan. But because of departures and defeats in three elections since, 32 percent of House members in the 110th Congress did not vote on the war — and those who did support it then account for less than a majority of the current membership. The change is less pronounced on the other side of the Capitol, where 18 of today's senators did not vote on the war, but there are still 62 who voted "yes."

SOURCE: CQ

HOUSE THEN:
107th Congress (2002)
Yes: 296   D 81   D 127*   No: 133
R 215   R 6

HOUSE NOW:
110th Congress (2007)
Yes: 190   D 56   D 102   No: 104
R 134   R 2
140 were not in office in 2002

SENATE THEN:
107th Congress (2002)
Yes: 77   D 29   D 22*   No: 23
R 48   R 1

SENATE NOW:
110th Congress (2007)
Yes: 62   D 21   D 20***   No: 20
R 41**   18 were not senators in 2002
No Republicans voted no.

* Includes one independent.
** Includes eight who were House members in 2002.
***Includes one Independent; also three Democrats and one independent who were House members in 2002.

After that happens, then people will probably have more confidence in where they want to be."

THE SEARCH FOR 60 VOTES

Judging from the barrage of criticism Bush's plan received from senators of both parties, it wouldn't seem too hard for Reid to get the Senate to take at least a symbolic stand against it.

When Rice arrived in a cavernous hearing room in the Dirksen Senate office building the morning after Bush's speech to make the case for Bush's plan, she came prepared for skeptical questions from the Foreign Relations Committee.

"I want you to know that I understand and, indeed, feel the heartbreak that Americans feel at the continued sacrifice of American lives, men and women who can never be replaced for their families," she told the senators. But the administration "really did consider the options before us," she said, and concluded that "the most urgent task before us now is to help the Iraqi government . . . establish confidence among the Iraqi population that it will and can protect all of its citizens."

But instead of closing the sale, Rice found herself on the receiving end of a full-fledged venting session. And not just from Democrats, but from Republicans as well.

"I think this speech given last night by this president represents the most dangerous foreign policy blunder in this country since Vietnam, if it's carried out. I will resist it," Republican Sen. Chuck Hagel of Nebraska, a potential presidential candidate, told Rice to applause from the standing-room-only audience.

Republican Sen. George V. Voinovich of Ohio echoed the theme, with only slightly more restraint. "I just must tell you that I've gone along with the president on this, and I bought into his dream," he told Rice, "and at this stage of the game I don't think it's going to happen."

Meanwhile, Sen. Sam Brownback of Kansas, a conservative Republican and another probable White House contender, issued a statement from Baghdad that made it clear he wasn't prepared to stake his political future on Bush's plan. "I do not believe that sending more troops to Iraq is the answer," he said. "The United States should not increase its involvement until Sunnis and Shi'a are more willing to cooperate with each other instead of shooting at each other."

What all those statements mean, however, is only that Reid might be able to get the 60 votes he needs for a non-binding resolution opposing the surge. Getting 60 votes for a measure that might actually deny Bush the funds or the authorization to go ahead with it is another matter entirely.

For Warner, for example, such a confrontation raises the prospect of yet another constitutional showdown over the president's authority as commander in chief. Even when Congress debated the War Powers Resolution, he said, lawmakers never resolved exactly how far they intended to go in curbing the president's powers. "We're in a gray area, and that's where we want to leave it," he said.

Reid's aides aren't even sure they could get all of the Democrats to go along with a confrontation with Bush. And they have good reason to worry. For all of their skepticism of Bush's plan, several of the Democratic senators from Republican-leaning states aren't anywhere near the point where they'd want to tie Bush's hands.

For example, Mark Pryor of Arkansas, a member of the Senate Armed Service Committee, said he has lots of questions to ask Joint Chiefs of Staff Chairman Gen. Peter Pace and other military leaders before he decides how he will respond to the surge proposal. When Pryor visited Baghdad a few months ago, he said, he noticed that one of the 13 precincts had no U.S. military presence at all, just Iraqi security forces — yet it seemed to be safer than the other neighborhoods. If so, he wondered, why wouldn't the other neighborhoods also be safer without U.S. troops?

The bottom line, though, is that Pryor knows how serious a showdown with Bush would be, and he isn't prepared to go there just yet.

"I think he has the authority to do this," said Pryor. "I would hate for us to get to the point of Congress cutting off funding. I just hope we don't get there."

In the House, Pelosi's challenge isn't as difficult as Reid's. She has a stronger margin of control — 233 Democrats, with only 218 votes needed for passage of most legislation — and no filibusters to worry about.

She also doesn't have to win over as many former supporters of the war. In the House, only 190 members are left who voted to authorize the Iraq War in 2002. By contrast, 62 senators who voted for the authorization are still serving today, including eight who were in the House in 2002.

CONVINCING THE NEW DEMOCRATS

But Pelosi's majority, like Reid's, rests on Democrats who were elected from Republican areas — and who are nervously biding their time before committing to a specific response to Bush's new strategy. It's an agonizing test for new lawmakers who are still getting up to speed on how to do their jobs.

Hours before the speech, Rep. Heath Shuler of North Carolina, who unseated Republican Charles H. Taylor in November, was part of a group of Democrats invited to the White House to be briefed in advance by administration officials. "I was not sold" on the plan, Shuler said. "So many times, we seem to have increased troop levels, increased troop levels, and it doesn't seem to have made any difference."

Still, Shuler wasn't prepared to say what he would do in response, other than asking "tough questions" of the military leaders. "I think we can come up with a policy that is a new direction, but is the right new direction," Shuler said. "We have a lot of troops in harm's way. We need to come up with something quickly."

Likewise, a group of newly elected House Democrats with military experience — including Iraq War veteran Patrick J. Murphy, retired Navy Vice Adm. Joe Sestak, and Navy Reserve Lt. Cmdr. Chris Carney, all of Pennsylvania — teamed up at a news conference the day after the speech to denounce the Bush proposal.

But even they weren't prepared to take the next step. "We're not at that point yet," Murphy said, but "we're champing at the bit to ask the tough questions." Carney suggested that lawmakers should talk to Bush some more, and wait to see what the next National Intelligence Estimate says: "If we have more information, we can make better decisions."

Sestak even suggested that Bush could win him over if he frames the surge proposal in the right way. "If the president says this increase in troops is necessary to guarantee the security of our troops who are already over there, I will support it," said Sestak. "If he does not, I will not support it."

Pelosi may well be able to count on all of their votes by the time the House is ready to act on the Bush plan. But she won't be able to take any of them for granted. And she'll have to balance their concerns with the liberals in her caucus, such as Kucinich, who don't think it's enough just to place conditions on more troops or even prevent the increase.

If Kucinich can talk enough House Democrats into supporting a full withdrawal of troops, he believes, Pelosi and the rest of the leadership will be emboldened to do the same. "Leaders respond to the will of the caucus," Kucinich said. "I supported Nancy Pelosi for Speaker, but she needs help."

It's not clear how helpful Pelosi will consider his efforts, given how often she has insisted that Democrats would never shut off money to the troops overseas. But whatever form the final showdown with Bush takes, if it comes to that, Kucinich may be right about one thing: Pelosi and Reid will need all the help they can get as they prepare their members to pull the trigger.

FOR FURTHER READING

Uncertain war costs, 2007 CQ Weekly, p. 14; 2006 key votes on troop withdrawals, pp. 63, 70.

Bracing for Default Day

Rising tide of foreclosures has Hill scrambling for ways to ease the blow to the U.S. economy

CQ / Scott J. Ferrell

PAIN AND RESPONSE: Evictions are common when homeowners default and lenders foreclose on their property. At a Capitol Hill summit last week, lawmakers, banking and housing officials, lenders and community organizers gather behind closed doors to talk about solutions to the current crisis affecting borrowers with poor credit ratings.

From *CQ Weekly,*
April 23, 2007.

Brian D. Montgomery will be forgiven if he starts to think his office is on Capitol Hill. The top government housing official, who can typically be found many blocks away at the headquarters of the Department of Housing and Urban Development, made no fewer than three separate appearances before members of Congress last week in his role as chief of the Federal Housing Administration.

He isn't alone. Banking regulators, community housing groups and representatives from the lending industry have been forced to set up camp in the halls and committee rooms of the Capitol in recent weeks. At least six hearings and one closed-door summit have been held since the first of March to directly address the widening crisis involving subprime mortgage loans and the rash of foreclosures that is forcing millions of people from their homes across the country. The subject arises in other settings as well, especially those in which the economy and the housing market generally are the topic of discussion.

One of every 92 U.S. households faced foreclosure last year and the number is expected to get larger. Over the next two years, monthly payments on millions of loans will surge as their low introductory interest rates balloon by as much as 50 percent. The nonprofit Center for Responsible Lending predicts that one in five subprime mortgages taken out in the past two years — those

Economically Troubled Regions Have High Foreclosure Rates

The rise in foreclosures over the 12 months ended in March has been felt nationally, but the largest percentage of foreclosures has occurred in states that either had loose regulation of mortgage brokers and lenders, or were already suffering from economic trouble. Foreclosures tend to be highest in urban areas.

Foreclosures in the U.S.
As a percentage of households over the past 12 months

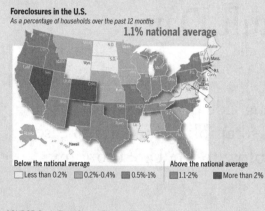

1.1% national average

Below the national average			Above the national average	
☐ Less than 0.2%	▨ 0.2%-0.4%	▨ 0.5%-1%	▨ 1.1-2%	■ More than 2%

SOURCE: RealtyTrac, Census Bureau; CQ / Marilyn Gates-Davis

Top 20 cities with high foreclosure rates
As a percentage of households in 2006

	Foreclosure rate	Total foreclosures
Detroit/Livonia/Dearborn	4.9%	40,219
Atlanta/Sandy Springs/Marietta	4.4	63,737
Indianapolis	4.3	27,598
Denver/Aurora	4.2	37,412
Dallas	3.9	51,730
Fort Worth/Arlington	3.7	25,625
Las Vegas/Paradise	3.3	19,578
Memphis	3.2	18,155
Fort Lauderdale	2.8	21,113
Miami	2.8	24,046
Stockton	2.7	5,153
San Antonio	2.7	14,754
Riverside/San Bernardino	2.6	30,255
Cleveland/Lorain/Elyria/Mentor	2.5	22,976
Dayton	2.3	8,493
Austin/Round Rock	2.3	11,513
Akron	2.3	6,754
Houston/Baytown/Sugarland	2.3	41,763
Columbus	2.2	15,175
Jacksonville	2.1	9,983

marketed to borrowers with poor credit histories and limited incomes — will end up in foreclosure. The crisis may eventually cost as much as $164 billion.

"It's subprime all the time," said one congressional aide of how the staggering figures have caught the attention of lawmakers suddenly frantic to prevent this still relatively confined problem from spreading both in their home districts and throughout the economy.

"We want to do everything possible to avoid foreclosures," said Connecticut Democrat Christopher J. Dodd, chairman of the Senate Banking, Housing and Urban Affairs Committee. "It's not in the interest of homeowners, neighborhoods, communities or the mortgage finance industry."

There is considerable fear that the pace of foreclosures, which jumped again in the first three months of this year, will continue to rise and jeopardize the entire economy. Although most foreclosures involve subprime borrowers, ordinary homeowners could be harmed, too,

if spreading neighborhood blight accelerates the decline of home prices. Falling prices will diminish the ability of homeowners to refinance their houses, as they have done repeatedly over the past decade to withdraw cash to pay for renovations, cars, vacations and college tuition. A resulting slowdown in consumer spending could then bring down the broader economy.

For that reason, lawmakers and other government officials say they want to act quickly to prevent such an escalation.

Still, the debate has just begun over which of several possible steps to take, or whether legislative action is required. Dodd is among those who would prefer to hand the task jointly to banking and housing regulators and to the mortgage industry, and have them work with troubled borrowers and put an end to abusive practices. But that alone may not be enough.

Lawmakers such as Barney Frank, the Massachusetts Democrat who is chairman of the House Financial

"We want to do every-thing possible to avoid foreclosures. It's not in the interest of home-owners, neighborhoods, communities or the mortgage finance industry."

— Christopher J. Dodd, chairman,
Senate Banking Committee

Only a year or so ago, lawmakers, regulators and mortgage industry representatives were lauding "creative" lending practices, and a furious pace of new loans that had boosted homeownership to near record levels was acting as the principal engine of the U.S. economy.

But millions of Americans took out mortgages they had little ability to repay, loans that came from lenders whose underwriting was lax at best and predatory at worst. For many of these borrowers, the dream of homeownership has already been shattered, or will be soon. Now, the question is how far Washington will go to remedy the situation.

SETTING THE RULES

Housing advocates who have long raised concerns about inappropriate loans to subprime borrowers often focus on the fact that no one regulator or set of regulations governs the mortgage industry. Federal regulators, including the Office of the Comptroller of the Currency, the Federal Deposit Insurance Corporation and the Federal Reserve, oversee bank lending. But most subprime loans are offered through mortgage brokers and financed by non-bank lenders, neither of which is subject to federal supervision. At most they are governed by an array of state laws that vary from strict to lax.

Some states, such as Louisiana and Washington, employ robust oversight efforts that include licensing brokers and lending officers individually and mandating minimum experience and continuing education requirements.

Others take a much more limited approach. For instance, Alaska law contains no rules at all governing mortgage brokers or lenders, according to a report this month by the Joint Economic Committee.

The chairman of the panel, Sen. Charles E. Schumer, a New York Democrat, has used the report to shine a spotlight on the subprime loan and foreclosure crisis. The committee has reported that 38 states plus the District of Columbia don't impose basic testing requirements on those who offer mortgage loans. And 17 of those states license companies rather than individuals.

The lack of supervision makes it easy for bad actors to find a foothold in the marketplace, said Richard F. Syron, chairman of mortgage financing giant Freddie Mac.

"As long as some institutions operate under different, or no, regulatory structures, the potential for these sorts

Services Committee, and Spencer Bachus of Alabama, the ranking Republican on the panel, join housing groups in saying that Congress needs to close gaps in the partly regulated and partly market-based system.

"Solutions to this problem will demand both stronger statutes on a federal level as well as some pragmatic work between Wall Street, loan servicers and various levels of government," said David Berenbaum, executive vice president of the National Community Reinvestment Coalition, a nonprofit advocacy group that also offers assistance to troubled borrowers.

Suggestions include creating a national licensing standard for mortgage brokers and lenders, mandating increased disclosure to borrowers and making lenders financially liable for steering home buyers into loans they cannot afford. Perhaps the most prominent and far-reaching idea — and the one of greatest import to taxpayers — is to create public-private "rescue funds" that ease the way for borrowers to rewrite the terms of their mortgages.

Some, like Berenbaum, say Congress needs to act because government officials were happy the housing market was surging earlier in this decade and allowed the current problem to grow and fester.

"We think regulatory failure is playing a role here," he said. "We've been crying out for greater oversight, but because the mortgage market has been driving the economy, I think there's been a political reluctance for regulators to do anything."

Market Without Risk — or Security

Any number of factors can be blamed for the collapse of the subprime mortgage market, but banking regulators and other experts say that one idea — the absence of market risk — underlies the current debacle.

A basic principle of financial market regulation is that attaching risk to an investment venture will make those who are putting up the money pay closer attention to the threat of adverse consequences, and their attention can go a long way toward putting the brakes on bad decisions. "Moral hazard" is the term that economists and regulators use to describe what happens when risk is diminished. It was present during the savings and loan crisis of almost two decades ago, and it is present today in some parts of the mortgage market.

"We did not have good market discipline," Sheila C. Bair, chairwoman of the Federal Deposit Insurance Corporation, told the House Financial Services Committee at a hearing last week.

Investors are supposed to be smart enough to put a price on a particular risk and create financial instruments that allow them to profit. In turn, the pricing mechanism is supposed to act as a check against excessive risky behavior.

But innovations in the way mortgage loans are made, and then packaged for sale to investors, have minimized the risks, even while these same changes were being applauded for helping borrowers with poor credit histories and limited incomes buy houses and push the rate of U.S. homeownership to record levels.

This all has to do with something called "securitization."

It used to be that mortgage loans were relatively simple instruments. Someone who wanted to buy a house would go to the local bank or credit union and apply for a loan, typically a 30-year fixed-rate mortgage. After collecting extensive information, the bank would decide whether to provide the money and then would collect the monthly payments of loan interest and principal. If a borrower fell behind on those payments, the bank would have the option of working with the borrower to find a solution that benefited both sides — or, in extreme cases, foreclosing on the property. The bank was responsible for the loan, so bad loans would hurt the bank's bottom line. As a result, loan officers and their institutions had an incentive to make sure the mortgages they gave out were made on terms that could be met.

No longer. Today, homebuyers or people who want to refinance their homes typically apply through a mortgage broker, who serves as an intermediary between borrowers and lenders in return for a fee paid for closing the deal. In the past the bank held on to the loan, but mortgages are now sold in blocks to so-called issuers, who package them in various combinations into securities that are backed by the interest payments or the principal amounts of the loans or both. These securities are sold to investors — many of whom are outside the United States — and the payments are passed along to them. The homeowner has no idea who owns the loan, and the investor who ultimately puts up the money has no real idea who the borrower is. Because the risk is so widely spread, it's a terrific way to increase the amount of capital available for home loans and for keeping down interest rates.

CQ / Scott J. Ferrell

ON THE SPOT: FDIC's Bair, left, FHA's Montgomery and Freddie Mac's Syron are among the regulators and market players being asked to solve the crisis.

No 'Plain Vanilla'

For a long time, most of these so-called mortgage-backed securities were sold through Fannie Mae and Freddie Mac, the two large government-created companies that finance a huge share of U.S. mortgages. They tended to package into securities the "plain vanilla" loans — mortgages that had very similar characteristics and whose risk was relatively easily assessed by investors. Fannie and Freddie say they have minimal involvement in the subprime loan market that is directed at borrowers with flimsy credit histories or uncertain income potential.

Things changed in recent years, when new players came into the mortgage-backed securities market and became sophisticated at packaging riskier subprime mortgages with more stable fixed-rate loans. Issuers quickly realized that they could slice and dice combinations of hundreds of different mortgages with varying risk profiles to suit the appetites of investors, who would be mostly protected from problems that can arise with an individual mortgage because so many loans, of so many different types, undergirded the security they purchased.

This system flourished during the first part of the decade, when low interest rates and rapidly rising home-price appreciation drove the market. But as issues and investors became used to the steady profits, concern about risk diminished.

"Subprime loans more than doubled as a share of all mortgage loan originations, from 7.9 percent in 2003 to 20 percent in 2005,"Bair testified last week. Moreover, she said, "approximately 75 percent of the estimated $600 billion of subprime mortgages originated in 2006 were funded by securitizations." And the volume of securities sold by new issuers — not Fannie and Freddie — also doubled since 2003.

Mortgage brokers who get paid to write loans needed to keep the process churning, and they increasingly offered special deals to non-traditional borrowers with blemished credit scores.

The market as a whole pushed borrowers into riskier and riskier loans to keep the profits coming, without regard for the individuals involved, said Allen Fishbein, director of housing and credit policy at the Consumer Federation of America. "The market can pool risk, but the borrower of course is an individual," he said. The fact that most loans in a mortgage-backed security do fine, he said, "doesn't do the borrower any good if they can't afford to repay their loan."

Mortgage Market Confusion

The mortgage market has become quite complex in recent years, funneling capital from thousands of investors through securities companies and lenders to borrowers who want loans. As a result, risk is thinly spread, and few participants have an incentive to guard against inappropriate loans.

A borrower obtains a loan from a lender, often with the assistance of a mortgage broker.
Risk: High because must repay the loan or face foreclosure

Mortgage broker often connects borrowers and lenders, generally for a fee.
Risk: None

The servicer collects payments from borrower and passes them to issuer.
Risk: Small because only fee income is in jeopardy, although servicer bears the obligation to force collection if borrower defaults.

The lender provides money to borrower and recovers that capital when the loan is sold to a securities issuer.
Risk: Small because most is passed to issuer.

The issuer provides capital to lender for new loans and packages groups of mortgages into securities to spread the risk widely to investors.
Risk: Small because most is passed to investor.

The investor re-capitalizes issuer by purchasing securities; receives regular payments from issuer.
Risk: Generally small because many loans are spread among many different investors.

SOURCE: Federal Deposit Insurance Corporation; CQ / Jamie Baylis

of excesses and abuses will exist," Syron told lawmakers at an April 17 hearing of the House Financial Services Committee.

In fact, there appears to be a strong correlation between states that are experiencing high levels of loan defaults and below-average levels of supervision, the Joint Economic Committee report showed. Indiana, Michigan and Ohio were among the top 10 states in the rate of foreclosures per household in 2006, and all "lack strict requirements for licensing brokers and lenders, and testing requirements for loan originators," the committee said.

Colorado, which was No. 1 with one foreclosure for every 33 households last year, has few rules intended to prevent lenders from making inappropriate loans, the report said. The state General Assembly in Denver is already considering ways to tighten the state's lending laws.

Such regulatory differences have led lawmakers such as Schumer and advocates such as Berenbaum to call for uniform regulation across the mortgage market, covering both federally supervised banks and state-supervised mortgage brokers.

Most suggestions wouldn't pull the entire mortgage industry under the federal umbrella. Rather, states would be required to adopt certain minimum standards. Still, a list of national minimums would probably include licensing for all individual brokers and lending officers, minimum education and experience standards, and criminal background checks, say lawmakers and critics of the current system.

"It should be one standard from Main Street — meaning the broker — to Wall Street and everyone in between," Berenbaum said.

Berenbaum and others suggest that lenders might be treated like brokers and dealers in the heavily regulated securities industry. Securities professionals have to pass rigorous examinations frequently and must be licensed to act in a professional capacity. Additionally, they have a legal fiduciary responsibility to operate on behalf of their clients and can be subject to lawsuits if they fail to uphold that standard.

Any push for increased scrutiny and regulation over non-bank mortgage brokers and lenders would be cheered by the banking industry, which contends that state regulation has been too lax.

"We very much support national standards," said James Ballentine, director of community outreach for the American Bankers Association. "There are 90,000 new brokers since 2000, and it's the easiest thing in the

Subprime Boom Leads to Many Busts

Foreclosures have been on the rise nationally for at least two years, driven in large part by a surge in subprime home loans, a high percentage of which eventually default. The number of loans that entered some stage of the foreclosure process was almost half a million in the first three months of 2007, more than twice the total in the first quarter of 2005. Meanwhile, the percentage of all mortgages that are subprime home loans was more than twice as large last year as it was in 2003. And the frequency with which subprime loans go into foreclosure has been rising as well. One in five subprime loans made last year is expected to go sour.

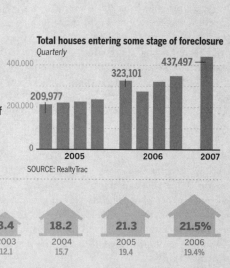

Total houses entering some stage of foreclosure
Quarterly

SOURCE: RealtyTrac

National percentage of new mortgage loans that are subprime

	1998	1999	2000	2001	2002	2003	2004	2005	2006
	10.3%	12.2	13.2	7.8	7.4	8.4	18.2	21.3	21.5%
Projected percentage that will end in ▶ foreclosure	9.8%	12.8	14.6	11.5	9.8	12.1	15.7	19.4	19.4%

SOURCES: Inside Mortgage Finance and Center for Responsible Lending; CQ / Marilyn Gates-Davis

world to do to toss a magnetic sign on the side of your car and say you make loans."

SHARING INFORMATION

Housing and consumer groups complain that borrowers of subprime loans often don't understand what they are getting into, and point to statistics showing a surge in both subprime borrowing and defaults as evidence of a lack of information.

Sheila C. Bair, chairwoman of the Federal Deposit Insurance Corporation, told Congress that subprime loans more than doubled as a share of new mortgages from 2003 to 2005, when they amounted to 20 percent of all loans.

And Syron said many borrowers default in the first few months after taking out a mortgage, suggesting that "many subprime borrowers have mortgages that should not have been made in the first place."

Why, then, would borrowers take out such loans? The answer may lie in part with the kinds of information required to be given to consumers: disclosure statements that are both extensive and confusing, as well as inconsistently applied.

Congress has enacted a number of laws aimed at providing consumers with the information they need to make sound decisions when taking out a loan or engaging in various other financial transactions. These measures, including the Home Ownership and Equity Protection Act, or HOEPA, and the Truth In Lending Act, require a variety of disclosure statements and direct federal regulators to set rules governing them.

During the mortgage closing process alone, lenders must provide borrowers with a booklet about the loan process and a good-faith estimate of total settlement costs, explain whether they intend to collect payments on the loan themselves or sell it off, and disclose any business relationships with other parties involved in the process.

Many of these disclosure requirements were designed with more traditional mortgages in mind, rather than the adjustable-rate subprime mortgages that are at the center of the foreclosure crisis.

The result is that consumers are flooded with information they are unable to understand, said Sen. Robert Menendez, a New Jersey Democrat. "The current disclo-

sures end up getting so difficult that I'm not sure what they are actually disclosing to the average consumer," he said.

Critics of current lending practices say that because not all mortgage brokers and lenders fall under federal regulations, a significant number engage in what is called "predatory lending," using dubious marketing tactics and limited disclosures to steer borrowers into higher-cost loans.

Predatory loans are frequently packed with excessive fees, unnecessary add-on costs and very high penalties for paying off a loan early, which occurs when a house is sold or a mortgage is refinanced. Predatory lenders frequently target minority and lower-income borrowers, using aggressive sales tactics to rope them into loans without assessing their ability to make payments.

"Subprime lenders have been routinely marketing the highest-risk loans to the most vulnerable families and those who already struggle with debt," said Michael Calhoun, president of the Center for Responsible Lending, in March testimony to Congress. "Lenders seek to attract borrowers by offering loans that start with deceptively low monthly payments, even though those payments are certain to increase."

The federal response to disclosure concerns will probably take place on multiple fronts. Lawmakers are already pressuring federal regulators to extend existing rules to non-bank mortgage brokers and lenders. That is especially true for HOEPA disclosures, which require lenders to notify borrowers when they are taking out a high-cost loan that has demonstrably higher fees or interest rates.

At a House hearing last month, lawmakers and fellow regulators urged Federal Reserve officials to broaden disclosure requirements to prevent predatory loans.

"The FDIC would strongly support the [Fed] should it decide to make greater use of the authorities provided by HOEPA to address predatory practices," Bair said. "Many abuses might be more effectively addressed by regulation rather than statute, especially in areas such as misleading marketing, in which the manner and types of abuse frequently change."

That may be a start, but lawmakers such as Menendez and Frank see a need for a legislative response as well to crack down on predatory lending.

Language for such a predatory lending bill is still being negotiated among Frank, Bachus and other panel members of both parties. Proposed legislation would probably establish a regulatory floor that would apply to all lenders. States that wanted to add additional protections for consumers would probably be allowed to do so.

Many lawmakers and consumer advocates would like to see additional clarity in the disclosures given to consumers, including easy-to-read charts that are tailored to non-traditional loans, that explain the full payment schedule over the life of a loan and that show all risks to the borrower.

"Consumers need to have confidence that they understand the implications of the mortgages they take out and are able and willing to meet their obligations," Syron said. "Mortgage disclosures must be understandable."

IMPOSING LIABILITY

The most contentious issue that lawmakers and housing industry representatives are debating is whether and how to impose liabilities on lenders and those who invest in mortgages in the so-called secondary market.

Nowadays, few loans remain on the books of the lender that writes them. They are almost instantaneously sold to securities companies that bundle hundreds of thousands of loans together and in effect sell them again to investors across the world who know only that they are guaranteed a certain return over time. These "mortgage-backed securities" are packaged in intricate ways designed to spread the risk of default from a single loan across a broad number of investors, with the goal of increasing the amount of capital in the mortgage market at the lowest possible interest rates.

Many observers say that one consequence of this spreading of risk is that no one in the marketplace is particularly concerned when a loan goes into default. No single investor is likely to sustain a significant loss, and few of these market players are liable to lawsuits from aggrieved borrowers. *(Mortgage market, p. 92)*

Current laws generally allow borrowers to pursue claims against lenders for fraudulent, abusive or otherwise illegal transactions. But as with other aspects of the subprime mortgage market, the patchwork of state and federal regulation muddies the legal waters for borrowers.

Additionally, because the subprime loan market is replete with minimally financed, "fly by night" mortgage brokers and lenders, it can be difficult for borrowers to find someone to sue by the time they realize the mortgage they received was predatory.

"The majority of people who are facing foreclosure today are facing it because they are in mortgages they shouldn't have been in," Bachus said.

Consumer groups say the solution is for Congress to create a "suitability" standard for mortgage brokers and lenders. Similar to fiduciary duty laws that apply to securities brokers and dealers, such a standard would make mortgage professionals responsible for not making loans that borrowers have no chance of repaying.

"We're not saying that loan originators ought to figure out what is the most suitable loan, but they ought to be able to not put people into unsuitable loans," said Allen Fishbein, director of housing and credit policy at the Consumer Federation of America.

Suitability standards are opposed by groups such as the Mortgage Bankers Association, which has expressed "grave concerns" about any standard that might expose its members to lawsuits.

"Mortgage lenders are not analogous to financial analysts in this way, and a subjective suitability standard could threaten decades of fair lending gains," said John M. Robbins, chairman of the Mortgage Bankers, in an April 11 statement.

Opponents say that enactment of a suitability standard would have a chilling effect on the mortgage market. Lenders would be less likely to do business with borrowers whose credit ratings were shaky, if they were more susceptible to lawsuits. The result might be a credit crunch that would be particularly harmful if it curtailed lending just as borrowers caught up in high-cost subprime mortgages were trying to refinance into more affordable loans.

The shape of the secondary market in mortgages further complicates the liability question. Since most loans are sold to securities issuers and then effectively on to investors, the servicing company responsible for collecting payments on a loan and enforcing its terms if a borrower falls behind on payments is seldom the original lender. As a result, a borrower who was saddled with an illegal or abusive loan and is pursuing legal action against the lender cannot stop the servicing company from foreclosing on the house while the lawsuit progresses. Laws governing mortgage-backed securities allow a foreclosure to move forward because investors have a claim on the borrower's promised payments.

New Jersey and a few other states have sought to address this situation by passing "assignee liability" laws

CQ / Scott J. Ferrell

CALLING ATTENTION: Schumer has used the Joint Economic Committee he chairs to raise concerns.

tized securities will compensate you for the risk you've taken."

PUTTING UP MONEY

Enhanced regulations, new disclosure requirements and making the marketplace assume liability for abusive practices are all aimed at preventing a wave of inappropriate loans and subsequent foreclosures in the future. For lawmakers concerned about conditions today, the bigger question is how to protect a million or more borrowers whose interest rates are set to skyrocket within the next two years, making their monthly payments vastly more expensive.

If last week was any indication, lawmakers are letting lenders, mortgage servicing companies and housing groups know they want help to prevent an even higher rate of foreclosures.

In hearings last week and in a closed-door summit convened by Senate Banking Chairman Dodd, the message was clear: While the range of possible solutions might eventually translate into tapping taxpayers for assistance, lawmakers are trying to put the burden on the industry to be more accountable.

According to Dodd, the group was broadly in agreement on a series of principles, the center of which is the idea that lenders and other participants in the mortgage market have a responsibility to work with community groups to reach out to borrowers whose loans are potentially in trouble. Whenever possible, lenders should modify loans to keep people in their homes, or offer refinancing terms that are appropriate for borrowers' financial conditions. *(Cost of foreclosures, p. 98)*

"We're calling on servicers and folks who hold the mortgage notes to assess from their consumers who are in non-traditional products who they should be reaching out to," Berenbaum said.

Citigroup, the nation's largest bank, applauded Dodd's principles and advocated adoption of the stan-

that allow a borrower to pursue legal claims against any party who has purchased or taken a legal interest in the loan. Housing advocates say assignee liability would encourage more appropriate mortgage underwriting and give secondary-market participants reasons to avoid investing in abusive loans. And homeowners who defaulted on their loans would have an opportunity to forestall foreclosure through the legal system.

The idea has support from lawmakers on both sides of the aisle, though some worry that Congress needs to be careful not to scare away mortgage market investors.

"It's very important to preserve the liquidity in the subprime lending market," Bachus said. "An ill-conceived assignee liability law restricts the ability to market mortgage securities, ultimately making it more difficult for low- and middle-income homebuyers to secure financing."

There is also a fear that allowing borrowers to sue investors would encourage bad decisions by homeowners.

"Taking out a loan will become a risk-free endeavor," wrote portfolio manager Vitaliy Katsenelson on minyanville.com, an investor-oriented Internet site, last week. "House price goes up — great; house price goes down — you claim to be a victim, and the purchasers of securi-

dards by the lending industry. In another sign of public-private cooperation, mortgage finance giants Fannie Mae and Freddie Mac announced initiatives intended to help troubled borrowers refinance their mortgages.

Freddie Mac's Syron said after the Senate meeting that his company would buy up to $20 billion in mortgages to help subprime borrowers. And earlier in the week, Fannie Mae rolled out a plan aimed at qualifying as many as 1.5 million borrowers.

While applauding such initiatives, those close to the problem say they won't be enough to rescue everyone.

"We should carefully distinguish between those borrowers who can be 'rescued' and those who cannot," Syron testified. And, he said, "such a triage will not be easy or popular."

The High Price of Foreclosure

The nationwide 42 percent rise in home mortgage foreclosures last year — a surge that is persisting into 2007 — is attracting so much attention because the fallout from one borrower's default can quickly become a contagion that infects neighbors, businesses, and whole cities and suburbs.

"This is not just a problem for the homeowners, it's a problem for the communities," Spencer Bachus of Alabama, the senior Republican on the House Financial Services Committee, said at a hearing last week. "A home is key to many things."

Foreclosure — essentially the process of a lender taking possession of a home on which the borrower can no longer afford to make mortgage payments — has an obvious and immediate impact on homeowners. They must deal with the financial and emotional consequences associated with giving up the most valuable asset most Americans will ever own. That includes any equity value that might have been built up in the property from a down payment, the amount of the principal paid each month on the mortgage and any market appreciation.

Not counting this loss of equity, however, the direct financial cost of foreclosure for an average homeowner is estimated at $7,200, according to a report earlier this month by the Joint Economic Committee of Congress. That amount includes charges from lawyers and other professionals, plus administrative fees.

Since people facing foreclosure are frequently already in financial trouble, there's also a good chance they will pay many of those foreclosure costs with credit cards, digging themselves further into debt. And homeowners struggling to make payments will frequently skip payments due on credit cards and other loans, adding to their woes.

The result is a cascade of trouble that is likely to ruin a foreclosed homeowner's credit rating for some time. That,

in turn, can lead to trouble in even finding a place to rent, and it makes future homeownership difficult if not impossible. The Center for Responsible Lending, a nonprofit research and advocacy group in Durham, N.C., says it takes a typical borrower at least 10 years to recover from foreclosure and buy a new house.

Community Costs

But the costs of foreclosure extend well beyond the homeowners themselves to their neighborhoods and subdivisions. That effect can be compounded in areas where a single mortgage broker or lender has concentrated its business, and where deteriorating economic conditions have widespread impact. "It affects the neighbor and the community because suddenly there's a rash of foreclosed homes and potentially vacant properties that will drive down property values and sock the locality with maintenance expenses," said Allen Fishbein, director of housing and credit policy at the Consumer Federation of America.

A study done for the Fannie Mae Foundation last year showed that in Chicago, sales prices of homes within one block of a foreclosed-upon property drop by an average 0.9 percent — and by at least 1.4 percent in some low- to moderate-income areas. Every additional foreclosure exacts an additional cost of the same magnitude, the study showed.

Supply-and-demand forces play a role in this price decline. A foreclosure means that yet another house is on the market competing for a buyer, and often at a fire-sale price or even at auction. Researchers have also found a correlation between a rise in foreclosures and an increase in violent crime. And, at the very least, a foreclosure typically results for a time in an abandoned house, which imposes social and economic stigmas on the surrounding neighborhood.

Some municipalities have taken on significant expenses to maintain abandoned and foreclosed properties, including

That thought was amplified by Alabama's Richard C. Shelby, the senior Republican on the Senate Banking panel, who said he would oppose any bailout for borrowers. "You can't save people from themselves," he said.

Many housing advocates and some lawmakers equate that argument with blaming the victim of a crime.

"Taxpayers should not be on the hook for deceptive practices by dubious mortgage brokers, but the federal government has a responsibility to protect those who were taken advantage of and also intervene where the markets have failed," Schumer said in a statement.

He and others are hoping that "rescue funds" of the sort run by Berenbaum's organization can form the core of aid to borrowers potentially facing foreclosure. The idea would be to offer refinancing help, as well as counseling and remediation efforts.

---

utility costs, grass mowing and general repairs, plus stepped-up police presence to prevent squatting and vandalism. Those costs rise even as the municipality's tax base erodes because of the decline in home values.

Cleveland and its suburbs, already in economic straits because of the decline of the U.S. auto industry, have spent millions of dollars on an anti-blight program to preserve the large number of abandoned households. The metropolitan area had almost 23,000 foreclosures in 2006 — one for every 40 households and more than twice the national average.

No End in Sight

The problem is likely to get much worse as defaults rise among subprime borrowers — those whose credit ratings are weak and who, for additional reasons, increasingly find themselves unable to make their loan payments. Data provided the Joint Economic Committee by LoanPerformance, a mortgage market information company, showed that at the end of February more than one in 10 of all outstanding subprime loans were delinquent by at least 60 days.

Rising foreclosures also threaten lenders. More than two dozen mortgage companies have gone out of business or filed for bankruptcy in the past few months as defaults climbed. Last year the Federal Reserve Bank in Chicago estimated that lenders can lose more than $50,000 for each foreclosed mortgage, even when they don't actually hold on to the mortgage as an investment. That loss includes both administrative costs and assessments owed to investors who purchased the mortgage.

An $80,000 Tab

The biggest cost of an average foreclosure is borne by the lender (and often spread to many investors). Borrowers incur legal expenses (not counting lost equity in the house); local governments lose tax revenue and incur maintenance costs; and neighbors must cope with falling property values.

Neighbor's home value $1,508
2%

Homeowner $7,200
9%

Local government $19,227
25%

64% Lender $50,000

Total: **$77,935**

SOURCE: Joint Economic Committee; CQ / Marilyn Gates-Davis

But while foreclosures have been especially hard on lenders that made large numbers of subprime loans, that was not the case earlier in the decade, when housing prices were rising. In that period, even when borrowers defaulted, increased home values allowed lenders to cover their expenses while putting the property back on the market.

The current state of the mortgage market suggests that the rate of foreclosure hasn't peaked. Analyzing loan data since 1998, the Center for Responsible Lending forecasts that as many as 2.2 million subprime borrowers have been stripped of their houses in the past few years or will lose them in the next few years, at an aggregate loss of $164 billion. The congressional Joint Economic Committee notes that interest rates on about 1.8 million subprime mortgages will increase in the next year and a half, and many of those borrowers are likely to have difficulty keeping up.

The bottom line, many lawmakers and experts say, will be a greater economic toll, unless government officials, lenders and borrowers all take steps to curtail the rise in loan defaults. "I think what some do not realize is that foreclosure does not help the taxpayers," Bachus said. "It does not help the economy, and it does not help communities."

About two-thirds of the time lenders are willing to adjust the terms of a loan without a need for refinancing, Berenbaum said.

In theory Congress could appropriate money to help finance such programs, but other sources might be used as well. Berenbaum said one option would be to assess a fee on mortgage lenders based on the risk of the loans they offer. The riskier the loan, the more they'd have to pay in to the fund.

A widely supported idea would be to expand the operations of the Federal Housing Administration and allow it to assist subprime borrowers. Founded in 1934, the FHA is supposed to help provide credit for home-buyers who are unable to obtain mortgages in the private market. But at an April 19 House Financial Services Committee hearing, FHA administrator Montgomery said his agency can't keep up with the industry, which has evolved rapidly as a result of technological and other innovations. As a result, many borrowers who probably should qualify for FHA loans turned toward other lenders, Montgomery said, sometimes with disastrous consequences.

"As the dynamic mortgage market passed FHA by, many homebuyers, especially those living in higher-cost states such as California, New York and Massachusetts, to name a few, purchased mortgage products with conditions and terms they would not be able to meet," he said.

In the last Congress, the House overwhelmingly passed a bill to expand the FHA's reach, although the Senate didn't act on it. A similar House measure that has been introduced this year would increase the size of FHA loans to account for high-cost real estate areas, allow lower down payments for FHA loans, and direct the agency to insure loans to subprime borrowers.

"Without a viable FHA, many low- and moderate-income borrowers are left with few safe and viable mortgage options," said Maxine Waters, the California Democrat who sponsored the bill.

The measure is supported by lenders, as well. Robbins of the Mortgage Bankers Association encouraged Congress to "empower FHA with the authority it needs to provide these consumers with affordable, viable lending options needed to help them achieve and maintain homeownership."

Dodd has said he hopes to avoid taking legislative steps to solve the crisis. But if worst-case scenarios develop and foreclosures multiply, Congress might have no choice.

As Ohio Democratic Rep. Marcy Kaptur put it at a recent hearing on subprime lending, the nation's economy is in jeopardy. "The cumulative impact of irresponsible lending, irresponsible borrowing and securitization of the mortgage market has threatened the safety and soundness of the financial system of this country," Kaptur said.

FOR FURTHER READING

Crisis brewing in subprime loans, 2007 CQ Weekly, p. 702; housing and the economy, 2006 CQ Weekly, p. 2614; regulators target questionable loans, 2006 CQ Weekly, p. 1215; Home Ownership and Equity Protection Act (PL 103-325), 1994 Almanac, p. 100; Truth in Lending Act (PL 90-321), 1968 Almanac, p. 205.

A General Digs In Against All Odds

Hill Republicans, Justice officials and the polls are against him, but Gonzales still has his boss's blessing

AP / Susan Walsh

HEAD DOWN: The attorney general, at an identity theft news conference last week, made clear he was staying. Support for him among Republicans in Congress, at Justice and in the polls all continued to sag significantly.

From *CQ Weekly,*
April 30, 2007.

The nation could clearly see Alberto R. Gonzales stumble through much of the Senate testimony that was billed as the make-or-break moment in his tenure at the Justice Department. But there was one response that he delivered with a polish that betrayed careful rehearsal.

"I have to know in my heart that I can continue to be effective as the leader of this department," the attorney general told the Judiciary Committee this month when Wisconsin Democrat Herb Kohl pressed Gonzales to say whether he'd remain even if the American public lost confidence in him. "Sitting here today, I believe that I can. And every day I ask myself that question, 'Can I continue to be effective as leader of this department?' The moment I believe I can no longer be effective, I will resign as attorney general."

Such overt self-confidence has done Gonzales little good in the past 10 days, when the circle of people sharing the view that he can remain effective as the nation's top law enforcement official has shrunk dramatically.

Even before this spring, the Democrats who now run Congress viewed him as ineffective, at best. But Gonzales' inability to fully explain the firings of eight U.S. attorneys last year has significantly tarnished his standing with fellow Republicans in Congress, with the remaining prosecutors and career Justice Department staff, and with the American public. Lawmakers have been left to conclude that the attorney general is either obscuring his own role in the affair or was remarkably uninvolved in a major shakeup of senior people under his command — and neither alternative is at all appealing to them.

Should Gonzales Resign?

April 20-24

Yes 44% No 28% Don't know 28%

April 9-12

36% 28% 36%

CBS / New York Times polls of 1,052 adults nationwide; margin of sampling error: +/- 3 percentage points

SOURCE: CQ / Marilyn Gates-Davis

By the end of last week, it appeared that Gonzales was still on the job only because he still enjoyed solid support from his most important constituent: the president himself. President Bush told reporters that Gonzales' testimony "increased my confidence in his ability to do the job," adding: "The attorney general broke no law, did no wrongdoing. And some senators didn't like his explanation, but he answered as honestly as he could. This is an honest, honorable man, in whom I have confidence."

Despite that, Gonzales has no real ammunition with which to rebut critics who say the administration has turned the Justice Department into a political arm of the White House. He also is ill-equipped to serve as the department's ambassador to Congress and the public on an array of issues, from budget matters to the flap over the FBI's misuse of its investigative powers.

"I think he's lost credibility on the Hill and around the country," said California Democrat Henry A. Waxman, chairman of the House Oversight and Government Reform Committee. "If he stays on, he's not going to be very effective at all."

The best senior Republicans could do was promise to make the most of a bad situation. "I will continue to deal with him, but whatever he has to say I will take with more than a grain of salt," said Senate Judiciary's senior GOP member, Arlen Specter of Pennsylvania. Added another committee member, Iowa's Charles E. Grassley: "The reality is that putting in a new attorney general with only 18 months left in this administration may not make much of a difference because of the heightened politicization that's taken hold in the Senate."

CREDIBILITY ISSUES

Gonzales' credibility problems predate the U.S. attorney dismissals. Some lawmakers have quietly seethed for his entire 26-month tenure about his refusal to distance himself from controversial administration policies such as the National Security Agency warrantless surveillance program. Many say Gonzales, who was White House counsel in Bush's first term and began his government service as Bush's gubernatorial counsel in Texas, wrongly continues to act first and foremost as the president's lawyer.

The attorney general's woes are compounded by the fact that he has no national legal reputation of his own making — or political power base apart from Bush, who put him on the Texas Supreme Court in 1999 — to insulate him from heightened criticism that he is not suited to be the nation's top law enforcement officer. The details about the firings of the prosecutors have highlighted how Gonzales had surrounded himself with a young, relatively inexperienced coterie of senior aides.

John E. Sununu of New Hampshire, the first GOP senator to call on Gonzales to resign, has criticized him for not working closely enough to assuage concerns about civil liberties when the anti-terrorism law known as the Patriot Act was updated in the last Congress. The attorney general "has, over a long period of time, lost the confidence of Republican and Democratic members of Congress," the senator said.

A handful of GOP senators have since joined Sununu — most prominently Arizona's John McCain, who called for resignation on the same day last week that he formally launched his bid for the presidency.

For now, the attorney general is trying to mend fences with his critics. Last week, he met with Democratic Sen. Mark Pryor of Arkansas, who said Gonzales should lose his job because he had inadequately explained the decision to remove the U.S. attorney in Little Rock, H.E. "Bud" Cummins III, and install Tim Griffin, a protégé of White House deputy chief of staff Karl Rove.

Gonzales has disavowed an e-mail by his former chief of staff, Kyle Sampson, outlining a plan to "gum this to death" and essentially ignore Pryor while pretending to deal with him in "good faith." But the attorney general failed to repair his standing with the senator, who afterward faulted Gonzales' memory and reiterated his call for resignation. "It's hard for me to see how he manages this very important department with all this stress and strain around him right now," Pryor said.

LOW MORALE

Indeed, Gonzales is going to have a hard time supervising the 93 U.S. attorneys around the country, despite his efforts to meet with most of them and offer reassurances that they have nothing to fear from "Main Justice" — as the Washington headquarters is known — when it comes to deciding which cases to prosecute.

Lawmakers and legal experts say Gonzales has damaged the relationship, whether he engineered the firings or merely acquiesced in them. They say other attorneys general would not have allowed U.S. attorneys to be targeted for removal based on whether or not they were prosecuting particular types of cases.

Philip Heymann, a Harvard law professor who was deputy attorney general in the Clinton administration, said Attorney General Janet Reno "wouldn't have gotten anywhere near the suggestion that a U.S. attorney should be removed because he was bringing the wrong kind of case."

People with ties to the Justice Department say its morale, particularly in U.S. attorneys' offices, has plummeted. "Frankly, out West, people are still pretty upset," said Laurie Levenson, a law professor at Loyola Law School in Los Angeles and a former assistant U.S. attorney. "It's not politics as usual out in California to have two U.S. attorneys canned."

Bob Barr, a former GOP congressman who was the U.S. attorney in Atlanta under attorneys general Edwin Meese III and Richard Thornburgh, said Gonzales has "lost the confidence" of his corps of prosecutors.

New York's Anthony Weiner, a Democrat on the House Judiciary Committee, said career prosecutors at the department have lamented that when conducting depositions or executing search warrants, they hear "wisecracks" about whether they are engaged in a politically motivated prosecution.

"There's a cloud that needs to be dispelled one way or another to the point where even a good U.S. attorney who's just doing his job now has the taint of the question 'Are you a loyal Bushie?' "said freshman Democratic Sen. Sheldon Whitehouse, who was the U.S. attorney in Rhode Island during the Clinton administration and now serves on the Judiciary Committee. "If you bring a voter fraud case, was it a phony case designed to make the politicos at the Department of Justice happy?"

At the daylong April 19 hearing, Gonzales was not able to offer senators a comprehensive explanation of why the eight former prosecutors were fired. He painted it all as the work of senior aides and had a hazy memory about his own involvement.

That did nothing to reassure lawmakers that Gonzales is an effective leader. Republicans and Democrats alike say, regardless of the reasons, the Justice Department just plain bungled the firings and did unnecessary damage to the reputations of the dismissed prosecutors.

The public appears to be increasingly blaming Gonzales. Polling by The New York Times and CBS News found 44 percent favoring his resignation in the days after he testified, up 8 percentage points from a week before he appeared in the Senate.

NO CONFIDENCE

Since the hearing, lawmakers have begun openly questioning whether Gonzales is up to his job. That means he lacks the confidence he needs among lawmakers to persuade Congress to support his priorities, as well as to fend off new legislation to restrict the FBI's investigative powers in the wake of a damning Justice inspector general's report in March that showed serious abuses of those powers.

Incensed by that report, Republicans and Democrats alike have already threatened to rewrite the Patriot Act. Justice's best hope for forestalling legislative curbs on its powers lies in FBI Director Robert S. Mueller III, who still enjoys most lawmakers' confidence despite the bureau's missteps.

The attorney general "has key responsibilities with respect to budget and other matters — there are a lot of issues that have emerged that are worrisome, like the national security letters and how that's all been mishandled — and if he has to come up and defend that and doesn't have any standing or confidence, it's disabling for the department," Whitehouse said.

Maryland Democrat Barbara A. Mikulski, chairwoman of the Senate Appropriations subcommittee that handles the Justice Department budget, pointedly postponed an April 12 hearing on the subject. "It would be very difficult in this environment to give the department's budget request the attention it deserves until the Senate has examined the department's leadership failures," she said.

For now, though, Bush and Gonzales have apparently made the calculation that, despite such widespread misgivings, there is no upside to Gonzales' stepping down. If he departs, the Democratic investigation into the firings of the prosecutors could shift away from the Justice Department, and Gonzales' own role, and focus more intently on the involvement of senior White House aides, especially Rove. And a confirmation hearing for Bush's replacement nominee would offer administration critics a prime opportunity to highlight their complaints.

Gonzales sought last week to portray himself as pursuing business as usual. "I can't just be focused on the U.S. attorney situation. I've also got to be focused on what's really important for the American people," he said at a news conference with the head of the Federal Trade Commission, Debra Platt Majoras, to release an administration plan to combat identity theft.

The attorney general sidestepped a question about whether he can carry out his agenda without the confidence of Capitol Hill.

"I'm intent on working with the Congress to reassure the Congress that we are identifying what happened here," he said. "We're going to correct mistakes that have been made."

During his Senate Judiciary appearance, Gonzales again denied that any U.S. attorneys were fired to thwart public corruption probes. He also tried to reassure lawmakers that the progress of individual criminal cases is not dramatically affected when a regional federal prosecutor leaves office. "This institution is built to withstand change and departures in leadership positions," he said.

But so much about the whole affair remains a mystery — such as precisely why each of the eight were targeted for dismissal and by whom, and whether and why any other U.S. attorneys were initially targeted but then kept on — that the possibility remains that additional revelations could implicate Gonzales more directly in politically untenable behavior. If that happens, he could still be spurred to heed his own implicit admonition that the Justice Department can carry on without him.

FOR FURTHER READING

Congressional probe of U.S. attorney firings, 2007 CQ Weekly, p. 1271; Gonzales' testimony, p. 1196; politics and federal prosecutors, p. 792; Justice Department inspector general's report, p. 755; reauthorization of the Patriot Act (PL 109-177), 2006 Weekly, p. 3360.

Lame Duck or Leapfrog?

George W. Bush joins a long list of his predecessors in discovering that when you can't push your agenda through Congress, there's another way around

In late October 2006, while most of Washington was riveted on the midterm election, President Bush began calling his Cabinet secretaries one by one and asking each to prepare a "to do" list of initiatives that could be accomplished without congressional approval.

The request, according to White House aides, was partly motivated by Bush's growing concern about Republicans losing control of the House and Senate. But the president, like many of his predecessors, also had come to the conclusion that a lame duck's waning influence cannot possibly support all of his ambitions, regardless of which party reigns on Capitol Hill. So, intent on enshrining his free-market principles and reducing the burden of federal regulations on businesses, Bush began focusing on the one lever of government he will control until the day he leaves office: the vast, sometimes overlooked rule-making process that resides within the executive branch agencies.

The president has not been shy about stressing the urgency of the task, telling his Cabinet at a Feb. 5, 2007 meeting that "he wants

From *CQ Weekly*,
February 12, 2007.

every Cabinet secretary to really be on the offense for the next 711 days" before the presidency ends, said Health and Human Services Secretary Michael O. Leavitt.

The to-do lists are beginning to bear fruit in a wide-ranging collection of regulations that are designed to make significant changes to environmental, health and labor laws; law enforcement; and even the space-age field of nanotechnology. The rules, which will be rolled out gradually over the next two years, will almost certainly spark a showdown with congressional Democrats, whose options include public expressions of disapproval, cutting off funding to actually implement the rules or playing catch-up by enacting new laws to undo Bush's initiatives.

The burst of rulemaking will be a fitting coda for an administration that has repeatedly relied on the assertive use of executive power to forge domestic and foreign policy. In truth, many initiatives now under way — including efforts to change the way

CQ Photos / Scott J. Ferrell

AGENDA MOVERS: The administration flexed its authority through rulemaking under Graham, above, and plans to centralize decisions further with OIRA's Dudley, below.

endangered species are designated, revamp the criteria for the Family and Medical Leave Act and cut entitlement spending — were too politically contentious to have been written into law even when the Republicans had control of Congress. The administration decision to act unilaterally through rulemaking thus has a twofold appeal because it accomplishes that task without the need to compromise with Democrats or accommodate dissenters within the GOP.

"When Congress is gridlocked or controlled by the other party, the president is likely to see rulemaking as a promising strategy to accomplish his or her agenda," said John D. Graham, who headed the Office of Information and Regulatory Affairs (OIRA) — the influential regulatory branch of the White House Office of Management and Budget — from 2001 to 2006 and is now dean of the Rand Graduate School of policy analysis. "Creative lawyers can find lots of lawful ways for a determined president to advance an agenda."

Wielding Power Step by Step

The federal rule-making process is one of the basic tools presidents use to make public policy. While the process can vary by agency or subject, it usually begins with an external event or important recommendation that the government take action, then proceeds through a series of drafting steps and public comment periods. Congress is largely left out of the loop until a final rule is issued. Rules can be scuttled by lawsuits or trumped by new legislation or denials of funding.

1 **AN EVENT**, such as a catastrophic accident or a recommendation from an outside body, kicks off the rulemaking process. Congress passes a law authorizing or requiring the appropriate federal agency to issue a rule.

SOURCE: Congressional Research Service

2 **THE AGENCY** develops draft rule and subjects it to an internal review. Under a new Bush administration directive, each agency has a regulatory policy office run by a political appointee to supervise the development of the rule and the issuance of documents giving guidance to the affected industry.

3 **MOST RULES** deemed "significant" are then submitted to the White House Office of Management and Budget's Office of Information and Regulatory Affairs (OIRA), which conducts a cost-benefit analysis.

4 **AN OFFICIAL** notice of rulemaking is published in the Federal Register.

5 **THE RULE** is published for public comment. Depending on circumstances, this may happen more than once.

Bush is hardly the first president to use executive fiat to cement a legacy in this way. Ronald Reagan in the 1980s became the first to use OIRA for the purpose of evaluating the economic impact of existing and proposed government rules and used it as an apparatus to promote deregulation within the executive branch. On the pro-regulation side, Bill Clinton imposed tough new environmental and workplace standards in his final months in office, over the strenuous objections of the Republican-controlled Congress, including a contentious rule dealing with workplace injuries. *(Clinton regulations, p. 110)*

"At the end of the presidency, the administration generally has a number of policies it wants to implement before exiting the White House," said Donald Arbuckle, who retired last year after serving for a quarter-century at the Office of Management and Budget, including 10 years as deputy administrator of OIRA from 1996 to 2006. "They want to push things through because, among other reasons, there is no long-term political downside to doing things, since everyone will be gone."

Arbuckle noted that every president in the past three decades has issued a spate of rules just before the conclusion of his term. "Administrative policy making by regulation seems to be an appealing activity at the end of a presidency, regardless of party and regardless of ideology toward regulation," he said.

Central to Bush's strategy is a desire to consolidate power within the office of the president and tamp down any potential dissent among the agencies' career staffs. The president took steps to centralize power over rule-making Jan. 18, 2007 by issuing an executive order requiring agencies to give political appointees more power to supervise all new rules and to inform industries about any changes in a broader range of policies. The order also requires agencies considering new rules to spell out the specific failure," or issue that justified government intervention.

Bush additionally brought on Susan E. Dudley, a conservative scholar who has long advocated pruning cumbersome or unnecessary federal rules on the books. Bush nominated Dudley to replace Graham as OIRA administrator in 2006, but the then-Republican-controlled Senate refused to confirm her. She joined OIRA as a senior adviser Jan. 30, 2007.

The administration in 2007 plans to require agencies to adopt OIRA's standards for "risk assessment," a controversial process that requires agencies to determine the risk of an occurrence that would necessitate regulation. Under this process, agencies could be pushed to rank risks and describe a range of possibilities, which might result in some threats being downplayed. The White House tried to impose this policy in 2006 but backed off after the National Academy of Sciences took the unusual step of urging the administration to reconsider, saying the process was fundamentally flawed. Instead of giving up on the idea, OIRA will issue a new version of the directive.

While they revamp the rule-making process, administration officials are soliciting input from business lobbyists about promising areas for policy changes and are getting plenty of feedback. Financial services firms are urging the Treasury Department to further streamline the so-called Sarbanes-Oxley corporate governance rules and limit the liability of accountants caught up in corporate accounting scandals. The chemical industry stands to benefit from a proposed Homeland Security Department rule that would set a national security standard for chemical plants and pre-empt state and local security laws — a policy the Senate Homeland Security and Governmental Affairs Committee expressly rejected in 2006. Technology companies are lobbying the admin-

6 THE AGENCY responds to comments and develops a draft of the final rule, which is then subjected to another internal review.

7 THE DRAFT final rule is submitted to OIRA, which reviews it and can make changes.

8 THE FINAL rule is published. In some instances, agencies publish a final rule without issuing a notice of proposed rulemaking.

9 THE RULE takes effect.

BUT THE FOLLOWING IS POSSIBLE...

➡ **CONGRESS REVIEWS** the rule. If there is opposition, lawmakers can vote on a resolution of disapproval or deny funding for the agency to implement the rule.

AND/OR...

➡ **INTEREST GROUPS** or other parties can file suit to block the rule. A court then determines the legality of the rule.

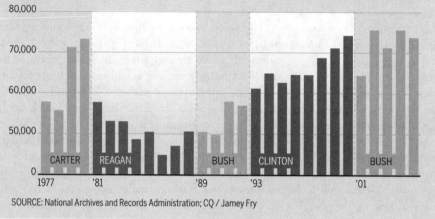

Busy Final Days

Presidents tend to issue more rules as their bargaining leverage with Congress wanes. Jimmy Carter, George Bush and Bill Clinton were particularly active during their final two years in office, as measured by the number of pages in the Federal Register. Ronald Reagan issued more rules at the beginning of his presidency, when he was revising Carter's regulations. So far, George W. Bush has been pretty consistent.

SOURCE: National Archives and Records Administration; CQ / Jamey Fry

istration to use a light touch regulating the emerging field of nanotechnology, which uses microscopic devices in thousands of consumer and health applications.

But the most far-reaching and contentious changes over 2007 and 2008 will address environmental protection, workplace regulations and health care — areas where the administration has seldom hesitated to impose its will on the legislative branch in the past. What follows is a look at five areas to watch in upcoming years.

ENDANGERED SPECIES

As one of its priorities before Bush leaves office, the administration wants to modify environmental laws that conservatives view as burdens on business and encroachments on property rights.

Interior Department officials are gathering information from business interests and property-rights groups with an eye toward drafting a rule this year that would change the process for protecting endangered species. The rule may relax a requirement in the 1973 Endangered Species Act that the Fish and Wildlife Service designate

"critical habitat" for a threatened animal or plant's recovery. The federal government may set aside an area as a critical habitat if officials believe it is necessary to protect the species. When an area is designated as a critical habitat, activities that are likely to destroy or damage the creature's habitat may be limited. Restrictions vary depending on the circumstances, but sometimes private-property owners have to change their plans to develop an area under critical habitat protection. More than one-fourth of the species that are protected by the law live in critical habitat areas.

The limits on land use have spawned numerous lawsuits by private landowners and prompted efforts to change the law. Former House Resources Chairman Richard W. Pombo, R-Calif., mounted an unsuccessful overhaul effort in the 109th Congress.

Interior Secretary Dirk Kempthorne, who was the governor of Idaho until 2006 and a U.S. senator before that, has similar sympathies. He and other administration officials believe such a rule could resolve unsettled legal questions about when habitat protection is an essential part of any long-term recovery plan. A congressionally commissioned study by the nonprofit Keystone Center of Colorado in early 2006 could not reach consensus on possible legislative clarifications to habitat protection.

Kempthorne also is concerned about complaints that it is too hard to get an endangered species off the list after the population has recovered. Idaho and Wyoming officials complain, for instance, that wolves in their states have recovered and should be de-listed.

The Bush administration has not aggressively enforced the Endangered Species Act, waiving the law's applicability in certain instances, such as when the

Department of Homeland Security wanted to start building a fence along the border with Mexico. But the envisioned rule would mark the first time the administration has actually tried to comprehensively rework the regulation. Interior officials are not commenting on or confirming their plans, though a spokeswoman said "there may be something new to report soon."

Many close to the issue expect that the rule will require more rigorous criteria for a designation of "critical habitat." The administration's point man for enforcing the rule will probably be incoming Deputy Fish and Wildlife Director Randall Luthi, a rancher and former Speaker of the Wyoming House of Representatives. Luthi criticized the Endangered Species Act at a 2004 congressional field hearing in his home state, lamenting what he called the law's "profound failure."

In private conversations with members of Congress, he has promised to balance conservation concerns with those of landowners and business interests, according to Wyoming Republican Sen. Craig Thomas, who strongly backed Luthi's candidacy. Luthi was an aide to Vice President Dick Cheney when Cheney served in the U.S. House.

Luthi, who does not require Senate confirmation and is expected to begin his new job Feb. 20, 2007, has in the past advocated requiring more evidence that a targeted species faces danger, increasing payments to owners of properties that fall within critical habitats and deferring to the views of state officials about whether a species should be protected. He also has advocates raising the standard for listing new threatened or endangered species.

Any major administrative changes to the law are likely to trigger the same kind of intense backlash from Democratic leaders in Congress and some moderate Republicans that sank Pombo's 2006 effort. But Democratic leaders could have difficulty finding enough support to cut off funding for such a rule. Some centrist Democrats from the West have also chafed at the Endangered Species Act's expansive reach and might support rule changes that accommodate "multiple use" of sensitive lands.

SMOG REGULATIONS

Since the Clean Air Act first required the EPA to track air pollutants, regulators have struggled to define what is an acceptable limit for ozone, or smog, in localities. The Bush administration's efforts to balance public health concerns with those of businesses have only complicated the task, triggering legal challenges and putting the administration on a collision course with the new Democratic majority in Congress.

In early 2007, the EPA revised its ozone standards and decided how much to clamp down on emissions from factory smokestacks, power plants and automobile tailpipes. Its last attempt was found by courts in 2004 to violate the spirit of the Clean Air Act.

The administration has not shown its cards yet, but the signs are that it will try to adopt a flexible approach that accommodates the interests of businesses. Democrats in the Senate are already warning the EPA that they won't tolerate a repeat of the 2004 rulemaking and intend to hold oversight hearings into the administration's decision making. The question is whether the Democrats can generate enough political pressure to persuade the administration to bend their way and impose strict new standards.

The dispute over smog began after the EPA in 2004 found that 474 counties in 31 states had unacceptable ground levels of ozone, a pervasive pollutant in urban areas that contributes to heart disease, asthma and other respiratory ailments.

The administration responded by requesting that non-compliant counties develop plans to reduce emissions, and set a standard of 84 parts per billion, measured over eight hours. An earlier standard for measuring levels over one hour was revoked because the agency reasoned that ozone can affect human health at lower levels and over longer exposure times than one hour.

But the EPA policy was quickly challenged in court by six Northeastern states and the District of Columbia, as well as California's South Coast Air Quality Management District. They argued the standards were designed to maximize the EPA's discretion in deciding what controls were necessary to make facilities comply with the act and that the EPA had ignored the intent of Congress. In December, the U.S. Court of Appeals for the District of Columbia found the standards actually weakened limits for some industrial plants and were in violation of the Clean Air Act. The ruling requires the EPA to address the court's concerns.

Separately, the agency is revising its standards. EPA career scientists have advocated tough new ozone regula-

Clinton's Rule by Rulemaking

Every president in the past three decades has gone on a rule-making binge in his final days in office. None were more driven than Bill Clinton, a consummate policy wonk who was prevented from getting his second-term priorities through Congress by scandals, impeachment and a hostile Republican majority.

Instead, Clinton used the Federal Register like a cudgel during his final months in office, issuing 88 proposed and final regulations during the last 17 days of his presidency alone. This enthusiastic embrace of executive power was best summed up by Clinton's political adviser Paul Begala, who at one point marveled, "Stroke of the pen, law of the land. Kinda cool."

Yet many of Clinton's most sweeping initiatives were short-lived. Within hours of taking control of the White House, President Bush's aides began using their administrative power to strike or change dozens of rules still under development. Republicans in Congress took care of others, most notably using a little-known law called the Congressional Review Act to kill a contentious workplace rule aimed at reducing repetitive-motion injuries in 2001.

Such tit-for-tat policy making illustrates a fundamental truth of Washington: While executive power is mighty, it also is ephemeral. One president's rules can be paved over by an equally determined successor's new regulations and executive orders — or by legislation with contrary aims. For this reason, many legal scholars and political scientists agree that the surest way for a president to build a legacy is by consulting with Congress and enshrining his policies into laws.

That may not be the most politically expedient approach, however. Clinton was eager to expand environmental protection of federal lands in the West but understood that he could not persuade congressional conservatives and Western Democrats friendly to resource industries. So he unilaterally issued rules, such as a U.S. Forest Service regulation banning the construction of new roads to accommodate logging on nearly 60 million acres in national forests, and an Interior Department regulation the same year that gradually banned snowmobile use in Yellowstone and Grand Teton national parks.

Neither rule survived. The Bush administration, within six months of taking power, ordered the Forest Service to review the rule. The agency eventually watered it down, setting individual protection standards for each forest district and allowing piecemeal road construction. Bush's Interior Department similarly issued a new rule on snowmobiles just before Clinton's rule would have completely banished the vehicles from the parks, during the 2003-2004 winter season. The Bush rule temporarily permitted up to 950 snowmobiles per day.

Clinton's conservation initiatives extended to consumer appliances. In the final days of his administration, the Energy Department released a new efficiency standard for central air conditioners and heat pumps that was designed to cut electricity consumption by 30 percent. Manufacturers like Carrier Corp. complained that the rule would be difficult to comply with. Within days of taking office, the Bush administration delayed the standards, eventually replacing them with a new standard requiring a 20 percent reduction.

In all, the Bush administration froze 371 Clinton regulations — including any that had not been issued in the Federal Register — pending further review. It allowed 281 to go forward with little delay. Seventy-five more went into effect after longer reviews, while 15 rules were killed outright or significantly changed, according to tallies by the Office of Information and Regulatory Affairs (OIRA), the rule-making arm of the White House Office of Management and Budget.

tions, though they haven't settled on a single recommendation. On Jan. 31, 2007, the scientists presented a range of options to EPA Administrator Stephen L. Johnson, stating that "the overall body of evidence [on ozone health effects] . . . provides strong support for consideration of an ozone standard that would provide increased health protection for sensitive groups, including asthmatic children and other people with lung disease, as well as all children and older adults."

The U.S. Chamber of Commerce and other business groups are strenuously arguing against toughening the standards, saying that would make it more difficult for non-compliant counties to attract new business, discourage expansions of existing plants and force owners of those plants to undertake costly renovations.

New smog rules are "a big-ticket item . . . a huge battle," said Bill Kovacs, vice president for environment, technology and regulatory affairs at the Chamber, which

Donald Arbuckle, OIRA's deputy administrator from 1996 to 2006, found himself in the unusual position of working overtime to get rules out the door until the morning Clinton left office. Then, just a few hours after Bush was sworn in, on Jan. 20, 2001, Arbuckle was called into a meeting with new Budget Director Mitchell E. Daniels Jr. and asked to discuss ways to reverse or halt the rules he had just released.

"After being the regulatory champion, OIRA now became the Cerberus at the regulatory gate, helping the Bush administration find ways to reverse what we had been assiduously doing for the past half-year," Arbuckle recalled in an interview.

Bush's former OIRA director, John Graham, said rules need to be completely out of the regulatory pipeline, with the blessing of both the White House and the agency that issued them, in order to escape reviews by a successive administration.

"It is critical that the rule be finalized and cleared by the Office of Management and Budget before the next president arrives," Graham said.

Some of Clinton's rules survived because of political and public pressure. One was an EPA rule that would have reduced the amount of arsenic in drinking water from a maximum of 50 parts per billion to 10 parts per billion — the level recommended by the World Health Organization. Mining companies and other businesses and officials in some small communities protested that they would not be able to comply. Bush immediately delayed the rule upon taking office, then said his administration wanted to change it. But Democrats in Congress, such as Rep. Henry A. Waxman of California and Sen. Joseph I. Lieberman of Connecticut, accused the administration of endangering public health by allowing the cancer-causing heavy metal to remain in unacceptable concentrations in drinking water. In the ensuing outcry, the White House said it would allow the Clinton rule to stand.

Another Clinton rule the Bush administration left untouched addressed pollution from diesel engines. The EPA had proposed regulations in 1997 to make heavy-duty trucks and buses run cleaner by reducing nitrogen oxides, soot, and other pollution emissions. It also proposed rules to require cleaner engines in bulldozers, forklifts and farm equipment.

Manufacturers lost court efforts to overturn the policies, weakening industry's appetite for a prolonged fight. And after states such as California began to adopt policies that mimicked the Clinton standards, manufacturers believed that clear-cut standards would help them plan ahead.

There was no such acquiescence on business's part when Clinton tried to address workplace injuries via rulemaking. In the final weeks of his administration, Clinton had the Occupational Safety and Health Administration issue regulations requiring employers to educate workers about how to prevent injuries from typing, sorting and other activities involving repetitive motion. Workers who reported injuries lasting seven days or longer would have been eligible for compensation of up to 90 percent of their salary for as long as 90 days if they were unable to work.

The business community quickly unified in opposition to the rules, saying they could cost companies upward of $100 billion. And lobbyists, working with Republicans in Congress, decided on a legislative gambit that would swiftly kill the rules rather than putting them on hold for more study.

Working swiftly and quietly, Republicans used special parliamentary procedures, created by the Congressional Review Act, that gave the House and Senate 60 days to erase major rules by a simple majority vote in each chamber. In effect, one stealthy maneuver trumped another, leaving Democrats frustrated.

"I'm still trying to figure out what the hell happened," said one Democratic aide after the Senate vote.

has listed the air-quality standards near the top of its agenda.

"When a company is looking to relocate, the first thing they do is scratch off the list every area that isn't in attainment [with the ozone standards]," Kovacs said. For non-compliant counties, he said, the result is, "No one is coming to your community."

Further complicating the debate is Bush's desire to promote ethanol as an alternative fuel. Adding ethanol to

gasoline contributes to smog problems because it increases the fuel's volatility and emits more organic compounds. Thus, tough smog standards could have the effect of discouraging use of the alternative fuel just as Bush is trying to make good on his State of the Union pledge to reduce gasoline consumption by 20 percent over 10 years by substituting alternative fuels.

Many observers expect the industry to issue a rule that heeds business concerns and will largely preserve the status quo. Even before Bush issued his executive order requiring political appointees to preside over rulemaking, EPA officials in December 2006 revised their internal rule-making procedures at the behest of the American Petroleum Institute, the oil industry's lobbying arm. The agency officials said they would eliminate the longstanding practice of allowing career employees to make recommendations on new rules in consultation with an advisory committee of scientists and replace it with a new process in which political and career staff evaluate proposed standards together, then release a consensus document for comment from the advisory committee, industry groups and the public.

"We fear that changing the process will mean weaker public health standards," said Frank O'Donnell, president of the environmental advocacy group Clean Air Watch.

O'Donnell and other skeptics note that the administration in 2003 opted to use rulemaking to replace several Clean Air Act provisions dealing with limits for sulfur dioxide and nitrogen oxides as well as mercury, after it failed to persuade Congress to revise the law.

But some Democrats are promising to hold the administration accountable. Senate Environment and Public Works Chairwoman Barbara Boxer of California has pledged to step up oversight of the administration's environmental policies, predicting that public outcry over rules seen as too industry-friendly — or not protecting the public health — will prod the EPA to enact tougher standards.

"In the light of day, people will change their minds," Boxer said in early January 2007. However, those oversight ambitions could conflict with her other priorities, including enacting broad restrictions on greenhouse-gas emissions that will need bipartisan support to succeed in the Senate and will also need White House backing to be signed into law.

FAMILY AND MEDICAL LEAVE

The Family and Medical Leave Act of 1993 was President Bill Clinton's first big legislative victory and the culmination of a decade's worth of efforts by congressional Democrats, family groups and organized labor to expand protections for rank-and-file workers. But the law, which authorizes time off for medical emergencies, has frequently been a flash point for criticism from business groups and conservatives, who view it as a mandate that both increases business costs and creates administrative nightmares.

The Department of Labor has begun soliciting public comment about the way the law is administered. Members of the business community believe — and hope — that the department will tighten the criteria that workers can cite for getting time off. The law requires businesses with up to 50 employees to grant up to 12 weeks of unpaid leave for serious illness, the birth or adoption of a child, or the illness of a close family member.

Democrats on Capitol Hill, such as Senate Health, Education, Labor and Pensions Chairman Edward M. Kennedy of Massachusetts, have been trying to expand the law by adding provisions that would require employers to pay workers during their leaves. However, the administration is sensitive to business concerns that the law is routinely being abused, especially by individuals who take unexpected leaves that can seriously disrupt some firms' operations.

"A lot of people, people on both sides, employers and employees, were probably surprised by our request for information," said Victoria A. Lipnic, assistant Labor secretary for employment standards. "But there are a lot of things where it's important for the department to make sure" and to ask, "are the regs working in the way they should work?"

Business lobbyists expect the administration to consider narrowing the definition of "serious health conditions" that would qualify for medical leave and also restricting employees' ability to take the 12 weeks of allotted leave in small increments, such as two hours at a time. Employer groups complain that the law, as written, allows workers to unexpectedly skip shifts citing medical emergencies, leaving employers scrambling at the last minute with personnel shortages.

"We certainly support what they're doing, and once they see the legitimate complaints of the business community, we believe they'll go forward with a rulemaking," said Randy Johnson, vice president of labor policy for the Chamber of Commerce. "This is clearly a serious effort by the agency."

The administration is not expected to take issue with provisions in the law dealing with leaves for birth or adoption. But the efforts are nonetheless drawing deep concern from organized labor and women's groups, who accuse the White House of plotting an end run around congressional Democrats.

"Congress seems to have a broad interest in expanding the Family and Medical Leave Act at the same time that the administration wants to restrict it," said Kim Gandy, the president of the National Organization for Women. "They're trying to do through regulation what they would not have been able to do through legislation."

Lipnic disputes that notion, saying, "To suggest that we're trying to do something that would thwart the majority — that's a little unfair at this point."

Democrats most likely would try to attach language to a spending bill denying the Labor Department funding to carry out any such rule change.

ENTITLEMENT CUTS

Having failed in 2006 to persuade Congress to make billions of dollars in cuts to Medicare and Medicaid last year, Bush is using rulemaking to pare spending in the entitlement programs.

The costs of the two government health care programs have surged over the past decade due to the increased use of new technologies, higher drug costs and the popularity of home care. These developments have contributed to widening federal budget deficits, much to the consternation of fiscal conservatives. Medicare provides health coverage to 42 million seniors and disabled individuals, while Medicaid is a jointly administered federal-state program that provides health care to the poor.

Bush fought hard in 2005 to persuade the Republican-controlled Congress to make $46 billion in cuts over 10 years to the programs, relying on Cheney's tie-breaking vote on a deficit-reduction bill in the Senate. In 2006, his call for more cuts prior to the mid-term election fell largely on deaf ears.

Democrats believe the government can get a handle on health care spending by paring payments to insurers who administer Medicare benefits and by allowing the government to negotiate prescription drug prices directly with manufacturers. But Bush and his GOP allies think the private sector is best equipped to control health spending and prefer to make targeted cuts in reimbursements to providers. To that end, Bush is relying on rulemaking to shave another $10.2 billion over five years

from Medicare and $12.7 billion over five years from Medicaid.

"They were having difficulties getting their proposals through even when Republicans controlled both houses of Congress, so now they are shifting to things that they can do through administrative means . . . so they don't have to go through Congress," said Leighton Ku, a health policy analyst at the liberal-leaning Center for Budget Priorities and Policy. "In some cases, they can do it regardless of what Congress thinks."

The administration is reviving a plan it broached in its fiscal 2005 and 2006 budgets — rejected each time by Congress — and issuing a regulation that would cut Medicaid payments to public hospitals, nursing homes and other institutional providers by $3.9 billion over five years. It also has proposed a rule in its fiscal 2008 budget to suspend about $1.8 billion worth of Medicaid reimbursements to train medical residents in teaching hospitals that see a disproportionate share of indigent patients.

"We believe that we need to have graduate medical education in our states, but we think Medicaid isn't the way to do that," Health and Human Services Secretary Michael O. Leavitt told the House Energy and Commerce Committee on Feb. 7, 2006.

The administration has not yet detailed the Medicare cuts, but it is expected to use rules to lower payments to some providers and tweak reimbursements for hospitals, home health agencies and, potentially, hospice care.

That tinkering doesn't sit well with Democrats in Congress, who believe the administration should collaborate on ways to strengthen the programs, while keeping an eye on the bottom line. They may seek to block the payment changes by placing restrictions in spending bills.

"The budget pre-empts Congress' annual review of Medicare payment policy, calling for permanent and long-term cuts that even Republican Congresses would be unlikely to enact," said Pete Stark of California, chairman of the House Ways and Means subcommittee on Health. "An unpopular president missed a historic opportunity to get off on the right foot with the new Congress."

DRUG SAFETY

Few of the government's regulatory functions have received more attention in recent years than its mechanism for tracking drug safety. In 2004, the Food and

Drug Administration was criticized for reacting slowly to warnings that Vioxx and other popular pain medicines increased the risk of heart attacks and stroke. The agency's response prompted numerous calls for change, especially in the way the FDA monitors drugs' performance after they have been approved for sale to the public. Congressional critics have charged that the FDA is too cozy with the companies it regulates, pointing to the way it uses industry advisory groups in making policy.

With Democrats now in charge, they, along with sympathetic Republicans such as Sen. Charles E. Grassley of Iowa, are expected to legislate a more robust regulatory scheme at FDA. The vehicle for their efforts is expected to be a rewrite this year of a 1992 law that allows the FDA to collect the user fees from drug companies that have become a significant source of FDA funding.

In the meantime, though, the agency has moved forward with its own proposal to rewrite the drug-approval process. In other words, this is a case in which the agency is acting, not to thwart the will of Congress, exactly, but to head lawmakers off at the pass.

The administration is proposing guidance policies that largely maintain the status quo in the face of intensifying efforts in the Senate to overhaul the FDA's operations. In January 2007, FDA officials announced a policy in which the agency will review the safety of selected prescription drugs for 18 months after they have been approved. The agency will also convene an advisory panel to help it improve the way it issues safety alerts and will collaborate with the Veterans Health Administration on studying patient reactions to medicines.

However, the pilot program could take more than a year to get started. And the FDA policies do not go nearly as far as the Institute of Medicine recommended in 2006. Many lawmakers say the FDA regulatory policies should be seen only as a starting point but that Congress should demand that the agency do far more to monitor drugs once they have been approved for use by U.S. consumers.

The new regulations may be intended to pre-empt efforts by such lawmakers as Grassley and Democratic Sen. Christopher J. Dodd of Connecticut to create a new drug-safety office within the FDA with the sole responsibility of tracking drugs on the market. The proposal would represent a major shift for an agency where resources are now primarily directed at evaluating drugs before they are approved for sale to the public. And, in the view of administration officials, Grassley and Dodd's effort would add an unnecessarily cumbersome layer to the federal bureaucracy.

Other senators such as Kennedy and Republican Michael B. Enzi of Wyoming want to expand the FDA's duties to policing drug-advertising claims. They are also proposing to give the agency the authority to demand additional studies or clinical trials after a drug is approved for sale and to fine companies that resist.

The administration may find itself waging an uphill battle in trying to defeat such proposals. As Congress rewrites the 1992 Prescription Drug User Fee Act this year, the legislation is likely to become a magnet for efforts to shift FDA resources to do more safety reviews, subject drug companies to higher fees and generally give the FDA more regulatory muscle.

"Only legislation can give FDA the tools it needs to ensure that the agency is the gold standard for safety," Kennedy said in January of 2007.

But business lobbyists are not under estimating the administration's desire to make a lasting imprint on the way government deals with regulated industries and say there is no shortage of ways the White House might thwart Congress with more rules and directives. "The change in Congress makes a big difference," said the U.S. Chamber's Kovacs. "Presidents have a tendency, when Congress isn't of their party, to realize that they can get out just as much policy through agencies as they can through Congress."

FOR FURTHER READING

Bush executive order on regulations, 2007 CQ Weekly, p. 293; promoting ethanol as an alternative fuel, 2006 CQ Weekly, p. 2166; turbulence at the FDA, p. 2161; Graham's legacy at OIRA, p. 226; Medicare prescription drug coverage (PL 108-173), 2003 Almanac, p. 11-3; Family and Medical Leave Act (PL 103-3), 1993 Almanac, p. 389; Endangered Species Act (PL 93-205), 1973 Almanac, p. 670.

Just Deserts or Just Harsh

In *Philip Morris v. Williams,* the
Supreme Court will decide if
the punitive damages awarded fit
the crime

Jesse Williams rationalized about the dangers of smoking cigarettes for more than 40 years. In part, he trusted the tobacco companies when they said that the link between smoking and lung cancer had not been proved. But when Williams was diagnosed with inoperable lung cancer in 1996, he told his wife Mayola, "Those darn cigarette people finally did it. They were lying all the time."

In 1999, two years after his death, an Oregon jury ordered the Philip Morris Co. — the maker of Williams' favorite brand, Marlboro — to pay Mayola $820,000 in compensatory damages and another $79.7 million in punitive damages. Oregon courts have twice upheld the punitive damage award, satisfied that the jury had reason to find that Philip Morris had perpetrated a fraud on Williams and other smokers in the state and that the company's conduct was both profitable and reprehensible in the extreme.

Next week, Philip Morris, the nation's biggest tobacco company, will ask the Supreme Court to throw out the punitive damage award. The company hopes to use the case to persuade the justices to set stricter rules for the federal courts to follow in an area traditionally left to the states.

From *CQ Weekly,*
October 23, 2006.

The war over punitive damages has now been raging for more than three decades. Business lobbies and other "tort reform" groups have planted in people's minds the image of an out-of-control civil justice system that frequently imposes outlandish punitive damage awards on companies based mostly on knee-jerk hostility to big corporations.

> **"Previously, the justices suggested that rarely should punitive damages be more than 10 times actual compensation."**

Any number of research reports and academic studies have shown that image to be essentially false. One report in the late 1990s by the Rand Corp. Institute for Civil Justice concluded that punitive damages are seldom sought and even more rarely awarded. A more recent study by University of Georgia professors Susette Talarico and Thomas Eaton found that out of 25,000 state civil lawsuits studied, punitive damages were sought in only about 3,700 cases and awarded in only 15.

As Talarico laments, such research gets far less attention from the public than the occasional spectacular case with a multimillion-dollar punitive damage award. "These become the basis for most people's generalizations about the tort system," she says.

A few of those spectacular cases have reached the Supreme Court and drawn the justices, very tentatively, into setting due process limits on punitive damages. A decade ago, the court threw out a $4 million punitive damage award against the German automaker BMW in a lawsuit stemming from a a flawed automobile paint job. Three years ago, the court threw out a $145 million punitive damage award against State Farm Mutual Automobile Insurance for mishandling a claim that cost the policyholder a $185,000 court judgment.

In both cases, plaintiffs presented strong evidence that the companies were guilty of patterns of fraudulent behavior toward customers. Juries may consider the companies' reprehensibility in awarding punitive damages, the justices said, but the disparity between compensatory and punitive damages was too high in both cases. In its State Farm ruling, the court suggested that rarely should punitive damages be more than 10 times actual compensation.

A WIDE DEGREE OF DISCRETION

By that standard, the Philip Morris case — with its 97-to-1 ratio — seems ripe for reversal. Yet, as pointed out by Mark Tushnet, a plaintiff-oriented professor at Georgetown University Law Center, Oregon courts tried to apply the Supreme Court precedents in upholding the award to Williams. The Oregon judges understood that the 10-to-1 formula was only a guide — and only one of several factors to be considered. And, unlike the other Supreme Court cases that have set precedent in this area, Philip Morris was found to have extremely reprehensible conduct over an extended period of time that did more than financial harm to the customer. It killed him.

Philip Morris contends that, historically, punitive damages have not been used to punish defendants for harm to anyone other than the individual plaintiff. It also warns that the next Oregon jury could hit the company with another, duplicative punitive damage award for the same conduct. And it notes that it was among the tobacco companies that in 1998 agreed to pay states more than $40 billion to settle smokers' health-related claims.

Williams' attorneys have rebuttals for each of those points. In particular, they note that Oregon law guards against repetitive punitive damage awards by providing that juries in subsequent cases would be told to take any prior awards into account. In any event, Philip Morris cites no actual case in which a corporate defendant has been hit with one after another punitive damage award.

Hard cases, it is said, make bad law. The justices may see *Philip Morris v. Williams* as an example of a civil justice system that runs roughshod over defendants in open defiance of the high court's own rulings. Both premises are at least somewhat misleading. Even if the court overturns the award, as many experts expect, the justices should leave juries and judges in state court systems a wide degree of discretion in meting out civil justice system as they — rather than corporate wrongdoers — think best.

Figure of Speech

Supreme Court weighs students' First Amendment rights to oppose objectives of school administrators

School administrators around the country are punishing students for speaking out on issues ranging from abortion and homosexuality to drug use and the war in Iraq. And the Supreme Court appears poised to side with school administrators and — for no compelling reason — limit a landmark 1960s precedent aimed at safeguarding pupils' free-speech rights.

In oral arguments in March 2007, the Juneau school board asked the justices to uphold an Alaska high school student's 10-day suspension for unfurling a pro-drug-use banner to display as the Olympic torch relay passed by the school in 2002. The 9th Circuit Court of Appeals ruled that the suspension violated Joseph Frederick's First Amendment rights. But the school board, backed by the National School Boards Association, maintains that upholding the ruling would hinder schools' anti-drug programs and subject school administrators to damage suits in a murky area of law.

Similar cases dot dockets around the country. In Williamstown, Vt., a student went to court after he was disciplined for wearing a T-shirt identifying President Bush as "Chicken-Hawk-in-Chief" and adorned with drug and alcohol imagery. A student in Poway, Calif., challenged his suspension for wearing a T-shirt inscribed with the words "Homosexuality Is Shameful." The Alliance Defense Fund, a Christian religious liberty advocacy group, is backing the

From *CQ Weekly*,
January 22, 2007.

California student's cause and also has filed federal lawsuits on behalf of students in New York, Pennsylvania and Virginia who were barred from wearing anti-abortion T-shirts or distributing anti-abortion literature.

The Supreme Court established the basic precedent in 1969, when it overturned the suspensions of three Iowa teenagers who came to school wearing black armbands to protest the Vietnam War. Students do not "shed their constitutional rights . . . at the schoolhouse gate," the court observed in *Tinker v. Des Moines Independent Community School District*. In subsequent rulings, the court decided to read that precedent narrowly. In 1986, it upheld the suspension of a Washington state student for injecting "patently offensive" sexual metaphors into his speech in favor of a candidate for high school student council president. In 1988, it said schools could censor student newspapers — in the case, by spiking a story on teenage pregnancy — if the newspaper was "an integral part of the school's educational function."

In the name of preventing drug use, the court has also allowed school authorities to limit students' constitutional rights against unreasonable searches. In 1985, it upheld the search of a student's purse (marijuana was found), even though the principal lacked probable cause to believe she was carrying drugs. In 1995 and again in 2002, the court said schools may require students to submit to random drug tests as a condition of participating in varsity athletics or any other extracurricular activity.

Even in *Tinker*, the court recognized that students' free speech rights could be limited when necessary to prevent disruption or to protect the rights of other students. But Justice Abe Fortas tellingly added that open discussion — "hazardous freedom," in his words — was "the basis of our national strength."

SCHOOL MISSION

Lower federal courts applying the Supreme Court's precedents have tended to favor students. In the Vermont case, for example, the 2nd Circuit Court of Appeals rejected the school board's view that the T-shirt's drug and alcohol images were "plainly offensive" or interfered with an "integral" school function of discouraging drug use.

> **"Justice Abe Fortas said that open discussion — 'hazardous freedom,' in his words — was 'the basis of our national strength.'"**

On the other hand, the 9th Circuit refused to stop the Poway school board from enforcing its rule against wearing anti-gay messages. School officials had grounds to believe such displays were "injurious to gay and lesbian students and interfered with their right to learn," the court said. The student has appealed to the Supreme Court.

Given the reality of anti-gay harassment and violence in public schools, the decision is not without justification. As in the anti-abortion cases, however, the Alliance Defense Fund lawyers have grounds to complain that school authorities sometimes single out "pro-life" or "pro-family" views for censorship. Indeed, the Poway teenager wore the T-shirt on the same day that many students were observing, with the school's apparent approval, a "Day of Silence" to support gay and lesbian schoolmates.

In Juneau, Frederick's stunt — displaying for TV cameras a banner that read "Bong Hits 4 Jesus" — can easily be dismissed as sophomoric. He muddied the case by saying the phrase was meaningless nonsense, not a pro-drug message. Still, school officials are making a far-reaching argument, that the banner was "offensive" and interfered with the school's "mission" of deterring illegal drug use. Under that reasoning, the Des Moines school board might have won the *Tinker* case by claiming support for U.S. troops in Vietnam as part of its "mission."

In fact, the public schools' most important mission is to prepare students for democratic governance in a country with what the Supreme Court has called "a profound national commitment to the principle that debate on public issues should be uninhibited, robust, and wide-open." That lesson is never too early for students to learn — or for teachers and principals to teach.

Judicial Retirement Strategy

The implication that Rehnquist may have edged O'Connor out makes a case for term limits

hief Justice Earl Warren tried to time his retirement so President Lyndon B. Johnson could appoint his successor before the 1968 election. But Senate Republicans filibustered Johnson's effort to put Abe Fortas in the top job, allowing President Richard M. Nixon to make the pivotal appointment of Warren E. Burger the next year.

Other justices have had more success in timing their departures for political effect. Republican Potter Stewart's decision to retire in 1981 gave his vacancy to Ronald Reagan to fill (with Sandra Day O'Connor). Byron R. White, at the time the court's only Democratic appointee, decided to leave in 1993 so Bill Clinton could name his successor (Ruth Bader Ginsburg).

Such episodes illustrate that politics plays a big part not only when justices join the court, but also when they leave. But new details about Chief Justice William H. Rehnquist's conversations with O'Connor as they both weighed retirement add a new twist: One justice — Rehnquist, in this case — influencing the timing of another's departure.

The events, as reported by Jan Crawford Greenburg of ABC News in her recent book, "Supreme Conflict," suggest that the gravely ill Rehnquist might have intentionally misled O'Connor about his own

From *CQ Weekly*,
February 29, 2007.

❝Law professors of diverse views want to set an 18-year limit on justices' active service.❞

likely tenure so as to ease her off the court earlier than she wanted. And even the hint of manipulation helps make the case for a proposal to limit active service on the Supreme Court to 18 years. By providing for a vacancy every two years, the proposal might reduce the Armageddon-like nature of some recent confirmation battles.

Rehnquist reportedly had his eye on confirmation politics in June 2005. As Greenburg tells the story, O'Connor approached the chief justice earlier in the year as she began thinking about retiring to care for her ailing husband, John. At the time, Rehnquist suggested that they talk again at the end of the term. Rehnquist, suffering from thyroid cancer, knew from his doctors that he probably had less than a year to live, but he had not told his colleagues. When O'Connor approached Rehnquist a second time, he surprised her by saying that he intended to stay for another term. And, according to Greenburg, Rehnquist pointedly added: "I don't think we need two vacancies."

In Greenburg's view, Rehnquist effectively forced O'Connor to retire then or wait two years, longer than she wanted. She took the first option. But then Rehnquist died two months later, creating the situation he had supposedly wanted to avoid.

Greenburg does not accuse Rehnquist of being deliberately misleading, but one conservative commentator saw the implication — and applauded. "If it is true that William Rehnquist effectively pushed Sandra Day O'Connor out the door," political science professor Matthew Franck wrote for National Review Online, "this fact would count as the last great service he did for his country."

TERM-LIMITED JUSTICES

Most court watchers, however, would probably disapprove of one justice manipulating another's retirement

decision. And Rehnquist's shielding information about his health had that effect, intentional or not.

Whatever the reasons, the political calculations that retiring justices make would appear to serve no legitimate constitutional purpose. In the modern era, justices often stay or leave depending on who is in the White House. And the president and Senate view each nomination as a chance to shape the court for years to come.

Law professors Roger Cramton and Paul Carrington want to reduce the stakes by setting an 18-year limit on justices' active service. The still life-tenured justice would then assume "senior status," available for temporary assignments to lower federal courts or even to the Supreme Court itself if a sitting justice was recused from a case. Cramton and Carrington developed the proposal in part because some aging justices have not carried their fair share of the court's work. More important, however, they say current arrangements create "incentives for strategic behavior" that may not be in the court's best interests — or the public's.

Skeptics argue that this proposal would have cut short the careers of many distinguished justices. But several justices made their marks in fewer than 18 years, including Robert H. Jackson, John Marshall Harlan and Lewis F. Powell Jr. And there seems to be little doubt but that any group of nine justices would have sufficient experience and knowledge to handle the court's work even if none had served for 20 or 30 years.

The Cramton-Carrington idea has support from law professors spanning the ideological spectrum. Their rationale is that, while no proposal can eliminate politics from Supreme Court successions, an orderly biennial vacancy could help make the court broadly responsive to changing political conditions and also lower the temperature on confirmation battles.

This is an interesting concept, probably worth an airing, but it has little prospect of serious consideration in Congress. Neither political party is likely to see much advantage in such a reform, and most scholars believe it would require a constitutional amendment. Thus, the process of replacing justices of the Supreme Court will probably remain unchanged, with all the resulting human drama that entails.

Politics and
Public Policy

The articles in this section consider political issues at the forefront of recent public debate in Washington, including the application of the death penalty, the centrist agenda of the Democratic majority in Congress, the Bush administration's current strategy for dealing with Iran, the shifting tactics of gun control advocates, and problems at the Department of Veterans Affairs.

The first article tackles the question of why the federal government has expanded the scope of the federal death sentence in recent years despite an overall decline in both death sentences and executions at the state level. Death penalty opponents attribute some of their recent progress to their shift in approach from challenging the morality of the death penalty toward focusing on the practical problems of administering the death penalty. At the same time, the Bush Justice Department has attempted to expand its reach by assuming responsibility for certain cases in states that do not have their own death penalty laws.

The Democrats' winning control of Congress last November was seen as a return of centrist and independent voters to the party. The challenge now facing Democratic leaders is to maintain the confidence of these voters by ruling from the center and addressing the concerns of the middle class. The second article discusses why centrist Democrats believe this will involve compromise, bipartisanship and rethinking the party's strategy on such controversial issues as abortion. The growing prominence of groups like the New Democratic Coalition and the Blue Dog Democrats supports the view that some congressional Democrats are heeding the mandate of the voters and focusing on a more practical and less ideological agenda.

The announcement earlier this year that the United States would reverse course and hold high-level diplomatic meetings with Iran, as well as other neighbors of Iraq, was made against a backdrop of continued United States military presence in the region. Experts disagree as to whether the military posturing will advance or thwart U. S. efforts to stabilize the region or resolve the core issue of the American diplomatic agenda—a demand for the abandonment of Iran's nuclear program. The third article in this section examines the mixed reviews of the administration's new strategy of combining diplomacy with implied military threat.

Unlike the response to the 1999 shooting at Columbine High School, Washington's response to the deadlier shooting at Virginia Tech has been marked by silence on the issue of gun control. As the fourth article illustrates, the American public has long been of two minds on gun control. In their efforts against the powerful National Rifle Association, advocates of gun control have shifted tactics toward incremental initiatives and fighting illegal gun trafficking.

The last article discusses inadequacies in the Department of Veterans Affairs that have become evident as service members return from the conflicts in Iraq and Afghanistan. Experts agree that the VA is facing unprecedented stresses and is ill equipped to handle the influx of injured and disabled soldiers. Problems include an enormous backlog of disability claims, a paralyzing bureaucracy and serious gaps in medical care. As Congress turns its attention to correcting the system, the VA and veterans advocates disagree about the source of the problem and possible solutions.

The Capital Punishment Crossroads

As opposition to executing criminals grows in some places, the federal government and some 'death belt' states move to expand the list of capital crimes

STATE OR FEDERAL? The U.S. attorney in Brooklyn took over Ronell Wilson's case after the New York death penalty was struck down by the state's top court. Wilson was convicted in January of executing two police officers.

From *CQ Weekly,*
February 19, 2007.

Three weeks ago, a federal judge in Brooklyn had an unusual request for prosecutors in a racketeering and "murder for hire" case. Judge Frederic Block wanted them to abandon their hopes of winning a death sentence, which he called "absurd" and "a total misappropriation" of taxpayer funds. He pleaded with them to ask their superiors at the Justice Department to give up the idea.

"Will you kindly advise Washington that, in this judge's opinion, there is no chance in the world there would be a death penalty verdict in this case?" Block said. "If I'm wrong, I will have egg on my face, but I will not be incorrect."

It's juries, not judges, who have the final say about death sentences. On the face of things, though, it seemed Block was on to something. Federal prosecutors have repeatedly sought capital convictions in New York but failed in 14 previous attempts. No federal jury in New York, in fact, had handed down a death sentence since 1954.

New York State itself does not have the death penalty in effect. Capital punishment had been a big issue in the gubernatorial elec-

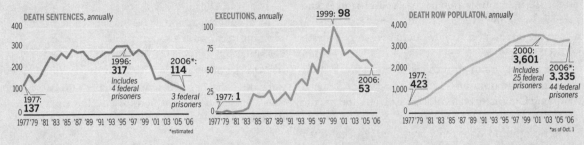

Executions Decline, But Death Row Is Still Packed

After the Supreme Court reinstated capital punishment in 1976, the number of death sentences accelerated, peaking 11 years ago. The pace of executions crested three years later. Since then, condemnations have declined by two-thirds, and executions have fallen by almost half. Yet, as of last fall, the population on the death rows in federal and state prisons topped 3,300, still 93 percent of the high point in 2000 and 2 percent more than at the end of 2005.

DEATH SENTENCES, *annually*

1996: **317** Includes 4 federal prisoners
2006*: **114** 3 federal prisoners
1977: **137**
1977 '79 '81 '83 '85 '87 '89 '91 '93 '95 '97 '99 '01 '03 '05 '06
*estimated

EXECUTIONS, *annually*

1999: **98**
2006: **53**
1977: **1**
1977 '79 '81 '83 '85 '87 '89 '91 '93 '95 '97 '99 '01 '03 '05 '06

DEATH ROW POPULATON, *annually*

2000: **3,601** Includes 25 federal prisoners
2006*: **3,335** 44 federal prisoners
1977: **423**
1977 '79 '81 '83 '85 '87 '89 '91 '93 '95 '97 '99 '01 '03 '05 '06
*as of Oct. 1

SOURCES: Bureau of Justice Statistics, Death Penalty Information Center, NAACP Legal Defense Fund; CQ / Jamie Baylis and Marilyn Gates-Davis

---

tion of 1994, and the state enacted a death penalty statute the following year. But it was rarely used: No one was ever executed by the state under the new law, and most of the few death sentences there were thrown out quickly on appeal. After the state's highest court struck down the statute in 2004, legislators showed little interest in reviving it.

Given that background, it was little wonder that Judge Block, who has a reputation for blunt talk from the bench, felt confident that the jury in his case would not return a verdict of death. But it turned out that he was wrong about the idea that federal prosecutors were wasting their time and taxpayer money by even trying.

Just six days after Block asked prosecutors to back down, a federal jury in the same Brooklyn courthouse sentenced Ronell Wilson to die for shooting two undercover detectives in the back of the head. Federal prosecutors, in fact, had taken over the Wilson case from state prosecutors after New York's death penalty law was invalidated.

Other states are finding out what New York has found: that a dip in the popularity of capital punishment, coupled with high-profile skepticism, does not mean the death penalty is going away for good.

Although there has been a recent decline in both death sentences and executions at the state level, statutes

Public Support Starts to Slip

As violent crime peaked during the 1990s, so did support for the death penalty. About two-thirds of the public still favors capital punishment, but support has declined due to concerns about wrongful convictions, disparities in sentencing and problems with execution methods.

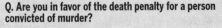

Q. Are you in favor of the death penalty for a person convicted of murder?

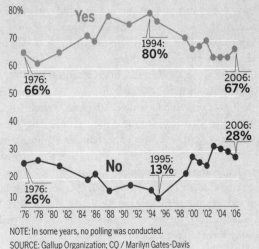

Yes
1994: **80%**
1976: **66%**
2006: **67%**

No
1995: **13%**
2006: **28%**
1976: **26%**
'76 '78 '80 '82 '84 '86 '88 '90 '92 '94 '96 '98 '00 '02 '04 '06

NOTE: In some years, no polling was conducted.
SOURCE: Gallup Organization; CQ / Marilyn Gates-Davis

are still being applied with regularity — particularly in Texas, which has carried out three of every eight executions in the nation during the past 30 years. And the federal death penalty is clearly a growth business: The roster of inmates on federal death row has more than doubled since 2000. That's because Congress has vastly expanded the scope of the federal death sentence in recent years, and the Bush administration has been pushing to extend its reach by taking over more and more death penalty cases in the dozen states that do not have their own death penalty laws.

"The willingness to pursue federal death cases reflects national public opinion," said John C. McAdams, a Marquette University political scientist who supports the penalty.

Public opinion does remain in favor of the death penalty, although not so strongly as a decade ago. And the country — which has always been divided on the topic — is becoming more divided than ever, not only in its views about the death penalty but also in its application. Like so many other social policies in a nation divided into liberal "blue" and conservative "red" slices, the death penalty's future looks starkly different depending on where you live. As a result, the federal government is therefore taking small but symbolically important steps to impose its view on the whole country.

As McAdams points out, "elite opinion" has turned against the death penalty in a number of Northeastern and Midwestern states. Several, including New Jersey and Maryland, are seriously considering abolishing executions altogether. And 11 other states have effectively put their use of capital punishment on hold, mainly out of concern that lethal injections are frequently botched, leading to pain that violates the constitutional ban on "cruel and unusual" punishment.

But there is the considerable interest within the Justice Department to push for capital verdicts — even in states, such as New York, that have no death penalty themselves. And the states that have imposed the death penalty most regularly, mostly in the South and Southwest, are showing few signs of slowing down. It's true that the growing ambivalence about the death penalty in "blue" states is having its effects even in distant places such as Texas. States within what the legal community terms the "death belt" recognize that greater scrutiny means they will inevitably have to create greater safeguards.

But those states aren't about to give the death penalty up, even if their neighbors to the north and a number of federal judges have turned sour on the idea. There may even be a bit of a backlash. Several states in the South and West are talking not about peeling back but rather expanding their death penalty laws, applying the ultimate sanction to a greater variety of crimes.

Last year, Oklahoma and South Carolina made sexual abuse of children a capital crime, even when the victim is not murdered. Other states, including Texas, may follow suit.

"On the one hand, we're seeing a decline in executions and people horrified by problems with lethal injections," said Deborah W. Denno, a death penalty critic at Fordham law school, "and on the other hand, we see leg-

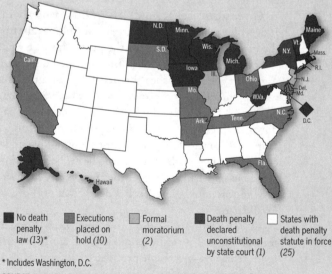

Executions Barred or On Hold

Although crimes are punishable by death in 38 states, as a practical matter there are only 25 states where an execution might be carried out today. In the others, capital punishment has been stopped by either the courts, the governors or the state legislatures — mainly out of concern about the pain and suffering of people being put to death by lethal injection.

No death penalty law (13)* | Executions placed on hold (10) | Formal moratorium (2) | Death penalty declared unconstitutional by state court (1) | States with death penalty statute in force (25)

* Includes Washington, D.C.

SOURCE: Death Penalty Information Center; CQ / Jamie Baylis and Marilyn Gates-Davis

islators broadening categories and making additional people eligible for the death penalty."

Since the Supreme Court reinstated the death penalty in 1976, the country has been split about its use. Even when concerns about violent crime during the 1980s and 1990s led states such as New York and New Jersey to impose the death penalty, they seldom used it.

Now that some of them are thinking about shutting down their death chambers, what was true at the start of the 1990s is becoming even truer today: The vast majority of executions occur in a relatively small number of states. Last year all but eight of the 53 executions nationwide took place in six states: Texas, Ohio, Virginia, Oklahoma, North Carolina and Florida.

A REMARKABLE SHIFT

"I don't think all states are going to be falling like dominoes and eliminating the death penalty after a few states do," said Richard Dieter, executive director of the Death Penalty Information Center in Washington, which is critical of the use of capital punishment.

Death penalty abolitionists feel they are making more headway with their arguments than they had for a generation. That has, in part, been the result of a fundamental change in their approach: from labeling immoral the idea of the state killing anyone to flagging problems in how the death penalty is administered. By pointing out practical concerns, they have managed to put death penalty supporters on the defensive.

Lethal injection, the main method for state and federal executions, has been successfully challenged for violating the Eighth Amendment protection against "cruel and unusual" punishment in numerous recent court cases, putting capital punishment on hold in 11 states.

Other tangible problems have cut into support for capital punishment, including instances of DNA evidence revealing the innocence of some death row inmates, questions about racial and geographic disparities in the application of the death penalty, and complaints that many convicted killers have not received adequate legal representation.

"We're in a period of national reconsideration of capital punishment," said Austin D. Sarat, an Amherst College political scientist who has written extensively on the subject. "It's become possible to say, 'I'm in favor of the death penalty in the abstract, but I'm against executing the innocent.'"

This week, both chambers of the Maryland General Assembly will hold hearings about a death penalty abolition bill that the new Democratic governor, Martin O'Malley, has pledged to sign.

It's a remarkable shift. A decade ago, the death penalty was a fixture in the nation's legal and political landscape. Today, many are wondering whether the death penalty is doomed. But while it's certain that a few states will abolish the death penalty within the next few years, if not this year, neither the federal government nor the states that have shown the greatest willingness to use the death penalty have any intention of surrendering it.

FALLING OUT OF FASHION

The total number of executions last year represented a 47 percent drop from the peak of 98 in 1999. There were 114 new death sentences handed down in 2006, only about one-third as many as the one-year high of 317 in 1996, according to the Death Penalty Information Center.

The public is increasingly open to the sentence of life without parole as an alternative to capital punishment. (Life without parole was instituted as a new option in 2005 for prosecutors in Texas, the most active death-penalty state.) That's reflected not only in polling, but in the behavior of juries. "The more juries are convinced that criminals won't get out, the less likely they are to sentence to death," Sarat said.

That dynamic — along with the expense and years of work involved in making a capital verdict stick — has discouraged many prosecutors from seeking the death penalty. It's simply much easier to make a life sentence stick.

In Indiana, for example, prosecutors sought the death penalty in 17 cases in 1994. But in recent years, they haven't asked for it more than a handful of times. "I would like to think the reason there are fewer death penalty cases these last few years are that people are taking it more seriously, both juries and prosecutors," said Robert Blecker, a professor at New York Law School.

A Political Death Knell No More

Politics, like show business, is largely a matter of giving the public what it wants. James E. Doyle, the Democratic governor of Wisconsin, has succeeded despite apparently violating this maxim.

Wisconsin has not executed anyone for 155 years. Most voters there think it's time to change that. A nonbinding referendum calling for the death penalty to be reinstated won 55 percent of the vote last November. Yet on the same day, Doyle — who openly opposes the death penalty — took 53 percent of the vote in winning a second term.

Doyle is one of 10 Democratic governors who have won elections in the past two years despite their opposition to the death penalty. A decade ago, such a stance was almost certainly a career stopper for politicians aspiring to statewide or national office. Today, the issue seems to have lost its salience, at least in some places.

"Some Republicans in the state legislature have seen this as an important issue to push for, but they have been frustrated in trying to get really strong electoral support for it," said Charles H. Franklin, a political scientist at the University of Wisconsin. "We have not had a case in Wisconsin that has made this a burning issue in everybody's daily newspaper."

Franklin and other political observers in the state say the referendum exaggerated public support for the death penalty because it included stipulations, such as the necessity for solid DNA evidence. Mark Green, the Republican congressman who was Doyle's challenger, supported the referendum but never made much of the issue — even though it would have marked a clear difference with his opponent. Similarly, continuing public support for the death penalty has not altered the priorities of the governors in two other states: Both Jon Corzine, who took office a year ago in New Jersey, and fellow Democrat Martin O'Malley, who took office last month in Maryland, are working to enact outright bans on executions.

But Republicans who have tried recently to make an issue out of opposition to the death penalty have not met with success. In November, Deval Patrick became the first Democrat elected governor of Massachusetts in 20 years, even though his opponent, Kerry Healey, produced television advertising accusing him of being "soft on crime." Patrick opposes the death penalty and had helped a cop killer get off death row when he was an NAACP Legal Defense Fund lawyer in the 1980s.

Similarly, former state Attorney General Jerry Kilgore gained little traction basing his unsuccessful 2005 campaign for governor of Virginia on complaints that Democrat Tim Kaine, then the lieutenant governor, was against the death penalty — even though the state

Although Blecker supports the death penalty, he is dubious about some of the cases that U.S. attorneys have pursued in states that don't have capital punishment laws. "The federal government is moving in with what are, to be generous, tenuous reasons," he said. "It's the wrong government prosecuting."

On Feb. 8, Alfonso Rodriguez Jr. became the first person sentenced to die in North Dakota since 1915. The state doesn't have a death penalty statute, but federal prosecutors stepped in because Rodriguez had carried across state lines the young woman whom he kidnapped, raped and killed. With his transfer last week to the federal penitentiary in Terre Haute, Ind., Rodriguez became the seventh inmate on federal death row sent from a state with no death penalty law. All told,

there are now 50 inmates sentenced to death under federal law, up from 18 when this decade began.

The federal death penalty was not restored until 1988, a dozen years after the Supreme Court reversed itself on capital punishment. But Congress has been adding to the list of federal offenses punishable by death ever since; today, the roster stands at more than five dozen, from presidential assassination to causing a death by damaging an offshore oil rig. *(List of crimes, p. 128)*

During the Clinton administration, the Justice Department in Washington seldom overruled its federal prosecutors across the country when they decided against recommending capital punishment, and it put no one on death row from a state that didn't support the death

trails only Texas in its use of the punishment during the past three decades. Kaine gave Kilgore plenty of ammunition, having worked as a defense attorney in death penalty cases. But Kaine promised that he would put his personal feelings aside to oversee executions as governor, and four men have been put to death so far on his watch.

"When the governor was running, he was very clear with people about what his personally held beliefs are but that he was committed to upholding the law," said Delacey Skinner, his communications director. "Once people understood that, they were ready to hear about education and transportation and some of the other big issues we deal with here every day."

Safety in Opposition

The fact that gubernatorial hopefuls now can run and win despite being opposed to the death penalty would have surprised political pundits during the 1980s and 1990s, when support for the issue was virtually a given. The death penalty was a central issue of the 1988 presidential campaign, and imposition of an "effective, enforceable death penalty" was part of the litany of issues that Newt Gingrich tried to have congressional candidates campaign on in the run-up to the GOP takeover of the House in 1994.

At a crucial point in Bill Clinton's nascent campaign for the presidency in early 1992, he raced home to Arkansas from New Hampshire to preside as governor over the execution of a convict with a low I.Q., hoping to prove to voters in both parties that he was tough on crime. Maryland state Del. Samuel I. Rosenberg, sponsor of the state's death penalty abolition bill, says the strategy worked. Clinton's actions as president, Rosenberg argues — signing laws that vastly expanded the reach of the federal death penalty, including a broad anti-crime package that also provided funding for thousands of new police officers — helped "diffuse the issue," inoculating not only the president but other Democrats against complaints that they are coddlers of criminals.

It may be the actual drop in crime over the past decade, though, coupled with the public's growing awareness that there are flaws in the systems of execution themselves, that has made it safe for at least some politicians to oppose the death penalty.

"The immediate sense of this as a high-priority national issue has faded a little bit," says Austin D. Sarat, author and editor of several books about the death penalty. "It's not a voting issue; it's not a mobilizing issue. People say they're in favor of the death penalty, but they care less about it."

Added Karlyn Bowman, a polling expert with the American Enterprise Institute: "You still have a solid majority in favor of the death penalty, but it may be that if crime is down, as it generally has been for a while, that it's not as strong a negative for a candidate."

penalty. That has changed under Attorney General Alberto R. Gonzales and his predecessor, John Ashcroft.

States and territories without the death penalty resent the federal intrusion. Eleanor Holmes Norton, the Democrat who is the District of Columbia's delegate in the House, sent a letter in January to the interim U.S. attorney for the city complaining "about the apparent emergence of a new and troubling pattern . . . of repeatedly seeking the death penalty in this strongly anti-death penalty jurisdiction despite consistent failure with juries and the federal court."

Justice officials counter that the same federal laws apply in abolitionist states such as Michigan and Iowa as in pro-death penalty states such as Missouri and Oklahoma. "The decision to seek the death penalty is made based on the unique facts of each case," said Erik Ablin, a department spokesman. "We do have a review process in place to ensure that the death penalty is applied in a consistent and fair manner nationwide."

But the death penalty has not been consistently applied nationwide at any point in the past three decades. Murderers may avoid it not only in states that don't impose it, but also in counties within death-penalty states where prosecutors are less likely to seek it, either because of financial or logistical limitations or ideological objections.

"We found a tremendous difference between jurisdictions, even ones side by side," said Parris N. Glendening, a Democrat who imposed a moratorium on executions during his final year as governor of Maryland, in 2002. "It became clear to me that the death penalty had become almost a lottery of jurisdiction."

Glendening notes a shift in the public mood around the issue since he left office. Many trace the current wave of skepticism to Illinois, one of the states outside the South most likely to put prisoners to death until 2000, when Republican Gov. George Ryan imposed a moratorium. "We have now freed more people than we have put to death under our system: Thirteen people have been exonerated, and 12 have been put to death,"

Ryan told CNN at the time. "There is a flaw in the system, without question." Ryan appointed a commission that indeed found numerous flaws in the system but did not recommend its abolition. Just before leaving office in 2003, he commuted the sentences of all 167 inmates on death row.

Ryan himself was convicted of corruption and racketeering charges in September 2006. But the doubts he raised about the possibility of innocent men being put to death started to spread throughout the political system. Public opinion began to soften, as stories entered the

Federal Crimes Punishable By Death

Although the Supreme Court effectively lifted the national moratorium on the death penalty in 1976, it was another 12 years before a law was enacted to permit executions for people convicted of federal crimes. The roster of federal offenses subject to the death penalty was significantly expanded in the anti-crime law a Democratic Congress wrote

Types of federal murder crimes punishable by death:

- Genocide in the United States or by a U.S. citizen or U.S. national
- Assassination of the president, president-elect, vice president, vice president-elect, acting president, the top 25 aides in the Executive Office of the President and the top five in the Office of the Vice President
- Assassination of a member of Congress, the Cabinet or the Supreme Court
- Assassination of a major presidential or vice presidential candidate
- First-degree murder of a foreign official, guest of the U.S. government or any "internationally protected person"
- First-degree murder of a federal official's relative in order to intimidate that official

- First-degree murder of a federal employee, or those assisting them, while on official business
- Murder of a state or local government employee aiding a federal criminal investigations or of a state corrections officer
- First-degree murder of a federal court officer or juror
- First-degree murder in retaliation against a federal criminal witness, victim or informant
- First-degree murder using a dangerous weapon at a federal facility
- First-degree murder in the maritime or territorial jurisdiction of the United States
- Murder overseas of a U.S. citizen or national
- Murder of a law enforcement official in furtherance of a drug crime

- Drive-by shootings to escape detection or to further a major drug crime
- Murder with a gun during a federal drug-trafficking or violent crime
- Intentional killing while violating the drug "kingpin" law
- Murder by a federal prisoner already sentenced to life
- Murder on behalf of a racketeering organization
- Murder-for-hire with any connection to interstate commerce
- Killing a federal poultry, meat or egg inspector, or an official engaged in protecting horses, while on official business or because of their decisions
- Murder of a child

SOURCES: Congressional Research Service, Death Penalty Information Center

wider culture about exonerations brought about through the introduction of genetic, or DNA, evidence — both in real life and in numerous movies and television shows. Congress responded three years ago with a law making it easier for convicts to gain access to DNA testing that could exonerate them.

All that has put what Franklin E. Zimring, a law professor at the University of California at Berkeley and a capital punishment skeptic, calls "an impossible burden on the proponents. What they've got to say is that not even one innocent person is going to be executed."

THE DRIP OF DEATH

The most pressing concern about the death penalty centers on the actual means of execution. Some capital punishment advocates argue that murderers should not be treated any more humanely than they treated their victims, but the Eighth Amendment's ban on cruel and unusual punishment has meant that the hunt for a quick and possibly pain-free procedure has lasted for more than a century.

States hoped they had cracked the problem 30 years ago with the development in Oklahoma of a protocol for

in 1994 and again in the 1996 law written by a Republican Congress to combat domestic and foreign terrorism. It was expanded most recently last year, with a law applying the death penalty to child abusers whose victims die. That brought to more than 60 the number of specific federal crimes punishable by death, and as of last week there were 50 people on federal death row. But only three — most famously Timothy McVeigh, who blew up a federal office building in Oklahoma City in 1995 — have been executed by the federal government in the past three decades.

Other federal crimes that, if they result in death, are punishable by death:

- Using or conspiring to use weapons of mass destruction
- Developing or transporting chemical weapons, or threatening to do so
- Taking explosive, biological or radioactive materials across state lines with intent to kill
- Damaging or attempting to damage federal property or any property used in interstate or international commerce
- Airline hijacking or attempted hijacking
- Destroying any aircraft in U.S. airspace or any commercial aviation facility,
- Violence aboard an aircraft that endangers flight
- Wrecking interstate-traveling trains or related structures
- Destroying trucks or cars engaged in interstate or international commerce
- Carjacking a vehicle engaged in interstate commerce

- Violence at an international airport, other than related to a labor dispute
- Violence on a fixed ocean platform in U.S. waters or against an American
- Violence against maritime navigation
- War crimes by or against a U.S. national or member of the military
- Espionage resulting in death of an American spy or compromising of national security
- Terrorist acts transcending national boundaries
- Delivering or detonating a bomb in a public place, government facility or public transit system
- Putting bombs in the mail
- Damaging religious property or obstructing freedom of religious exercise
- Smuggling people into the United States
- Depriving or conspiring to deprive others of their civil rights
- Tampering with federal witnesses, victims or informants

- Torturing or attempting torture by a government official
- Taking hostages
- Robbing a bank
- Kidnapping, other than by parents
- Sexually abusing an adult
- Sexually abusing or exploiting a child
- Injuring a child

Other federal crimes punishable by death:

- Treason
- Attempting murder to obstruct justice by a federal "kingpin," someone convicted of running a major drug-trafficking enterprise
- Operating a drug operation twice as big as that which defines a federal drug "kingpin"
- Spying for the enemy in wartime

lethal injection that was soon widely adopted. Three drugs are injected intravenously: The first leads to unconsciousness, the second prevents movement (to avoid jerking motions that could upset witnesses), and the third stops the heart.

Lethal injection is now the preferred method of execution in every death-penalty state except Nebraska, which uses electrocution. But because of rising complaints about botched injections, the death penalty has been put on hold in 11 states, either by courts or the governor, as lawmakers try to come up with a new, safer protocol.

Details about death penalty procedures are closely guarded secrets, so it's been difficult for outside experts to know whether correct doses have been given. (Veterinary euthanasia is more uniformly regulated.) Injections are typically administered by guards or other prison volunteers, not by doctors or nurses. And because of the high incidence of past drug use among death row felons, it's sometimes hard for the guards to find a usable vein. Needles stuck into tissue rather than veins have resulted in many instances of the condemned enduring gruesome and long-lasting pain before dying.

It was once difficult for attorneys for death row inmates to get any information about how lethal injections were used — the first evidentiary hearing about the method was not held until 15 years after states began to use it — but they have pieced together a considerable body of evidence that has recently led judges in several states to call the practice into question. Some states, such as South Dakota, are now working on legislation to clarify the rules surrounding the procedure. Lawmakers in other states, Missouri among them, are having to negotiate with judges to find altered methods that will pass muster. That task has been made more difficult by the unwillingness of the medical community to participate.

"We've called this the Hippocratic paradox," said Jonathan Groner, a physician at Ohio State University opposed to the death penalty. "It's immoral for health care professionals to participate because of their irreversible obligation only to use their skills for healing and not for killing." And, says Groner, it's just as immoral for prison guards without medical training to use the necessary equipment.

Others dispute that, but the resistance of the medical profession to capital punishment is having effects throughout the system. A 2005 article in the British

A Few States, One Procedure Dominate the Death Penalty

Of the 38 states with death penalties, lethal injection is the preferred method everywhere but Nebraska. Three of every eight executions in the past 30 years have been in Texas, but one in five death row inmates is in California. And Alabama, Oklahoma and Nevada have sentenced the biggest shares of their populations to death.

Jan. 17, 1977, through Feb. 7, 2007
Total executions: 1,062

Method of execution
(number executed)
Hanging **0.3%** (3)
Delaware, Washington
Firing squad **0.2%** (2)
Utah
Gas chamber **1%** (11)
Five states
Electrocution
14% (153)
Ten states
Lethal injection
84% (893)

SOURCE: Death Penalty Information Center

	Executions since 1977	Exonerations 1973-2006	Death row population in October	Death row inmates per million population
Texas	383	8	392	16.7
Virginia	98	1	20	2.6
Oklahoma	84	7	89	24.9
Missouri	66	1	50	8.6
Florida	64	22	398	22.0
North Carolina	43	5	184	20.8
Georgia	39	5	107	11.4
South Carolina	36	2	66	15.3
Alabama	35	5	192	41.7
Arkansas	27	—	37	13.2
Louisiana	27	8	88	20.5
Ohio	24	5	192	16.7
Arizona	22	8	124	20.1
Indiana	17	2	24	3.8
Delaware	14	—	18	21.1
California	13	3	657	18.0
Illinois	12	18	11	0.9
Nevada	12	1	79	31.7
Mississippi	8	3	66	22.7
Utah	6	—	9	3.5
Maryland	5	3	8	1.4
Washington	4	1	9	1.4
Montana	3	2	2	2.1
Nebraska	3	1	9	5.1
Pennsylvania	3	6	228	18.3
Federal (*civilian*)	3	—	44	0.1
Kentucky	2	1	39	9.3
Oregon	2	—	33	8.9
Tennessee	2	—	108	17.9
Colorado	1	—	2	0.4
Connecticut	1	—	8	2.3
Idaho	1	1	20	13.6
New Mexico	1	4	2	1.0
Wyoming	1	—	2	3.9
Kansas	—	—	9	3.3
New Jersey	—	—	11	1.3
New York	—	—	1	0.1
South Dakota	—	—	4	5.1
New Hampshire	—	—	—	—
TOTALS:	**1,062**	**123**	**3,342**	**11.2**

SOURCES: Death Penalty Information Center, NAACP Legal Defense Fund, Census Bureau; CQ / Marilyn Gates-Davis

Capital Punishment and the Supreme Court

There appears to be no chance that the Supreme Court, which banned capital punishment in 1972 only to reinstate it four years later, will reverse itself again in the near future. But the court has restricted the use of the death penalty in recent years and frequently seeks to insure that states and lower courts follow proper methodologies. Last month, for example, the justices heard oral arguments in three cases challenging death sentences in Texas, one regarding a constitutional mistake that the Texas Court of Criminal Appeals deemed "harmless" and the other two concerning habeas corpus cases. The court's most important decisions of the modern era include:

Furman v. Georgia (1972) invalidated all existing death penalty statutes, 5-4, on the grounds that they violated the Eighth Amendment's stricture against "cruel and unusual" punishment.

Gregg v. Georgia (1976) upheld discretionary death penalty statutes enacted by states after the *Furman* decision but struck down those that made capital punishment mandatory for specific crimes.

Coker v. Georgia (1977) struck down the death penalty in cases of rape when no murder had occurred, an expression of the high court's prohibition on capital punishment for all crimes save murder.

Pulley v. Harris (1984) held that states did not need to ensure death sentences were proportional to punishments imposed on others convicted of similar crimes.

Wainwright v. Witt (1985) made it easier for prosecutors to exclude jurors who said they would not support the death penalty.

McCleskey v. Kemp (1987) held that the disproportionate imposition of capital punishment in cases where the victims were white did not require striking down the death penalty itself.

Penny v. Lynaugh (1989) rejected the idea of banning executions of mentally retarded offenders.

Stanford v. Kentucky (1989) permitted the execution of offenders as young as 16 at the time of their crimes. A year earlier, the court had barred executions for capital crimes committed by 15-year-olds.

Atkins v. Virginia (2002) reversed the *Penny* decision and barred executions of the mentally retarded, based on what Justice John Paul Stevens called a "national consensus" against the practice.

Ring v. Arizona (2002) extended an earlier ruling that only juries, not judges, may make factual determinations in imposing a death sentence.

Roper v. Simmons (2005) reversed *Stanford*, ruling that the execution of minors was "disproportionate." Justice Antonin Scalia complained about the weight given in the majority opinion to "like-minded foreigners," a reference to international law on the death penalty. Roper was one of the five decisions in 2005 striking down death sentences, leading to speculation that the court was becoming swayed not just by international opinion but by public uneasiness in the United States.

Hill v. McDonough (2006) allowed death row inmates to use civil rights law rather than more restrictive habeas corpus petitions to challenge the specific methods of lethal injections.

Adapted from Kenneth Jost, *The Supreme Court A to Z*, 4th ed. (Washington, D.C.; CQ Press, 2007).

medical journal The Lancet has also had a wide influence in the battle against "medical collusion."

A federal judge in California found the state's injection method unconstitutional, forcing it to call off the most recently scheduled execution at nearly the last minute in February 2006. The longstanding refusal of the California Medical Association to allow physicians to administer the death penalty — the group won statutory protection in 2001 to prevent physicians from being forced to participate directly in executions — has made the state's job of finding a workable compromise more difficult.

"That's absolutely going to slow us down, because the courts want to see the medical profession weigh in on how you make sure they're not feeling pain while you stop their heart," said Lance Corcoran, chief of governmental affairs for the California Correctional Peace Officers Association, a prison guard union.

Kent Scheidegger, legal director for the Criminal Justice Legal Foundation in Sacramento, which supports capital punishment, is confident the problems regarding methodology will be resolved. The complaints about lethal injection spread quickly, he said, "but once a state comes up with an acceptable method, that will be approved and copied by other states."

But Denno, the Fordham law professor, says the concerns about lethal injections will not fade away. "No responsible death penalty attorney these days would not challenge it," she said. "Not every inmate is going to be innocent, and not all of them are affected by questions about racial disparities, but all of them are going to be able to make this appeal."

PRESSURE ON PUNISHERS

Denno contends that even the states that are most ardent in their pursuit of the death penalty have to be aware that there is now greater scrutiny placed on executions. The various issues that have left the death penalty out of favor in states such as Illinois and New York are also drawing attention in states that execute many people. The Supreme Court has also been reviewing the death penalty applications of many states, with three cases from Texas due to be decided this term.

As a result, states that are eager to maintain the death penalty may have to put in place greater safeguards. The same federal law that expanded DNA testing also requires states to have mechanisms in place to investigate forensic misconduct and errors in order to receive federal funding for their crime labs.

Even in Texas there is a growing recognition of flaws within its system. The legislature, the state bar and the courts are all looking for ways to address the chronic lack of adequate counsel, particularly during the stage of the state appeals process that defines the issues that will be relevant during federal appeals.

"It is refreshing that the debate here is not about whether there are problems, but what can be done to fix the problems," said Andrea Keilen, executive director of the Texas Defender Service, which represents defendants in capital cases. "For many years, every public official would argue that there's nothing wrong."

The climate of debate has clearly changed. As governor of Massachusetts in 2005, Mitt Romney — who declared himself a candidate last week for the 2008 GOP presidential nomination — sought to reinstate the death penalty. His proposal failed, but the limitations Romney himself put on his prospective capital punishment system were just as instructive about how tough a sell the death penalty has become. He would have

restricted capital punishment to a short list of "the most heinous of crimes," required "conclusive scientific evidence" linking the defendant to the crime and proposed that juries be instructed to apply a "no doubt" standard of proof. Romney openly acknowledged criticisms of the death penalty systems in other states but challenged the notion that such complaints couldn't be solved by a commission.

"The proponents of capital punishment are more and more on the defensive," said Sarat, the Amherst professor. "It's much less prevalent, and the burden of proof is higher."

It's certainly the case that death penalty supporters are on the defensive in certain states. The Colorado General Assembly is considering a bill that would end the death penalty and devote the expected monetary savings to "cold case" investigations of unsolved crimes. A commission created by the New Jersey Legislature recommended in January that the state's little-used death penalty system be abolished altogether — an outcome being explored by the legislature and pushed by the Democratic governor, Jon Corzine.

"As a practical matter, we are already operating under the system that the commission has proposed, namely a system in which we have life sentences without parole," says Peter G. Verniero, a former state Supreme Court justice and Republican attorney general, who thinks his state should drop the death penalty.

"Capital punishment is not something that you should have on the books unless there is a very clear consensus that it is the correct policy."

REDEFINING 'MONSTER'

In states where the abolitionist streak is not so wide, however, there are not only efforts to ensure that lethal injections and the death penalty system as a whole pass constitutional muster, but to expand the list of crimes that might result in capital convictions.

Some states are also hopeful that they may soon be spared the agony and expense of appeals that drag on for a decade or more. As part of a 1996 anti-crime law, Congress promised states "fast track" federal death penalty appeals, with strict time limits, if they could show that they had provided adequate counsel to defendants during state-level appeals. But the federal courts,

Alone Among the Rich

The rate of executions in the United States is not high by world standards, but the country has become isolated among the world's rich nations in carrying them out. Abolition has become virtually a prerequisite for membership in the European Union, leading to its decline among Eastern European countries.

	Executions in 2005	Executions per million people
China	1,770 *	1.35
Iran	94 *	1.38
Saudi Arabia	86 *	3.26
United States	60	0.20
Pakistan	31	0.19
Yemen	24	1.16
Vietnam	21	0.25
Jordan	11	1.91
Mongolia	8	2.87
Singapore	8	1.81
Kuwait	7	3.00
Libya	6	1.04
Palestinian Authority	5	1.33
Taiwan	3	0.13
Iraq	3	0.12
Bangladesh	3	0.02
Uzbekistan	2 *	0.07
Indonesia	2 *	0.01
Somalia	1 *	0.12
North Korea	1 *	0.04
Belarus	1	0.10
Japan	1	0.01

* Minimum estimate

SOURCES: Amnesty International (execution statistics), CIA World Factbook (population figures)

which were given the job of determining whether counsel had in fact been adequate, have never declared that a state has qualified for an expedited appeals process.

In hopes of speeding things up, Congress last year, in reauthorizing the anti-terrorism law known as the Patriot Act, shifted the job of certifying state-provided counsel as "adequate" from the courts to the U.S. attorney general.

Death penalty opponents argue that a prosecutor has no business determining adequacy of defense counsel. They also say that the faster cases move, the more likely they are to end in error. But supporters are confident that the switch will ease a notoriously slow-grinding process. "Most of the delay at present is not making sure that we

have the right guy, but reviewing the penalty verdict five or six times over," said Scheidegger of the Criminal Justice Legal Foundation.

Some states may soon have new sets and types of cases to contend with. In Missouri, where the death penalty has been put on hold because of judicial objections to the state's lethal injection procedures, GOP Gov. Matt Blunt has proposed making cop killers automatically subject to capital punishment. In Georgia, legislators are considering a proposal to permit the death penalty in cases where as few as nine of the 12 jurors vote to impose it. Texas is considering imposing the death penalty on sexual abusers of children.

The Utah House this month passed two bills that would expand the death penalty in cases involving children. One would make the murder of children younger than 14 a capital crime, while the other would impose the death penalty on those who killed children as a result of abuse, even if they lacked intent.

The second measure was prompted by the death of a 10-year-old girl who had been abused over a two-week period and whose body was found covered with bites and bruises. "We couldn't get it declared a capital offense, even though this one absolutely deserved it," said state Rep. Paul Ray, the legislation's sponsor. "Both the father and mother were monsters."

Death penalty supporters often invoke the specter of monsters — people who are incorrigibly evil and deserve to die. The death penalty is already reserved for the most part for particularly gruesome killers, torturers and terrorists, and others who create "aggravating circumstances."

Even as abolitionists have largely abandoned their moral arguments in favor of drawing attention to practical and legal problems, death penalty supporters now often couch their arguments not in terms of deterrence but in terms of the moral necessity of executing killers whose crimes scour the heart.

Corcoran, the guard union official in California, cites the example of Richard Ramirez, known as the Night Stalker, who was convicted of 13 murders in 1989. "If we execute Richard Ramirez, we can debate all day whether it's going to have an impact on other psychopaths," he said. "But when we execute Richard Ramirez, he is specifically deterred from ever murdering anyone again."

It is the most brutal killers that most people think about when they think about preserving the death

New Champion for an Old Cause

Kenneth W. Starr has wracked up a pretty good record as a defense attorney in death penalty cases. What's surprising is that he has been willing to take on such work at all.

Now the dean of Pepperdine University's law school, Starr earned a national reputation, whether fairly or not, as a particularly zealous prosecutor during his years as an independent counsel. His extraordinarily detailed investigation of President Bill Clinton's affair with Monica Lewinsky, a White House intern, led to the first presidential impeachment in 120 years — and also made Starr a figure of derision among liberals.

Now many of those same critics are applauding his work helping convicted murderers avoid execution. "I never, ever expected to write the following words but — gulp — here goes: Three cheers for Ken Starr," E.J. Dionne Jr., a generally liberal columnist for The Washington Post, wrote in 2005.

Starr does not oppose capital punishment; he described himself as "a non-abolitionist" during a telephone interview from his office in California last week. But, he said, "If we're going to maintain the death penalty system, it needs to be significantly improved."

One particular area that needs addressing, he said, is the adequacy and experience of defense attorneys in capital cases, many of whom are assigned by the states because the accused murderers cannot afford to hire their own counsels.

Starr argues that these defense lawyers should also be more generously compensated. "The fundamental problem that I have seen in my work is the quality of representation at the trial level," he said. "That is the enduring, systemic problem that cries out for thoughtful reform."

Starr would like to see all the major law firms in the country take on death penalty defense cases as part of their pro bono caseload. That is how Starr himself became involved in such work. He had returned to private practice following his turn as an independent counsel, and his firm, Kirkland & Ellis, had decided to represent Robin M. Lovitt, a convicted murderer in Virginia. Starr and Lovitt's other defenders objected to the fact that a court clerk had destroyed DNA material pertinent to the case not long after the commonwealth had outlawed eliminating such evidence. Mark Warner, the Democrat who was then governor, commuted Lovitt's sentence in 2005.

Since his work on that case, Starr has been on something of a crusade, speaking at panels and conferences around the country about problems with the death penalty. "Ken Starr, there's an example of an unexpected skeptic," said David Bruck, a death penalty opponent at the Washington and Lee University law school.

Starr has since worked on the clemency appeal of Michael Morales, a convicted killer in California. A fellow Republican, Gov. Arnold Schwarzenegger, rejected Starr's appeal last year, but Morales' execution was blocked by a judge who found the state's method of lethal injection unconstitutional.

Starr is one of several prominent conservatives and prosecutors to express newfound doubts about the death penalty in recent years. Starr himself credits former Virginia Attorney General Mark Earley, a nationally prominent social conservative who has become a prison reformer, with helping to convince Warner of the justice of commuting Lovitt's sentence. (He's serving a life sentence instead.)

"There is a wing of conservatism that believes that unless the death penalty is reformed from within, it's abolition will come about — a kind of 'mend it so they don't end it' approach," said Benjamin Wittes, the author of a 2002 book about Starr. "I think he fits within that vision."

Starr's liberal allies at the death penalty bar scoff at the idea that the lawyer who earned a place in American history as Clinton's principal legal antagonist is engaged in any sort of effort to polish his image. There are far easier ways to win public favor, they note, than representing notorious death row inmates. Instead, the credibility that Starr brings to their cause — he staked a claim as one of the nation's most prominent legal conservatives as solicitor general in the first Bush administration and then during six years on the U.S. Circuit of Appeals of the District of Columbia — is clearly a public relations coup for them.

"Overwhelmingly, conservatives remain in favor of the death penalty," said John C. McAdams, a Marquette University political scientist. "If a few defect, they're going to get an overwhelming amount of media attention."

penalty. It is because of them — the Jeffrey Dahmers and the Osama bin Ladens — that the death penalty, for all its flaws and declining application, is unlikely to disappear entirely in this country.

A few states may in fact abolish it, determining that it's better to wipe it from the books after years of not using it. That's what happened in Europe, where after several years of moratoriums politicians decided they might as well abolish it. But in most states, even the ones that impose capital punishment rarely or not at all, the death penalty serves a symbolic purpose, said Dieter of the Death Penalty Information Center. "We need it for those worst offenses, to keep anarchy from slipping in the door."

FOR FURTHER READING

Anti-terrorism law reauthorization (PL109-177), 2006 CQ Weekly, p. 3360; DNA testing and forensic misconduct (PL 108-405), 2004 Almanac, p. 12-8; federal death penalty statutes: PL 104-132, 1996 Almanac, p. 5-18; PL 103-332, 1994 Almanac, p. 273; PL 100-690, 1988 Almanac, p. 111.

On a Mission to the Middle

The voters gave Democrats control of Congress with instructions attached: Meet in the center and focus on middle-class concerns. Can the party get its act together?

For most of this year, Tim Mahoney was on track to be another Democratic also-ran in a Republican congressional district. Smart, thoughtful and more conservative than the average Democrat — he's a budget hawk with strong anti-abortion and pro-gun views — Mahoney still made little headway until the GOP incumbent, Mark Foley, self-destructed.

This time, it was his opponent's behavior and national worries such as Iraq that got Mahoney elected, not so much his centrist views. The next time around, though, those views could make all the difference. Mahoney won't keep his seat if his Republican district decides he has tacked too far to the left — or, for that matter, if his party does. If Democrats can produce accomplishments on what he calls "bread-and-butter issues that will really affect people's lives in a tangible way" and avoid destructive infighting, Mahoney thinks he and his party will be fine.

If not, though, Democratic control of Congress won't last very long. That's why the party's new challenge is to keep centrist and independent voters — the ones who gave them the majority this

From *CQ Weekly*, December 4, 2006.

year and could just as easily take it away — on its side. To stay in power, the Democrats will have to hold on to those red states and districts, and that will happen only if they can govern with a huge dose of pragmatism — fixing what those voters thought was wrong with Republican policies while keeping their usual tensions between center and left on the back burner.

The Congress that convenes in January will be full of freshman Democrats who got in because national issues made it easy for them to break the Republicans' hold. For some, it was the seemingly endless Iraq War; for others, the public's anxiety about the economy and the squeeze on the middle class. Ethics scandals, such as the one that helped Mahoney, left many voters feeling that Washington had lost its way.

But this election was about more than just a series of bad breaks for the GOP. This was also the year in which the Republicans lost the middle — and the Democrats grabbed it. In a year when the GOP's losses came disproportionately from among its moderates, many of the newly elected Democrats came from either marginal or solidly Republican states or districts.

While some Democrats were able to win on traditionally liberal platforms, the party generally owes its majority to the election of a large class of centrists, skeptical of ideology and determined to search for practical solutions to problems they believe have been neglected during years of partisan wars in Congress. Those views helped them swing independent voters decisively away from the Republican Party this year, allowing them to win unlikely victories and bring the Democratic Party to power despite an electoral map that was tilted against it.

In 2004, President Bush won a majority of votes in 255 out of the 435 House districts, according to a Congressional Quarterly study published last year, suggesting that Republican congressional candidates had an edge in far more House seats than the 218 needed to win a majority. Democrats, by contrast, could count on an advantage in only 180 districts. (The redrawing of districts in Texas and Georgia since then leaves that figure virtually unchanged.)

As a result of this year's election, though, Democrats are expected to hold 232 House seats next year — meaning they will have roughly 50 members who had to run against the grain in Republican-leaning districts. Now, the Democrats' challenge is to find the key to keeping centrist and independent voters on their side in most of those districts — and suffer no net losses at all in the Senate races — or their majority could slip away as quickly as it arrived.

"It's really the moderate and unaffiliated voters who swung this election," said Ed Perlmutter of Colorado, who won Republican Rep. Bob Beauprez's seat in the Denver suburbs, in a district that boasts a nearly even split of Republican, Democratic and independent voters. "If they don't like the way we're going, they'll swing right back. And that will be bad for me."

The key to holding on to the middle, according to these newly elected centrists and the outside advisers they will rely upon for ideas, is to prove that Democrats understand why they were given a chance in this election.

They have to demonstrate they can work together to correct the flaws many voters saw with Bush's foreign and domestic policies, and they have to avoid the kind of internal warfare that has bedeviled the party in the past. Moreover, they will have to convince middle-class voters — a group the party had been losing until this election — that Democrats will fight as hard for their needs as they do for low-income people.

A BROADER AGENDA

It shouldn't be an impossible task, say the advisers who will be giving centrist Democrats their ideas. They say the party just needs to make sure its domestic agenda doesn't begin and end with its traditional proposals aimed at low-income people, such as increasing the minimum wage and expanding the earned income tax credit for low-wage workers.

"That's not to say they shouldn't raise the minimum wage, because they should," said Matt Bennett, a founder of the centrist policy group Third Way. But "what you need to focus on are the things they don't know you care about," he said, like helping with day care expenses or the cost of caring for aging parents — concerns that speak more specifically to the middle class.

In the short term, House Democrats are counting on passing proposals backed by centrists that are part of incoming Speaker Nancy Pelosi's "first 100 hours" agenda, such as reviving the pay-as-you-go approach to federal budgeting and letting the government use its bulk purchasing power to negotiate lower Medicare prescription drug prices. Many Democrats want to pass the

Idea Factories' for a New Majority

Jim Kessler and Matt Bennett want to find ways to help Democrats talk to centrist and independent voters more effectively. Their group, Third Way, is a small policy and message shop that proposes ways to fix weaknesses in the party's appeal to voters, particularly on national security and middle class issues.

John Podesta sees the political landscape differently. The president and chief executive officer of the Center for American Progress, a think tank full of former advisers to President Bill Clinton and various Democratic congressional leaders, doesn't dwell on how to tweak liberal policies to appeal to centrists. Instead, he and his colleagues churn out reams of policy suggestions for the Democrats and argue that the middle will respond to good ideas, whether they're liberal or centrist.

Both groups will have the ear of the newly expanded ranks of centrist Democrats next year — and a better chance of seeing their ideas popping up on the congressional agenda now that the party will control both houses of Congress. These groups, as well as the Progressive Policy Institute (PPI), a centrist think tank that helped shape the policies of the Clinton administration, are the organizations moderate Democrats cite most often as their sources of the policies they will try to advance next year.

"They're idea factories," said Rep. Ellen O. Tauscher of California, who chairs the New Democrat Coalition, one of the party's two groups of moderate lawmakers.

The appeal of these groups is rooted in the pragmatic views of the Democratic centrists, who generally say they're suspicious of ideology and are just looking for experienced policy experts with a fresh take on how to solve pressing problems. "I don't go into any issue with an ideological view. I want to listen to what people from all sides have to say about it and make up my mind," said Rep.-elect Jason Altmire of Pennsylvania, a self-described "policy wonk" who praises the work of PPI and the Center for American Progress.

CQ / Scott J. Ferrell

NEW APPROACH: Kessler, left, and Bennett of Third Way advise Democrats on ideas and how to better communicate them to the public.

The groups have already inspired some of the initiatives Democrats proposed during their years in the minority. Third Way, for example, helped Reps. Tim Ryan of Ohio and Rosa DeLauro of Connecticut write a bill designed to reduce abortions. It was a major departure for a party that has struggled to win the support of what Kessler, the group's vice president for policy, calls the "abortion grays" — the six out of 10 voters who support abortion rights but also have moral qualms about the procedure.

But that bill, like so many other Democratic initiatives over the last 12 years, never even got a hearing. Now these groups are savoring the idea that their proposals might actually go somewhere in Congress. And centrist Democrats are planning to spend a lot more time reading their memos.

"Now we can think bigger because our ideas actually have a chance of passing," said Rep. Debbie Wasserman-Schultz of Florida, a member of the New Democrat Coalition.

Fixing the Weak Spots

The groups have different specialties. PPI, the oldest of the organizations, was founded in 1989 to generate specific policy ideas to help steer the Democratic Party in a more centrist direction — complementing the more general arguments of the Democratic Leadership Council, its affiliate.

Will Marshall, PPI's president and founder, says the organization's goal is to "think strategically" about the obstacles that prevent Democrats from building a lasting majority and suggest new policies that could help them overcome those obstacles. "I don't get up every day to fight for moderation," he says. PPI's goal, he says, is to develop "a platform for modernizing progressive politics."

Marshall's group has been around long enough to claim credit for ideas that helped define Clinton's presidency, such as the 1996 welfare overhaul and the creation of the AmeriCorps national service program. Now it is trying to generate ideas to bolster the Democrats' credibility on fighting terrorism, an issue where the party is just beginning to catch up to the Republicans in public support.

PPI has called for a "national competition strategy," including a beefed-up tax credit for research and experimentation and charter high schools that would focus on math, science and engineering. And to help parents whose job demands are forcing them to work longer hours, Marshall's group says, Congress should require employers to offer more paid and unpaid leave and flexible work schedules.

Third Way is the newest of the groups, created in January 2005 to put out short, user-friendly policy and strategy memos that could be used by busy politicians. They contain some policy advice, but the group's leaders also spend a lot of time advising Democrats on how to talk about their ideas.

One example is immigration, on which "voters think Democrats are compassionate about illegal immigrants to a fault," according to Bennett, the group's vice president for public affairs. Rather than just saying illegal immigrants deserve a chance to become citizens, Democrats can be more persuasive by arguing that such a policy would be fairer to taxpayers, since immigrants who became citizens would start paying taxes, he said.

But Third Way generates specific policy proposals as well, and one of the areas where it has placed the most focus is on appealing to the middle class — a theme shared by many of the Democratic centrists who were elected this year. The reason the effort is so crucial, Kessler said, is that until this year, congressional Democrats were losing the majority of votes from white middle class voters. In 2004, for example, voters were more likely to vote for Republicans than Democrats once their incomes exceeded $23,700 a year, he said.

Starting at this relatively low income level, "white voters didn't see a lot in what the Democrats were offering in 2004 that appealed to them," Kessler said. This year, he said, the Democrats did better. The "tipping point" at which voters started to vote for Republicans over Democrats rose to $39,000 a year. One of the reasons, he says, is that candidates started to talk more specifically about middle class tax relief and other issues that appeal directly to those voters.

Still, the group says Democrats will have to keep middle class voters' concerns in their sights if they want to stay in

CQ / Scott J. Ferrell

IDEA FACTORY: Former Clinton aide Podesta says voters will respond to good ideas whether they are centrist or liberal.

power. It has proposed ideas like a bigger tax deduction for college tuition expenses, a "new baby tax credit" to help parents raise young children, paid family leave, a tax credit for first-time homebuyers, and tax relief to help people care for elderly parents.

The Power of Ideas

When Podesta, who had been Clinton's chief of staff, launched the Center for American Progress in October 2003, he wasn't worried about the strength of liberal ideas. He just wanted a better vehicle for distributing them to the public. At the time, the organization billed itself as a "Heritage of the left" — referring to the conservative Heritage Foundation.

Two days after the midterm election, Podesta wrote a memo calling the Republican Party's loss of Congress "The End of the Grand Conservative Experiment." Now, Podesta says, the midterm election has given Democrats a chance to win over swing voters for the long term.

Last week, the group's advocacy arm, the Center for American Progress Action Fund, proposed a "first 100 days" agenda for the new majority. It has some ambitious ideas that have long been in circulation among Democratic advisers, such as the creation of a "universal 401(k)" that would follow workers between jobs, with a government match for low- and middle-income families. It also includes some bite-sized specifics — in the style of the Clinton presidency — such as creating a new special inspector general to oversee the reconstruction of Afghanistan and cracking down on excessive credit card fees.

Even though there is no special centrist tilt to it, Podesta's organization is cited frequently by Democratic centrists as a likely source of ideas for the next two years — suggesting that Podesta may not be off base when he suggests that swing voters will stick with Democrats if their ideas are practical and relevant to most people's lives.

"Our thinking is that political success follows substantive success," said Podesta. "If progressive leaders can achieve success in tackling problems that affect people's lives, if they can fix a broken Congress, if they advance substantive solutions, then they will be politically rewarded. The middle will see who's on which side."

Winning Against the Grain

To gain control of Congress, Democrats had to reach into what had been Republican territory. Of the 29 House members-elect who took away seats from the GOP last month, 19 did so in districts that President Bush carried in his 2004 re-election. Of the six Democratic pickups in the Senate, four were in states that Bush won two years ago. To help hold their new seats, most of the House takeover winners have joined at least one of the caucuses for more-conservative Democrats.

HOUSE	DISTRICT	2004 PRESIDENTIAL MARGIN (percentage points)	2006 WINNER'S VOTE SHARE	AFFILIATIONS ■ New Democrats ● BlueDogs
		KERRY		
Dave Loebsack	Iowa 2	+11	51.4%	
Joe Courtney	Connecticut 2	10	50.0	■
Bruce Braley	Iowa 1	7	55.1	■
Joe Sestak	Pennsylvania 7	6	56.4	■
Paul W. Hodes	New Hampshire 2	5	52.7	
Ed Perlmutter	Colorado 7	3	54.8	■
Patrick J. Murphy	Pennsylvania 8	3	50.3	■●
Ron Klein	Florida 22	2	50.9	■
John Yarmuth	Kentucky 3	2	50.6	
Christopher S. Murphy	Connecticut 5	<1	56.2	■
		BUSH		
Carol Shea-Porter	New Hampshire 1	+3	51.3	
Tim Walz	Minnesota 1	4	52.7	
Michael Arcuri	New York 24	6	53.8	■●
Gabrielle Giffords	Arizona 8	7	54.1	■
John Hall	New York 19	8	51.0	
Kirsten Gillibrand	New York 20	8	53.1	■●
Harry E. Mitchell	Arizona 5	9	50.5	
Jerry McNerney	California 11	9	53.1	
Jason Altmire	Pennsylvania 4	9	51.9	■
Tim Mahoney	Florida 16	10	49.6	■●
Steven L. Kagen	Wisconsin 8	11	51.2	
Joe Donnelly	Indiana 2	13	54.0	●
Heath Shuler	North Carolina 11	14	53.8	■●
Zack Space	Ohio 18	15	61.5	
Baron P. Hill	Indiana 9	19	50.0	■●
Nancy Boyda	Kansas 2	20	50.6	
Chris Carney	Pennsylvania 10	20	53.0	■
Brad Ellsworth	Indiana 8	24	60.7	●
Nick Lampson	Texas 22	29	51.8	■
SENATE	STATE	**KERRY**		
Sheldon Whitehouse	Rhode Island	+20	53.5	
Bob Casey	Pennsylvania	3	58.7	
		BUSH		
Sherrod Brown	Ohio	+2	55.8	
Claire McCaskill	Missouri	7	49.5	
Jim Webb	Virginia	9	49.6	
Jon Tester	Montana	20	49.1	

strongest possible ethics package to show they understood voters' concerns about corruption.

"There was a perception that things just weren't right in Washington," said Harry E. Mitchell, who unseated conservative Republican Rep. J.D. Hayworth in Arizona. A few days after the election, Mitchell said, a man stopped him in downtown Tempe and passed on one simple request: "Just be honest." It's about the least a voter can ask of any politician, but Mitchell said the advice stuck in his mind this time because "he wasn't the first person who told me that."

Over the long term, Democrats will have to try to advance solutions to more intractable problems, the new lawmakers say. The war in Iraq heads the list, but many of the centrist Democrats say they have been bombarded with requests to encourage renewable energy sources and address the rising cost of health care. They know they will have to live within the tight fiscal policies they have promised, rather than immediately jacking up spending on priorities they believe have been underfunded for years, such as the education law known as No Child Left Behind.

"It really is about priorities," said Senator-elect Jon Tester of Montana, a farmer and small-business owner who defeated Republican Conrad Burns. "I was just thinking about how much I'd like to have a new tractor. But can I afford it? No, I can't." Democrats don't necessarily have to sacrifice funding increases for priorities such as education, Tester said, but they should make sure the money isn't lost in bureaucracy — and they should look for wasted spending, particularly in Iraq, that could be better used elsewhere in the war on terrorism or even eliminated entirely.

Democrats will also have to learn to get along with each other if they are to hang on to power, political experts say. That means accepting the handful of anti-abortion, pro-gun Democrats who got elected this time around.

Most of those Democrats say they're not too worried. Tester, an opponent of gun control, doesn't see the issue on the party's agenda. Rather than a partisan issue, he thinks it will become more of an urban vs. rural debate.

And Mahoney doesn't think either abortion or guns will be hotly debated issues over the next two years. Instead, he says, his constituents will want evidence that the party lived up to its promises to strengthen Washington's lobbying and ethics rules, since "so many of us got elected on the issue of ethics and cronyism and corruption."

He thinks the public wants Democrats to show the discipline to resist deficit spending, even on programs they believe have been shortchanged under Bush. They will look for a successful resolution to the war in Iraq, Mahoney says, and for measures to strengthen national security, lower the cost of prescription drugs and make college tuition more affordable.

If divisive issues such as abortion come up, some centrists think the way to handle them is to find a compromise, such as the bill negotiated by Rosa DeLauro of Connecticut, a supporter of abortion rights, and Tim Ryan of Ohio, an abortion opponent, that would attempt to reduce abortions by funding programs to prevent unwanted pregnancies while boosting health care coverage and other support services for low-income parents.

By shifting the focus of the debate from the legality of abortions to the need to reduce them, Democrats have "a chance to move forward and get past some of the stumbling blocks that have tripped us up for so long," said DeLauro.

That much give and take might be difficult for Democrats regaining power after 12 years, but compromise and bipartisanship will be important to holding swing districts and independent voters.

Bipartisanship is a standard promise everybody makes after an election, and it's usually abandoned shortly after the new Congress is gaveled into session. In this Congress, the two parties will have an especially tough time making deals with each other. Bush will still be around to veto bills; many Republicans will be in no mood to help Democrats after the bitterness of the campaign; and the 2008 presidential race is just around the corner.

But bipartisanship is one of the demands voters made in the elections, Perlmutter says, and outside advisers agree. "I think the voters decisively rejected the politics of polarization as practiced by Karl Rove and Tom DeLay," said Will Marshall, president of the Progressive Policy Institute, another centrist group. "It's not just that they didn't solve the most important problems. They didn't even talk about them."

That point underscores the most important challenge centrist Democrats say they need to meet in order to keep their seats: accomplishments on issues that matter to middle-class and rural voters, such as health care, jobs and education. And it means rejecting the kind of overt appeals to particular interest groups that helped cost Republicans the support of moderate and independent voters.

"This time, more than in years past, it's going to be about how I do my job," said Nancy Boyda of Kansas, who unseated Republican Rep. Jim Ryun in a district that includes Topeka and many rural farm communities. "They're going to say, 'What have you done about health care? What have you done to make sure the rural voice is heard?' "

RISE OF THE CENTRISTS

Not all of the newly elected Democrats fit the centrist mold, a fact that liberal commentators have been quick to point out.

Senator-elect Sherrod Brown of Ohio, a seven-term House member who unseated Republican Mike DeWine, wages populist crusades against the health care industry and free-trade agreements. Another new senator, Bernard Sanders of Vermont, an independent who will caucus with the Democrats, calls himself a "Democratic socialist." Carol Shea-Porter of New Hampshire is a social worker who unseated Republican Rep. Jeb Bradley through a grass-roots anti-war campaign.

And the issues that were key in the election — the Iraq War, the economic squeeze on the middle class and corruption in Congress — aren't inherently centrist subjects. In fact, it may be hard to tell Democratic centrists from liberals on such issues.

For example, Claire McCaskill of Missouri, a state auditor who campaigned on fiscal responsibility, spent much of her time railing against waste in government spending. She promised to be the Government Accountability Office's "best friend." But she also wants to make sure any of Bush's tax cuts that are renewed will benefit the middle class. The ones that mainly help upper-income people, she says, should be allowed to expire so the money can be used for other middle-class tax relief, such as help with college tuition.

And John Yarmuth of Kentucky, who defeated GOP Rep. Anne M. Northup, said the election turned mainly on the war and economic security. The Democratic leadership's agenda, he said, is "very much in keeping with the mandate of this election: make the country work better for everyone, not just the rich, and have a change of direction in Iraq. Is that a centrist agenda? I think it's a progressive agenda."

Still, the majority of the newly elected Democrats who took seats away from Republicans have at least some centrist leanings, and keeping them in the fold will mean a constant set of compromises for the party.

Of the 29 seats Democrats gained to win control of the House, 18 were won by candidates who belong to the pro-business New Democrat Coalition, the fiscally conservative Blue Dog Coalition, or both. And that total doesn't capture all of the Democrats who are likely to depart from the party line on issues other than budget and economics.

Boyda, for example, hasn't joined either group, but she shies away from liberal positions on some cultural issues. "I support gun rights. I do not support abortion on demand," said Boyda. "It's not a political choice to take these positions. It's just where I am."

In the Senate, it will be even more important to keep the centrists satisfied, since the Democrats will have a one-vote majority. Four of the six seats that Democrats won away from Republicans will be filled by centrists such as McCaskill and Tester, as well as Bob Casey of Pennsylvania, who takes conservative stands on abortion and other social issues, and Jim Webb of Virginia, a former Republican.

Marshall of the Progressive Policy Institute argues that because more voters identify themselves as conservatives than liberals, Democrats have to reach further into the middle than Republicans do to stay in power. In national exit polls at this year's election, 21 percent of voters described themselves as liberals, 32 percent said they were conservatives, and 47 percent called themselves moderates.

"The lesson for Democrats is that we have to put together a broad center-left coalition and manage it," said Marshall. "Ideological purity can only lead us down the same path that doomed the Republicans."

SHAPING THE AGENDA

The election of so many centrists is sure to bolster the influence of the coalitions within Congress that speak for them. For example, groups such as the New Democrat Coalition and the Blue Dogs are sure to grow in prominence and thus help shape the party's agenda.

Pelosi has already used some of their ideas. The New Democrats, for example, were instrumental in the "innovation agenda" Pelosi proposed in March, which called for expanding broadband Internet service, speeding up the approval of patents, and making the research and development tax credit permanent.

The Blue Dogs, meanwhile, pushed hard to return to pay-as-you-go budget rules — a rallying cry for many of the Democratic centrists. "Our government needs to start living within a budget, just like every American family does," said Rep. Dennis Moore of Kansas, who will serve as the Blue Dogs' policy co-chairman next year.

Pelosi has already adopted an agenda of moderate issues for the House, said Rep. Debbie Wasserman-Schultz of Florida, a member of the New Democrat Coalition. "It was important that we embraced an agenda that had broad appeal. We're going to have to continue on that same path."

Democratic leaders who have advanced centrist ideas will benefit as well. Rahm Emanuel of Illinois, who as chairman of the Democratic Congressional Campaign Committee recruited many of the new centrists, is expected to have a hand in promoting centrist policies in his new role as Democratic caucus chairman.

"His influence will go well beyond the job description. He'll have a substantial voice on policy as well," said Rep. Adam B. Schiff of California, a member of both the New Democrats and the Blue Dogs.

The key to their success, however, will be whether the rest of the leadership and the caucus gives the centrists an outlet for their ideas and accepts their occasional votes against the party's agenda as the cost of staying in the majority.

"If Democrats don't embrace and do everything we can to help these new members," said Rep. Martin T. Meehan of Massachusetts, "our majority won't last very long."

COMMON GOALS

Just defining these new centrist lawmakers and their goals is a challenge for the Democratic Party.

Most of the Republicans swept into office in 1994 were conservatives who shared a commitment to fight for smaller government, lower taxes and less regulation. This year's Democratic centrists are not as united on broad philosophical principles. Many are fiscal conservatives. But for the most part, their agendas are defined by practical efforts to address long-stalled issues such as energy and immigration.

Where they mainly find common cause is in their determination to correct the problems that caused voters to turn away from Bush and the Republican Party.

"The centrists are reformers," Schiff said. "It will take many forms — ethics reform, earmark reform" and a general push for more civility in how Congress is run.

When Perlmutter — who has joined the New Democrat Coalition — got to Washington for new member orientation the week after the election, he decided that he and a number of his newly elected Democratic colleagues were on the same wavelength.

"It was like we'd been on panels together for 20 years," Perlmutter said. "I just felt very comfortable with how they looked at things." Many of them talked about the need for fiscal restraint, he said, as a reaction to "the borrow and spend approach that has driven this country deeply into debt." Several also talked about the need for renewable energy sources, such as solar and wind power, to make foreign oil less of a necessity.

Mitchell, who has not joined either of the centrist groups, said the new class agreed that their constituents mainly wanted to make sure Congress spent its time on issues that actually affected their lives, rather than on some of the social questions that absorbed Republicans. "How much time did they spend on Terri Schiavo, for example, rather than trying to do something about immigration or asking oversight questions about Iraq and Katrina?" he asked.

Given that the election was mainly a reaction to the record of the Bush administration and the GOP, it may be no surprise that those are the issues that unite the newly elected Democrats. But that may make it hard for them to convince the public that they won a mandate to do much other than fight Bush's agenda for the next two years.

"The mandate the Democrats got in this election wasn't so much to pursue an agenda of their own. It was more to oppose what the administration has been doing," said Alan I. Abramowitz, a political science professor at Emory University who studies the realignment of political parties. The 2008 presidential election will give Democrats a better chance to present a more positive agenda, he said.

Still, the policy groups that supply ideas to congressional Democrats are already cranking out ambitious lists of legislative proposals. Their argument: Democrats can create a market for their ideas and use it to consolidate their hold on centrist voters.

"We think of it as an opportunity rather than a mandate," said John Podesta, the former Clinton chief of staff who is president of the Center for American Progress. Last week, his group proposed a "first 100 days" agenda full of ideas for energy, education, the environment and consumer protection.

And most of the newly elected Democrats say they don't want to wait until after 2008 to try to tackle the big issues — even if the odds aren't great for solving long-term problems heading into a presidential campaign.

Boyda, for instance, is eager to attack health care problems of small business. "When I talk to small businesses in my district, they can't figure out how they can make health care work in 2007 and 2008," she said. "Whether we can get health care costs under control will determine whether many of these businesses will still be in business in five years."

CAN THE TRUCE HOLD?

The urgency of some issues, such as the Iraq War and the squeeze on the middle class, may help centrist Democrats by muting the usual tension between moderates and liberals in the party on so many issues. The big issues certainly made it easier for Democrats of all stripes to campaign on the same themes this year. And liberal Democrats who might otherwise be suspicious of their centrist colleagues insist they have plenty of common ground on major issues, such as their determination to wind down the war.

Boyda, for example, sounds like more of a populist than a centrist when she talks about the needs of her rural constituents. "The rural economy is being left out of a lot of the gains the national economy has made. They've been thrown a lot of bones over the years, but the huge, massive corporations have been thrown steak dinners," she said. "And now, small businesses and independent farmers are understanding that they've been left out."

But the Democratic unity over such front-burner issues could easily break down over such questions as abortion and gun control — if the Democrats or their supporters let it.

Jason Altmire of Pennsylvania, who defeated Republican Melissa A. Hart in suburban Pittsburgh, says his anti-abortion views allowed him to "get the hot buttons off the table" and talk about Democratic staple issues such as health care, education and Social Security.

He's also a supporter of gun rights, and says he would have to oppose his party if, for example, it tried to reinstate the ban on assault weapons. The same is true of immigration, where he says he would take a harder line than most of his party in favor of enforcing the borders and against a guest worker program. In all of these cases, he says, he needs to be free to break from the party if the issues come up.

"If you knock on someone's door and the first question you get is, 'Are you pro-life?' and you answer wrong, they shut the door and you don't get to talk about health care or education or Social Security," said Altmire, who has joined the New Democrat Coalition.

At the same time, some liberal advocacy groups aren't convinced the party needs to bend over backwards to accommodate anti-abortion Democrats. Most of the newly elected Democrats are supporters of abortion rights who unseated anti-abortion Republicans, said Terry O'Neill, executive director of the National Council of Women's Organizations.

Moreover, she doesn't believe the Democrats needed to run an anti-abortion candidate such as Casey to defeat Republican Sen. Rick Santorum in Pennsylvania. Former state Treasurer Barbara Hafer, a supporter of abortion rights who had planned to run until party officials rallied behind Casey, would have unseated Santorum, too, given the anti-Republican tide, O'Neill said.

So far, though, Altmire likes what he has heard from Pelosi. When he and other newly elected Democrats arrived for orientation, he said, Pelosi told them: "You guys represent your constituents and your districts first. Don't even think about the party." That speech, Altmire said, proved the Democratic leadership understands that "in order to keep the majority, they're going to have to return a lot of us to our seats."

Senate Democratic leaders are trying to play down the importance of the cultural issues as well. Richard J. Durbin of Illinois, who will become Senate majority whip next year, says Casey's opposition to abortion and Tester's support for gun rights are "bumper sticker" issues, and he insists the new Democrats all have similar goals on more meaningful issues such as energy, health care and the minimum wage. "Will we have our differences? Will we split up from time to time? Of course," said Durbin. "But on the core issues, I think we have a real opportunity."

Tester, however, is under no illusions that Democrats have an easy task even if they stay focused on the core issues. "I can't tell you what the solution is" on rising health care costs, he said, and "it's going to be difficult to get everyone on the same page because health care is so complex."

They're going to have to try, Tester says, because "everyone knows the system is broken." But as Tester's health care dilemma illustrates, simply staying focused on the core issues doesn't mean the new majority can agree on the solutions. That will be the ultimate challenge for the Democratic centrists who pledged to make Washington work again — and the one that may determine whether they're still in power in two years.

FOR FURTHER READING

Democrats' agenda, 2006 CQ Weekly, p. 3104; election coverage, p. 2962; study of 2004 presidential vote, 2005 CQ Weekly, p. 878.

Full Metal Diplomacy

As the White House talks about talking with Iran, it makes clear that U.S. military force will remain a prominent backdrop for any negotiations

IMPLIED THREAT: An F/A-18 from the USS *John C. Stennis* in the Arabian Sea could easily reach Iran.

From *CQ Weekly*,
March 5, 2007.

Last week, Secretary of State Condoleezza Rice won a round for diplomacy by announcing that the United States would hold high-level meetings on Iraq later this month with some of its neighbors, including Iran and Syria. In an administration that has stubbornly refused to have anything to do with Tehran, Rice's announcement was a victory of sorts over those in the administration who seemingly would rather fight Iran than converse with it.

Even as Rice set the stage for the highest-level contact between U.S. and Iranian officials in more than two years, two U.S. Navy carrier battle groups held training exercises in the Persian Gulf and the Arabian Sea. Squadrons of F/A-18 warplanes took off and landed from flight decks within easy striking distance of Iran.

In the conduct of critical international affairs, it is common for nations to back up their diplomacy with a credible threat of force. But as the White House takes a tentative step toward negotiations with Iran, the question is whether its military posture — and blustery rhetoric — is louder than its diplomacy. That question applies not only to the upcoming talks on Iraq, but to the most critical area of diplomacy with Iran: the effort to halt its nuclear program.

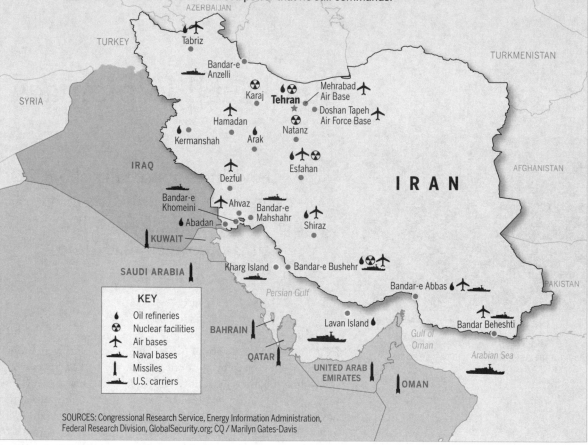

The Potential Battlefield

In a move to convince Iran that the Iraq War has not weakened U.S. resolve, Bush is backing up his nuclear diplomacy with the credible threat of military force. Over the past month, the administration has supplied Arab allies in the Persian Gulf with advanced Patriot missiles to deter any Iranian air attack. Bush also has sent two carrier battle groups to the region as a reminder of the massive air and sea power that he still commands.

KEY
- Oil refineries
- Nuclear facilities
- Air bases
- Naval bases
- Missiles
- U.S. carriers

SOURCES: Congressional Research Service, Energy Information Administration, Federal Research Division, GlobalSecurity.org; CQ / Marilyn Gates-Davis

Ever since last May, the State Department has been saying the United States is willing to negotiate with Iran, as long as the Iranians have first stopped enriching nuclear fuel — material that could be used to make weapons. Until Iran agrees, U.S. diplomats will demand ever tighter economic sanctions against Iran and its leaders, and will continue pressuring U.S. allies in Europe, Asia and the Middle East to do the same.

Eventually, those officials confidently predict, Iran will give in and come to the negotiating table.

But some officials in the administration doubt that diplomatic efforts and economic pressure will bring Iran's rulers around. Only the threat of force, they think, will put iron in the diplomacy and disabuse Tehran of any notion that the Iraq War has debilitated the United States and sapped its resolve.

"The Iranians think we're weak, but we're going to show them they are wrong," is the way Patrick Clawson, an Iran expert at the Washington Institute for Near East Policy, explains the theory.

If the military side of the administration's policy toward Iran appears to have overshadowed the diplomacy, that is because there has been so much rattling of weapons lately. Not only has the Pentagon stationed the

> **❝We have got time. There is no one arguing . . . inside the administration or outside to the effect that we have to exhaust diplomacy in the next few months.❞**

— Undersecretary of State for political affairs
R. Nicholas Burns

two carrier groups in Middle East waters, but military planners have been studying options for strikes against Iran, a country four times the size of Iraq with two and a half times the population.

Administration officials have made a show of supplying advanced Patriot missile batteries to Arab allies in the Gulf region for protection against an Iranian air attack. And they have described in detail how Iran has been supplying weapons to Shiite groups in Iraq and the subsequent steps taken by U.S. troops to round up and interrogate Iranian diplomats and agents suspected of complicity in attacks on U.S. forces.

The risk is that the threatening tone of Bush's Iran policy has created the impression, both at home and abroad, that his real intention is regime change in Tehran. In Iran, President Mahmoud Ahmadinejad has used Bush's threats to strengthen his political standing and ignore U.S. demands. And here at home, some members of Congress and foreign policy experts worry that they are witnessing a replay of the administration's tactics that led to the 2003 invasion of Iraq. For that reason, Democratic leaders are considering legislation that would require Bush to at least seek congressional permission for military action against Iran. *(Congress, p. 150)*

"It looks like Iraq all over again," said Sam Gardiner, a retired U.S. Air Force colonel who taught at the National War College.

Bush and his top aides respond by insisting that they have no intention of attacking Iran. "For the umpteenth time," Defense Secretary Robert M. Gates told a group of reporters on Feb. 15, "we are not looking for an excuse to go to war with Iran." But nine days later, during a visit to Australia, Vice President Dick Cheney warned that "all options are still on the table," a phrase that, especially after the Iraq invasion, has come to mean that military action is still a possibility.

A policy that can't find the right balance between its diplomatic and military missions runs the risk of accomplishing neither. Despite Rice's readiness to engage Iran on the subject of stabilizing Iraq, critics say the centerpiece of the administration's diplomatic strategy — its willingness to talk to Iran, but only after Iran stops trying to build nuclear weapons — has built-in problems. The biggest is that it confines U.S. diplomacy to the issue of disarmament, on which the administration must move in concert with other nations, some of which do not share Bush's agenda. Such divisions would only encourage Iran to continue its nuclear program.

At the same time, there is a very real danger that the administration's military moves to thwart Iran's designs could touch off a new war in the Gulf that might spread along religious alliances to the entire region.

Some Middle East experts say U.S. interests would be better served if the White House toned down its bluster and let its military maneuvers in and around the Persian Gulf speak for themselves. There is no guarantee that such an approach would work, since negotiations also depend on Iran's readiness to talk. And over the past three decades, the United States and Iran have rarely been on speaking terms.

At home, however, Bush must worry that his administration's tough talk might goad Congress into further steps to limit his freedom of action toward Iran. A quieter policy might soften some of those suspicions, experts say.

"We don't need the bluster," said Martin S. Indyk, the director of the Brookings Institution's Saban Center for Middle East Policy. "The bluster is counterproductive."

A NEW CONTAINMENT STRATEGY

The problem of devising an effective policy toward Iran is not a new one. Ever since the 1979 revolution that brought radical Islamic clerics to power, U.S. policy toward Tehran has oscillated between military confrontation and back-room negotiation. In between, the

United States has tried to topple Iranian rulers and at other times sold them weapons. More recently, in 2001, the two countries reached agreement on U.S. military action in neighboring Afghanistan.

The only common thread in all these efforts has been a U.S. desire to contain Iran's influence in the region, and none of the efforts have worked.

Now, the Bush administration faces an Iran that feels strengthened by the U.S. invasions that toppled Saddam Hussein in Iraq and the Taliban in Afghanistan — the two principal threats on its borders. Moreover, Iran's Ahmadinejad regards the United States, exhausted after four years of combat in Iraq, as a spent force that will eventually withdraw, leaving Iran to assert its historic role as the region's major power.

Iran has already assumed a greater role with its support for Hezbollah in Lebanon, which fought Israel to a standstill in a month-long war last summer, and its backing for Hamas, which won parliamentary elections in the Palestinian territories in January 2006. But the greatest threat posed by Iran to the region is its nuclear program, which the United States charges is aimed at producing nuclear weapons but which Iran says is meant only to produce nuclear energy.

Against that backdrop of challenges, the administration has come up with a new containment strategy that combines diplomacy and military threat to deny Iran a nuclear weapons capability, diminish Tehran's support for terrorists groups such as Hezbollah and Hamas, and prevent Iran from supplying sophisticated explosives to Iraqi insurgents who have been using them to deadly effect against U.S. forces there.

Because of the long history of distrust and animosity between the United States and Iran, as well as Iran's support for terrorism, administration officials say they have no choice but to pursue a strategy that has a threat of force as its underpinning. In addition to Arab allies, the administration must protect U.S. troops in Iraq who have been targeted by insurgents using sophisticated bombs supplied by Iran, officials say.

"We have a fundamental responsibility to protect American soldiers," R. Nicholas Burns, the undersecretary of State for political affairs and the State Department's point man on Iran, said at a Feb. 14 appearance at the Brookings Institution. "That message has gone out to the Iranians, and we hope they will hear that message."

> **"We worked with the European community and the United Nations to put together a set of policies to persuade the Iranians to give up their [nuclear] aspirations and resolve the matter peacefully, and that is still our preference. But I've also made the point, and the president has made the point, that all options are on the table."**
>
> — Vice President Dick Cheney

The central focus of the administration's diplomatic track has been to persuade Iran to abandon its nuclear program. In this regard, the White House has shown some flexibility. Bush had insisted that Iran permanently and verifiably abandon its nuclear program before any talks could take place. But in May of last year, Rice announced that a coalition consisting of the five permanent members of the U.N. Security Council, plus Germany, would be prepared to negotiate with Iran on a broad range of issues as long as Tehran temporarily suspended its uranium enrichment activities during the negotiations.

Iran rejected the offer, citing its right to enrich uranium for peaceful purposes under the 1970 Treaty for the Non-Proliferation of Nuclear Weapons. In response, U.S. diplomats focused their efforts on isolating Iran. In December, the U.N. Security Council approved sanctions against Iran that banned the import or export of materials and technology used in uranium enrichment, reprocessing and ballistic missiles. The sanctions also froze the assets of a dozen Iranians and 10 companies said to be involved in nuclear and ballistic missile programs.

The administration had sought a much tougher resolution, including a travel ban on Iranian officials involved in nuclear activities and sanctions against Iran's nuclear installation at Bushehr, which Russia is helping to build. So the administration took a number of unilateral steps against Iran, which included prohibiting it from doing business in U.S. dollars and persuading several European and Asian banks to stop lending Iran money.

Burns said the sanctions are beginning to bite. "The Iranians are telling people in Japan, Europe and the Arab world that they are worried about this," he said. "So that is an effective measure we have taken."

Some policy experts praise the administration's diplomacy. "It's "deft, and it's skillful," said Clawson of the Washington Institute for Near East Policy. "We're having an effect."

After Tehran failed to comply with a U.N. deadline of Feb. 21 to halt its nuclear program, the White House called for a new resolution to tighten the sanctions, including a ban on travel and blocking the financial transactions of senior Iranian officials.

U.S. officials acknowledge that drafting the next round of sanctions won't be easy. Russia has already indicated that it may balk at stricter measures, particularly any that target its investments in Iran, such as the nuclear power plant at Bushehr.

But administration officials say they will be patient. "We have got time," Burns said. "There is no one arguing that I know of inside the administration or outside to the effect that we have to exhaust diplomacy in the next few months."

TRYING TO BE HEARD

Those who want a muscular approach to Iran think that too much delay might be dangerous. For instance, supporters of Israel warn that Iran's government is rapidly reaching the point where it will have the knowledge and capacity to build nuclear weapons and the missiles to deliver them — a clear threat in the region. And then there is Cheney, who has never softened his message about the possibility of a U.S. military move against Iran.

"We worked with the European community and the United Nations to put together a set of policies to persuade the Iranians to give up their [nuclear] aspirations and resolve the matter peacefully, and that is still our preference," Cheney said on Feb. 24. "But I've also made the point, and the president has made the point, that all options are on the table."

Bush, Cheney and other administration officials have been warning of possible military action against Iran for more than a year now. But Cheney's latest warning is the first since Bush sent the two carrier battle groups to the Gulf, began distributing Patriot missiles to Arab allies and started cracking down on Iranian agents inside Iraq. Foreign policy experts say administration hard-liners are trying to make sure their concerns are heard above the diplomacy of those such as Burns and Rice.

"These guys always think that force is the right answer," said Kenneth M. Pollack, an Iran specialist on the National Security Council during the Clinton administration.

To build their case for a harder-edged approach to Iran, Cheney and those with similar views emphasize the Iranian activities that they say prompted the administration's military steps so far. In recent interviews and public appearances, the vice president has focused on Iran's sponsorship of terrorist groups such as Hezbollah and Hamas, its alleged supplying of explosives to Iraqi insurgents and the inflammatory statements by Ahmadinejad, who has questioned whether the Holocaust ever occurred and has called for Israel to be wiped off the map.

Meanwhile, officials from the White House, the Pentagon, and the Treasury and State departments are coordinating additional plans to counter the perceived Iranian threat. According to administration officials, they include the possibility of sending a third carrier battle group to the region and further economic sanctions. The administration has also launched a campaign to publicize Tehran's role in supporting terrorism as a way to further isolate the country diplomatically and economically.

Though these officials say the aim of this policy initiative is to contain Iran's ambitions in the region, some experts suspect that administration hard-liners quietly hope that such moves might goad Iran into a military confrontation with the United States.

"It's entirely possible that the hard-liners want to provoke Iran into taking the first swing, giving us the excuse

Preparing for the Worst on Iran

Democratic congressional leaders are reluctant to limit President Bush's options for dealing with Iran, given the strategic and political risks, but they want him to ask permission before taking any military action.

What form that insistence might take has not been finally settled, and it's not clear what course Democrats might pursue in order to influence Bush's Iran policy. Congress has been focused on Iraq and the administration's troop increase there, and the potential for a confrontation with Iran has arisen only recently.

"Iraq is a reality. Iran is a possibility," said Larry Diamond, an authority on foreign policy with experience in the region. He is a senior fellow at the Hoover Institution in California.

House Speaker Nancy Pelosi of California and her close ally, John P. Murtha of Pennsylvania, chairman of the Appropriations Defense Subcommittee, are said to favor adding a provision to the fiscal 2007 supplemental spending bill that would require the president to seek Congress' authorization before using force against Iran. Democrats working on the bill have that in their initial package. The language would be similar to resolutions introduced by two liberals and opponents of the Iraq War: Rep. Peter A. DeFazio, an Oregon Democrat, and Sen. Bernard Sanders, an independent from Vermont.

"I think that there would be absolute outrage," Sanders said, "if we woke up one day and learned suddenly that the president had attacked Iran without getting permission from the Congress."

DeFazio said he did not think a resolution alone would stop Bush if he thought he already had the authority to take military action. Presidents have a number of times committed troops on their own and have refused to recognize the constitutionality of the 1973 War Powers Resolution that limited a president's ability to wage war without a congressional declaration. In Bush's case, DeFazio said, "Hopefully with some push back from Congress, they might reconsider" a war stance.

In the Senate, Majority Leader Harry Reid of Nevada also has said Bush should have to seek congressional approval for war with Iran. So, too, has the chairman of the Foreign Relations Committee, Democrat Joseph R. Biden Jr. of Delaware.

Reid has no current plans for a resolution on the subject, though he has asked committees to analyze what the administration is doing and saying on Iran, and he has been pushing the White House to finish a National Intelligence Estimate on Iran, a report that is overdue. An aide to Biden said the senator has doubts about the wisdom of a resolution, because if Congress tells Bush he must ask permission to take military action against Iran, that in itself might imply that Bush already has authority to use force.

The Senate probably will have to debate the question, if only over a floor amendment to the supplemental spending bill. Freshman Democrat Jim Webb of Virginia, a member of the Armed Services Committee, said last week that the bill should prohibit, with some exceptions, the use of funds "for unilateral military action against Iran" without prior congressional approval.

If Congress passed such a provision on the spending bill, Bush would have to sign or veto it, running a political risk either way. A veto would defy Congress. If he signed it and later went to war, Diamond said, Congress should impeach him.

Tough Questions; Few Answers

Though almost six in 10 Americans lack confidence in Bush to handle the current tensions with Iran, according to a recent poll by ABC News and The Washington Post, Democrats are approaching the issue cautiously.

The options for Congress include imposing tighter sanctions on Iran to dissuade it from continuing its nuclear program; pressure on the administration to pursue diplomacy; oversight hearings to scrutinize administration claims about the scope of the threat; and legislative language that might slow a drive to war.

Democrats already are holding hearings on Iran, and the schedule will doubtless get more crowded over the next month as lawmakers weigh in. But legislative action is doubtful beyond the resolution requiring Bush to seek approval for military action.

Even some Republicans might support such a resolution, but that's as far as it goes. As Rep. Peter Hoekstra, a Michigan Republican and a hardliner on Iran, said, "I think Congress needs to be very, very careful about the limitations that we put on the executive branch or trying on a tactical basis to conduct foreign policy."

Some Democrats, in fact, do not want to restrict at all the president's option to attack. Lawmakers pursuing the resolution of the use of force make clear that they are not necessarily opposing military action against Iran, only that

Bush should seek their approval first if he considers using force.

If that situation arose, Congress would probably demand more information from Bush, and analyze it more closely, than it did before authorizing military action against Iraq in 2002. That was an election year, Bush was at the height of his power, and he was able to apply pressure on Democrats to back a war resolution. Many did.

Stung by misleading or erroneous intelligence in the lead-up to the Iraq War, the Intelligence and Armed Services committees, now run by Democrats, have turned their attention to intelligence on Iran.

The chairman of the House Intelligence Committee, Silvestre Reyes of Texas, said he found it "more than a little upsetting" that the Pentagon held a background briefing with reporters on Iranian weapons found in Iraq before his committee was even briefed.

"I believe we have to be very cautious about accepting any hyped up or ginned up faulty intelligence as it pertains to Iran, because we don't want a repetition of Iraq," Reyes said.

His Senate counterpart, Democrat John D. Rockefeller IV of West Virginia, together with ranking Republican Christopher S. Bond of Missouri, have tried without success to obtain from the administration its review of the intelligence work used to inform assessments about the threat of Iran. Rockefeller has formed a study group specifically to examine Iran intelligence; so far, he says, it looks like the quality of the analysis is better than it has been on Iraq, but that intelligence collection is slower than it should be.

But Rockefeller says he's not as worried about the prospect of war with Iran as he was a few weeks ago when he publicly warned about a potential conflict. He thinks the administration has wisely ratcheted down its rhetoric.

As skeptical as Democrats and some Republicans are of Bush's policies on Iraq and Iran, they have to weigh the political and policy consequences of trying to influence Bush's course and intervening to halt any military action.

Most military and foreign policy experts predict a war with Iran could be disastrous when compared with Iraq. The large antiwar contingent of the Democratic Party is growing more nervous by the day about the threat of a new Middle East conflict, and if war broke out, Democrats might share the blame for it.

However, even with the support of the public, Democrats are wary of challenging Bush and being attacked, either by the White House or future election opponents, as being weak on national security and perhaps encouraging U.S. enemies. White House spokesman Tony Snow speculated in an interview with CNN on Feb. 18 that some lawmakers who have said the administration is laying the groundwork for a war with Iran "maybe are trying to protect Iran."

The Iraq War overshadows the debate, though, and Democrats overwhelmingly oppose the Iraq War and expect Congress to take a skeptical approach to Bush's policy on Iran. In a story in The Nation, a magazine with influence among liberals, Scott Ritter, the former Iraq weapons inspector who is now working on a book about Iran, warned that Democrats in Congress would share the blame if the Bush administration attacked Iran. "Congress," he said in an interview, "postured itself to be the party of change, rather than stay the course. If we go to Iran, unlike in the lead-up to the war in Iraq, it will be Congress that will be held accountable."

Ruling Nothing Out

Even some members of Congress who have said they want to avoid war with Iran have refused to rule it out as an option. They are more worried about the prospect of an Iran with nuclear weapons that it could use to attack Israel and other U.S. allies. Groups such as the American Israel Public Affairs Committee have emphasized the threat that Iran's rulers pose in the region. "It is our hope," AIPAC spokesman Josh Block said, "that Congress and the administration will work together to maintain maximum flexibility and maximum pressure to prevent Iran from developing nuclear weapons."

New York Sen. Hillary Rodham Clinton, a Democratic presidential candidate, favors the use of tighter sanctions to bring Iran into negotiations. But "no option can be taken off the table," she said. In January, she told an audience at Princeton, "Let's be clear about the threat we face now: A nuclear Iran is a danger to Israel, to its neighbors and beyond."

Most Democrats prefer to stick with sanctions and other diplomatic measures and hope the chance of a war diminishes. One senior Democratic aide said it would be worth waiting to see whether the U.S. talks with Iran and Syria later this month over the situation in Iraq produce any results. The talks involve a number of countries in the Middle East and Europe along with international organizations.

Lawmakers like Webb worry that a war might start by accident, perhaps because of the U.S. naval maneuvers under way in the Persian Gulf. If Iran attacked U.S. forces in such a scenario, Congress could be even more hard-pressed to resist signing off on an administration return of fire.

MAKING A CASE: At a press conference on February 14, 2007, in Baghdad, evidence gathered by the U.S. military is displayed. The evidence is intended to support the case that Iran is supplying militant Iraqis who are fighting American forces.

to go to war," said Pollack, now the director of research at the Brookings Institution's Saban Center.

In the event of such an Iranian reaction, Pollack said, hard-liners in the administration would urge Bush to respond with a devastating campaign of air and naval strikes on Iran's military and nuclear installations.

"Normally, I don't like conspiracy theories," Pollack added. "But I believe in this one."

THE RISKS OF FAILURE

To hear Burns tell it, it is only a matter of time before the U.S. strategy of hard-nosed diplomacy and military threat forces Iran to negotiate an end to its nuclear program.

"We are convinced," he said, "that sooner or later the cost to Iran of its isolation are going to be so profoundly important to them, destructive to their economic potential, that they are going to have to come to the negotiating table."

Iranians are already restless about their economy. After international sanctions took effect, a majority of the 290 members of Iran's parliament, called the Majlis, signed a letter criticizing Ahmadinejad's handling of economic affairs. Ahmadinejad has also been criticized by some Iranian politicians for hosting a conference last year of people who deny that the Holocaust took place. The meeting attracted white supremacists such as former Ku Klux Klan leader David Duke.

But there is little evidence that U.S. moves have weakened the hard-line Ahmadinejad's grip on power.

"He remains popular," J. Michael McConnell, the new director of national intelligence, told the Senate Armed Services Committee on Feb. 27. "He has staffed the Cabinet and those around him with hard-liners. The economy is strong because of the oil revenues."

With oil almost $60 a barrel, Iran's earnings create other problems for the administration's diplomatic strategy. China, a permanent member of the U.N. Security Council with a veto over any further sanctions, depends on Iran for 11 percent of its oil. And Iran is tapping those revenues to pay billions of dollars to Russia — another permanent Security Council member — for civilian nuclear technology and advanced conventional arms.

Despite administration assurances that the Security Council will eventually agree on tightened sanctions, Bush must now tread carefully or risk the refusal of Russia and China to go along with such measures. At the same time, hard-liners warn that anemic sanctions will not prevent Iran from developing nuclear weapons.

"Current policy . . . will not by itself lead the Iranians to abandon their nuclear weapons program," Richard Perle, a former director of the Defense Policy Board Advisory Committee, told a security conference in Israel in January. "If we continue to do what we are doing, Iran will become a nuclear weapons state."

On the military front, administration hard-liners run the risk of provoking the kind of war that neither side wants.

Gary G. Sick, a former National Security Council expert on Iran and now a professor at Columbia University, said the White House is kidding itself if it thinks it can incite an Iranian attack and then subdue the country with a quick campaign of air strikes.

Such a move, he says, would strengthen the Ahmadinejad government and provoke Iranian retaliation against the United States somewhere else, most likely in Iraq. Other experts agree that Iranian attacks inevitably would lead to a U.S. response.

"And from there, you can end up in an escalatory cycle that results in the end in all-out conflict," said Indyk, a former Middle East adviser on President Bill Clinton's National Security Council.

NO WAY OUT

Shortly after the U.S. invasion of Iraq in 2003, Washington was abuzz with reports that Iran had quietly offered the administration a so-called "grand bargain": If the United States would lift its sanctions and stop supporting the Mujahedeen al Khalq, an Iranian opposition group with bases in Iraq, then the Iranian government would end its military support for Hezbollah and Hamas and help the United States stabilize Iraq. Former U.S. officials in touch with Iranian diplomats say Tehran also offered to be more open with the details of its nuclear program.

Lawrence Wilkerson, the chief of staff to then-Secretary of State Colin L. Powell, recalls that the Iranian overture came in a letter delivered by a Swiss diplomat.

"We thought it was a very propitious moment," Wilkerson told the BBC in January. "But as soon as it got to the White House, and as soon as it got to the vice president's office, the old mantra of 'we don't talk to evil' reasserted itself." Nothing further happened.

The episode illustrates another fact about the tortured history of U.S.-Iranian relations over the past three decades: When one side has been ready to talk, the other side has not. That was true during Clinton's second term, when Iran spurned a U.S. offer to negotiate, having concluded that the Republican election victories in 1994 left Clinton too weak to make a deal. In 2003, it was the Iranians who were ready to talk, worried about the U.S. military presence on their borders.

"At that particular moment, our influence was at its high point," said Indyk. "And that, of course, was the moment when we should have engaged them — when they were weak and we were strong."

That moment passed. Today, both sides say they are willing to negotiate, and the upcoming multination talks on stabilizing Iraq offer the possibility of a wider diplomatic opening. But on the principal issue separating the two sides — suspension of Iran's nuclear program — Tehran continues to resist the administration's condition to begin talks.

In the debate over Bush's Iran policy, some experts argue that the administration's nuclear diplomacy doesn't begin to address the major political and strategic issues that divide the two countries, which include Iran's role in the Persian Gulf and its widening influence in the region through its support of Hezbollah and Hamas.

As hard as it would be for this administration to swallow, the best policy option, these experts suggest, is a strategy of diplomatic détente in which the United States would acknowledge Iran's emergence as a major power player in the Persian Gulf and seek ways to co-exist with it.

In an article in the current issue of Foreign Affairs, Ray Takeyh, a senior fellow at the Council on Foreign Relations and an expert on Iran, suggests an initial negotiation whose aim would be normalizing ties, including a timetable for the resumption of diplomatic relations, the phasing out of U.S. sanctions and the return of Iran's assets that have been frozen. A successful negotiation, he says, would go a long way toward re-establishing good will between Washington and Tehran and facilitating productive negotiations on the nuclear and regional issues.

Administration officials say the United States would be making a grave error if it were to normalize relations with Iran before resolving the nuclear issue. They note that under such an agreement, Tehran could conclude that Washington had tacitly accepted its nuclear program and turned its back on U.N. Security Council resolutions condemning Iran's uranium enrichment. For better or worse, they say, the United States must first resolve the nuclear issue one way or another.

Indyk suggests that the administration could help clear up some of the confusion over its Iran policy by simply turning down the volume on its threatening state-ments. Such threats, he says, are unnecessary and only serve to strengthen Ahmadinejad, who is refusing to negotiate, and to sideline Iranian pragmatists who would like to engage the Americans.

"The Iranians will understand the message of a second carrier battle group very clearly," he said. "They'll understand it even better if there's a third there. They'll understand the message of increased sanctions. We don't need to be saber rattling at the same time. We make a lot of people nervous about what our real intentions are."

But even with a lower volume, mixing diplomacy and the threat of force might not work. And at that point, the administration will be faced with a stark choice.

"If the diplomacy doesn't work," Indyk said, "then you're left with the choice of either using the force or having your bluff called." Perhaps it is no wonder, then, that for now the administration prefers its mixed messages to the consequences of clarity.

FOR FURTHER READING

Congressional opposition to Bush's troop increase, p. 79; details of Bush surge plan, p. 80. Iran sanctions, 2007 CQ Weekly, p. 552; Middle East diplomacy, p. 442.

AP Images / The Roanoke Times / Matt Gentry

CLASSMATES GRIEVE: Thousands attend a candle-light vigil on the Virginia Tech campus for 32 students and faculty members gunned down on April 16 by 23-year-old Cho Seung Hui.

Gun Control's Strategy Shift

Lobbyists hope an NRA-style grass-roots approach can reverse a decade of sobering losses

Within days of the shootings in 1999 at Columbine High School in Colorado, members of Congress responded with new gun control measures, including child safety locks and background checks at gun shows. Nothing was enacted, but the debate took place.

Now, precisely eight years later, as the nation struggles to come to terms with the even deadlier shootings at Virginia Tech in Blacksburg, Va., gun control is not even on the agenda in Washington, beyond a bill to ensure that background records for gun purchases are complete and up to date.

There are a number of reasons for this, including the power of the National Rifle Association and divisions in the Democratic party. But the main result is that gun control advocates have adopted a new strategy of disciplined, incremental initiatives, building grass-roots support and momentum from the state level up.

They are, in fact, using much the same strategy as the NRA.

Should the climate suddenly change and the public demand federal action, the gun control groups would respond and push for legislation, such as banning the kind of high-capacity ammunition magazines that Seung-Hui Cho used to kill 32 people and himself at Virginia Tech.

But the public has long been of two minds on gun control. Before grass-roots groups pour their limited resources into another

From *CQ Weekly*, April 23, 2007.

A Patchwork of Handgun Laws

Handguns are easy to buy and carry concealed in most states. Thirteen require a permit or license for purchases; just four demand registration. Only the District of Columbia bans acquisitions. Most states have a "shall issue" policy to grant concealed-weapon permits to anyone meeting basic criteria; eight leave it to police discretion with a "may issue" rule. Only Illinois, Wisconsin and D.C. ban the practice.

Required to buy a handgun

*Registration required in Chicago

■ License or permit and registration (4) □ License or permit (13) □ No requirement (34)

Required to carry a concealed handgun

■ Banned (2) ■ "May-issue" permit (8) □ "Shall-issue" permit (38) □ No permit required (2)

SOURCES: National Rifle Association, Wisconsin Legislative Reference Bureau; CQ / Jamey Fry

against the trade in illegal guns, a top concern of the gun control movement.

"We've got to put our toe in the water first, before we go willy-nilly after something," he said. "In the past, we just charged ahead. We need to be smarter."

In some cases, the movement's successes were later weakened or rescinded. The 1994 ban on assault weapons, which was prompted by high-profile cases including a schoolyard shooting in Stockton, Calif., and the killing of two people on the highway near CIA headquarters in northern Virginia, was allowed to expire in 2004.

National and state gun control groups did a lot of soul-searching and strategizing after losing the assault weapons law, a low point that revealed fissures among state and national groups. They decided to refocus their energy on an issue where they might build a broad consensus: fighting the traffic in illegal guns. They have managed to organize the movement around that goal, with an alliance of mayors.

That issue does not speak directly to the outrage over the Virginia Tech shootings, since authorities say the killer bought his guns from licensed dealers, not on the street. But they intend to keep working it hard. Their immediate target at the federal level is to get rid of legislative language added year after year to appropriations bills that restricts the release of federal trace data on guns used in crimes, something mayors say undercuts the ability of law enforcement agencies to fight the flow of illegal guns that fuels violence on their streets.

One initiative linked to the latest shootings is stronger background checks with more complete data that might have prevented Cho, who had documented instances of mental illness, from buying two handguns.

To get such a bill passed, though, sponsors say they would probably need the acquiescence of the NRA.

THE 'THIRD RAIL'

The political realities in Washington are stacked against activists like Miller. Many Democrats in Washington have concluded that the gun issue is a divisive one that their party needs to avoid.

"There's a widespread perception among Democrats that guns are the third rail," said Kristen Goss, a political scientist at North Carolina's Duke University who has

campaign, they need to be sure that it really has a chance of success, according to Bryan Miller, executive director of Cease Fire NJ, one of the groups leading a campaign

written about the trouble gun control advocates have had building a widespread movement.

The circumstances of the Democrats' return to power last fall reinforced that notion. As Democratic Rep. Jim Moran of Virginia, an advocate of stricter gun control, put it, "it has not gone unnoticed" by Democrats that staying away from the gun issue may have been one of the factors behind their return to power last fall. The party made headway in rural and conservative districts and states previously held by Republicans.

Public opinion actually leans in favor of tougher gun regulation. But in an analysis last week, the Pew Research Center for the People & the Press pointed out that polls taken before the Blacksburg shooting showed that the public has been cooling on stricter gun laws, even as the image of the NRA has been improving.

The percentage of people telling the Gallup Poll that they favor stricter laws on gun sales went from 78 percent in 1990 to a low of 51 percent in 2002. It's been mostly in the mid-50s since. Given a choice between new laws or stricter enforcement of existing laws, 53 percent of respondents last fall chose enforcement.

At the same time, Pew's nationwide polling showed that the percentage of people holding a favorable view of the NRA rose from 44 percent in 1995 to 52 percent this past January.

Even the names gun control groups have adopted speak to the limits of the debate: They have dropped "gun control," fearing it made the public think they were out to take guns from law-abiding people. North Carolinians for Gun Control, for example, has become North Carolinians Against Gun Violence.

In the campaign against illegal guns, activists and mayors also are careful to say that their aim is crime control, not gun control — and being able to frame the issue that way is one of the big reasons advocates involved in the campaign see it as politically viable.

CHECKING BACKGROUNDS

But the main question raised by the shootings in Blacksburg is how a mentally disturbed young man was able to buy two lethal handguns.

A leading gun control advocate in Congress, Democratic Rep. Carolyn McCarthy of New York, is focusing on efforts to improve the FBI's National Instant

Criminal Background Check System, which gun dealers use to search for information that would disqualify a person from buying a handgun. The instant check replaced a five-day waiting period required by the 1993 Brady handgun law.

McCarthy's bill passed the House in 2002 but died in the Senate.

The Virginia Tech shootings add new urgency to the legislation, McCarthy says, because a more complete background check system could have caught the fact that a judge had earlier found Cho mentally ill, which should have disqualified him from buying a handgun. McCarthy's bill aims to ensure that such records are quickly added to the nationwide electronic system, rather than sitting in a courthouse file someplace.

"I think it stands an excellent chance of getting passed, and it would save lives," she said.

She's been working with Democratic Rep. John Dingell, an ally of the NRA, to convince the gun rights group to at least stand aside and let the legislation through. The two have worked together on the bill for some years. McCarthy said. Speaker Nancy Pelosi earlier this week expressed support for strengthening background checks.

So far, Democratic leaders haven't publicly committed to anything, though. Pelosi spokesman Nadeam Elshami said the leaders are weighing their options. "Speaker Pelosi appreciates Congresswoman McCarthy's commitment to make our country safer," Elshami said. "House leaders are taking a closer look at this and other proposals to determine the best legislative way forward."

An NRA spokesman declined to comment on the legislation.

Before the Virginia Tech shootings, McCarthy also introduced a bill that would restrict large-capacity magazines. But she doesn't think she would have the votes to get it passed, so she's not trying.

BETTER COORDINATION

One piece of potentially encouraging news for gun control advocates is that their movement is showing some signs of new unity.

McCarthy, who was frustrated with fractiousness among the groups during efforts to extend the assault weapons ban in 2004, said "the smarter leaders" in the movement are telling groups to stay focused and stop fighting among themselves.

"In other words, let's try to use the model followed by the NRA," she said.

The Brady Campaign recently named a new president, Paul Helmke, and having a fresh face at that large national group has helped open new lines of communication among national and state organizations, activists say. The campaign against illegal guns has galvanized the groups, too.

But what direction they should push after the Virginia Tech shootings is less clear.

There was widespread agreement that strengthening the background checks would be a good thing — and that groups ought to stay open to other legislative initiatives that seem necessary and possible as the facts come in from Blacksburg.

But resources are limited, and the movement can't afford to react precipitously and get scattered across multiple fights, said Thomas Mannard, president of States United to Prevent Gun Violence. It has to pick carefully.

"If you're not focused on one or two things, you're spread all over the place," Mannard said. "You're not as effective as you could be."

Gun control advocates also have reason to be wary of putting Democrats — or friendly Republicans for that matter — in a political bind. The new Democratic Congress, built in large measure on seats won in conservative, pro-gun country, may not be embracing their cause, but it still looks friendlier than the previous Republican majorities, which actively worked for the NRA's agenda.

Gun control groups don't buy the idea that their agenda is a losing proposition for Democrats, said Josh Horwitz, executive director of the Coalition to Stop Gun Violence. But party leaders do, and activists are "not interested in putting our friends in a position that would hurt them," he said.

Particularly with new members, groups can't build credibility and support for their issues by asking for big steps immediately, Horwitz said. The goal at first needs to be "baby steps."

Still, even those who see the wisdom of such counsel say they are frustrated and disheartened by it. "To be offering these small, incremental steps" — like the effort to roll back the restrictions on gun trace data at the federal level — "is what we've been reduced to by the power of the gun lobby," said Lisa Price, executive director of North Carolinians Against Gun Violence and the wife of Democratic Rep. David E. Price.

"Unless there's strong congressional and presidential leadership on this issue — and a demand from the public — I don't think the gun violence prevention movement will accomplish very much," she said. "Or even try."

FOR FURTHER READING

Background check bill is HR 297; ban on large-capacity magazines is HR 1859; mayors focus on illegal guns, 2006 CQ Weekly, p. 1294; assault weapons ban (PL 103-322), 1994 Almanac, p. 276; Brady law (PL 103-159), 1993 Almanac, p. 300.

Wounded Vets, Broken System

America's injured servicemembers are coming home to face another battle: with red tape, delays and a VA ill-prepared to handle a long war's crushing caseload

CQ / Scott J. Ferrell

FILING CLAIMS: Adam Kave, 23, who was discharged from the Air Force after serving in Iraq, Kuwait and Uzbekistan, recently sought help from the Disabled American Veterans to file a claim for VA compensation for a personality disorder.

From *CQ Weekly,* April 30, 2007.

The downtown Washington offices of Disabled American Veterans hummed with activity on a recent weekday as four staff counselors helped ex-servicemembers navigate the bureaucracy of the Department of Veterans Affairs.

James Mack, a stern-looking veteran of the first Gulf War, welcomed recent returnees from the conflicts in Iraq and Afghanistan by handing them copies of VA Form 21-526 — a two-sided, 13-page application for benefits — then tearing out the first four pages of fine-print instructions.

"For folks who just want to know what they're entitled to, that's a little bit too much information," said Mack, who patiently guided some veterans through questions about service-related injuries and the care they received, and signed others up for a biweekly class on veterans' benefits that he teaches Monday nights. It is fully subscribed until July.

Elsewhere in the office, workers tracked the progress of hundreds of appeals filed by veterans in response to VA denials, stepping around piles of inch-thick files detailing the particulars of each case

CQ / Scott J. Ferrell

LENDING A HAND: Mack of the Disabled American Veterans, with paperwork from hundreds of appeals of denied claims, helps returning veterans from Iraq and Afghanistan navigate the VA's bureaucracy.

that threatened to inundate their cubicles. Phones constantly rang with big and small requests. One frantic ex-servicemember could not find the room in VA headquarters where he was supposed to participate in a teleconference about his appeal. By the time Mack sorted out the matter and provided directions, the hearing had been postponed. Mack then spent an hour rescheduling the hearing and briefing the veteran on what to expect.

Disabled veterans of the Iraq War already have braved insurgent attacks and the threat of improvised explosive devices. But few are prepared for the nerve-wracking experience of dealing with the VA system. The government is trying to hack away at a backlog of more than 405,500 disability claims while marshaling more injured soldiers through its bureaucracy. It now takes an average of 177 days for a disabled soldier to get a VA claim processed — nearly double the 89.5-day wait civilians

face in a private health-insurance system widely acknowledged to be underperforming. And with recent revelations about neglect of care at the Army's flagship Walter Reed Medical Center, the political pressure is mounting for the government to improve its performance.

But there aren't many signs that the crush is dissipating at critical junctures like the Disabled American Veterans office and similar facilities run by nearly a dozen veterans' service groups. Academic experts and veterans' advocates say the VA is facing unprecedented stresses due to the conflicts in Iraq and Afghanistan and is ill-equipped to handle an influx of returning soldiers that would come from any troop withdrawal in Iraq.

Beyond the paperwork hassles and delays, there are serious gaps in medical care, especially for treating traumatic brain injuries and psychological problems that have arisen from extended deployments and stressful ground warfare, according to health professionals and veterans' groups.

"We have not paid careful enough attention, or devoted sufficient resources, to planning for how to take care of these men and women who have served the nation," said Linda Bilmes, a lecturer in public policy at Harvard University's John F. Kennedy School of Government who has studied the long-term costs of caring for veterans.

Congress, rattled by the problems at Walter Reed and public concern over returning servicemembers, is pledging to spend considerably more on veterans' programs. The House's 2008 budget resolution would increase the budget for VA health care and claims processing by $6.6 billion over 2007 levels. Congress in February included $3.6 billion for veterans' programs in a budget package to fund much of the government for the remainder of the fiscal year. A supplemental spending bill cleared April 26 would give the department $1.8 billion more.

But experts such as Bilmes warn that the extra money will do little good unless Congress and the VA fix deep-rooted problems in the way the government processes disability claims, screens veterans for health problems and handles appeals for denied benefits. These problems will loom over Congress for the rest of the session as the House and Senate debate the direction of the war and how to provide for what a bipartisan majority have come to call "wounded warriors."

"All of the things we're seeing — the problems at Walter Reed, people getting lost in the process — can all relate back to the fact that the VA and the Department of Defense did not plan for a long war and the impacts of that," said Democratic Sen. Patty Murray of Washington, a member of the chamber's Veterans' Affairs Committee and the Appropriations subcommittee that oversees the VA. "If I was sitting in the VA, I'd be in the president's face all the time, saying we have to deal with these huge issues and I want resources to educate people."

The Bush administration says it is addressing the most serious concerns. An interagency task force headed by VA Secretary Jim Nicholson released recommendations April 24 that include adding case managers to help guide troops and their families through the system and improving the process for handing off medical records when an active-duty soldier is discharged and enters the VA's network.

"The federal government must be responsive and efficient in delivering our benefits and services to these heroes," Nicholson said in announcing the recommendations. "They should not have to fight bureaucratic red tape for benefits earned by their courageous service."

Some of the problems are due to the unique nature of the Iraq and Afghanistan conflicts. Better battlefield care has allowed more servicemembers to survive roadside bombs, suicide attacks, rocket-propelled grenades and other incidents that probably would have killed soldiers in past conflicts. But many are returning home with complicated, sometimes catastrophic wounds that require much more elaborate treatment and rehabilitation.

The government has not prepared itself for such demands. Harvard's Bilmes notes that while the VA has steadfastly maintained that it can cope, the agency ran out of money to provide health care for the past two years and had to submit emergency budget requests to Congress for $2 billion in fiscal 2006 and $1 billion in 2005. A Government Accountability Office analysis of the shortfalls concluded that the VA was basing its cost projections on 2002 data that was generated before the war in Iraq began.

FLAWED CLAIMS PROCESS

The concern about the VA goes beyond just how it calculates costs to how efficiently it provides veterans with their benefits. Experts are particularly worried about the claims process that returning soldiers must confront to

"We have not paid careful enough attention, or devoted sufficient resources, to planning for how to take care of these men and women who have served the nation."

— Linda Bilmes, Harvard University

qualify for disability payments — a system that has been widely criticized for delays and excessive bureaucracy.

Servicemembers file claims in one of 57 regional offices belonging to the Veterans Benefits Administration, a branch of the VA that assesses service-related injuries on a sliding scale from 0 percent to 100 percent in 10 percent increments. Veterans must submit to medical evaluations for each condition they are claiming. If a claim is rejected, the veteran can appeal to a VA board that renders a decision or sends the case back to the regional office.

Government audits have uncovered fundamental flaws in the process. The GAO last March reported that even though medical problems that veterans report are becoming more complex — including those based on environmental risks, infectious diseases and brain injuries — the VA's criteria for disability decisions continue to be based on estimates made in 1945 about how service-connected impairments could affect the average individual's ability to perform manual labor.

The GAO also found that the Veterans Benefits Administration has to wait a year or longer to obtain military records to verify some claims of post-traumatic stress disorder. Auditors suggested that the VA try using an electronic library of medical records instead of submitting requests to the Army and Joint Services Records Research Center. The VA responded that it would study the matter.

Piecemeal efforts to streamline claims processing in the regional offices have left big disparities in service, with significant delays in some cities. The advocacy group Amvets found that 63 percent of claims filed at the VA's Washington, D.C., office took six months or longer to resolve. By contrast, 7 percent or fewer claims filed in offices in Providence, R.I., Fargo, N.D. and Boise, Idaho, took that long.

The VA's reliance on medical checkups to verify claims is adding to the bureaucratic headaches by lengthening waiting times at VA medical centers around the country and delaying some patients from getting access to specialists. "People are just clamoring to get VA medical treatment in order to be able to get into the VA disability benefits ladder,"Bilmes said.

She expects the situation to worsen, projecting that the VA will receive roughly 400,000 new claims from servicemembers returning from Iraq and Afghanistan over the next two years. Many will be submitted after the veterans exhaust the two free years of medical care the VA provides upon discharge. "The main stress is yet to come,"Bilmes said. "There will be a huge increase in the number of claims."

The claims process also does not treat every returning servicemember equally. Active-duty soldiers have a better chance of getting claims evaluated promptly and approved than reservists and members of the National Guard. That is because active-duty soldiers often have the option of having their condition reviewed earlier by the VA before they are discharged from service. Reservists and guardsmen typically cannot get a ruling because they are discharged much faster. The result is that some ex-servicemembers

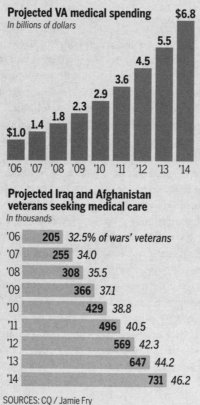

Upward Slopes

Projections by Linda Bilmes, an expert in veterans policy at Harvard University, conclude that VA medical spending on servicemembers returning from Iraq and Afghanistan will triple by fiscal 2010, to almost $3 billion, and then will more than double during the following four years. By 2014, she estimates, almost three-quarters of a million troops from those conflicts will be seeking VA treatment, about half the wars' veterans — even assuming no new troops are deployed.

Projected VA medical spending
In billions of dollars

'06	$1.0
'07	1.4
'08	1.8
'09	2.3
'10	2.9
'11	3.6
'12	4.5
'13	5.5
'14	$6.8

Projected Iraq and Afghanistan veterans seeking medical care
In thousands

Year	Number	Percent
'06	205	32.5% of wars' veterans
'07	255	34.0
'08	308	35.5
'09	366	37.1
'10	429	38.8
'11	496	40.5
'12	569	42.3
'13	647	44.2
'14	731	46.2

SOURCES: CQ / Jamie Fry

start collecting their disability payments later.

"They typically don't remain in place long enough for us to go ahead and make the arrangements for the necessary medical exams and the other steps needed . . . to give them the same types of service we give the active-duty members," said Ron Aument, the VA's deputy undersecretary for benefits.

Data the VA released in February confirmed that active-duty servicemembers are nearly twice as likely as reservists to have claims approved.

"The result is devastating and scandalous,"said Paul Sullivan, executive director of Veterans for Common Sense and a former project manager at the Veterans Benefits Administration. "The VA should immediately and aggressively investigate this problem and then correct it."

Congress tried to address claim denials last year by including language in a VA authorization bill allowing claimants to retain attorneys to represent them at some stages of the appeals process. But VA officials and veterans' groups have said the addition of attorneys has made the claims process more adversarial, encouraging claimants to file more, and more complicated, appeals. Veterans' groups predict additional delays as the system gets increasingly clogged.

"You have an entire system that's been designed around the notion of being a non-adversarial process," Aument said. "You are now bringing attorneys into the process whose very training is to be a zealous advocate and actually conduct themselves in many cases in an adversarial manner on behalf of their clients."

Nicholson, in announcing improvements April 24, attributed some of the backlog in the system to the VA's improved outreach to the veterans' community, which made some ex-servicemembers aware of benefits and, in turn, encouraged more claims.

"We're challenged really because we're . . . a victim, maybe is the best way to say it, of our own success," Nicholson said. "The result of that is that while we are working diligently, the time it's taking is too long."

The VA and Congress propose solving many of the problems by hiring more claims processors. The agency, in its fiscal 2008 budget request, requested 450 processors to help cut through red tape. Congress will probably authorize money in this year's supplemental spending measure, and again in 2008 spending bills. VA officials say the additional staff will help the agency reach a goal of shortening the time it takes veterans to get a ruling on initial claims to 125 days, although Aument said that this may not be realized until fiscal 2009 at earliest.

However, some veterans' groups predict that extra staff at claims centers could increase waiting times even more. That is because it takes two to three years for senior staff to train claims processors. Meanwhile, some longtime processors are expected to retire, with the net effect being a shortage of experienced personnel available to process the veterans' paperwork.

"They're going to have to pull some of their best people off to train" the new hires, said Dennis Cullinan, legislative director of the Veterans of Foreign Wars. "Things are going to get worse for a while rather than better."

SHIFTING THE BURDEN

Some in Congress, such as House Veterans' Affairs Chairman Bob Filner of California, have embraced a new approach proposed by Bilmes in which the government would assume that all claims are valid, then audit a fraction at some later date. That would effectively shift the burden of proving a claim was valid from the veteran to the government.

"I do favor the principle of shifting the burden," Filner said in an interview, adding that the VA "had enough time to deal with this, and they have refused."

VA officials have stated publicly that they are concerned that the extra auditing of claims will sap the agency's resources. The department this spring announced its opposition to a bill by Indiana Democratic Rep. Joe Donnelly, a member of the Veterans' Affairs panel, that would essentially implement the system Bilmes proposes, citing projections that the change would cost an extra $173 billion over 10 years.

Groups such as Disabled American Veterans, which for decades have guided returning servicemembers through the claims process, also believe the change would unwisely divert VA funding for the sake of shaking up the present system. Carl Blake, legislative director of the Paralyzed Veterans of America, even suggests that blanket approval of all claims would encourage fraud and abuse.

"We believe if Congress lowers this threshold . . . the results would be an overwhelming number of claims filed for compensation," Blake said.

But opinion within the VA could be shifting on the issue. While Aument testified against Donnelly's legislation and said in an interview that such a proposal probably would cause "serious unintended consequences," VA Secretary Nicholson has made statements to the contrary. In an interview April 24, he said he is considering the possibility of creating a pilot program modeled on Bilmes' proposal, and has discussed the matter with the White House Office of Management and Budget.

Bilmes said that during a recent meeting with her, Nicholson "definitely was intrigued at the concept of changing the presumption."

But even if the VA gets behind such a change, the prospect of offering blanket approval of claims would face tough scrutiny in the Senate.

"There are serious procedural questions, but far more importantly, the cost implications suggest this has little chance of enactment," said a Senate Democratic aide.

Another change proposed by Bilmes would streamline the VA's 10-point disability rating system and create four classifications: none, low, medium and high. Bilmes believes the change would cut down on the number of appeals in the system.

Some lawmakers, such as New York Democratic Rep. John Hall, who also serves on the House Veterans' Affairs Committee, would provide financial assistance to veterans whose claims were languishing by providing a $500 monthly benefit to those whose appeals were not taken up within 180 days.

But such proposals face stiff opposition in the Senate, where lawmakers from both parties are worried

A Little War of Their Own

For all their frustrating encounters with government bureaucracy, former members of the military services could always count on the two Veterans Affairs' committees of Congress to be models of bipartisanship and comity.

Under chairmen such as Mississippi Democrat G.V. "Sonny" Montgomery in the 1980s and 1990s and New Jersey Republican Christopher H. Smith earlier this decade, Democrats and Republicans on the House Veterans' Affairs Committee collaborated to increase spending on veterans' programs and make disability benefits more generous. A similar spirit prevails in the Senate, where the current chairman, Daniel K. Akaka of Hawaii, maintains a collegial relationship with the senior Republican, Larry E. Craig of Idaho.

But over the past two years, the House committee has been riven by tension between the top two members: Democrat Bob Filner of California and Republican Steve Buyer of Indiana. The disdain the two have displayed for each other worries veterans' groups, who are counting on the panel to address problems with the disability claims, medical care and other issues at a time when public support of returning service members is running especially high.

CQ / Scott J. Ferrell

RUFFLING FEATHERS: Filner survived an intra-party challenge for the VA panel chairmanship, then overhauled the committee's Democratic staff after taking the gavel.

"I think there will be quite a bit of disappointment in the veterans' community if we don't see some substantial gains and enhancements to veterans' programs," says Joe Violante, legislative director for the Disabled American Veterans.

Filner and Buyer are widely regarded as two of the most partisan members of the panel. The friction between them became evident after House Republican leaders deposed Smith in 2005 for defying them on veterans' spending issues and installed Buyer, a Gulf War veteran and colonel in the Army Reserve. Filner's ascension to the chairmanship when Democrats took control of the House this year brought the conflict into full view.

Buyer has roundly criticized Filner's leadership this year, attacking him even on procedural issues, such as the committee's budget. When legislation requiring the Pentagon and Veterans Affairs Department to better coordinate the transfer of servicemembers between the two bureaucracies was referred to the House Armed Services Committee in March, Buyer said that Filner "refused to assert jurisdiction and to assert an active role in this bill." Buyer also used parliamentary rules to disrupt a hearing on servicemembers' transition into civilian life, successfully keeping a recently discharged veteran from speaking on the same panel as a VA official.

Even non-controversial legislation, such as a bill to expand benefits for blinded veterans, got bogged down in partisan battles during a March markup, although the House eventually passed it.

Buyer has also strongly criticized one of Filner's pet initiatives — to extend retroactive benefits to Filipino and Merchant Mariner World War II veterans — suggesting that it was hypocritical to make payments to these two groups while ignoring others who did not receive full VA benefits for years. Buyer, in an interview, assailed Filner for partisanship he displayed in the past and all but said he can't work with the eight-term Democrat.

about the extra costs and inclined to wait for the recommendations of a congressionally mandated 13-member commission convened to study the VA's disability benefits programs.

Sen. Larry E. Craig of Idaho, the ranking Republican on the Senate Veterans' Affairs Committee, says he hopes the commission "will provide the foundation for the types of fundamental changes that may be needed to

"You can't just wake up after 12 years and say I'm going to be bipartisan because I'm chairman," Buyer, who is also in his eighth term, said in an interview. "He has been the most partisan member of the committee."

"I'm going to give Buyer all the chances he wants," Filner responded. "I think everybody else on the committee is going to join me. Whether Buyer does or not is another issue. I can't answer for him."

A Tough Partisan

Filner comes to the chairmanship with a reputation for being something of a bomb thrower. A 1960s civil rights activist who was arrested during a sit-in at a Mississippi lunch counter, he assailed Buyer early in 2006 for rescheduling annual legislative hearings on veterans' programs and later accused Veterans Affairs Secretary Jim Nicholson of overstating how much the Bush administration wanted to increase the agency's budget. After a VA-issued laptop computer containing personal information belonging to at least 26.5 million veterans and active-duty personnel was stolen from a department employee's home last May, Filner called for Nicholson's resignation and decried the Bush administration's stewardship of the department in an expletive-laden tirade during a news conference outside VA headquarters.

Filner faced an unexpected and unusual intraparty challenge for the VA chairmanship from third-term Maine Democrat Michael H. Michaud when Democrats reorganized the House last December. Michaud's bid was supported by the previous top Democrat on the committee, Lane Evans of Illinois, a well-respected member who retired last year due to the effects of Parkinson's disease.

Filner won the gavel in an 112-69 Democratic caucus vote, and most Democratic members — including

CQ / Scott J. Ferrell

ERECTING ROADBLOCKS: As ranking Republican, Buyer has put up procedural hurdles and has assailed Filner's leadership, implying that he can't work with the Californian.

Michaud — have publicly supported him since. But the new chairman soon generated comment by dismissing the committee's Democratic staff director and two subcommittee staff directors in January. Two other subcommittee aides held over from Evans' tenure resigned in the following weeks.

"They had gotten used to the last four or five years that Lane was a ranking member," Filner said of the dismissed aides. "He didn't have much to say about what was happening, and the staff ran the place, and there wasn't the accountability that needs to be done there . . . I was going to make sure that changed."

Several former senior members of the committee staff, in interviews, took issue with what they referred to as Filner's top-down management style. Routine requests often have to be conveyed through Filner's personal office, specifically chief of staff Tony Buckles. Today, Filner's committee staff is composed almost solely of new hires, led by former Department of the Army official Malcom Shorter.

"He and his staff are still coming up to speed with respect to their total grasp of the issues in front of them," says Dennis Cullinan, the Veterans of Foreign Wars legislative director. "We see them as making progress, but they probably have a little ways to go."

Filner says he is trying to reach out to GOP members after years of being a combative minority member in Republican Congresses. "I was in the minority for 12 years, and I thought my job was to sharpen the differences, and to show what we were doing, and sometimes that gets people upset," Filner said.

"People don't know if I can act differently. If I have to govern, I'll do that."

ensure lasting improvement to the disability compensation system" and possibly lead to a bipartisan reform package. "The system as currently structured cannot provide veterans with timely, accurate and consistent decisions on their claims," Craig said.

GAPS IN MEDICAL CARE

In contrast to the troubled claims process, the VA's medical system has received widespread praise from politicians and veterans' groups for the way it treats more than

The Claims Crush

Disability claims pending before the Department of Veterans Affairs surged and then abated at the start of the decade. But the number has grown by 49 percent during the past three years as troops wounded in Iraq and Afghanistan enter the VA system, often with complex injuries that are difficult to quantify and often facing delays in obtaining evidence to support their disability claims. As a result, about one-fifth of all cases now take more than half a year to process.

In thousands

	Total pending on Sept. 30	■ Pending over six
2000	57	Total: 228
'01	172	421
'02	122	346
'03	47	254
'04	67	321
'05	72	346
'06	83	378

SOURCE: Government Accountability Office; CQ / Jamey Fry

5 million veterans annually. The network's well-regarded rehabilitation services have become vital for many of the recent returnees from Iraq, who suffer from head trauma, spinal injuries, amputations, blindness or deafness.

But experts contend that the system is ill-equipped to cope with increased caseloads because the VA has regularly underestimated the cost of care, workloads and the length of waiting lists. Harvard's Bilmes noted that the VA's fiscal 2006 request for emergency funding included $677 million to cover an unexpected 2 percent increase in the number of patients, another $600 million to correct inaccurate estimates of long-term care costs and $400 million more for an unexpected 1.2 percent increase in per-patient costs.

Some professional organizations and veterans' groups are particularly concerned about the VA's ability to treat mental health and brain disorders — including traumatic brain injuries and behavioral problems such as post-traumatic stress disorder, depression and substance abuse — that are fast becoming the war's signature medical issues.

Frances M. Murphy, the VA's deputy undersecretary for health policy coordination, stoked fears last year when she told a presidential commission on mental health that some VA clinics do not provide mental health or substance abuse care, and that in other locations, "waiting lists render that care virtually inaccessible." The remarks triggered a huge flap in which Murray and other congressional Democrats questioned whether Nicholson was giving returning veterans the services they need.

The American Psychological Association reported in February that the armed forces and veterans' systems both suffer a shortage of qualified specialists, noting that the VA employs 1,839 psychologists to serve some 24.3 million veterans. Veterans' groups contend that the shortage has meant some returning servicemembers — especially National Guard members and reservists — are subjected to perfunctory screenings lasting only several minutes that are geared toward treating easily apparent physical disabilities.

"Funding for the VA was based more on hope than projectable data," said Paul Rieckhoff, executive director of the advocacy group Iraq and Afghanistan Veterans of America. "They hoped people wouldn't have casualties, wouldn't have brain injuries. The reality is those things happened. There was an absurd lack of planning."

The VA has disputed the psychological association's study, saying the findings were flawed because the group did not contact the department for information about VA programs, staffing data and other information.

However, veterans' groups and experts contend that staffing shortages within the military medical establishment hinder the ability to diagnose mental health problems in the field, before servicemembers return home. The American Psychological Association says the number of active-duty psychologists has been slipping in recent years because of heavy caseloads, job stress and declining morale. And only 10 to 20 percent have been trained to counsel soldiers suffering from post-traumatic stress disorder.

Harvard's Bilmes says the cumulative effect of these gaps in care is that veterans are at higher risk of unemployment, homelessness, family violence, crime, alcoholism and drug abuse — problems that will impose societal and financial burdens on states and localities.

VA officials say they are addressing shortcomings in their system by beginning to screen discharged servicemembers for traumatic brain injuries as soon as they are admitted into the veterans system. The department also will hire 100 new patient advocates to travel to medical facilities and help wounded servicemembers and their families cut through bureaucratic red tape and obtain information about disability compensation and options for rehabilitation. And the department is asking Congress for money to expand a network of 21 "polytrauma" centers across the country so that veterans who live in outlying areas can have better access to facilities that can simultaneously treat injuries to more than one body part.

The task force recommendations that Nicholson issued April 24 call for making VA and military medical records systems interoperable sometime between mid-2008 and January 2009.

"VA has worked hard to improve the transition process for our deserving servicemen and women. Yet we are not satisfied that we have achieved all that is possible," VA Undersecretary for Benefits Daniel Cooper told a joint hearing of the Senate Armed Services and Veterans' Affairs committees April 12.

HELPING 'WOUNDED WARRIORS'

While Congress has always supported the principle of improving veterans' health care, the disclosure of problems at Walter Reed Army Medical Center has inspired more detailed proposals that address kinks in the system.

After the Walter Reed disclosure, the House in late March overwhelmingly passed a plan to improve the coordination of VA and military health services by adding caseworkers and counselors to the military's medical system. The plan also required the Pentagon and VA to better coordinate the transfer of servicemembers between the two bureaucracies. The changes would cost at least $300 million over the next five years, according to the Congressional Budget Office.

There is no identical companion legislation in the Senate yet. An effort by Democrats Barack Obama of Illinois and Claire McCaskill of Missouri to add caseworkers and mental health counselors to military hospitals and provide money for the military to develop a system allowing soldiers to submit medical paperwork over the Internet was defeated by Republicans during a debate on a war spending bill in late March. The Bush administration says it prefers that Congress wait until a presidentially appointed commission studying problems in the military's medical system issues a report, due by July 31. The commission is headed by former Republican Sen. Bob Dole and Donna Shalala, former secretary of Health and Human Services in the Clinton administration.

House members and senators also are trying to confront the problems by earmarking more money in spending bills. The 2007 supplemental spending bill, for example, designated $100 million for mental health services, another $30 million for a new polytrauma center and $20 million to improve services at "Vet Centers" — a network of more than 200 storefront centers the VA operates around the country where veterans and their families can receive counseling.

Beyond such narrow remedies, VA officials and medical researchers are trying to gain a better understanding of the new types of injuries veterans are bringing home. With as many as one in five soldiers projected to suffer mild traumatic brain injuries, researchers at the W.G. Hefner Medical Center in North Carolina are collaborating with scientists at the Massachusetts Institute of Technology to establish how the force of an explosion affects brain cells and their ability to communicate with one another. The answers could yield clues about whether veterans with brain injuries are more susceptible to the effects of alcohol or certain medicines, and help VA screeners differentiate between physical brain injuries and stress-related disorders.

Murray, a leading Democratic voice on veterans' issues, gives the administration some credit for recognizing the scope of the problems and taking constructive steps. But she says the VA needs to be a much more vocal advocate for veterans' needs, especially in the area of health care.

She predicts that unless there is more initiative, the Democratic Congress will impose more oversight when it draws up fiscal 2008 spending bills and takes up a defense authorization bill later this year.

FOR FURTHER READING

Supplemental spending bill (HR 1591), 2007 CQ Weekly, p. 1266; House veterans' health care plan (HR 1538), p. 975; VA's rising medical caseload, 2005 CQ Weekly, p. 1362.

Appendix

The Legislative Process in Brief

INTRODUCTION OF BILLS

A House member (including the resident commissioner of Puerto Rico and nonvoting delegates of the District of Columbia, Guam, the Virgin Islands and American Samoa) may introduce any one of several types of bills and resolutions by handing it to the clerk of the House or placing it in a box called the hopper. A senator first gains recognition of the presiding officer to announce the introduction of a bill.

As the usual next step in either the House or Senate, the bill is numbered, referred to the appropriate committee, labeled with the sponsor's name and sent to the Government Printing Office so that copies can be made for subsequent study and action. House and Senate bills may be jointly sponsored and carry several senators' names. A bill written in the executive branch and proposed as an administration measure usually is introduced by the chairman of the congressional committee that has jurisdiction, as a courtesy to the White House.

Bills — Prefixed with HR in the House, S in the Senate, followed by a number. Used as the form for most legislation, whether general or special, public or private.

Joint Resolutions — Designated H J Res or S J Res. Subject to the same procedure as bills, with the exception of a joint resolution proposing an amendment to the Constitution. The latter must be approved by two-thirds of both houses and is then sent directly to the administrator of general services for submission to the states for ratification instead of being presented to the president for his approval.

Note: Parliamentary terms used are defined in the glossary.

Concurrent Resolutions — Designated H Con Res or S Con Res. Used for matters affecting the operations of both houses. These resolutions do not become law.

Resolutions — Designated H Res or S Res. Used for a matter concerning the operation of either house alone and adopted only by the chamber in which it originates.

COMMITTEE ACTION

With few exceptions, bills are referred to the appropriate standing committees. The job of referral formally is the responsibility of the Speaker of the House and the presiding officer of the Senate, but this task usually is carried out on their behalf by the parliamentarians of the House and Senate. Precedent, statute and the jurisdictional mandates of the committees as set forth in the rules of the House and Senate determine which committees receive what kinds of bills. Bills are technically considered "read for the first time" when referred to House committees.

When a bill reaches a committee it is placed on the committee's calendar. Failure of a committee to act on a bill is equivalent to killing it and most fall by the legislative roadside. The measure can be withdrawn from the committee's purview only by a discharge petition signed by a majority of the House membership on House bills, or by adoption of a special resolution in the Senate. Discharge attempts rarely succeed and the Senate procedure has not been used for decades.

The first committee action taken on a bill usually is a request for comment on it by interested agencies of the government. The committee chairman may assign the bill to a subcommittee for study and hearings, or it may be considered by the full committee. Hearings may be public, closed (executive session) or both. A subcommittee, after considering a bill, reports to the full committee its recommendations for action and any proposed amendments.

The full committee then votes on its recommendation to the House or Senate. This procedure is called "ordering a bill reported." Occasionally a committee may order a bill reported unfavorably; most of the time a report, submitted by the chairman of the committee to the House or Senate, calls for favorable action on the measure since the committee can effectively "kill" a bill by simply failing to take any action.

After the bill is reported, the committee chairman instructs the staff to prepare a written report. The report describes the purposes and scope of the bill, explains the committee revisions, notes proposed changes in existing law and, usually, includes the views of the executive branch agencies consulted. Often committee members opposing a measure issue dissenting minority statements that are included in the report.

Usually, the committee "marks up" or proposes amendments to the bill. If the amendments are substantial and the measure is complicated, the committee may order a "clean bill" introduced, which will embody the proposed amendments. The original bill then is put aside and the clean bill, with a new number, is reported to the floor.

The chamber must approve, alter or reject the committee amendments before the bill itself can be put to a vote.

FLOOR ACTION

After a bill is reported back to the house where it originated, it is placed on the calendar.

There are five legislative calendars in the House, issued in one cumulative calendar titled *Calendars of the United States House of Representatives and History of Legislation*. The House calendars are:

The Union Calendar to which are referred bills raising revenues, general appropriations bills and any measures directly or indirectly appropriating money or property. It is the Calendar of the Committee of the Whole House on the State of the Union.

The House Calendar to which are referred bills of public character not raising revenue or appropriating money.

The Corrections Calendar to which are referred bills to repeal rules and regulations deemed excessive or unnecessary when the Corrections Calendar is called the second and fourth Tuesday of each month. (Instituted in the 104th Congress to replace the seldom-used Consent Calendar.) A three-fifths majority is required for passage.

The Private Calendar to which are referred bills for relief in the nature of claims against the United States or private immigration bills that are passed without debate when the Private Calendar is called the first and third Tuesdays of each month.

The Discharge Calendar to which are referred motions to discharge committees when the necessary signatures are signed to a discharge petition.

There is only one legislative calendar in the Senate and one "executive calendar" for treaties and nominations submitted to the Senate.

How a Bill Becomes a Law

This graphic shows the most typical way in which proposed legislation is enacted into law. There are more complicated, as well as simpler, routes, and most bills never become law. The process is illustrated with two hypothetical bills, House bill No. 1 (HR 1) and Senate bill No. 2 (S 2). Bills must be passed by both houses in identical form before they can be sent to the president. The path of HR 1 is traced by a gray line, that of S 2 by a black line. In practice, most bills begin as similar proposals in both houses.

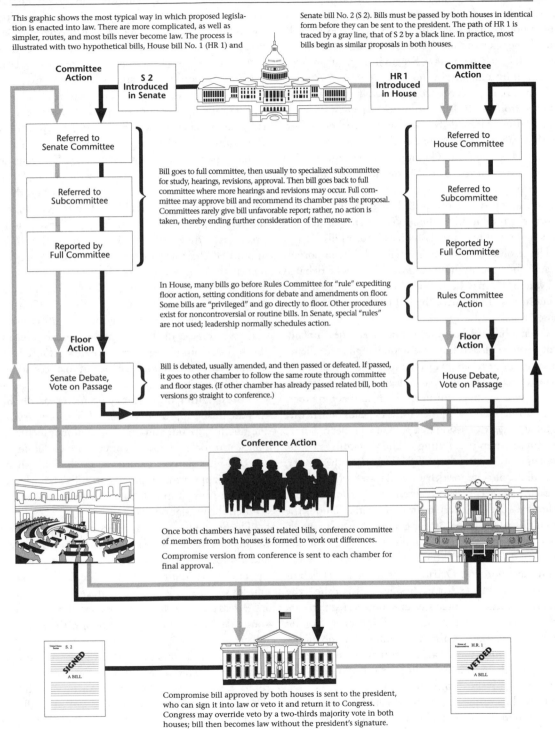

Committee Action

S 2 Introduced in Senate

HR 1 Introduced in House

Committee Action

Referred to Senate Committee

Referred to Subcommittee

Reported by Full Committee

Referred to House Committee

Referred to Subcommittee

Reported by Full Committee

Rules Committee Action

Bill goes to full committee, then usually to specialized subcommittee for study, hearings, revisions, approval. Then bill goes back to full committee where more hearings and revisions may occur. Full committee may approve bill and recommend its chamber pass the proposal. Committees rarely give bill unfavorable report; rather, no action is taken, thereby ending further consideration of the measure.

In House, many bills go before Rules Committee for "rule" expediting floor action, setting conditions for debate and amendments on floor. Some bills are "privileged" and go directly to floor. Other procedures exist for noncontroversial or routine bills. In Senate, special "rules" are not used; leadership normally schedules action.

Floor Action

Floor Action

Senate Debate, Vote on Passage

House Debate, Vote on Passage

Bill is debated, usually amended, and then passed or defeated. If passed, it goes to other chamber to follow the same route through committee and floor stages. (If other chamber has already passed related bill, both versions go straight to conference.)

Conference Action

Once both chambers have passed related bills, conference committee of members from both houses is formed to work out differences.

Compromise version from conference is sent to each chamber for final approval.

Compromise bill approved by both houses is sent to the president, who can sign it into law or veto it and return it to Congress. Congress may override veto by a two-thirds majority vote in both houses; bill then becomes law without the president's signature.

Debate. A bill is brought to debate by varying procedures. In the Senate the majority leader, in consultation with the minority leader and others, schedules the bills that will be taken up for debate. If it is urgent or important it can be taken up in the Senate either by unanimous consent or by a majority vote.

In the House, precedence is granted if a special rule is obtained from the Rules Committee. A request for a special rule usually is made by the chairman of the committee that favorably reported the bill. The request is considered by the Rules Committee in the same fashion that other committees consider legislative measures. The committee proposes a resolution providing for immediate consideration of the bill. The Rules Committee reports the resolution to the House where it is debated and voted on in the same fashion as regular bills.

The resolutions providing special rules are important because they specify how long the bill may be debated and whether it may be amended from the floor. If floor amendments are banned, the bill is considered under a "closed rule."

When a bill is debated under an "open rule," amendments may be offered from the floor. Committee amendments always are taken up first but may be changed, as may all amendments up to the second degree; that is, an amendment to an amendment to an amendment is not in order.

Duration of debate in the House depends on whether the bill is under discussion by the House proper or before the House when it is sitting as the Committee of the Whole House on the State of the Union. In the former, the amount of time for debate is allocated with an hour for each member if the measure is under consideration without a rule. In the Committee of the Whole the amount of time agreed on for general debate is equally divided between proponents and opponents. At the end of general discussion, the bill is often read section by section for amendment. Debate on an amendment is limited to five minutes for each side; this is called the "five-minute rule." In practice, amendments regularly are debated more than ten minutes, with members gaining the floor by offering pro forma amendments or obtaining unanimous consent to speak longer than five minutes.

Senate debate usually is unlimited. It can be halted only by unanimous consent or by "cloture," which requires a three-fifths majority of the entire Senate except for proposed changes in the Senate rules. The latter requires a two-thirds vote.

The House considers almost all important bills within a parliamentary framework known as the Committee of the Whole. It is not a committee as the word usually is understood; it is the full House meeting under another name for the purpose of speeding action on legislation. Technically, the House sits as the Committee of the Whole when it considers any tax measure or bill dealing with public appropriations. Upon adoption of a special rule, the Speaker declares the House resolved into the Committee of the Whole and appoints a member of the majority party to serve as the chairman. The rules of the House permit the Committee of the Whole to meet when a quorum of 100 members is present on the floor and to amend and act on bills. When the Committee of the Whole has acted, it "rises," the Speaker returns as the presiding officer of the House and the member appointed chairman of the Committee of the Whole reports the action of the committee and its recommendations. The Committee of the Whole cannot pass a bill; instead it reports the measure to the full House with whatever changes it has approved. The full House then may pass or reject the bill — or, on occasion, recommit the bill to committee. Amendments adopted in the Committee of the Whole may be put to a second vote in the full House.

Votes. Voting on bills may occur repeatedly before they are finally approved or rejected. The House votes on the rule for the bill and on various amendments to the bill. Voting on amendments often is a more illuminating test of a bill's support than is the final tally. Sometimes members approve final passage of bills after vigorously supporting amendments that, if adopted, would have scuttled the legislation.

The Senate has three different methods of voting: an untabulated voice vote, a standing vote (called a division) and a recorded roll call to which members answer "yea" or "nay" when their names are called. The House also employs voice and standing votes, but since January 1973 yeas and nays have been recorded by an electronic voting device, eliminating the need for time-consuming roll calls.

After amendments to a bill have been voted upon, a vote may be taken on a motion to recommit the bill to committee. If carried, this vote is usually a death blow to the bill. If the motion is unsuccessful, the bill then is "read for the third time." After the third reading a vote on passage is taken. The final vote may be followed by a motion to reconsider, and this motion may be followed by a move to lay the motion on the table. Usually, those voting for the bill's passage vote for the tabling motion, thus safeguarding the final passage action. With that, the bill has been formally passed by the chamber.

ACTION IN SECOND CHAMBER

After a bill is passed it is sent to the other chamber. This body may then take one of several steps. It may pass the bill as is — accepting the other chamber's language. It may send the bill to committee for scrutiny or alteration, or reject the entire bill, advising the other chamber of its actions. Or it simply may ignore the bill submitted while it continues work on its own version of the proposed legislation. Frequently, one chamber may approve a version of a bill that is greatly at variance with the version already passed by the other chamber, and then substitute its contents for the language of the other, retaining only the latter's bill number.

Often the second chamber makes only minor changes. If these are readily agreed to by the other chamber, the bill then is routed to the president. However, if the opposite chamber significantly alters the bill submitted to it, the measure usually is "sent to conference." The chamber that has possession of the "papers" (engrossed bill, engrossed amendments, messages of transmittal) requests a conference and the other chamber may agree to it. If the second chamber does not agree, the bill dies.

CONFERENCE ACTION

A conference works out conflicting House and Senate versions of a legislative bill. The conferees usually are senior members from the committees that managed the legislation who are appointed by the presiding officers of the two houses. Under this arrangement the conferees of one house have the duty of trying to maintain their chamber's position in the face of amending actions by the conferees (also referred to as "managers") of the other house.

The number of conferees from each chamber may vary, the range usually being from seven to nine members in each group, depending on the length or complexity of the bill involved. But a majority vote controls the action of each group so that a large representation does not give one chamber a voting advantage over the other chamber's conferees.

Theoretically, conferees are not allowed to write new legislation in reconciling the two versions before them, but this curb sometimes is bypassed. Many bills have been put into acceptable compromise form only after new language was provided by the conferees. Frequently the ironing out of difficulties takes days or even weeks. Conferences on involved, complex and controversial bills sometimes are particularly drawn out.

As a conference proceeds, conferees reconcile differences between the versions, but generally they grant concessions only insofar as they remain sure that the chamber they represent will accept the compromises. Occasionally, uncertainty over how either house will react, or the positive refusal of a chamber to back down on a disputed amendment, results in an impasse, and the bills die in conference even though each was approved by its sponsoring chamber.

When the conferees have reached agreement, they prepare a conference report embodying their recommendations (compromises) and a joint explanatory statement. The report, in document form, must be submitted to each house. The conference report must be approved by each house. Consequently, approval of the report is approval of the compromise bill. In the order of voting on conference reports, the chamber that asked for a conference yields to the other chamber the opportunity to vote first.

FINAL ACTION

After a bill has been passed by both the House and Senate in identical form, all of the original papers are sent to the enrolling clerk of the chamber in which the bill originated. The clerk then prepares an enrolled bill, which is printed on parchment paper.

When this bill has been certified as correct by the secretary of the Senate or the clerk of the House, depending on which chamber originated the bill, it is signed first (no matter whether it originated in the Senate or House) by the Speaker of the House and then by the president of the Senate. It is next sent to the White House to await action.

If the president approves the bill, he signs it, dates it and usually writes the word "approved" on the document. If the president does not sign it within 10 days (Sundays excepted) and Congress is in session, the bill becomes law without his signature.

If Congress adjourns *sine die* at the end of the second session the president can pocket veto a bill and it dies without Congress having the opportunity to override.

A president vetoes a bill by refusing to sign it and, before the ten-day period expires, returning it to Congress with a message stating his reasons. The message is sent to the chamber that originated the bill. If no action is taken on the message, the bill dies. Congress, however, can attempt to override the president's veto and enact the bill, "the objections of the president to the contrary notwithstanding." Overriding a veto requires a two-thirds vote of those present in each chamber, who must number a quorum and vote by roll call.

If the president's veto is overridden by a two-thirds vote in both houses, the bill becomes law. Otherwise it is dead.

When bills are passed finally and signed, or passed over a veto, they are given law numbers in numerical order as they become law. There are two series of numbers, one for public and one for private laws, starting at the number "1" for each two-year term of Congress. They are then identified by law number and by Congress — for example, Private Law 10, 105th Congress; Public Law 33, 106th Congress (or PL 106-33).

The Budget Process in Brief

Through the budget process, the president and Congress decide how much to spend and tax during the upcoming fiscal year. More specifically, they decide how much to spend on each activity, ensure that the government spends no more than that and spends it only for that activity and report on that spending at the end of each budget cycle.

THE PRESIDENT'S BUDGET

The law requires that, by the first Monday in February, the president submit to Congress his proposed federal budget for the next fiscal year, which begins on October 1. To accomplish this the president establishes general budget and fiscal policy guidelines. Based on these guidelines, executive branch agencies make requests for funds and submit them to the White House's Office of Management and Budget (OMB) nearly a year before the start of a new fiscal year. The OMB, receiving direction from the president and administration officials, reviews the agencies' requests and develops a detailed budget by December. From December to January the OMB prepares the budget documents, so that the president can deliver it to Congress in February.

The president's budget is the executive branch's plan for the next year — but it is just a proposal. After receiving it, Congress has its own budget process to follow from February to October. Only after Congress passes the required spending bills — and the president signs them — has the government created its actual budget.

ACTION IN CONGRESS

Congress first must pass a "budget resolution" — a framework within which the members of Congress will make their decisions about spending and taxes. It includes targets for total spending, total revenues and the deficit, and allocations within the spending target for the two types of spending — discretionary and mandatory.

Discretionary spending, which currently accounts for about 33 percent of all federal spending, is what the president and Congress must decide to spend for the next year through the thirteen annual appropriations bills. It includes money for such activities as the FBI and the Coast Guard, for housing and education, for NASA and highway and bridge construction and for defense and foreign aid.

Mandatory spending, which currently accounts for 67 percent of all spending, is authorized by laws that have already been passed. It includes entitlement spending — such as for Social Security, Medicare, veterans' benefits and food stamps — through which individuals receive benefits because they are eligible based on their age, income or other criteria. It also includes interest on the national debt, which the government pays to individuals and institutions that hold Treasury bonds and other government securities. The only way the president and Congress can change the spending on entitlement and other mandatory programs is if they change the laws that authorized the programs.

Currently, the law requires that legislation that would raise mandatory spending or lower revenues — compared to existing law — be offset by spending cuts or revenue increases. This requirement, called "pay-as-you-go" is designed to prevent new legislation from increasing the deficit.

Once Congress passes the budget resolution, legislators turn their attention to passing the 13 annual appropriations bills and, if they choose, "authorizing" bills to change the laws governing mandatory spending and revenues.

Congress begins by examining the president's budget in detail. Scores of committees and subcommittees hold hearings on proposals under their jurisdiction. The House and Senate Armed Services Authorizing Committees, and the Defense and Military Construction Subcommittees of the Appropriations Committees, for instance, hold hearings on the president's defense budget. The White House budget director, cabinet officers and other administration officials work with Congress as it accepts some of the president's proposals, rejects others and changes still others. Congress can change funding levels, eliminate programs or add programs not requested by the president. It can add or eliminate taxes and other sources of revenue, or make other changes that affect the amount of revenue collected. Congressional rules require that these committees and subcommittees take actions that reflect the congressional budget resolution.

The president's budget, the budget resolution and the appropriations or authorizing bills measure spending in two ways — "budget authority" and "outlays." Budget authority is what the law authorizes the federal government to spend for certain programs, projects or activities. What the government actually spends in a particular year, however, is an outlay. For example, when the government decides to build a space exploration system, the president and Congress may agree to appropriate $1 billion in budget authority. But the space system may take ten years to build. Thus, the government may spend $100 million in outlays in the first year to begin construction and the remaining $900 million during the next nine years as the construction continues.

Congress must provide budget authority before the federal agencies can obligate the government to make outlays. When Congress fails to complete action on one or more of the regular annual appropriations bills before the fiscal year begins on October 1, budget authority may be made on a temporary basis through continuing resolutions. Continuing resolutions make budget authority available for limited periods of time, generally at rates related through some formula to the rate provided in the previous year's appropriation.

MONITORING THE BUDGET

Once Congress passes and the president signs the federal appropriations bills or authorizing laws for the fiscal year, the government monitors the budget through (1) agency program managers and budget officials, including the Inspectors General, who report only to the agency head; (2) the Office of Management and Budget; (3) congressional committees; and (4) the Government Accountability Office, an auditing arm of Congress.

This oversight is designed to (1) ensure that agencies comply with legal limits on spending and that agencies use budget authority only for the purposes intended; (2) see that programs are operating consistently with legal requirements and existing policy; and (3) ensure that programs are well managed and achieving the intended results.

The president may withhold appropriated amounts from obligation only under certain limited circumstances — to provide for contingencies, to achieve savings made possible through changes in requirements or greater effi-ciency of operations or as otherwise provided by law. The Impoundment Control Act of 1974 specifies the procedures that must be followed if funds are withheld. Congress can also cancel previous authorized budget authority by passing a rescissions bill — but it also must be signed by the president.

Glossary of Congressional Terms

AA — (See Administrative Assistant.)

Absence of a Quorum — Absence of the required number of members to conduct business in a house or a committee. When a quorum call or roll-call vote in a house establishes that a quorum is not present, no debate or other business is permitted except a motion to adjourn or motions to request or compel the attendance of absent members, if necessary by arresting them.

Absolute Majority — A vote requiring approval by a majority of all members of a house rather than a majority of members present and voting. Also referred to as constitutional majority.

Account — Organizational units used in the federal budget primarily for recording spending and revenue transactions.

Act — (1) A bill passed in identical form by both houses of Congress and signed into law by the president or enacted over the president's veto. A bill also becomes an act without the president's signature if he does not return it to Congress within ten days (Sundays excepted) and if Congress has not adjourned within that period. (2) Also, the technical term for a bill passed by at least one house and engrossed.

Ad Hoc Select Committee — A temporary committee formed for a special purpose or to deal with a specific subject. Conference committees are ad hoc joint committees. A House rule adopted in 1975 authorizes the Speaker to refer measures to special ad hoc committees, appointed by the Speaker with the approval of the House.

Adjourn — A motion to adjourn is a formal motion to end a day's session or meeting of a house or a committee. A motion to adjourn usually has no conditions attached to it, but it sometimes may specify the day or time for reconvening or make reconvening subject to the call of the chamber's presiding officer or the committee's chairman. In both houses, a motion to adjourn is of the highest privilege, takes precedence over all other motions, is not debatable and must be put to an immediate vote. Adjournment of a house ends its legislative day. For this reason, the House or Senate sometimes adjourns for only one minute, or some other very brief period of time, during the course of a day's session. The House does not permit a motion to adjourn after it has resolved into Committee of the Whole or when the previous question has been ordered on a measure to final passage without an intervening motion.

Adjourn for More Than Three Days — Under Article I, Section 5 of the Constitution, neither house may adjourn for more than three days without the approval of the other. The necessary approval is given in a concurrent resolution to which both houses have agreed.

Adjournment *Sine Die* — Final adjournment of an annual or two-year session of Congress; literally, adjournment without a day. The two houses must agree to a privileged concurrent resolution for such an adjournment. A sine die adjournment precludes Congress from meeting again until the next constitutionally fixed date of a session (Jan. 3 of the following year) unless Congress determines otherwise by law or the president calls it into special session. Article II, Section 3 of the Constitution authorizes the president to adjourn both houses until such time as the president thinks proper when the two houses cannot agree to a time of adjournment. No president, however, has ever exercised this authority.

Adjournment to a Day (and Time) Certain — An adjournment that fixes the next date and time of meeting for one or both houses. It does not end an annual session of Congress.

Administration Bill — A bill drafted in the executive office of the president or in an executive department or agency to implement part of the president's program. An administration bill is introduced in Congress by a member who supports it or as a courtesy to the administration.

Administrative Assistant (AA) — The title usually given to a member's chief aide, political advisor and head of office staff. The administrative assistant often represents the member at meetings with visitors or officials when the member is unable (or unwilling) to attend.

Adoption — The usual parliamentary term for approval of a conference report. It is also commonly applied to amendments.

Advance Appropriation — In an appropriation act for a particular fiscal year, an appropriation that does not become available for spending or obligation until a subsequent fiscal year. The amount of the advance appropriation is counted as part of the budget for the fiscal year in which it becomes available for obligation.

Advance Funding — A mechanism whereby statutory language may allow budget authority for a fiscal year to be increased, and obligations to be incurred, with an offsetting decrease in the budget authority available in the succeeding fiscal year. If not used, the budget authority remains available for obligation in the succeeding fiscal year. Advance funding is sometimes used to provide contingency funding of a few benefit programs.

Adverse Report — A committee report recommending against approval of a measure or some other matter. Committees usually pigeonhole measures they oppose instead of reporting them adversely, but they may be required to report them by a statutory rule or an instruction from their parent body.

Advice and Consent — The Senate's constitutional role in consenting to or rejecting the president's nominations to executive branch and judicial offices and treaties with other nations. Confirmation of nominees requires a simple majority vote of senators present and voting. Treaties must be approved by a two-thirds majority of those present and voting.

Aisle — The center aisle of each chamber. When facing the presiding officer, Republicans usually sit to the right of the aisle, Democrats to the left. When members speak of "my side of the aisle" or "this side," they are referring to their party.

Amendment — A formal proposal to alter the text of a bill, resolution, amendment, motion, treaty or some other text. Technically, it is a motion. An amendment may strike out (eliminate) part of a text, insert new text or strike out and insert — that is, replace all or part of the text with new text. The texts of amendments considered on the floor are printed in full in the *Congressional Record*.

Amendment in the Nature of a Substitute — Usually, an amendment to replace the entire text of a measure. It strikes out everything after the enacting clause and inserts a version that may be somewhat, substantially or entirely different. When a committee adopts extensive amendments to a measure, it often incorporates them into such an amendment. Occasionally, the term is applied to an amendment that replaces a major portion of a measure's text.

Amendment Tree — A diagram showing the number and types of amendments that the rules and practices of a house permit to be offered to a measure before any of the amendments is voted on. It shows the relationship of one amendment to the others, and it may also indicate the degree of each amendment, whether it is a perfecting or substitute amendment, the order in which amendments may be offered and the order in which they are put to a vote. The same type of diagram can be used to display an actual amendment situation.

Annual Authorization — Legislation that authorizes appropriations for a single fiscal year and usually for a specific amount. Under the rules of the authorization-appropriation process, an annually authorized agency or program must be reauthorized each year if it is to receive appropriations for that year. Sometimes Congress fails to enact the reauthorization but nevertheless provides appropriations to continue the program, circumventing the rules by one means or another.

Appeal — A member's formal challenge of a ruling or decision by the presiding officer. On appeal, a house or a committee may overturn the ruling by majority vote. The right of appeal ensures the body against arbitrary control by the chair. Appeals are rarely made in the House and are even more rarely successful. Rulings are more frequently appealed in the Senate and occasionally overturned, in part because its presiding officer is not the majority party's leader, as in the House.

Apportionment — The action, after each decennial census, of allocating the number of members in the House of Representatives to each state. By law, the total number of House members (not counting delegates and a resident commissioner) is fixed at 435. The number allotted to each state is based approximately on its proportion of the nation's total population. Because the Constitution guarantees each state one representative no matter how small its population, exact proportional distribution is virtually impossible. The mathematical formula currently used to determine the apportionment is called the Method of Equal Proportions. (See Method of Equal Proportions.)

Appropriated Entitlement — An entitlement program, such as veterans' pensions, that is funded through annual appropriations rather than by a permanent appropriation. Because such an entitlement law requires the government to provide eligible recipients the benefits to which they are entitled, whatever the cost, Congress must appropriate the necessary funds.

Appropriation — (1) Legislative language that permits a federal agency to incur obligations and make payments from the Treasury for specified purposes, usually during a specified period of time. (2) The specific amount of money made available by such language. The Constitution prohibits payments from the Treasury except "in Consequence of Appropriations made by Law." With some exceptions, the rules of both houses forbid consideration of appropriations for purposes that are unauthorized in law or of appropriation amounts larger than those authorized in law. The House of Representatives claims the exclusive right to originate appropriation bills — a claim the Senate denies in theory but accepts in practice.

At-Large — Elected by and representing an entire state instead of a district within a state. The term usually refers to a representative rather than to a senator. (See Apportionment; Congressional District; Redistricting.)

August Adjournment — A congressional adjournment during the month of August in odd-numbered years, required by the Legislative Reorganization Act of 1970. The law instructs the two houses to adjourn for a period of at least thirty days before the second day after Labor Day, unless Congress provides otherwise or if, on July 31, a state of war exists by congressional declaration.

Authorization — (1) A statutory provision that establishes or continues a federal agency, activity or program for a fixed or indefinite period of time. It may also establish policies and restrictions and deal with organizational and administrative matters. (2) A statutory provision, as described in (1), may also, explicitly or implicitly, authorize congressional action to provide appropriations for an agency, activity or program. The appropriations may be authorized for one year, several years or an indefinite period of time, and the authorization may be for a specific amount of money or an indefinite amount ("such sums as may be necessary"). Authorizations of specific amounts are construed as ceilings on the amounts that subsequently may be appropriated in an appropriation bill, but not as minimums; either house may appropriate lesser amounts or nothing at all.

Authorization-Appropriation Process — The two-stage procedural system that the rules of each house require for establishing and funding federal agencies and programs: first, enactment of authorizing legislation that creates or continues an agency or program; second, enactment of appropriations legislation that provides funds for the authorized agency or program.

Automatic Roll Call — Under a House rule, the automatic ordering of the yeas and nays when a quorum is not present on a voice or division vote and a member objects to the vote on that ground. It is not permitted in the Committee of the Whole.

Backdoor Spending Authority — Authority to incur obligations that evades the normal congressional appropriations process because it is provided in legislation other than appropriation acts. The most common forms are borrowing authority, contract authority and entitlement authority.

Baseline — A projection of the levels of federal spending, revenues and the resulting budgetary surpluses or deficits for the upcoming and subsequent fiscal years, taking into account laws enacted to date and assuming no new policy decisions. It provides a benchmark for measuring the budgetary effects of proposed changes in federal revenues or spending, assuming certain economic conditions.

Bells — A system of electric signals and lights that informs members of activities in each chamber. The type of activity taking place is indicated by the number of signals and the interval between them. When the signals are sounded, a corresponding number of lights are lit around the perimeter of many clocks in House or Senate offices.

Bicameral — Consisting of two houses or chambers. Congress is a bicameral legislature whose two houses have an equal role in enacting legislation. In most other national bicameral legislatures, one house is significantly more powerful than the other.

Bigger Bite Amendment — An amendment that substantively changes a portion of a text including language that had previously been amended. Normally, language that has been amended may not be amended again. However, a part of a sentence that has been changed by amendment, for example, may be changed again by an amendment that amends a "bigger bite" of the text — that is, by an amendment that also substantively changes the unamended parts of the sentence or the entire section or title in which the previously amended language appears. The biggest possible bite is an amendment in the nature of a substitute that amends the entire text of a measure. Once adopted, therefore, such an amendment ends the amending process.

Bill — The term for the chief vehicle Congress uses for enacting laws. Bills that originate in the House of Representatives are designated as HR, those in the Senate as S, followed by a number assigned in the order in which they are introduced during a two-year Congress. A bill becomes a law if passed in identical language by both houses and signed by the president, or passed over the president's veto, or if the president fails to sign it within ten days after receiving it while Congress is in session.

Bill of Attainder — An act of a legislature finding a person guilty of treason or a felony. The Constitution prohibits the passage of such a bill by the U.S. Congress or any state legislature.

Bills and Resolutions Introduced — Members formally present measures to their respective houses by delivering them to a clerk in the chamber when their house is in session. Both houses permit any number of members to join in introducing a bill or resolution. The first member listed on the measure is the sponsor; the other members listed are its cosponsors.

Bills and Resolutions Referred — After a bill or resolution is introduced, it is normally sent to one or more committees that have jurisdiction over its subject, as defined by House and Senate rules and precedents. A Senate measure is usually referred to the committee with jurisdiction over the predominant subject of its text, but it may be sent to two or more committees by unanimous consent or on a motion offered jointly by the majority and minority leaders. In the House, a rule requires the Speaker to refer a measure to the committee that has primary jurisdiction. The Speaker is also authorized to refer measures sequentially to additional committees and to impose time limits on such referrals.

Bipartisan Committee — A committee with an equal number of members from each political party. The House Committee on Standards of Official Conduct and the Senate Select Committee on Ethics are the only bipartisan, permanent full committees.

Borrowing Authority — Statutory authority permitting a federal agency, such as the Export-Import Bank, to borrow money from the public or the Treasury to finance its operations. It is a form of backdoor spending. To bring such spending under the control of the congressional appropriation process, the Congressional Budget Act requires that new borrowing authority shall be effective only to the extent and in such amounts as are provided in appropriations acts.

Budget — A detailed statement of actual or anticipated revenues and expenditures during an accounting period. For the national government, the period is the federal fiscal year (Oct. 1 to Sept. 30). The budget usually refers to the president's budget submission to Congress early each calendar year. The president's budget estimates federal government income and spending for the upcoming fiscal year and contains detailed recommendations for appropriation, revenue and other legislation. Congress is not required to accept or even vote directly on the president's proposals, and it often revises the president's budget extensively. (See Fiscal Year.)

Budget Act — Common name for the Congressional Budget and Impoundment Control Act of 1974, which established the basic procedures of the current congressional budget process; created the House and Senate Budget Committees; and enacted procedures for reconciliation, deferrals and rescissions. (See Budget Process; Deferral; Impoundment; Reconciliation; Rescission. See also Gramm-Rudman-Hollings Act of 1985.)

Budget and Accounting Act of 1921 — The law that, for the first time, authorized the president to submit to Congress an annual budget for the entire federal government. Before passage of the act, most federal agencies sent their budget requests to the appropriate congressional committees without review by the president.

Budget Authority — Generally, the amount of money that may be spent or obligated by a government agency or for a government program or activity. Technically, it is statutory authority to enter into obligations that normally result in outlays. The main forms of budget authority are appropriations, borrowing authority and contract authority. It also includes authority to obligate and expend the proceeds of offsetting receipts and collections. Congress may make budget authority available for only one year, several years or an indefinite period, and it may specify definite or indefinite amounts.

Budget Enforcement Act of 1990 — An act that revised the sequestration process established by the Gramm-Rudman-Hollings Act of 1985, replaced the earlier act's fixed deficit targets with adjustable ones, established discretionary spending limits for fiscal years 1991 through 1995, instituted pay-as-you-go rules to enforce deficit neutrality on revenue and mandatory spending legislation and reformed the budget and accounting rules for federal credit activities. Unlike the Gramm-Rudman-Hollings Act, the 1990 act emphasized restraints on legislated changes in taxes and spending instead of fixed deficit limits.

Budget Enforcement Act of 1997 — An act that revised and updated the provisions of the Budget Enforcement Act of 1990, including by extending the discretionary spending caps and pay-as-you-go rules through 2002.

Budget Process — (1) In Congress, the procedural system it uses (a) to approve an annual concurrent resolution on the budget that sets goals for aggregate and functional categories of federal expenditures, revenues and the surplus or deficit for an upcoming fiscal year; and (b) to implement those goals in spending, revenue and, if necessary, reconciliation and debt-limit legislation. (2) In the executive branch, the process of formulating the president's annual budget, submitting it to Congress, defending it before congressional committees, implementing subsequent budget-related legislation, impounding or sequestering expenditures as permitted by law, auditing and evaluating programs and compiling final budget data. The Budget and Accounting Act of 1921 and the Congressional Budget and Impoundment Control Act of 1974 established the basic elements of the current budget process. Major revisions were enacted in the Gramm-Rudman-Hollings Act of 1985 and the Budget Enforcement Act of 1990.

Budget Resolution — A concurrent resolution in which Congress establishes or revises its version of the federal budget's broad financial features for the upcoming fiscal year and several additional fiscal years. Like other concurrent resolutions, it does not have the force of law, but it provides the framework within which Congress subsequently considers revenue, spending and other budget-implementing legislation. The framework consists of two basic elements: (1) aggregate budget amounts (total revenues, new budget authority, outlays, loan obligations and loan guarantee commitments, deficit or surplus and debt limit); and (2) subdivisions of the relevant aggregate amounts among the functional categories of the budget. Although it does not allocate funds to specific programs or accounts, the budget committees' reports accompanying the resolution often discuss the major program assumptions underlying its functional amounts. Unlike those amounts, however, the assumptions are not binding on Congress.

By Request — A designation indicating that a member has introduced a measure on behalf of the president, an executive agency or a private individual or organization. Members often introduce such measures as a courtesy because neither the president nor any person other than a member of Congress can do so. The term, which appears next to the sponsor's name, implies that the member who introduced the measure does not necessarily endorse it. A House rule dealing with by-request introductions dates from 1888, but the practice goes back to the earliest history of Congress.

Byrd Rule — The popular name of an amendment to the Congressional Budget Act that bars the inclusion of extraneous matter in any reconciliation legislation considered in the Senate. The ban is enforced by points of order that the presiding officer sustains. The provision defines different categories of extraneous matter, but it also permits certain exceptions. Its chief sponsor was Sen. Robert C. Byrd, D-W.Va.

Calendar — A list of measures or other matters (most of them favorably reported by committees) that are eligible for floor consideration. The House has five calendars; the Senate has two. A place on a calendar does not guarantee consideration. Each house decides which measures and matters it will take up, when and in what order, in accordance with its rules and practices.

Calendar Wednesday — A House procedure that on Wednesdays permits its committees to bring up for floor consideration nonprivileged measures they have reported. The procedure is so cumbersome and susceptible to dilatory tactics, however, that it is rarely used.

Call Up — To bring a measure or report to the floor for immediate consideration.

Casework — Assistance to constituents who seek assistance in dealing with federal and local government agencies. Constituent service is a high priority in most members' offices.

Caucus — (1) A common term for the official organization of each party in each house. (2) The official title of the organization of House Democrats. House and Senate Republicans and Senate Democrats call their organizations "conferences." (3) A term for an informal group of members who share legislative interests, such as the Black Caucus, Hispanic Caucus and Children's Caucus.

Censure — The strongest formal condemnation of a member for misconduct short of expulsion. A house usually adopts a resolution of censure to express its condemnation, after which the presiding officer reads its rebuke aloud to the member in the presence of his or her colleagues.

Chairman — The presiding officer of a committee, a subcommittee or a task force. At meetings, the chairman preserves order, enforces the rules, recognizes members to speak or offer motions and puts questions to a vote. The chairman of a committee or subcommittee usually appoints its staff and sets its agenda, subject to the panel's veto.

Chamber — The Capitol room in which a house of Congress normally holds its sessions. The chamber of the House of Representatives, officially called the Hall of the House, is considerably larger than that of the Senate because it must accommodate 435 representatives, four delegates and one resident commissioner. Unlike the Senate chamber, members have no desks or assigned seats. In both chambers, the floor slopes downward to the well in front of the presiding officer's raised desk. A chamber is often referred to as "the floor," as when members are said to be on or going to the floor. Those expressions usually imply that the member's house is in session.

Christmas Tree Bill — Jargon for a bill adorned with amendments, many of them unrelated to the bill's subject, that provide benefits for interest groups, specific states, congressional districts, companies and individuals.

Classes of Senators — A class consists of the thirty-three or thirty-four senators elected to a six-year term in the same general election. Because the terms of approximately one-third of the senators expire every two years, there are three classes.

Clean Bill — After a House committee extensively amends a bill, it often assembles its amendments and what is left of the bill into a new measure that one or more of its members introduces as a "clean bill." The revised measure is assigned a new number.

Clerk of the House — An officer of the House of Representatives responsible principally for administrative support of the legislative process in the House. The clerk is invariably the candidate of the majority party.

Cloakrooms — Two rooms with access to the rear of each chamber's floor, one for each party's members, where members may confer privately, sit quietly or have a snack. The presiding officer sometimes urges members who are conversing too loudly on the floor to retire to their cloakrooms.

Closed Hearing — A hearing closed to the public and the media. A House committee may close a hearing only if it determines that disclosure of the testimony to be taken would endanger national security, violate any law or tend to defame, degrade or incriminate any person. The Senate has a similar rule. Both houses require roll-call votes in open session to close a hearing.

Closed Rule — A special rule reported from the House Rules Committee that prohibits amendments to a measure or that only permits amendments offered by the reporting committee.

Cloture — A Senate procedure that limits further consideration of a pending proposal to thirty hours in order to end a filibuster. Sixteen senators must first sign and submit a cloture motion to the presiding officer. One hour after the Senate meets on the second calendar day thereafter, the chair puts the motion to a yea-and-nay vote following a live quorum call. If three-fifths of all senators (sixty if there are no vacancies) vote for the motion, the Senate must take final action on the cloture proposal by the end of the thirty hours of consideration and may consider no other business until it takes that action. Cloture on a proposal to amend the Senate's standing rules requires approval by two-thirds of the senators present and voting.

Code of Official Conduct — A House rule that bans certain actions by House members, officers and employees; requires them to conduct themselves in ways that "reflect creditably" on the House; and orders them to adhere to the spirit and the letter of House rules and those of its committees. The code's provisions govern the receipt of outside compensation, gifts and honoraria and the use of campaign funds; prohibit members from using their clerk-hire allowance to pay anyone who does not perform duties commensurate with that pay; forbids discrimination in members' hiring or treatment of employees on the grounds of race, color, religion, sex, handicap, age or national origin; orders members convicted of a crime who might be punished by imprisonment of two or more years not to participate in committee business or vote on the floor until exonerated or reelected; and restricts employees' contact with federal agencies on matters in which they have a significant financial interest. The Senate's rules contain some similar prohibitions.

College of Cardinals — A popular term for the subcommittee chairmen of the appropriations committees, reflecting their influence over appropriation measures. The chairmen of the full appropriations committees are sometimes referred to as popes.

Comity — The practice of maintaining mutual courtesy and civility between the two houses in their dealings with each other and in members' speeches on the floor. Although the practice is largely governed by long-established customs, a House rule explicitly cautions its members not to characterize any Senate action or inaction, refer to individual senators except under certain circumstances, or quote from Senate proceedings except to make legislative history on a measure. The Senate has no rule on the subject but references to the House have been held out of order on several occasions. Generally the houses do not interfere with each other's appropriations although minor conflicts sometimes occur. A refusal to receive a message from the other house has also been held to violate the practice of comity.

Committee — A panel of members elected or appointed to perform some service or function for its parent body. Congress has four types of committees: standing, special or select, joint, and, in the House, a Committee of the Whole. Committees conduct investigations, make studies, issue reports and recommendations and, in the case of standing committees, review and prepare measures on their assigned subjects for action by their respective houses. Most committees divide their work among several subcommittees. With rare exceptions, the majority party in a house holds a majority of the seats on its committees, and their chairmen are also from that party.

Committee Jurisdiction — The legislative subjects and other functions assigned to a committee by rule, precedent, resolution or statute. A committee's title usually indicates the general scope of its jurisdiction but often fails to mention other significant subjects assigned to it.

Committee of the Whole — Common name of the Committee of the Whole House on the State of the Union, a committee consisting of all members of the House of Representatives. Measures from the union calendar must be considered in the Committee of the Whole before the House officially completes action on them; the committee often considers other major bills as well. A quorum of the committee is 100, and it meets in the House chamber under a chairman appointed by the Speaker. Procedures in the Committee of the Whole expedite consideration of legislation because of its smaller quorum requirement, its ban on certain motions and its five-minute rule for debate on amendments. Those procedures usually permit more members to offer amendments and participate in the debate on a measure than is normally possible. The Senate no longer uses a Committee of the Whole.

Committee Ratios — The ratios of majority to minority party members on committees. By custom, the ratios of most committees reflect party strength in their respective houses as closely as possible.

Committee Report on a Measure — A document submitted by a committee to report a measure to its parent chamber. Customarily, the report explains the measure's purpose, describes provisions and any amendments recommended by the committee and presents arguments for its approval.

Committee Veto — A procedure that requires an executive department or agency to submit certain proposed policies, programs or action to designated committees for review before implementing them. Before 1983, when the Supreme Court declared that a legislative veto was unconstitutional, these provisions permitted committees to veto the proposals. Committees no longer conduct this type of policy review, and the term is now something of a misnomer. Nevertheless, agencies usually take the pragmatic approach of trying to reach a consensus with the committees before carrying out their proposals, especially when an appropriations committee is involved.

Concur — To agree to an amendment of the other house, either by adopting a motion to concur in that amendment or a motion to concur with an amendment to that amendment. After both houses have agreed to the same version of an amendment, neither house may amend it further, nor may any subsequent conference change it or delete it from the measure. Concurrence by one house in all amendments of the other house completes action on the measure; no vote is then necessary on the measure as a whole because both houses previously passed it.

Concurrent Resolution — A resolution that requires approval by both houses but does not need the president's signature and therefore cannot have the force of law. Concurrent resolutions deal with the prerogatives or internal affairs of Congress as a whole. Designated H. Con. Res. in the House and S. Con. Res. in the Senate, they are numbered consecutively in each house in their order of introduction during a two-year Congress.

Conferees — A common title for managers, the members from each house appointed to a conference committee. The Senate usually authorizes its presiding officer to appoint its conferees. The Speaker appoints House conferees, and under a rule adopted in 1993, can remove conferees "at any time after an original appointment" and also appoint additional conferees at any time. Conferees are expected to support the positions of their houses despite their personal views, but in practice this is not always the case. The party ratios of conferees generally reflect the ratios in their houses. Each house may appoint as many conferees as it pleases. House conferees often outnumber their Senate colleagues; however, each house has only one vote in a conference, so the size of its delegation is immaterial.

Conference — (1) A formal meeting or series of meetings between members representing each house to reconcile House and Senate differences on a measure (occasionally several measures). Because one house cannot require the other to agree to its proposals, the conference usually reaches agreement by compromise. When a conference completes action on a measure, or as much action as appears possible, it sends its recommendations to both houses in the form of a conference report, accompanied by an explanatory statement. (2) The official title of the organization of all Democrats or Republicans in the Senate and of all Republicans in the House of Representatives. (See Party Caucus.)

Conference Committee — A temporary joint committee formed for the purpose of resolving differences between the houses on a measure. Major and controversial legislation usually requires conference committee action. Voting in a conference committee is not by individuals but within the House and Senate delegations. Consequently, a conference committee report requires the support of a majority of the conferees from each house. Both houses require that conference committees open their meetings to the public. The Senate's rule permits the committee to close its meetings if a majority of conferees in each delegation agree by a roll-call vote. The House rule permits closed meetings only if the House authorizes them to do so on a roll-call vote. Otherwise, there are no congressional rules governing the organization of, or procedure in, a conference committee. The committee chooses its chairman, but on measures that go to conference annually, such as general appropriation bills, the chairmanship traditionally rotates between the houses.

Conference Report — A document submitted to both houses that contains a conference committee's agreements for resolving their differences on a measure. It must be signed by a majority of the conferees from each house separately and must be accompanied by an explanatory statement. Both houses prohibit amendments to a conference report and require it to be accepted or rejected in its entirety.

Congress — (1) The national legislature of the United States, consisting of the House of Representatives and the Senate. (2) The national legislature in office during a two-year period. Congresses are numbered sequentially; thus, the 1st Congress of 1789-1791 and the 106th Congress of 1999-2001. Before 1935, the two-year period began on the first Monday in December of odd-numbered years. Since then it has extended from January of an odd-numbered year through noon on Jan. 3 of the next odd-numbered year. A Congress usually holds two annual sessions, but some have had three sessions and the 67th Congress had four. When a Congress expires, measures die if they have not yet been enacted.

Congressional Accountability Act of 1995 (CAA) — An act applying eleven labor, workplace and civil rights laws to the legislative branch and establishing procedures and remedies for legislative branch employees with grievances in violation of these laws. The following laws are covered by the CAA: the Fair Labor Standards Act of 1938; Title VII of the Civil Rights Act of 1964; Americans with Disabilities Act of

1990; Age Discrimination in Employment Act of 1967; Family and Medical Leave Act of 1993; Occupational Safety and Health Act of 1970; Chapter 71 of Title 5, U.S. Code (relating to federal service labor-management relations); Employee Polygraph Protection Act of 1988; Worker Adjustment and Retraining Notification Act; Rehabilitation Act of 1973; and Chapter 43 of Title 38, U.S. Code (relating to veterans' employment and reemployment).

Congressional Budget and Impoundment Control Act of 1974 — The law that established the basic elements of the congressional budget process, the House and Senate Budget Committees, the Congressional Budget Office and the procedures for congressional review of impoundments in the form of rescissions and deferrals proposed by the president. The budget process consists of procedures for coordinating congressional revenue and spending decisions made in separate tax, appropriations and legislative measures. The impoundment provisions were intended to give Congress greater control over executive branch actions that delay or prevent the spending of funds provided by Congress.

Congressional Budget Office (CBO) — A congressional support agency created by the Congressional Budget and Impoundment Control Act of 1974 to provide nonpartisan budgetary information and analysis to Congress and its committees. CBO acts as a scorekeeper when Congress is voting on the federal budget, tracking bills to ensure they comply with overall budget goals. The agency also estimates what proposed legislation would cost over a five-year period. CBO works most closely with the House and Senate Budget Committees.

Congressional Directory — The official who's who of Congress, usually published during the first session of a two-year Congress.

Congressional District — The geographical area represented by a single member of the House of Representatives. For states with only one representative, the entire state is a congressional district. As of 2001 seven states had only one representative each: Alaska, Delaware, Montana, North Dakota, South Dakota, Vermont and Wyoming.

Congressional Record — The daily, printed and substantially verbatim account of proceedings in both the House and Senate chambers. Extraneous materials submitted by members appear in a section titled "Extensions of Remarks." A "Daily Digest" appendix contains highlights of the day's floor and committee action plus a list of committee meetings and floor agendas for the next day's session.

Although the official reporters of each house take down every word spoken during the proceedings, members are permitted to edit and "revise and extend" their remarks before they are printed. In the Senate section, all speeches, articles and other material submitted by senators but not actually spoken or read on the floor are set off by large black dots, called bullets. However, bullets do not appear when a senator reads part of a speech and inserts the rest. In the House section, undelivered speeches and materials are printed in a distinctive typeface. The term "permanent Record" refers to the bound volumes of the daily Records of an entire session of Congress.

Congressional Research Service (CRS) — Established in 1917, a department of the Library of Congress whose staff provide nonpartisan, objective analysis and information on virtually any subject to committees, members and staff of Congress. Originally the Legislative Reference Service, it is the oldest congressional support agency.

Congressional Support Agencies — A term often applied to three agencies in the legislative branch that provide nonpartisan information and analysis to committees and members of Congress: the Congressional Budget Office, the Congressional Research Service of the Library of Congress and the General Accounting Office. A fourth support agency, the Office of Technology Assessment, formerly provided such support but was abolished in the 104th Congress.

Congressional Terms of Office — A term normally begins on Jan. 3 of the year following a general election and runs two years for representatives and six years for senators. A representative chosen in a special election to fill a vacancy is sworn in for the remainder of the predecessor's term. An individual appointed to fill a Senate vacancy usually serves until the next general election or until the end of the predecessor's term, whichever comes first. Some states, however, require their governors to call a special election to fill a Senate vacancy shortly after an appointment has been made.

Constitutional Rules — Constitutional provisions that prescribe procedures for Congress. In addition to certain types of votes required in particular situations, these provisions include the following: (1) the House chooses its Speaker, the Senate its president pro tempore and both houses their officers; (2) each house requires a majority quorum to conduct business; (3) less than a majority may adjourn from day to day and compel the attendance of absent members; (4) neither house may adjourn for more than three days without the consent of the other; (5) each house must keep a journal; (6) the yeas and nays are ordered when supported by one-fifth of the members present; (7) all revenue-raising bills must originate in the House, but the Senate may propose amendments to them. The Constitution also sets out the procedure in the House for electing a president, the procedure in the Senate for electing a vice president, the procedure for filling a vacancy in the office of vice president and the procedure for overriding a presidential veto.

Constitutional Votes — Constitutional provisions that require certain votes or voting methods in specific situations. They include (1) the yeas and nays at the desire of one-fifth of the members present; (2) a two-thirds vote by the yeas and nays to override a veto; (3) a two-thirds vote by one house to expel one of its members and by both houses to propose a constitutional amendment; (4) a two-thirds vote of senators present to convict someone whom the House has impeached and to consent to ratification of treaties; (5) a two-thirds vote in each house to remove political disabilities from persons who have engaged in insurrection or rebellion or given aid or comfort to the enemies of the United States; (6) a majority vote in each house to fill a vacancy in the office of vice president; (7) a majority vote of all states to elect a president in the House of Representatives when no candidate receives a majority of the electoral votes; (8) a majority vote of all senators when the Senate elects a vice president under the same circumstances; and (9) the casting vote of the vice president in case of tie votes in the Senate.

Contempt of Congress — Willful obstruction of the proper functions of Congress. Most frequently, it is a refusal to obey a subpoena to appear and testify before a committee or to produce documents demanded by it. Such obstruction is a misdemeanor and persons cited for contempt are subject to prosecution in federal courts. A house cites an individual for contempt by agreeing to a privileged resolution to that effect reported by a committee. The presiding officer then refers the matter to a U.S. attorney for prosecution.

Continuing Body — A characterization of the Senate on the theory that it continues from Congress to Congress and has existed continuously since it first convened in 1789. The rationale for the theory is that under the system of staggered six-year terms for senators, the terms of only about one-third of them expire after each Congress and, therefore, a quorum of the Senate is always in office. Consequently, under this theory, the Senate, unlike the House, does not have to adopt its rules at the beginning of each Congress

because those rules continue from one Congress to the next. This makes it extremely difficult for the Senate to change its rules against the opposition of a determined minority because those rules require a two-thirds vote of the senators present and voting to invoke cloture on a proposed rules change.

Continuing Resolution (CR) — A joint resolution that provides funds to continue the operation of federal agencies and programs at the beginning of a new fiscal year if their annual appropriation bills have not yet been enacted; also called continuing appropriations. Continuing resolutions are enacted shortly before or after the new fiscal year begins and usually make funds available for a specified period. Additional resolutions are often needed after the first expires. Some continuing resolutions have provided appropriations for an entire fiscal year. Continuing resolutions for specific periods customarily fix a rate at which agencies may incur obligations based either on the previous year's appropriations, the president's budget request, or the amount as specified in the agency's regular annual appropriation bill if that bill has already been passed by one or both houses. In the House, continuing resolutions are privileged after Sept. 15.

Contract Authority — Statutory authority permitting an agency to enter into contracts or incur other obligations even though it has not received an appropriation to pay for them. Congress must eventually fund them because the government is legally liable for such payments. The Congressional Budget Act of 1974 requires that new contract authority may not be used unless provided for in advance by an appropriation act, but it permits a few exceptions.

Correcting Recorded Votes — The rules of both houses prohibit members from changing their votes after a vote result has been announced. Nevertheless, the Senate permits its members to withdraw or change their votes, by unanimous consent, immediately after the announcement. In rare instances, senators have been granted unanimous consent to change their votes several days or weeks after the announcement. Votes tallied by the electronic voting system in the House may not be changed. But when a vote actually given is not recorded during an oral call of the roll, a member may demand a correction as a matter of right. On all other alleged errors in a recorded vote, the Speaker determines whether the circumstances justify a change. Occasionally, members merely announce that they were incorrectly recorded; announcements can occur hours, days or even months after the vote and appear in the *Congressional Record*.

Cosponsor — A member who has joined one or more other members to sponsor a measure.

Credit Authority — Authority granted to an agency to incur direct loan obligations or to make loan guarantee commitments. The Congressional Budget Act of 1974 bans congressional consideration of credit authority legislation unless the extent of that authority is made subject to provisions in appropriation acts.

C-SPAN — Cable-Satellite Public Affairs Network, which provides live, gavel-to-gavel coverage of Senate floor proceedings on one cable television channel and coverage of House floor proceedings on another channel. C-SPAN also televises important committee hearings in both houses. Each house also transmits its televised proceedings directly to congressional offices.

Current Services Estimates — Executive branch estimates of the anticipated costs of federal programs and operations for the next and future fiscal years at existing levels of service and assuming no new initiatives or changes in existing law. The president submits these estimates to Congress with the annual budget and includes an explanation of the underlying economic and policy assumptions on which they are based, such as anticipated rates of inflation, real economic growth and unemployment, plus program caseloads and pay increases.

Custody of the Papers — Possession of an engrossed measure and certain related basic documents that the two houses produce as they try to resolve their differences over the measure.

Dance of the Swans and the Ducks — A whimsical description of the gestures some members use in connection with a request for a recorded vote, especially in the House. When members want their colleagues to stand in support of the request, they move their hands and arms in a gentle upward motion resembling the beginning flight of a graceful swan. When they want their colleagues to remain seated to avoid such a vote, they move their hands and arms in a vigorous downward motion resembling a diving duck.

Dean — Within a state's delegation in the House of Representatives, the member with the longest continuous service.

Debate — In congressional parlance, speeches delivered during consideration of a measure, motion or other matter, as distinguished from speeches in other parliamentary situations, such as one-minute and special order speeches when no business is pending. Virtually all debate in the House of Representatives is under some kind of time limitation. Most debate in the Senate is unlimited; that is, a senator, once recognized, may speak for as long as he or she chooses, unless the Senate invokes cloture.

Debt Limit — The maximum amount of outstanding federal public debt permitted by law. The limit (or ceiling) covers virtually all debt incurred by the government except agency debt. Each congressional budget resolution sets forth the new debt limit that may be required under its provisions.

Deferral — An impoundment of funds for a specific period of time that may not extend beyond the fiscal year in which it is proposed. Under the Impoundment Control Act of 1974, the president must notify Congress that he is deferring the spending or obligation of funds provided by law for a project or activity. Congress can disapprove the deferral by legislation.

Deficit — The amount by which the government's outlays exceed its budget receipts for a given fiscal year. Both the president's budget and the annual congressional budget resolution provide estimates of the deficit or surplus for the upcoming and several future fiscal years.

Degrees of Amendment — Designations that indicate the relationships of amendments to the text of a measure and to each other. In general, an amendment offered directly to the text of a measure is an amendment in the first degree, and an amendment to that amendment is an amendment in the second degree. Both houses normally prohibit amendments in the third degree — that is, an amendment to an amendment to an amendment.

Delegate — A nonvoting member of the House of Representatives elected to a two-year term from the District of Columbia, the territory of Guam, the territory of the Virgin Islands or the territory of American Samoa. By law, delegates may not vote in the full House but they may participate in debate, offer motions (except to reconsider) and serve and vote on standing and select committees. On their committees, delegates possess the same powers and privileges as other members and the Speaker may appoint them to appropriate conference committees and select committees.

Denounce — A formal action that condemns a member for misbehavior; considered by some experts to be equivalent to censure. (See Censure.)

Dilatory Tactics — Procedural actions intended to delay or prevent action by a house or a committee. They include, among others, offering numerous motions, demanding quorum calls and recorded votes at every opportunity, making numerous points of order and parliamentary inquiries and speaking as long as the applicable rules permit. The Senate rules permit a battery of dilatory tactics, especially lengthy speeches, except under cloture. In the House, possible dilatory tactics are more limited. Speeches are always subject to time limits and debate-ending motions. Moreover, a House rule instructs the Speaker not to entertain dilatory motions and lets the Speaker decide whether a motion is dilatory. However, the Speaker may not override the constitutional right of a member to demand the yeas and nays, and in practice usually waits for a point of order before exercising that authority. (See Cloture.)

Discharge a Committee — Remove a measure from a committee to which it has been referred in order to make it available for floor consideration. Noncontroversial measures are often discharged by unanimous consent. However, because congressional committees have no obligation to report measures referred to them, each house has procedures to extract controversial measures from recalcitrant committees. Six discharge procedures are available in the House of Representatives. The Senate uses a motion to discharge, which is usually converted into a discharge resolution.

District Office — Representatives maintain one or more offices in their districts for the purpose of assisting and communicating with constituents. The costs of maintaining these offices are paid from members' official allowances. Senators can use the official expense allowance to rent offices in their home state, subject to a funding formula based on their state's population and other factors.

District Work Period — The House term for a scheduled congressional recess during which members may visit their districts and conduct constituency business.

Division Vote — A vote in which the chair first counts those in favor of a proposition and then those opposed to it, with no record made of how each member votes. In the Senate, the chair may count raised hands or ask senators to stand, whereas the House requires members to stand; hence, often called a standing vote. Committees in both houses ordinarily use a show of hands. A division usually occurs after a voice vote and may be demanded by any member or ordered by the chair if there is any doubt about the outcome of the voice vote. The demand for a division can also come before a voice vote. In the Senate, the demand must come before the result of a voice vote is announced. It may be made after a voice vote announcement in the House, but only if no intervening business has transpired and only if the member was standing and seeking recognition at the time of the announcement. A demand for the yeas and nays or, in the House, for a recorded vote, takes precedence over a division vote.

Doorkeeper of the House — A former officer of the House of Representatives who was responsible for enforcing the rules prohibiting unauthorized persons from entering the chamber when the House is in session. The doorkeeper was usually the candidate of the majority party. In 1995 the office was abolished and its functions transferred to the sergeant at arms.

Effective Dates — Provisions of an act that specify when the entire act or individual provisions in it become effective as law. Most acts become effective on the date of enactment, but it is sometimes necessary or prudent to delay the effective dates of some provisions.

Electronic Voting — Since 1973 the House has used an electronic voting system to record the yeas and nays and to conduct recorded votes. Members vote by inserting their voting cards in one of the boxes at several locations in the chamber. They are given at least fifteen minutes to vote. When several votes occur immediately after each other, the Speaker may reduce the voting time to five minutes on the second and subsequent votes. The Speaker may allow additional time on each vote but may also close a vote at any time after the minimum time has expired. Members can change their votes at any time before the Speaker announces the result. The House also uses the electronic system for quorum calls. While a vote is in progress, a large panel above the Speaker's desk displays how each member has voted. Smaller panels on either side of the chamber display running totals of the votes and the time remaining. The Senate does not have electronic voting.

Enacting Clause — The opening language of each bill, beginning "Be it enacted by the Senate and House of Representatives of the United States of America in Congress assembled..." This language gives legal force to measures approved by Congress and signed by the president or enacted over the president's veto. A successful motion to strike it from a bill kills the entire measure.

Engrossed Bill — The official copy of a bill or joint resolution as passed by one chamber, including the text as amended by floor action and certified by the clerk of the House or the secretary of the Senate (as appropriate). Amendments by one house to a measure or amendments of the other also are engrossed. House engrossed documents are printed on blue paper; the Senate's are printed on white paper.

Enrolled Bill — The final official copy of a bill or joint resolution passed in identical form by both houses. An enrolled bill is printed on parchment. After it is certified by the chief officer of the house in which it originated and signed by the House Speaker and the Senate president pro tempore, the measure is sent to the White House for the president's signature.

Entitlement Program — A federal program under which individuals, businesses or units of government that meet the requirements or qualifications established by law are entitled to receive certain payments if they seek such payments. Major examples include Social Security, Medicare, Medicaid, unemployment insurance and military and federal civilian pensions. Congress cannot control their expenditures by refusing to appropriate the sums necessary to fund them because the government is legally obligated to pay eligible recipients the amounts to which the law entitles them.

Equality of the Houses — A component of the Constitution's emphasis on checks and balances under which each house is given essentially equal status in the enactment of legislation and in the relations and negotiations between the two houses. Although the House of Representatives initiates revenue and appropriation measures, the Senate has the right to amend them. Either house may initiate any other type of legislation, and neither can force the other to agree to, or even act on, its measures. Moreover, each house has a potential veto over the other because legislation requires agreement by both. Similarly, in a conference to resolve their differences on a measure, each house casts one vote, as determined by a majority of its conferees. In most other national bicameral legislatures, the powers of one house are markedly greater than those of the other.

Ethics Rules — Several rules or standing orders in each house that mandate certain standards of conduct for members and congressional employees in finance, employment, franking and other areas. The Senate Permanent Select Committee on Ethics and the House Committee on Standards of Official Conduct investigate alleged violations of conduct and recommend appropriate actions to their respective houses.

Exclusive Committee — (1) Under the rules of the Republican Conference and House Democratic Caucus, a standing committee whose members usually cannot serve on any other standing committee. As of 2000 the Appropriations, Energy and Commerce (beginning in the 105th Congress), Ways and Means and Rules Committees were designated as exclusive committees. (2) Under the rules of

the two party conferences in the Senate, a standing committee whose members may not simultaneously serve on any other exclusive committee.

Executive Calendar — The Senate's calendar for committee reports on its executive business, namely treaties and nominations. The calendar numbers indicate the order in which items were referred to the calendar but have no bearing on when or if the Senate will consider them. The Senate, by motion or unanimous consent, resolves itself into executive session to consider them.

Executive Document — A document, usually a treaty, sent by the president to the Senate for approval. It is referred to a committee in the same manner as other measures. Resolutions to ratify treaties have their own "treaty document" numbers. For example, the first treaty submitted in the 106th Congress would be "Treaty Doc 106-1."

Executive Order — A unilateral proclamation by the president that has a policy-making or legislative impact. Members of Congress have challenged some executive orders on the grounds that they usurped the authority of the legislative branch. Although the Supreme Court has ruled that a particular order exceeded the president's authority, it has upheld others as falling within the president's general constitutional powers.

Executive Privilege — The assertion that presidents have the right to withhold certain information from Congress. Presidents have based their claim on (1) the constitutional separation of powers; (2) the need for secrecy in military and diplomatic affairs; (3) the need to protect individuals from unfavorable publicity; (4) the need to safeguard the confidential exchange of ideas in the executive branch; and (5) the need to protect individuals who provide confidential advice to the president.

Executive Session — (1) A Senate meeting devoted to the consideration of treaties or nominations. Normally, the Senate meets in legislative session; it resolves itself into executive session, by motion or by unanimous consent, to deal with its executive business. It also keeps a separate Journal for executive sessions. Executive sessions are usually open to the public, but the Senate may choose to close them.

Expulsion — A member's removal from office by a two-thirds vote of his or her house; the supermajority is required by the Constitution. It is the most severe and most rarely used sanction a house can invoke against a member. Although the Constitution provides no explicit grounds for expulsion, the courts have ruled that it may be applied only for misconduct during a member's term of office, not for conduct before the member's election. Generally, neither house will consider expulsion of a member convicted of a crime until the judicial processes have been exhausted. At that stage, members sometimes resign rather than face expulsion. In 1977 the House adopted a rule urging members convicted of certain crimes to voluntarily abstain from voting or participating in other legislative business.

Extensions of Remarks — An appendix to the daily *Congressional Record* that consists primarily of miscellaneous extraneous material submitted by members. It often includes members' statements not delivered on the floor, newspaper articles and editorials, praise for a member's constituents and noteworthy letters received by a member, among other material. Representatives supply the bulk of this material; senators submit very little. "Extensions of Remarks" pages are separately numbered, and each number is preceded by the letter "E." Materials may be placed in the Extensions of Remarks section only by unanimous consent. Usually, one member of each party makes the request each day on behalf of his or her party colleagues after the House has completed its legislative business of the day.

Federal Debt — The total amount of monies borrowed and not yet repaid by the federal government. Federal debt consists of public debt and agency debt. Public debt is the portion of the federal debt borrowed by the Treasury or the Federal Financing Bank directly from the public or from another federal fund or account. For example, the Treasury regularly borrows money from the Social Security trust fund. Public debt accounts for about 99 percent of the federal debt. Agency debt refers to the debt incurred by federal agencies such as the Export-Import Bank but excluding the Treasury and the Federal Financing Bank, which are authorized by law to borrow funds from the public or from another government fund or account.

Filibuster — The use of obstructive and time-consuming parliamentary tactics by one member or a minority of members to delay, modify or defeat proposed legislation or rules changes. Filibusters are also sometimes used to delay urgently needed measures to force the body to accept other legislation. The Senate's rules permitting unlimited debate and the extraordinary majority it requires to impose cloture make filibustering particularly effective in that chamber. Under the stricter rules of the House, filibusters in that body are short-lived and therefore ineffective and rarely attempted.

Fiscal Year — The federal government's annual accounting period. It begins Oct. 1 and ends on the following Sept. 30. A fiscal year is designated by the calendar year in which it ends and is often referred to as FY. Thus, fiscal year 1998 began Oct. 1, 1997, ended Sept. 30, 1998, and is called FY98. In theory, Congress is supposed to complete action on all budgetary measures applying to a fiscal year before that year begins. It rarely does so.

Five-Minute Rule — A House rule that limits debate on an amendment offered in Committee of the Whole to five minutes for its sponsor and five minutes for an opponent. In practice, the committee routinely permits longer debate by two devices: the offering of pro forma amendments, each debatable for five minutes, and unanimous consent for a member to speak longer than five minutes. Consequently, debate on an amendment sometimes continues for hours. At any time after the first ten minutes, however, the committee may shut off debate immediately or by a specified time, either by unanimous consent or by majority vote on a nondebatable motion. The motion, which dates from 1847, is also used in the House as in Committee of the Whole, where debate also may be shut off by a motion for the previous question.

Floor — The ground level of the House or Senate chamber where members sit and the houses conduct their business. When members are attending a meeting of their house they are said to be on the floor. Floor action refers to the procedural actions taken during floor consideration such as deciding on motions, taking up measures, amending them and voting.

Floor Manager — A majority party member responsible for guiding a measure through its floor consideration in a house and for devising the political and procedural strategies that might be required to get it passed. The presiding officer gives the floor manager priority recognition to debate, offer amendments, oppose amendments and make crucial procedural motions.

Frank — Informally, members' legal right to send official mail postage free under their signatures; often called the franking privilege. Technically, it is the autographic or facsimile signature used on envelopes instead of stamps that permits members and certain congressional officers to send their official mail free of charge. The franking privilege has been authorized by law since the first Congress, except for a few months in 1873. Congress reimburses the U.S. Postal Service for the franked mail it handles.

Function or Functional Category — A broad category of national need and spending of budgetary significance. A category provides an accounting method for allocating and keeping track of budgetary resources and expenditures for that function because it includes all budget accounts related to the function's subject or purpose such as agriculture, administration of justice, commerce and housing and energy. Functions do not necessarily correspond with appropriations acts or with the budgets of individual agencies. As of 2000 there were twenty functional categories, each divided into a number of subfunctions.

Gag Rule — A pejorative term for any type of special rule reported by the House Rules Committee that proposes to prohibit amendments to a measure or only permits amendments offered by the reporting committee.

Galleries — The balconies overlooking each chamber from which the public, news media, staff and others may observe floor proceedings.

General Appropriation Bill — A term applied to each of the thirteen annual bills that provide funds for most federal agencies and programs and also to the supplemental appropriation bills that contain appropriations for more than one agency or program.

Germaneness — The requirement that an amendment be closely related — in terms of subject or purpose, for example — to the text it proposes to amend. A House rule requires that all amendments be germane. In the Senate, only amendments offered to general appropriation bills and budget measures or proposed under cloture must be germane. Germaneness rules can be waived by suspension of the rules in both houses, by unanimous consent agreements in the Senate and by special rules from the Rules Committee in the House. Moreover, presiding officers usually do not enforce germaneness rules on their own initiative; therefore, a nongermane amendment can be adopted if no member raises a point of order against it. Under cloture in the Senate, however, the chair may take the initiative to rule amendments out of order as not being germane, without a point of order being made. All House debate must be germane except during general debate in the Committee of the Whole, but special rules invariably require that such debate be "confined to the bill." The Senate requires germane debate only during the first three hours of each daily session. Under the precedents of both houses, an amendment can be relevant but not necessarily germane. A crucial factor in determining germaneness in the House is how the subject of a measure or matter is defined. For example, the subject of a measure authorizing construction of a naval vessel is defined as being the construction of a single vessel; therefore, an amendment to authorize an additional vessel is not germane.

Gerrymandering — The manipulation of legislative district boundaries to benefit a particular party, politician or minority group. The term originated in 1812 when the Massachusetts legislature redrew the lines of state legislative districts to favor the party of Gov. Elbridge Gerry, and some critics said one district looked like a salamander. (See also Congressional District; Redistricting.)

Government Accountability Office (GAO) — A congressional support agency, often referred to as the investigative arm of Congress. It evaluates and audits federal agencies and programs in the United States and abroad on its initiative or at the request of congressional committees or members.

Gramm-Rudman-Hollings Act of 1985 — Common name for the Balanced Budget and Emergency Deficit Control Act of 1985, which established new budget procedures intended to balance the federal budget by fiscal year 1991. (The timetable subsequently was extended and then deleted.) The act's chief sponsors were senators Phil Gramm (R-Texas), Warren Rudman (R-N.H.) Ernest Hollings (D-S.C.).

Grandfather Clause — A provision in a measure, law or rule that exempts an individual, entity or a defined category of individuals or entities from complying with a new policy or restriction. For example, a bill that would raise taxes on persons who reach the age of sixty-five after a certain date inherently grandfathers out those who are sixty-five before that date. Similarly, a Senate rule limiting senators to two major committee assignments also grandfathers some senators who were sitting on a third major committee before a specified date.

Grants-in-Aid — Payments by the federal government to state and local governments to help provide for assistance programs or public services.

Hearing — Committee or subcommittee meetings to receive testimony on proposed legislation during investigations or for oversight purposes. Relatively few bills are important enough to justify formal hearings. Witnesses often include experts, government officials, spokespersons for interested groups, officials of the Government Accountability Office and members of Congress.

Hold — A senator's request that his or her party leaders delay floor consideration of certain legislation or presidential nominations. The majority leader usually honors a hold for a reasonable period of time, especially if its purpose is to assure the senator that the matter will not be called up during his or her absence or to give the senator time to gather necessary information.

Hold (or Have) the Floor — A member's right to speak without interruption, unless he or she violates a rule, after recognition by the presiding officer. At the member's discretion, he or she may yield to another member for a question in the Senate or for a question or statement in the House, but may reclaim the floor at any time.

Hold-Harmless Clause — In legislation providing a new formula for allocating federal funds, a clause to ensure that recipients of those funds do not receive less in a future year than they did in the current year if the new formula would result in a reduction for them. Similar to a grandfather clause, it has been used most frequently to soften the impact of sudden reductions in federal grants. (See Grandfather Clause.)

Hopper — A box on the clerk's desk in the House chamber into which members deposit bills and resolutions to introduce them. In House jargon, to drop a bill in the hopper is to introduce it.

Hour Rule — A House rule that permits members, when recognized, to hold the floor in debate for no more than one hour each. The majority party member customarily yields one-half the time to a minority member. Although the hour rule applies to general debate in Committee of the Whole as well as in the House, special rules routinely vary the length of time for such debate and its control to fit the circumstances of particular measures.

House As In Committee of the Whole — A hybrid combination of procedures from the general rules of the House and from the rules of the Committee of the Whole, sometimes used to expedite consideration of a measure on the floor.

House Calendar — The calendar reserved for all public bills and resolutions that do not raise revenue or directly or indirectly appropriate money or property when they are favorably reported by House committees.

House Manual — A commonly used title for the handbook of the rules of the House of Representatives, published in each Congress. Its official title is *Constitution, Jefferson's Manual and Rules of the House of Representatives.*

House of Representatives — The house of Congress in which states are represented roughly in proportion to their populations, but every state is guaranteed at least one representative. By law, the number of voting representatives is fixed at 435. Four delegates and one resident commissioner also serve in the House; they may vote in their committees but not on the House floor. Although the House and Senate have equal legislative power, the Constitution gives the House sole authority to originate revenue measures. The House also claims the right to originate appropriation measures, a claim the Senate disputes in theory but concedes in practice. The House has the sole power to impeach, and it elects the president when no candidate has received a majority of the electoral votes. It is sometimes referred to as the lower body.

Immunity — (1) Members' constitutional protection from lawsuits and arrest in connection with their legislative duties. They may not be tried for libel or slander for anything they say on the floor of a house or in committee. Nor may they be arrested while attending sessions of their houses or when traveling to or from sessions of Congress, except when charged with treason, a felony or a breach of the peace. (2) In the case of a witness before a committee, a grant of protection from prosecution based on that person's testimony to the committee. It is used to compel witnesses to testify who would otherwise refuse to do so on the constitutional ground of possible selfincrimination. Under such a grant, none of a witness's testimony may be used against him or her in a court proceeding except in a prosecution for perjury or for giving a false statement to Congress. (See also Contempt of Congress.)

Impeachment — The first step to remove the president, vice president or other federal civil officers from office and to disqualify them from any future federal office "of honor, Trust or Profit." An impeachment is a formal charge of treason, bribery or "other high Crimes and Misdemeanors." The House has the sole power of impeachment and the Senate the sole power of trying the charges and convicting. The House impeaches by a simple majority vote; conviction requires a two-thirds vote of all senators present.

Impeachment Trial, Removal and Disqualification — The Senate conducts an impeachment trial under a separate set of twenty-six rules that appears in the Senate Manual. Under the Constitution, the chief justice of the United States presides over trials of the president, but the vice president, the president pro tempore or any other senator may preside over the impeachment trial of another official.

The Constitution requires senators to take an oath for an impeachment trial. During the trial, senators may not engage in colloquies or participate in arguments, but they may submit questions in writing to House managers or defense counsel. After the trial concludes, the Senate votes separately on each article of impeachment without debate unless the Senate orders the doors closed for private discussions. During deliberations senators may speak no more than once on a question, not for more than ten minutes on an interlocutory question and not more than fifteen minutes on the final question. These rules may be set aside by unanimous consent or suspended on motion by a two-thirds vote.

The Senate's impeachment trial of President Clinton in 1999 was only the second such trial involving a president. It continued for five weeks, with the Senate voting not to convict on the two impeachment articles.

Senate impeachment rules allow the Senate, at its own discretion, to name a committee to hear evidence and conduct the trial, with all senators thereafter voting on the charges. The impeachment trials of three federal judges were conducted this way, and the Supreme Court upheld the validity of these rules in *Nixon v. United States*, 506 U.S. 224, 1993.

An official convicted on impeachment charges is removed from office immediately. However, the convicted official is not barred from holding a federal office in the future unless the Senate, after its conviction vote, also approves a resolution disqualifying the convicted official from future office. For example, federal judge Alcee L. Hastings was impeached and convicted in 1989, but the Senate did not vote to bar him from office in the future. In 1992 Hastings was elected to the House of Representatives, and no challenge was raised against seating him when he took the oath of office in 1993.

Impoundment — An executive branch action or inaction that delays or withholds the expenditure or obligation of budget authority provided by law. The Impoundment Control Act of 1974 classifies impoundments as either deferrals or rescissions, requires the president to notify Congress about all such actions and gives Congress authority to approve or reject them.

Inspector General (IG) In the House of Representatives — A position established with the passage of the House Administrative Reform Resolution of 1992. The duties of the office have been revised several times and are now contained in House Rule II. The inspector general (IG), who is subject to the policy direction and oversight of the Committee on House Administration, is appointed for a Congress jointly by the Speaker and the majority and minority leaders of the House. The IG communicates the results of audits to the House officers or officials who were the subjects of the audits and suggests appropriate corrective measures. The IG submits a report of each audit to the Speaker, the majority and minority leaders and the chair-

man and ranking minority member of the House Administration Committee; notifies these five members in the case of any financial irregularity discovered; and reports to the Committee on Standards of Official Conduct on possible violations of House rules or any applicable law by any House member, officer or employee. The IG's office also has certain duties to audit various financial operations of the House that had previously been performed by the Government Accountability Office.

Instruct Conferees — A formal action by a house urging its conferees to uphold a particular position on a measure in conference. The instruction may be to insist on certain provisions in the measure as passed by that house or to accept a provision in the version passed by the other house. Instructions to conferees are not binding because the primary responsibility of conferees is to reach agreement on a measure and neither House can compel the other to accept particular provisions or positions.

Investigative Power — The authority of Congress and its committees to pursue investigations, upheld by the Supreme Court but limited to matters related to, and in furtherance of, a legitimate task of the Congress. Standing committees in both houses are permanently authorized to investigate matters within their jurisdictions. Major investigations are sometimes conducted by temporary select, special or joint committees established by resolutions for that purpose.

Some rules of the House provide certain safeguards for witnesses and others during investigative hearings. These permit counsel to accompany witnesses, require that each witness receive a copy of the committee's rules and order the committee to go into closed session if it believes the testimony to be heard might defame, degrade or incriminate any person. The committee may subsequently decide to hear such testimony in open session. The Senate has no rules of this kind.

Item Veto — Item veto authority, which is available to most state governors, allows governors to eliminate or reduce items in legislative measures presented for their signature without vetoing the entire measure and sign the rest into law. A similar authority was briefly granted to the U.S. president under the Line Item Veto Act of 1996. According to the majority opinion of the Supreme Court in its 1998 decision overturning that law, a constitutional amendment would be necessary to give the president such item veto authority.

Jefferson's Manual — Short title of *Jefferson's Manual of Parliamentary Practice*, prepared by Thomas Jefferson for his guidance when he was president of the Senate from 1797 to 1801. Although it reflects English parliamentary practice in his day, many procedures in both houses of Congress are still rooted in its basic precepts. Under a House rule adopted in 1837, the manual's provisions govern House procedures when applicable and when they are not inconsistent with its standing rules and orders. The Senate, however, has never officially acknowledged it as a direct authority for its legislative procedure.

Johnson Rule — A policy instituted in 1953 under which all Democratic senators are assigned to one major committee before any Democrat is assigned to two. The Johnson Rule is named after its author, Sen. Lyndon B. Johnson, D-Texas, then the Senate's Democratic leader. Senate Republicans adopted a similar policy soon thereafter.

Joint Committee — A committee composed of members selected from each house. The functions of most joint committees involve investigation, research or oversight of agencies closely related to Congress. Permanent joint committees, created by statute, are sometimes called standing joint committees. Once quite numerous, only four joint committees remained as of 2002: Joint Economic, Joint Taxation, Joint Library and Joint Printing. None has authority to report legislation.

Joint Resolution — A legislative measure that Congress uses for purposes other than general legislation. Similar to a bill, it has the force of law when passed by both houses and either approved by the president or passed over the president's veto. Unlike a bill, a joint resolution enacted into law is not called an act; it retains its original title. Most often, joint resolutions deal with such relatively limited matters as the correction of errors in existing law, continuing appropriations, a single appropriation or the establishment of permanent joint committees. Unlike bills, however, joint resolutions also are used to propose constitutional amendments; these do not require the president's signature and become effective only when ratified by three-fourths of the states. The House designates joint resolutions as H.J. Res., the Senate as S.J. Res. Each house numbers its joint resolutions consecutively in the order of introduction during a two-year Congress.

Joint Session — Informally, any combined meeting of the Senate and the House. Technically, a joint session is a combined meeting to count the electoral votes for president and vice president or to hear a presidential address, such as the State of the Union message; any other formal combined gathering of both houses is a joint meeting. Joint sessions are authorized by concurrent resolutions and are held in the House chamber, because of its larger seating capacity. Although the president of the Senate and the Speaker sit side by side at the Speaker's desk during combined meetings, the former presides over the electoral count and the latter presides on all other occasions and introduces the president or other guest speaker. The president and other guests may address a joint session or meeting only by invitation.

Joint Sponsorship — Two or more members sponsoring the same measure.

Journal — The official record of House or Senate actions, including every motion offered, every vote cast, amendments agreed to, quorum calls and so forth. Unlike the *Congressional Record*, it does not provide reports of speeches, debates, statements and the like. The Constitution requires each house to maintain a *Journal* and to publish it periodically.

Junket — A member's trip at government expense, especially abroad, ostensibly on official business but, it is often alleged, for pleasure.

Killer Amendment — An amendment that, if agreed to, might lead to the defeat of the measure it amends, either in the house in which the amendment is offered or at some later stage of the legislative process. Members sometimes deliberately offer or vote for such an amendment in the expectation that it will undermine support for the measure in Congress or increase the likelihood that the president will veto it.

King of the Mountain (or Hill) Rule — (See Queen of the Hill Rule.)

LA — (See Legislative Assistant.)

Lame Duck — Jargon for a member who has not been reelected, or did not seek reelection, and is serving the balance of his or her term.

Lame Duck Session — A session of a Congress held after the election for the succeeding Congress, so-called after the lame duck members still serving.

Last Train Out — Colloquial name for last must-pass bill of a session of Congress.

Law — An act of Congress that has been signed by the president, passed over the president's veto or allowed to become law without the president's signature.

Lay on the Table — A motion to dispose of a pending proposition immediately, finally and adversely; that is, to kill it without a direct vote on its substance. Often simply called a motion to table, it is not debatable and is adopted by majority vote or without objection. It is a highly privileged motion, taking precedence over all others except the motion to adjourn in the House and all but three additional motions in the Senate. It can kill a bill or resolution, an amendment, another motion, an appeal or virtually any other matter.

Tabling an amendment also tables the measure to which the amendment is pending in the House, but not in the Senate. The House does not allow the motion against the motion to recommit, in Committee of the Whole, and in some other situations. In the Senate it is the only permissible motion that immediately ends debate on a proposition, but only to kill it.

(The) Leadership — Usually, a reference to the majority and minority leaders of the Senate or to the Speaker and minority leader of the House. The term sometimes includes the majority leader in the House and the majority and minority whips in each house and, at other times, other party officials as well.

Legislation — (1) A synonym for legislative measures: bills and joint resolutions. (2) Provisions in such measures or in substantive amendments offered to them. (3) In some contexts, provisions that change existing substantive or authorizing law, rather than provisions that make appropriations.

Legislation on an Appropriation Bill — A common reference to provisions changing existing law that appear in, or are offered as amendments to, a general appropriation bill. A House rule prohibits the inclusion of such provisions in general appropriation bills unless they retrench expenditures. An analogous Senate rule permits points of order against amendments to a general appropriation bill that propose general legislation.

Legislative Assistant (LA) — A member's staff person responsible for monitoring and preparing legislation on particular subjects and for advising the member on them; commonly referred to as an LA.

Legislative Day — The day that begins when a house meets after an adjournment and ends when it next adjourns. Because the House of Representatives normally adjourns at the end of a daily session, its legislative and calendar days usually coincide. The Senate, however, frequently recesses at the end of a daily session, and its legislative day may extend over several calendar days, weeks or months. Among other uses, this technicality permits the Senate to save time by circumventing its morning hour, a procedure required at the beginning of every legislative day.

Legislative History — (1) A chronological list of actions taken on a measure during its progress through the legislative process. (2) The official documents relating to a measure, the entries in the *Journals* of the two houses on that measure and the *Congressional Record* text of its consideration in both houses. The documents include all committee reports and the conference report and joint explanatory statement, if any. Courts and affected federal agencies study a measure's legislative history for congressional intent about its purpose and interpretation.

Legislative Process — (1) Narrowly, the stages in the enactment of a law from introduction to final disposition. An introduced measure that becomes law typically travels through reference to committee; committee and subcommittee consideration; report to the chamber; floor consideration; amendment; passage; engrossment; messaging to the other house; similar steps in that house, including floor amendment of the measure; return of the measure to the first house; consideration of amendments between the houses or a conference to resolve their differences; approval of the conference report by both houses; enrollment; approval by the president or override of the president's veto; and deposit with the Archivist of the United States. (2) Broadly, the political, lobbying and other factors that affect or influence the process of enacting laws.

Legislative Veto — A procedure, declared unconstitutional in 1983, that allowed Congress or one of its houses to nullify certain actions of the president, executive branch agencies or independent agencies. Sometimes called congressional vetoes or congressional disapprovals. Following the Supreme Court's 1983 decision, Congress amended several legislative veto statutes to require enactment of joint resolutions, which are subject to presidential veto, for nullifying executive branch actions.

Limitation on a General Appropriation Bill — Language that prohibits expenditures for part of an authorized purpose from funds provided in a general appropriation bill. Precedents require that the language be phrased in the negative: that none of the funds provided in a pending appropriation bill shall be used for a specified authorized activity. Limitations in general appropriation bills are permitted on the grounds that Congress can refuse to fund authorized programs and, therefore, can refuse to fund any part of them as long as the prohibition does not change existing law. House precedents have established that a limitation does not change existing law if it does not impose additional duties or burdens on executive branch officials, interfere with their discretionary authority or require them to make judgments or determinations not required by existing law. The proliferation of limitation amendments in the 1970s and early 1980s prompted the House to adopt a rule in 1983 making it more difficult for members to offer them. The rule bans such amendments during the reading of an appropriation bill for amendments, unless they are specifically authorized in existing law. Other limitations may be offered after the reading, but the Committee of the Whole can foreclose them by adopting a motion to rise and report the bill back to the House. In 1995 the rule was amended to allow the motion to rise and report to be made only by the majority leader or his or her designee. The House Appropriations Committee, however, can include limitation provisions in the bills it reports.

Line Item — An amount in an appropriation measure. It can refer to a single appropriation account or to separate amounts within the account. In the congressional budget process, the term usually refers to assumptions about the funding of particular programs or accounts that underlie the broad functional amounts in a budget resolution. These assumptions are discussed in the reports accompanying each resolution and are not binding.

Line-Item Veto — (See Item Veto.)

Line Item Veto Act of 1996 — A law, in effect only from January 1997 until June 1998, that granted the president authority intended to be functionally equivalent to an item veto, by amending the Impoundment Control Act of 1974 to incorporate an approach known as enhanced rescission. Key provisions established a new procedure that permitted the president to cancel amounts of new discretionary appropriations (budget authority), new items of direct spending (entitlements) or certain limited tax benefits. It also required the president to notify Congress of the cancellation in a special message within five calendar days after signing the measure. The cancellation would become permanent unless legislation disapproving it was enacted within thirty days. On June 25, 1998, in *Clinton v. City of New York* the Supreme Court held the Line Item Veto Act unconstitutional, on the grounds that its cancellation provisions violated the presentment clause in Article I, clause 7, of the Constitution.

Live Pair — A voluntary and informal agreement between two members on opposite sides of an issue, one of whom is absent for a recorded vote, under which the member who is present withholds or withdraws his or her vote to offset the failure to vote by the member who is absent. Usually the member in attendance announces that he or she has a live pair, states how each would have voted and votes

"present." In the House, under a rules change enacted in the 106th Congress, a live pair is only permitted on the rare occasions when electronic voting is not used.

Live Quorum — In the Senate, a quorum call to which senators are expected to respond. Senators usually suggest the absence of a quorum, not to force a quorum to appear, but to provide a pause in the proceedings during which senators can engage in private discussions or wait for a senator to come to the floor. A senator desiring a live quorum usually announces his or her intention, giving fair warning that there will be an objection to any unanimous consent request that the quorum call be dispensed with before it is completed.

Loan Guarantee — A statutory commitment by the federal government to pay part or all of a loan's principal and interest to a lender or the holder of a security in case the borrower defaults.

Lobby — To try to persuade members of Congress to propose, pass, modify or defeat proposed legislation or to change or repeal existing laws. Lobbyists attempt to promote their preferences or those of a group, organization or industry. Originally the term referred to persons frequenting the lobbies or corridors of legislative chambers in order to speak to lawmakers. In a general sense, lobbying includes not only direct contact with members but also indirect attempts to influence them, such as writing to them or persuading others to write or visit them, attempting to mold public opinion toward a desired legislative goal by various means and contributing or arranging for contributions to members' election campaigns. The right to lobby stems from the First Amendment to the Constitution, which bans laws that abridge the right of the people to petition the government for a redress of grievances.

Lobbying Disclosure Act of 1995 — The principal statute requiring disclosure of — and also, to a degree, circumscribing — the activities of lobbyists. In general, it requires lobbyists who spend more than 20 percent of their time on lobbying activities to register and make semiannual reports of their activities to the clerk of the House and the secretary of the Senate, although the law provides for a number of exemptions. Among the statute's prohibitions, lobbyists are not allowed to make contributions to the legal defense fund of a member or high government official or to reimburse for official travel. Civil penalties for failure to comply may include fines of up to $50,000. The act does not include grassroots lobbying in its definition of lobbying activities.

The act amends several other lobby laws, notably the Foreign Agents Registration Act (FARA), so that lobbyists can submit a single filing. Since the measure was enacted, the number of lobby registrations has risen from about 12,000 to more than 20,000. In 1998 expenditures on federal lobbying, as disclosed under the Lobbying Disclosure Act, totaled $1.42 billion. The 1995 act supersedes the 1946 Federal Regulation of Lobbying Act, which was repealed in Section 11 of the 1995 Act.

Logrolling — Jargon for a legislative tactic or bargaining strategy in which members try to build support for their legislation by promising to support legislation desired by other members or by accepting amendments they hope will induce their colleagues to vote for their bill.

Lower Body — A way to refer to the House of Representatives, which is considered pejorative by House members.

Mace — The symbol of the office of the House sergeant at arms. Under the direction of the Speaker, the sergeant at arms is responsible for preserving order on the House floor by holding up the mace in front of an unruly member, or by carrying the mace up and down the aisles to quell boisterous behavior. When the House is in session, the mace sits on a pedestal at the Speaker's right; when the House is in Committee of the Whole, it is moved to a lower pedestal. The mace is forty-six inches high and consists of thirteen ebony rods bound in silver and topped by a silver globe with a silver eagle, wings outstretched, perched on it.

Majority Leader — The majority party's chief floor spokesperson, elected by that party's caucus — sometimes called floor leader. In the Senate, the majority leader also develops the party's political and procedural strategy, usually in collaboration with other party officials and committee chairmen. The majority leader negotiates the Senate's agenda and committee ratios with the minority leader and usually calls up measures for floor action. The chamber traditionally concedes to the majority leader the right to determine the days on which it will meet and the hours at which it will convene and adjourn. In the House, the majority leader is the Speaker's deputy and heir apparent and helps plan the floor agenda and the party's legislative strategy and often speaks for the party leadership in debate.

Managers — (1) The official title of members appointed to a conference committee, commonly called conferees. The ranking majority and minority managers for each house also manage floor consideration of the committee's conference report. (2) The members who manage the initial floor consideration of a measure. (3) The official title of House members appointed to present impeachment arti-

cles to the Senate and to act as prosecutors on behalf of the House during the Senate trial of the impeached person.

Mandatory Appropriations — Amounts that Congress must appropriate annually because it has no discretion over them unless it first amends existing substantive law. Certain entitlement programs, for example, require annual appropriations.

Markup — A meeting or series of meetings by a committee or subcommittee during which members mark up a measure by offering, debating and voting on amendments to it.

Means-Tested Programs — Programs that provide benefits or services to low-income individuals who meet a test of need. Most are entitlement programs, such as Medicaid, food stamps and Supplementary Security Income. A few — for example, subsidized housing and various social services — are funded through discretionary appropriations.

Members' Allowances — Official expenses that are paid for or for which members are reimbursed by their houses. Among these are the costs of office space in congressional buildings and in their home states or districts; office equipment and supplies; postage-free mailings (the franking privilege); a set number of trips to and from home states or districts, as well as travel elsewhere on official business; telephone and other telecommunications services; and staff salaries.

Member's Staff — The personal staff to which a member is entitled. The House sets a maximum number of staff and a monetary allowance for each member. The Senate does not set a maximum staff level, but it does set a monetary allowance for each member. In each house, the staff allowance is included with office expenses allowances and official mail allowances in a consolidated allowance. Representatives and senators can spend as much money in their consolidated allowances for staff, office expenses or official mail, as long as they do not exceed the monetary value of the three allowances combined. This provides members with flexibility in operating their offices.

Method of Equal Proportions — The mathematical formula used since 1950 to determine how the 435 seats in the House of Representatives should be distributed among the fifty states in the apportionment following each decennial census. It minimizes as much as possible the proportional difference between the average district population in any two states. Because the Constitution guarantees each state at least one representative, fifty seats are automatically apportioned. The formula calculates priority numbers for each state, assigns the first of the 385 remaining seats to the state with the highest priority number, the second to the state with the next highest number and so on until all seats are distributed. (See Apportionment.)

Midterm Election — The general election for members of Congress that occurs in November of the second year in a presidential term.

Minority Leader — The minority party's leader and chief floor spokesman, elected by the party caucus; sometimes called minority floor leader. With the assistance of other party officials and the ranking minority members of committees, the minority leader devises the party's political and procedural strategy.

Minority Staff — Employees who assist the minority party members of a committee. Most committees hire separate majority and minority party staffs but they also may hire nonpartisan staff. Senate rules state that a committee's staff must reflect the relative number of its majority and minority party committee members, and the rules guarantee the minority at least one-third of the funds available for hiring partisan staff. In the House, each committee is authorized thirty professional staff, and the minority members of most committees may select up to ten of these staff (subject to full committee approval). Under House rules, the minority party is to be "treated fairly" in the apportionment of additional staff resources. Each House committee determines the portion of its additional staff it allocates to the minority; some committees allocate one-third; and others allot less.

Modified Rule — A special rule from the House Rules Committee that permits only certain amendments to be offered to a measure during its floor consideration or that bans certain specified amendments or amendments on certain subjects.

Morning Business — In the Senate, routine business that is to be transacted at the beginning of the morning hour. The business consists, first, of laying before the Senate, and referring to committees, matters such as messages from the president and the House, federal agency reports and unreferred petitions, memorials, bills and joint resolutions. Next, senators may present additional petitions and memorials. Then committees may present their reports, after which senators may introduce bills and resolutions. Finally, resolutions coming over from a previous day are taken up for consideration. In practice, the Senate adopts standing orders that permit senators to introduce measures and file reports at any time, but only if there has been a morning business period on that day. Because the Senate often remains in the same legislative day for several days, weeks or months at a time, it orders a morning business period almost every calendar day for the convenience of senators who wish to introduce measures or make reports.

Morning Hour — A two-hour period at the beginning of a new legislative day during which the Senate is supposed to conduct routine business, call the calendar on Mondays and deal with other matters described in a Senate rule. In practice, the morning hour very rarely, if ever, occurs, in part because the Senate frequently recesses, rather than adjourns, at the end of a daily session. Therefore the rule does not apply when the senate next meets. The Senate's rules reserve the first hour of the morning for morning business. After the completion of morning business, or at the end of the first hour, the rules permit a motion to proceed to the consideration of a measure on the calendar out of its regular order (except on Mondays). Because that normally debatable motion is not debatable if offered during the morning hour, the majority leader may, but rarely does, use this procedure in anticipating a filibuster on the motion to proceed. If the Senate agrees to the motion, it can consider the measure until the end of the morning hour, and if there is no unfinished business from the previous day it can continue considering it after the morning hour. But if there is unfinished business, a motion to continue consideration is necessary, and that motion is debatable.

Motion — A formal proposal for a procedural action, such as to consider, to amend, to lay on the table, to reconsider, to recess or to adjourn. It has been estimated that at least eighty-five motions are possible under various circumstances in the House of Representatives, somewhat fewer in the Senate. Not all motions are created equal; some are privileged or preferential and enjoy priority over others. Some motions are debatable, amendable or divisible, while others are not.

Multiple and Sequential Referrals — The practice of referring a measure to two or more committees for concurrent consideration (multiple referral) or successively to several committees in sequence (sequential referral). A measure may also be divided into several parts, with each referred to a different committee or to several committees sequentially (split referral). In theory this gives all committees that have jurisdiction over parts of a measure the opportunity to consider and report on them.

Before 1975, House precedents banned such referrals. A 1975 rule required the Speaker to make concurrent and sequential referrals "to the maximum extent feasible." On sequential referrals, the Speaker could set deadlines for reporting the measure. The Speaker ruled that this provision authorized him to discharge a committee from further consideration of a measure and place it on the appropriate calendar of the House if the committee fails to meet the Speaker's deadline. The Speaker also used combinations of concurrent and sequential referrals. In 1995 joint referrals were prohibited. Now each measure is referred to a primary committee and also may be referred, either concurrently or sequentially, to one or more other committees, but usually only for consideration of portions of the measure that fall within the jurisdiction of each of those other committees.

In the Senate, before 1977 concurrent and sequential referrals were permitted only by unanimous consent. In that year, a rule authorized a privileged motion for such a referral if offered jointly by the majority and minority leaders. Debate on the motion and all amendments to it is limited to two hours. The motion may set deadlines for reporting and provide for discharging the committees involved if they fail to meet the deadlines. To date, this procedure has never been invoked; multiple referrals in the Senate continue to be made by unanimous consent.

Multiyear Appropriation — An appropriation that remains available for spending or obligation for more than one fiscal year; the exact period of time is specified in the act making the appropriation.

Multiyear Authorization — (1) Legislation that authorizes the existence or continuation of an agency, program or activity for more than one fiscal year. (2) Legislation that authorizes appropriations for an agency, program or activity for more than one fiscal year.

Nomination — A proposed presidential appointment to a federal office submitted to the Senate for confirmation. Approval is by majority vote. The Constitution explicitly requires confirmation for ambassadors, consuls, "public Ministers" (department heads) and Supreme Court justices. By law, other federal judges, all military promotions of officers and many high-level civilian officials must be confirmed.

Oath of Office — Upon taking office, members of Congress must swear or affirm that they will "support and defend the Constitution...against all enemies, foreign and domestic," that they will "bear true faith and allegiance" to the Constitution, that they take the obligation "freely, without any mental reservation or purpose of evasion," and that they will "well and faithfully discharge the duties" of their office. The oath is required by the Constitution, and the wording is prescribed by a statute. All House members must take the oath at the beginning of each new Congress. Usually, the member with the longest continuous service in the House swears in the Speaker, who then swears in the other members. The president of the Senate or a surrogate administers the oath to newly elected or reelected senators.

Obligation — A binding agreement by a government agency to pay for goods, products, services, studies and the like, either immediately or in the future. When an agency enters into such an agreement, it incurs an obligation. As the agency makes the required payments, it liquidates the obligation. Appropriation laws usually make funds available for obligation for one or more fiscal years but do not require agencies to spend their funds during those specific years. The actual outlays can occur years after the appropriation is obligated, as with a contract for construction of a submarine that may provide for payment to be made when it is delivered in the future. Such obligated funds are often said to be "in the pipeline." Under these circumstances, an agency's outlays in a particular year can come from appropriations obligated in previous years as well as from its current-year appropriation. Consequently, the money Congress appropriates for a fiscal year does not equal the total amount of appropriated money the government will actually spend in that year.

Off-Budget Entities — Specific federal entities whose budget authority, outlays and receipts are excluded by law from the calculation of budget totals, although they are part of government spending and income. As of early 2001, these included the Social Security trust funds (Federal Old-Age and Survivors Insurance Fund and the Federal Disability Insurance Trust Fund) and the Postal Service. Government-sponsored enterprises are also excluded from the budget because they are considered private rather than public organizations.

Office of Management and Budget (OMB) — A unit in the Executive Office of the President, reconstituted in 1970 from the former Bureau of the Budget. The Office of Management and Budget (OMB) assists the president in preparing the budget and in formulating the government's fiscal program. The OMB also plays a central role in supervising and controlling implementation of the budget, pursuant to provisions in appropriations laws, the Budget Enforcement Act and other statutes. In addition to these budgetary functions, the OMB has various management duties, including those performed through its three statutory offices: Federal Financial Management, Federal Procurement Policy and Information and Regulatory Affairs.

Officers of Congress — The Constitution refers to the Speaker of the House and the president of the Senate as officers and declares that each house "shall chuse" its "other Officers," but it does not name them or indicate how they should be selected. A House rule refers to its clerk, sergeant at arms and chaplain as officers. Officers are not named in the Senate's rules, but Riddick's Senate Procedure lists the president pro tempore, secretary of the Senate, sergeant at arms, chaplain and the secretaries for the majority and minority parties as officers. A few appointed officials are sometimes referred to as officers, including the parliamentarians and the legislative counsels. The House elects its officers by resolution at the beginning of each Congress. The Senate also elects its officers, but once elected Senate officers serve from Congress to Congress until their successors are chosen.

Omnibus Bill — A measure that combines the provisions of several disparate subjects into a single and often lengthy bill.

One-Minute Speeches — Addresses by House members that can be on any subject but are limited to one minute. They are usually permitted at the beginning of a daily session after the chaplain's prayer, the pledge of allegiance and approval of the *Journal*. They are a customary practice, not a right granted by rule. Consequently, recognition for one-minute speeches requires unanimous consent and is entirely within the Speaker's discretion. The Speaker sometimes refuses to permit them when the House has a heavy legislative schedule or limits or postpones them until a later time of the day.

Open Rule — A special rule from the House Rules Committee that permits members to offer as many floor amendments as they wish as long as the amendments are germane and do not violate other House rules.

Order of Business (House) — The sequence of events prescribed by a House rule during the meeting of the House on a new legislative day that is supposed to take place, also called the general order of business. The sequence consists of (1) the chaplain's prayer; (2) reading and approval of the *Journal*; (3) the pledge of allegiance; (4) correction of the reference of public bills to committee; (5) disposal of business on the Speaker's table; (6) unfinished business; (7) the morning hour call of committees and consideration of their bills; (8) motions to go into Committee of the Whole; and (9) orders of the day. In practice, the House never fully complies with this rule. Instead, the items of business that follow the pledge of allegiance are supplanted by any special

orders of business that are in order on that day (for example, conference reports; the corrections, discharge or private calendars; or motions to suspend the rules) and by other privileged business (for example, general appropriation bills and special rules) or measures made in order by special rules or unanimous consent. The regular order of business is also modified by unanimous consent practices and orders that govern recognition for one-minute speeches (which date from 1937) and for morning-hour debates, begun in 1994. By this combination of an order of business with privileged interruptions, the House gives precedence to certain categories of important legislation, brings to the floor other major legislation from its calendars in any order it chooses and provides expeditious processing for minor and noncontroversial measures.

Order of Business (Senate) — The sequence of events at the beginning of a new legislative day, as prescribed by Senate rules and standing orders. The sequence consists of (1) the chaplain's prayer; (2) the pledge of allegiance; (3) the designation of a temporary presiding officer if any; (4) *Journal* reading and approval; (5) recognition of the majority and minority leaders or their designees under the standing order; (6) morning business in the morning hour; (7) call of the calendar during the morning hour (largely obsolete); and (8) unfinished business from the previous session day.

Organization of Congress — The actions each house takes at the beginning of a Congress that are necessary to its operations. These include swearing in newly elected members, notifying the president that a quorum of each house is present, making committee assignments and fixing the hour for daily meetings. Because the House of Representatives is not a continuing body, it must also elect its Speaker and other officers and adopt its rules.

Original Bill — (1) A measure drafted by a committee and introduced by its chairman or another designated member when the committee reports the measure to its house. Unlike a clean bill, it is not referred back to the committee after introduction. The Senate permits all its legislative committees to report original bills. In the House, this authority is referred to in the rules as the "right to report at any time," and five committees (Appropriations, Budget, House Administration, Rules and Standards of Official Conduct) have such authority under circumstances specified in House Rule XIII, clause 5.

(2) In the House, special rules reported by the Rules Committee often propose that an amendment in the nature of a substitute be considered as an original bill for purposes

of amendment, meaning that the substitute, as with a bill, may be amended in two degrees. Without that requirement, the substitute may only be amended in one further degree. In the Senate, an amendment in the nature of a substitute automatically is open to two degrees of amendment, as is the original text of the bill, if the substitute is offered when no other amendment is pending.

Original Jurisdiction — The authority of certain committees to originate a measure and report it to the chamber. For example, general appropriation bills reported by the House Appropriations Committee are original bills, and special rules reported by the House Rules Committee are original resolutions.

Other Body — A commonly used reference to a house by a member of the other house. Congressional comity discourages members from directly naming the other house during debate.

Outlays — Amounts of government spending. They consist of payments, usually by check or in cash, to liquidate obligations incurred in prior fiscal years as well as in the current year, including the net lending of funds under budget authority. In federal budget accounting, net outlays are calculated by subtracting the amounts of refunds and various kinds of reimbursements to the government from actual spending.

Override a Veto — Congressional enactment of a measure over the president's veto. A veto override requires a recorded two-thirds vote of those voting in each house, a quorum being present. Because the president must return the vetoed measure to its house of origin, that house votes first, but neither house is required to attempt an override, whether immediately or at all. If an override attempt fails in the house of origin, the veto stands and the measure dies.

Oversight — Congressional review of the way in which federal agencies implement laws to ensure that they are carrying out the intent of Congress and to inquire into the efficiency of the implementation and the effectiveness of the law. The Legislative Reorganization Act of 1946 defined oversight as the function of exercising continuous watchfulness over the execution of the laws by the executive branch.

Oxford-Style Debate — The House held three Oxford-style debates in 1994, modeled after the famous debating format favored by the Oxford Union in Great Britain. Neither chamber has held Oxford-style debates since then. The Oxford-style debates aired nationally over C-SPAN television and National Public Radio. The organized event featured eight participants divided evenly into two teams, one team representing the Democrats (then holding the majority in the chamber) and the other the Republicans. Both teams argued a single question chosen well ahead of the event. A moderator regulated the debate, and began it by stating the resolution at issue. The order of the speakers alternated by team, with a debater for the affirmative speaking first and a debater for the opposing team offering a rebuttal. The rest of the speakers alternated in kind until all gained the chance to speak.

Parliamentarian — The official advisor to the presiding officer in each house on questions of procedure. The parliamentarian and his or her assistants also answer procedural questions from members and congressional staff, refer measures to committees on behalf of the presiding officer and maintain compilations of the precedents. The House parliamentarian revises the *House Manual* at the beginning of every Congress and usually reviews special rules before the Rules Committee reports them to the House. Either a parliamentarian or an assistant is always present and near the podium during sessions of each house.

Party Caucus — Generic term for each party's official organization in each house. Only House Democrats officially call their organization a caucus. House and Senate Republicans and Senate Democrats call their organizations conferences. The party caucuses elect their leaders, approve committee assignments and chairmanships (or ranking minority members, if the party is in the minority), establish party committees and study groups and discuss party and legislative policies. On rare occasions, they have stripped members of committee seniority or expelled them from the caucus for party disloyalty.

Pay-as-You-Go (PAYGO) — A provision first instituted under the Budget Enforcement Act of 1990 that applies to legislation enacted before Oct. 1, 2002. It requires that the cumulative effect of legislation concerning either revenues or direct spending should not result in a net negative impact on the budget. If legislation does provide for an increase in spending or decrease in revenues, that effect is supposed to be offset by legislated spending reductions or revenue increases. If Congress fails to enact the appropriate offsets, the act requires presidential sequestration of sufficient offsetting amounts in specific direct spending accounts. Congress and the president can circumvent this requirement if both agree that an emergency requires a particular action or if a law is enacted declaring that deteriorated economic circumstances make it necessary to suspend the requirement.

Permanent Appropriation — An appropriation that remains continuously available, without current action or renewal by Congress, under the terms of a previously enacted authorization or appropriation law. One such appropriation provides for payment of interest on the public debt and another the salaries of members of Congress.

Permanent Authorization — An authorization without a time limit. It usually does not specify any limit on the funds that may be appropriated for the agency, program or activity that it authorizes, leaving such amounts to the discretion of the appropriations committees and the two houses.

Permanent Staff — Term used formerly for committee staff authorized by law, who were funded through a permanent authorization and also called statutory staff. Most committees were authorized thirty permanent staff members. Most committees also were permitted additional staff, often called investigative staff, who were authorized by annual or biennial funding resolutions. The Senate eliminated the primary distinction between statutory and investigative staff in 1981. The House eliminated the distinction in 1995 by requiring that funding resolutions authorize money to hire both types of staff.

Personally Obnoxious (or Objectionable) — A characterization a senator sometimes applies to a president's nominee for a federal office in that senator's state to justify his or her opposition to the nomination.

Pocket Veto — The indirect veto of a bill as a result of the president withholding approval of it until after Congress has adjourned sine die. A bill the president does not sign but does not formally veto while Congress is in session automatically becomes a law ten days (excluding Sundays) after it is received. But if Congress adjourns its annual session during that ten-day period the measure dies even if the president does not formally veto it.

Point of Order — A parliamentary term used in committee and on the floor to object to an alleged violation of a rule and to demand that the chair enforce the rule. The point of order immediately halts the proceedings until the chair decides whether the contention is valid.

Pork or Pork Barrel Legislation — Pejorative terms for federal appropriations, bills or policies that provide funds to benefit a legislator's district or state, with the implication that the legislator presses for enactment of such benefits to ingratiate himself or herself with constituents rather than on the basis of an impartial, objective assessment of need or merit. The terms are often applied to such benefits

as new parks, post offices, dams, canals, bridges, roads, water projects, sewage treatment plants and public works of any kind, as well as demonstration projects, research grants and relocation of government facilities. Funds released by the president for various kinds of benefits or government contracts approved by him allegedly for political purposes are also sometimes referred to as pork.

Postcloture Filibuster — A filibuster conducted after the Senate invokes cloture. It employs an array of procedural tactics rather than lengthy speeches to delay final action. The Senate curtailed the postcloture filibuster's effectiveness by closing a variety of loopholes in the cloture rule in 1979 and 1986.

Power of the Purse — A reference to the constitutional power Congress has over legislation to raise revenue and appropriate monies from the Treasury. Article I, Section 8 states that Congress "shall have Power To lay and collect Taxes, Duties, Imposts and Excises, [and] to pay the Debts." Section 9 declares: "No Money shall be drawn from the Treasury, but in Consequence of Appropriations made by Law."

Preamble — Introductory language describing the reasons for and intent of a measure, sometimes called a whereas clause. It occasionally appears in joint, concurrent and simple resolutions but rarely in bills.

Precedent — A previous ruling on a parliamentary matter or a long-standing practice or custom of a house. Precedents serve to control arbitrary rulings and serve as the common law of a house.

President of the Senate — One constitutional role of the vice president is serving as the presiding officer of the Senate, or president of the Senate. The Constitution permits the vice president to cast a vote in the Senate only to break a tie, but the vice president is not required to do so.

President Pro Tempore — Under the Constitution, an officer elected by the Senate to preside over it during the absence of the vice president of the United States. Often referred to as the "pro tem," this senator is usually a member of the majority party with the longest continuous service in the chamber and also, by virtue of seniority, a committee chairman. When attending to committee and other duties the president pro tempore appoints other senators to preside.

Presiding Officer — In a formal meeting, the individual authorized to maintain order and decorum, recognize members to speak or offer motions and apply and interpret the chamber's rules, precedents and practices. The Speaker of the House and the president of the Senate are the chief presiding officers in their respective houses.

Previous Question — A nondebatable motion which, when agreed to by majority vote, usually cuts off further debate, prevents the offering of additional amendments and brings the pending matter to an immediate vote. It is a major debate-limiting device in the House; it is not permitted in Committee of the Whole in the House or in the Senate.

Private Bill — A bill that applies to one or more specified persons, corporations, institutions or other entities, usually to grant relief when no other legal remedy is available to them. Many private bills deal with claims against the federal government, immigration and naturalization cases and land titles.

Private Calendar — Commonly used title for a calendar in the House reserved for private bills and resolutions favorably reported by committees. The private calendar is officially called the Calendar of the Committee of the Whole House.

Private Law — A private bill enacted into law. Private laws are numbered in the same fashion as public laws.

Privilege — An attribute of a motion, measure, report, question or proposition that gives it priority status for consideration. Privileged motions and motions to bring up privileged questions are not debatable.

Privilege of the Floor — In addition to the members of a house, certain individuals are admitted to its floor while it is in session. The rules of the two houses differ somewhat but both extend the privilege to the president and vice president, Supreme Court justices, cabinet members, state governors, former members of that house, members of the other house, certain officers and officials of Congress, certain staff of that house in the discharge of official duties and the chamber's former parliamentarians. They also allow access to a limited number of committee and members' staff when their presence is necessary.

Pro Forma Amendment — In the House, an amendment that ostensibly proposes to change a measure or another amendment by moving "to strike the last word" or "to strike the requisite number of words." A member offers it not to make any actual change in the measure or amendment but only to obtain time for debate.

Pro Tem — A common reference to the president pro tempore of the Senate or, occasionally, to a Speaker pro tempore. (See President Pro Tempore; Speaker Pro Tempore.)

Procedures — The methods of conducting business in a deliberative body. The procedures of each house are governed first by applicable provisions of the Constitution, and then by its standing rules and orders, precedents, traditional practices and any statutory rules that apply to it. The authority of the houses to adopt rules in addition to those specified in the Constitution is derived from Article I, Section 5, clause 2, of the Constitution, which states: "Each House may determine the Rules of its Proceedings...." By rule, the House of Representatives also follows the procedures in *Jefferson's Manual* that are not inconsistent with its standing rules and orders. Many Senate procedures also conform with Jefferson's provisions, but by practice rather than by rule. At the beginning of each Congress, the House uses procedures in general parliamentary law until it adopts its standing rules.

Proxy Voting — The practice of permitting a member to cast the vote of an absent colleague in addition to his or her own vote. Proxy voting is prohibited on the floors of the House and Senate, but the Senate permits its committees to authorize proxy voting, and most do. In 1995, House rules were changed to prohibit proxy voting in committee.

Public Bill — A bill dealing with general legislative matters having national applicability or applying to the federal government or to a class of persons, groups or organizations.

Public Debt — Federal government debt incurred by the Treasury or the Federal Financing Bank by the sale of securities to the public or borrowings from a federal fund or account.

Public Law — A public bill or joint resolution enacted into law. It is cited by the letters "PL" followed by a hyphenated number. The digits before the hyphen indicate the number of the Congress in which it was enacted; the digits after the hyphen indicate its position in the numerical sequence of public measures that became law during that Congress. For example, the Budget Enforcement Act of 1990 became PL 101-508 because it was the 508th measure in that sequence for the 101st Congress. (See also Private Law.)

Qualification (of Members) — The Constitution requires members of the House of Representatives to be twenty-five years of age at the time their terms begin. They must have been citizens of the United States for seven years before that date and, when elected, must be "Inhabitant[s]" of the state from which they were elected. There is no constitutional requirement that they reside in the districts they represent. Senators are required to be thirty years of age at the time their terms begin. They must have been citizens of the United States for nine years before that date and, when elected, must be "Inhabitant[s]" of the states in which they were elected. The "Inhabitant" qualification is broadly interpreted, and in modern times a candidate's declaration of state residence has generally been accepted as meeting the constitutional requirement.

Queen of the Hill Rule — A special rule from the House Rules Committee that permits votes on a series of amendments, especially complete substitutes for a measure, in a specified order, but directs that the amendment receiving the greatest number of votes shall be the winning one. This kind of rule permits the House to vote directly on a variety of alternatives to a measure. In doing so, it sets aside the precedent that once an amendment has been adopted, no further amendments may be offered to the text it has amended. Under an earlier practice, the Rules Committee reported "king of the hill" rules under which there also could be votes on a series of amendments, again in a specified order. If more than one of the amendments was adopted under this kind of rule, it was the last amendment to receive a majority vote that was considered as having been finally adopted, whether or not it had received the greatest number of votes.

Quorum — The minimum number of members required to be present for the transaction of business. Under the Constitution, a quorum in each house is a majority of its members: 218 in the House and 51 in the Senate when there are no vacancies. By House rule, a quorum in Committee of the Whole is 100. In practice, both houses usually assume a quorum is present even if it is not, unless a member makes a point of no quorum in the House or suggests the absence of a quorum in the Senate. Consequently, each house transacts much of its business, and even passes bills, when only a few members are present. For House and Senate committees, chamber rules allow a minimum quorum of one-third of a committee's members to conduct most types of business.

Quorum Call — A procedure for determining whether a quorum is present in a chamber. In the Senate, a clerk calls the roll (roster) of senators. The House usually employs its electronic voting system.

Ramseyer Rule — A House rule that requires a committee's report on a bill or joint resolution to show the changes the measure, and any committee amendments to it, would make in existing law. The rule requires the report to present the text of any statutory provision that would be repealed and a comparative print showing, through typo-graphical devices such as stricken-through type or italics, other changes that would be made in existing law. The rule, adopted in 1929, is named after its sponsor, Rep. Christian W. Ramseyer, R-Iowa. The Senate's analogous rule is called the Cordon Rule.

Rank or Ranking — A member's position on the list of his or her party's members on a committee or subcommittee. When first assigned to a committee, a member is usually placed at the bottom of the list, then moves up as those above leave the committee. On subcommittees, however, a member's rank may not have anything to do with the length of his or her service on it.

Ranking Member — (1) Most often a reference to the minority member with the highest ranking on a committee or subcommittee. (2) A reference to the majority member next in rank to the chairman or to the highest ranking majority member present at a committee or subcommittee meeting.

Ratification — (1) The president's formal act of promulgating a treaty after the Senate has approved it. The resolution of ratification agreed to by the Senate is the procedural vehicle by which the Senate gives its consent to ratification. (2) A state legislature's act in approving a proposed constitutional amendment. Such an amendment becomes effective when ratified by three-fourths of the states.

Reapportionment — (See Apportionment.)

Recess — (1) A temporary interruption or suspension of a meeting of a chamber or committee. Unlike an adjournment, a recess does not end a legislative day. Because the Senate often recesses from one calendar day to another, its legislative day may extend over several calendar days, weeks or even months. (2) A period of adjournment for more than three days to a day certain, especially over a holiday or in August during odd-numbered years.

Recess Appointment — A presidential appointment to a vacant federal position made after the Senate has adjourned sine die or has adjourned or recessed for more than thirty days. If the president submits the recess appointee's nomination during the next session of the Senate, that individual can continue to serve until the end of the session even though the Senate might have rejected the nomination. When appointed to a vacancy that existed thirty days before the end of the last Senate session, a recess appointee is not paid until confirmed.

Recommit — To send a measure back to the committee that reported it; sometimes called a straight motion to recommit to distinguish it from a motion to recommit with instructions. A successful motion to recommit kills the measure unless it is accompanied by instructions.

Recommit a Conference Report — To return a conference report to the conference committee for renegotiation of some or all of its agreements. A motion to recommit may be offered with or without instructions.

Recommit with Instructions — To send a measure back to a committee with instructions to take some action on it. Invariably in the House and often in the Senate, when the motion recommits to a standing committee, the instructions require the committee to report the measure "forthwith" with specified amendments.

Reconciliation — A procedure for changing existing revenue and spending laws to bring total federal revenues and spending within the limits established in a budget resolution. Congress has applied reconciliation chiefly to revenues and mandatory spending programs, especially entitlements. Discretionary spending is controlled through annual appropriation bills.

Recorded Vote — (1) Generally, any vote in which members are recorded by name for or against a measure; also called a record vote or roll-call vote. The only recorded vote in the Senate is a vote by the yeas and nays and is commonly called a roll-call vote. (2) Technically, a recorded vote is one demanded in the House of Representatives and supported by at least one-fifth of a quorum (forty-four members) in the House sitting as the House or at least twenty-five members in Committee of the Whole.

Recorded Vote by Clerks — A voting procedure in the House where members pass through the appropriate "aye" or "no" aisle in the chamber and cast their votes by depositing a signed green (yea) or red (no) card in a ballot box. These votes are tabulated by clerks and reported to the chair. The electronic voting system is much more convenient and has largely supplanted this procedure. (See Committee of the Whole; Recorded Vote; Teller Vote.)

Redistricting — The redrawing of congressional district boundaries within a state after a decennial census. Redistricting may be required to equalize district populations or to accommodate an increase or decrease in the number of a state's House seats that might have resulted from the decennial apportionment. The state governments determine the district lines. (See Apportionment; Congressional District; Gerrymandering.)

Referral — The assignment of a measure to committee for consideration. Under a House rule, the Speaker can

refuse to refer a measure if the Speaker believes it is "of an obscene or insulting character."

Report — (1) As a verb, a committee is said to report when it submits a measure or other document to its parent chamber. (2) A clerk is said to report when he or she reads a measure's title, text or the text of an amendment to the body at the direction of the chair. (3) As a noun, a committee document that accompanies a reported measure. It describes the measure, the committee's views on it, its costs and the changes it proposes to make in existing law; it also includes certain impact statements. (4) A committee document submitted to its parent chamber that describes the results of an investigation or other study or provides information it is required to provide by rule or law.

Representative — An elected and duly sworn member of the House of Representatives who is entitled to vote in the chamber. The Constitution requires that a representative be at least twenty-five years old, a citizen of the United States for at least seven years and an inhabitant of the state from which he or she is elected. Customarily, the member resides in the district he or she represents. Representatives are elected in even-numbered years to two-year terms that begin the following January.

Reprimand — A formal condemnation of a member for misbehavior, considered a milder reproof than censure. The House of Representatives first used it in 1976. The Senate first used it in 1991. (See also Censure; Code of Official Conduct; Denounce; Ethics Rules; Expulsion; Seniority Loss.)

Rescission — A provision of law that repeals previously enacted budget authority in whole or in part. Under the Impoundment Control Act of 1974, the president can impound such funds by sending a message to Congress requesting one or more rescissions and the reasons for doing so. If Congress does not pass a rescission bill for the programs requested by the president within forty-five days of continuous session after receiving the message, the president must make the funds available for obligation and expenditure. If the president does not, the comptroller general of the United States is authorized to bring suit to compel the release of those funds. A rescission bill may rescind all, part or none of an amount proposed by the president, and may rescind funds the president has not impounded.

Reserving the Right To Object — Members' declaration that at some indefinite future time they may object to a unanimous consent request. It is an attempt to circumvent the requirement that members may prevent such an action only by objecting immediately after it is proposed.

Resident Commissioner from Puerto Rico — A non-voting member of the House of Representatives, elected to a four-year term. The resident commissioner has the same status and privileges as delegates. Like the delegates, the resident commissioner may not vote in the House or Committee of the Whole.

Resolution — (1) A simple resolution; that is, a non-legislative measure effective only in the house in which it is proposed and not requiring concurrence by the other chamber or approval by the president. Simple resolutions are designated H. Res. in the House and S. Res. in the Senate. Simple resolutions express nonbinding opinions on policies or issues or deal with the internal affairs or prerogatives of a house. (2) Any type of resolution: simple, concurrent or joint. (See Concurrent Resolution; Joint Resolution.)

Resolution of Inquiry — A resolution usually simple rather than concurrent calling on the president or the head of an executive agency to provide specific information or papers to one or both houses.

Resolution of Ratification — The Senate vehicle for agreeing to a treaty. The constitutionally mandated vote of two-thirds of the senators present and voting applies to the adoption of this resolution. However, it may also contain amendments, reservations, declarations or understandings that the Senate had previously added to it by majority vote.

Revenue Legislation — Measures that levy new taxes or tariffs or change existing ones. Under Article I, Section 7, clause 1 of the Constitution, the House of Representatives originates federal revenue measures, but the Senate can propose amendments to them. The House Ways and Means Committee and the Senate Finance Committee have jurisdiction over such measures, with a few minor exceptions.

Revise and Extend One's Remarks — A unanimous consent request to publish in the *Congressional Record* a statement a member did not deliver on the floor, a longer statement than the one made on the floor or miscellaneous extraneous material.

Revolving Fund — A trust fund or account whose income remains available to finance its continuing operations without any fiscal year limitation.

Rider — Congressional slang for an amendment unrelated or extraneous to the subject matter of the measure to which it is attached. Riders often contain proposals that are less likely to become law on their own merits as separate bills, either because of opposition in the committee of juris-diction, resistance in the other house or the probability of a presidential veto. Riders are more common in the Senate.

Roll Call — A call of the roll to determine whether a quorum is present, to establish a quorum or to vote on a question. Usually, the House uses its electronic voting system for a roll call. The Senate does not have an electronic voting system; its roll is always called by a clerk.

Rule — (1) A permanent regulation that a house adopts to govern its conduct of business, its procedures, its internal organization, behavior of its members, regulation of its facilities, duties of an officer or some other subject it chooses to govern in that form. (2) In the House, a privileged simple resolution reported by the Rules Committee that provides methods and conditions for floor consideration of a measure or, rarely, several measures.

Rule Twenty-Two — A common reference to the Senate's cloture rule. (See Cloture)

Second-Degree Amendment — An amendment to an amendment in the first degree. It is usually a perfecting amendment.

Secretary of the Senate — The chief financial, administrative and legislative officer of the Senate. Elected by resolution or order of the Senate, the secretary is invariably the candidate of the majority party and usually chosen by the majority leader. In the absence of the vice president and pending the election of a president pro tempore, the secretary presides over the Senate. The secretary is subject to policy direction and oversight by the Senate Committee on Rules and Administration. The secretary manages a wide range of functions that support the administrative operations of the Senate as an organization as well as those functions necessary to its legislative process, including record keeping, document management, certifications, housekeeping services, administration of oaths and lobbyist registrations. The secretary is responsible for accounting for all funds appropriated to the Senate and conducts audits of Senate financial activities. On a semiannual basis the secretary issues the Report of the Secretary of the Senate, a compilation of Senate expenditures.

Section — A subdivision of a bill or statute. By law, a section must be numbered and, as nearly as possible, contain "a single proposition of enactment."

Select or Special Committee — A committee established by a resolution in either house for a special purpose and, usually, for a limited time. Most select and special committees are assigned specific investigations or studies but are not authorized to report measures to their chambers.

However, both houses have created several permanent select and special committees and have given legislative reporting authority to a few of them: the Ethics Committee in the Senate and the Intelligence Committees in both houses. There is no substantive difference between a select and a special committee; they are so called depending simply on whether the resolution creating the committee calls it one or the other.

Senate — The house of Congress in which each state is represented by two senators; each senator has one vote. Article V of the Constitution declares that "No State, without its Consent, shall be deprived of its equal Suffrage in the Senate." The Constitution also gives the Senate equal legislative power with the House of Representatives. Although the Senate is prohibited from originating revenue measures, and as a matter of practice it does not originate appropriation measures, it can amend both. Only the Senate can give or withhold consent to treaties and nominations from the president. It also acts as a court to try impeachments by the House and elects the vice president when no candidate receives a majority of the electoral votes. It is often referred to as "the upper body," but not by members of the House.

Senate Manual — The handbook of the Senate's standing rules and orders and the laws and other regulations that apply to the Senate, usually published once each Congress.

Senator — A duly sworn elected or appointed member of the Senate. The Constitution requires that a senator be at least thirty years old, a citizen of the United States for at least nine years and an inhabitant of the state from which he or she is elected. Senators are usually elected in even-numbered years to six-year terms that begin the following January. When a vacancy occurs before the end of a term, the state governor can appoint a replacement to fill the position until a successor is chosen at the state's next general election or, if specified under state law, the next feasible date for such an election, to serve the remainder of the term. Until the Seventeenth Amendment was ratified in 1913, senators were chosen by their state legislatures.

Senatorial Courtesy — The Senate's practice of declining to confirm a presidential nominee for an office in the state of a senator of the president's party unless that senator approves.

Seniority — The priority, precedence or status accorded members according to the length of their continuous service in a house or on a committee.

Seniority Loss — A type of punishment that reduces a member's seniority on his or her committees, including the

loss of chairmanships. Party caucuses in both houses have occasionally imposed such punishment on their members, for example, for publicly supporting candidates of the other party.

Seniority Rule — The customary practice, rather than a rule, of assigning the chairmanship of a committee to the majority party member who has served on the committee for the longest continuous period of time.

Seniority System — A collection of long-standing customary practices under which members with longer continuous service than their colleagues in their house or on their committees receive various kinds of preferential treatment. Although some of the practices are no longer as rigidly observed as in the past, they still pervade the organization and procedures of Congress.

Sequestration — A procedure for canceling budgetary resources — that is, money available for obligation or spending — to enforce budget limitations established in law. Sequestered funds are no longer available for obligation or expenditure.

Sergeant at Arms — The officer in each house responsible for maintaining order, security and decorum in its wing of the Capitol, including the chamber and its galleries. Although elected by their respective houses, both sergeants at arms are invariably the candidates of the majority party.

Session — (1) The annual series of meetings of a Congress. Under the Constitution, Congress must assemble at least once a year at noon on Jan. 3 unless it appoints a different day by law. (2) The special meetings of Congress or of one house convened by the president, called a special session. (3) A house is said to be in session during the period of a day when it is meeting.

Severability (or Separability) Clause — Language stating that if any particular provisions of a measure are declared invalid by the courts the remaining provisions shall remain in effect.

Sine Die — Without fixing a day for a future meeting. An adjournment sine die signifies the end of an annual or special session of Congress.

Slip Law — The first official publication of a measure that has become law. It is published separately in unbound, single-sheet form or pamphlet form. A slip law usually is available two or three days after the date of the law's enactment.

Speaker — The presiding officer of the House of Representatives and the leader of its majority party. The Speaker is selected by the majority party and formally elected by the House at the beginning of each Congress. Although the Constitution does not require the Speaker to be a member of the House, in fact, all Speakers have been members.

Speaker Pro Tempore — A member of the House who is designated as the temporary presiding officer by the Speaker or elected by the House to that position during the Speaker's absence.

Speaker's Vote — The Speaker is not required to vote, and the Speaker's name is not called on a roll-call vote unless so requested. Usually, the Speaker votes either to create a tie vote, and thereby defeat a proposal or to break a tie in favor of a proposal. Occasionally, the Speaker also votes to emphasize the importance of a matter.

Special Session — A session of Congress convened by the president, under his constitutional authority, after Congress has adjourned sine die at the end of a regular session. (See Adjournment *Sine Die*; Session.)

Spending Authority — The technical term for backdoor spending. The Congressional Budget Act of 1974 defines it as borrowing authority, contract authority and entitlement authority for which appropriation acts do not provide budget authority in advance. Under the Budget Act, legislation that provides new spending authority may not be considered unless it provides that the authority shall be effective only to the extent or in such amounts as provided in an appropriation act.

Spending Cap — The statutory limit for a fiscal year on the amount of new budget authority and outlays allowed for discretionary spending. The Budget Enforcement Act of 1997 requires a sequester if the cap is exceeded.

Split Referral — A measure divided into two or more parts, with each part referred to a different committee.

Sponsor — The principal proponent and introducer of a measure or an amendment.

Staff Director — The most frequently used title for the head of staff of a committee or subcommittee. On some committees, that person is called chief of staff, clerk, chief clerk, chief counsel, general counsel or executive director. The head of a committee's minority staff is usually called minority staff director.

Standing Committee — A permanent committee established by a House or Senate standing rule or standing order. The rule also describes the subject areas on which the committee may report bills and resolutions and conduct oversight. Most introduced measures must be referred to one or more standing committees according to their jurisdictions.

Standing Order — A continuing regulation or directive that has the force and effect of a rule, but is not incorporated into the standing rules. The Senate's numerous standing orders, like its standing rules, continue from Congress to Congress unless changed or the order states otherwise. The House uses relatively few standing orders, and those it adopts expire at the end of a session of Congress.

Standing Rules — The rules of the Senate that continue from one Congress to the next and the rules of the House of Representatives that it adopts at the beginning of each new Congress.

Standing Vote — An alternative and informal term for a division vote, during which members in favor of a proposal and then members opposed stand and are counted by the chair.

Star Print — A reprint of a bill, resolution, amendment or committee report correcting technical or substantive errors in a previous printing; so called because of the small black star that appears on the front page or cover.

State of the Union Message — A presidential message to Congress under the constitutional directive that the president shall "from time to time give to the Congress Information of the State of the Union, and recommend to their Consideration such Measures as he shall judge necessary and expedient." Customarily, the president sends an annual State of the Union message to Congress, usually late in January.

Statutes at Large — A chronological arrangement of the laws enacted in each session of Congress. Though indexed, the laws are not arranged by subject matter nor is there an indication of how they affect or change previously enacted laws. The volumes are numbered by Congress, and the laws are cited by their volume and page number. The Gramm-Rudman-Hollings Act, for example, appears as 99 Stat. 1037.

Straw Vote Prohibition — Under a House precedent, a member who has the floor during debate may not conduct a straw vote or otherwise ask for a show of support for a proposition. Only the chair may put a question to a vote.

Strike From the *Record* — Expunge objectionable remarks from the *Congressional Record*, after a member's words have been taken down on a point of order.

Subcommittee — A panel of committee members assigned a portion of the committee's jurisdiction or other functions. On legislative committees, subcommittees hold hearings, mark up legislation and report measures to their full committee for further action; they cannot report directly to the chamber. A subcommittee's party composition usually reflects the ratio on its parent committee.

Subpoena Power — The authority granted to committees by the rules of their respective houses to issue legal orders requiring individuals to appear and testify, or to produce documents pertinent to the committee's functions, or both. Persons who do not comply with subpoenas can be cited for contempt of Congress and prosecuted.

Subsidy — Generally, a payment or benefit made by the federal government for which no current repayment is required. Subsidy payments may be designed to support the conduct of an economic enterprise or activity, such as ship operations, or to support certain market prices, as in the case of farm subsidies.

Sunset Legislation — A term sometimes applied to laws authorizing the existence of agencies or programs that expire annually or at the end of some other specified period of time. One of the purposes of setting specific expiration dates for agencies and programs is to encourage the committees with jurisdiction over them to determine whether they should be continued or terminated.

Sunshine Rules — Rules requiring open committee hearings and business meetings, including markup sessions, in both houses, and also open conference committee meetings. However, all may be closed under certain circumstances and using certain procedures required by the rules.

Supermajority — A term sometimes used for a vote on a matter that requires approval by more than a simple majority of those members present and voting; also referred to as extraordinary majority.

Supplemental Appropriation Bill — A measure providing appropriations for use in the current fiscal year, in addition to those already provided in annual general appropriation bills. Supplemental appropriations are often for unforeseen emergencies.

Suspension of the Rules (House) — An expeditious procedure for passing relatively noncontroversial or emergency measures by a two-thirds vote of those members voting, a quorum being present.

Suspension of the Rules (Senate) — A procedure to set aside one or more of the Senate's rules; it is used infrequently, and then most often to suspend the rule banning legislative amendments to appropriation bills.

Task Force — A title sometimes given to a panel of members assigned to a special project, study or investigation. Ordinarily, these groups do not have authority to report measures to their respective houses.

Tax Expenditure — Loosely, a tax exemption or advantage, sometimes called an incentive or loophole; technically, a loss of governmental tax revenue attributable to some provision of federal tax laws that allows a special exclusion, exemption or deduction from gross income or that provides a special credit, preferential tax rate or deferral of tax liability.

Televised Proceedings — Television and radio coverage of the floor proceedings of the House of Representatives has been available since 1979 and of the Senate since 1986. They are broadcast over a coaxial cable system to all congressional offices and to some congressional agencies on channels reserved for that purpose. Coverage is also available free of charge to commercial and public television and radio broadcasters. The Cable-Satellite Public Affairs Network (C-SPAN) carries gavel-to-gavel coverage of both houses.

Teller Vote — A voting procedure, formerly used in the House, in which members cast their votes by passing through the center aisle to be counted, but not recorded by name, by a member from each party appointed by the chair. The House deleted the procedure from its rules in 1993, but during floor discussion of the deletion a leading member stated that a teller vote would still be available in the event of a breakdown of the electronic voting system.

Third-Degree Amendment — An amendment to a second-degree amendment. Both houses prohibit such amendments.

Third Reading — A required reading to a chamber of a bill or joint resolution by title only before the vote on passage. In modern practice, it has merely become a pro forma step.

Three-Day Rule — (1) In the House, a measure cannot be considered until the third calendar day on which the committee report has been available. (2) In the House, a conference report cannot be considered until the third calendar day on which its text has been available in the *Congressional Record*. (3) In the House, a general appropriation bill cannot be considered until the third calendar day on which printed hearings on the bill have been available. (4) In the Senate, when a committee votes to report a measure, a committee member is entitled to three calendar days within which to submit separate views for inclusion in the committee report. (In House committees, a member is entitled to two calendar days for this purpose, after the day on which the committee votes to report.) (5) In both houses, a majority of a committee's members may call a special meeting of the committee if its chairman fails to do so within three calendar days after three or more of the members, acting jointly, formally request such a meeting.

In calculating such periods, the House omits holiday and weekend days on which it does not meet. The Senate makes no such exclusion.

Tie Vote — When the votes for and against a proposition are equal, it loses. The president of the Senate may cast a vote only to break a tie. Because the Speaker is invariably a member of the House, the Speaker is entitled to vote but usually does not. The Speaker may choose to do so to break, or create, a tie vote.

Title — (1) A major subdivision of a bill or act, designated by a roman numeral and usually containing legislative provisions on the same general subject. Titles are sometimes divided into subtitles as well as sections. (2) The official name of a bill or act, also called a caption or long title. (3) Some bills also have short titles that appear in the sentence immediately following the enacting clause. (4) Popular titles are the unofficial names given to some bills or acts by common usage. For example, the Balanced Budget and Emergency Deficit Control Act of 1985 (short title) is almost invariably referred to as Gramm-Rudman (popular title). In other cases, significant legislation is popularly referred to by its title number (see definition (1) above). For example, the federal legislation that requires equality of funding for women's and men's sports in educational institutions that receive federal funds is popularly called Title IX.

Track System — An occasional Senate practice that expedites legislation by dividing a day's session into two or more specific time periods, commonly called tracks, each reserved for consideration of a different measure.

Transfer Payment — A federal government payment to which individuals or organizations are entitled under law and for which no goods or services are required in return. Payments include welfare and Social Security benefits, unemployment insurance, government pensions and veterans benefits.

Treaty — A formal document containing an agreement between two or more sovereign nations. The Constitution authorizes the president to make treaties, but the president must submit them to the Senate for its approval by a two-thirds vote of the senators present. Under the Senate's rules, that vote actually occurs on a resolution of ratification. Although the Constitution does not give the House a direct role in approving treaties, that body has sometimes insisted that a revenue treaty is an invasion of its prerogatives. In any case, the House may significantly affect the application of a treaty by its equal role in enacting legislation to implement the treaty.

Trust Funds — Special accounts in the Treasury that receive earmarked taxes or other kinds of revenue collections, such as user fees, and from which payments are made for special purposes or to recipients who meet the requirements of the trust funds as established by law. Of the more than 150 federal government trust funds, several finance major entitlement programs, such as Social Security, Medicare and retired federal employees' pensions. Others fund infrastructure construction and improvements, such as highways and airports.

Unanimous Consent — Without an objection by any member. A unanimous consent request asks permission, explicitly or implicitly, to set aside one or more rules. Both houses and their committees frequently use such requests to expedite their proceedings.

Uncontrollable Expenditures — A frequently used term for federal expenditures that are mandatory under existing law and therefore cannot be controlled by the president or Congress without a change in the existing law. Uncontrollable expenditures include spending required under entitlement programs and also fixed costs, such as interest on the public debt and outlays to pay for prior-year obligations. In recent years, uncontrollables have accounted for approximately three-quarters of federal spending in each fiscal year.

Unfunded Mandate — Generally, any provision in federal law or regulation that imposes a duty or obligation on a state or local government or private sector entity without providing the necessary funds to comply. The Unfunded Mandates Reform Act of 1995 amended the Congressional Budget Act of 1974 to provide a mechanism for the control of new unfunded mandates.

Union Calendar — A calendar of the House of Representatives for bills and resolutions favorably reported by committees that raise revenue or directly or indirectly appropriate money or property. In addition to appropriation bills, measures that authorize expenditures are also placed on this calendar. The calendar's full title is the Calendar of the Committee of the Whole House on the State of the Union.

Upper Body — A common reference to the Senate, but not used by members of the House.

U.S. Code — Popular title for the United States Code: Containing the General and Permanent Laws of the United States in Force on.... It is a consolidation and partial codification of the general and permanent laws of the United

States arranged by subject under 50 titles. The first six titles deal with general or political subjects, the other forty-four with subjects ranging from agriculture to war, alphabetically arranged. A supplement is published after each session of Congress, and the entire Code is revised every six years.

User Fee — A fee charged to users of goods or services provided by the federal government. When Congress levies or authorizes such fees, it determines whether the revenues should go into the general collections of the Treasury or be available for expenditure by the agency that provides the goods or services.

Veto — The president's disapproval of a legislative measure passed by Congress. The president returns the measure to the house in which it originated without his signature but with a veto message stating his objections to it. When Congress is in session, the president must veto a bill within ten days, excluding Sundays, after the president has received it; otherwise it becomes law without his signature. The ten-day clock begins to run at midnight following his receipt of the bill. (See also Committee Veto; Item Veto; Line Item Veto Act of 1996; Override a Veto; Pocket Veto.)

Voice Vote — A method of voting in which members who favor a question answer aye in chorus, after which those opposed answer no in chorus, and the chair decides which position prevails.

Voting — Members vote in three ways on the floor: (1) by shouting "aye" or "no" on voice votes; (2) by standing for or against on division votes; and (3) on recorded votes (including the yeas and nays), by answering "aye" or "no" when their names are called or, in the House, by recording their votes through the electronic voting system.

War Powers Resolution of 1973 — An act that requires the president "in every possible instance" to consult Congress before committing U.S. forces to ongoing or imminent hostilities. If the president commits them to a combat situation without congressional consultation, the president must notify Congress within forty-eight hours. Unless Congress declares war or otherwise authorizes the operation to continue, the forces must be withdrawn within sixty or ninety days, depending on certain conditions. No president has ever acknowledged the constitutionality of the resolution.

Well — The sunken, level, open space between members' seats and the podium at the front of each chamber. House members usually address their chamber from their party's lectern in the well on its side of the aisle. Senators usually speak at their assigned desks.

Whip — The majority or minority party member in each house who acts as assistant leader, helps plan and marshal support for party strategies, encourages party discipline and advises his or her leader on how colleagues intend to vote on the floor. In the Senate, the Republican whip's official title is assistant leader.

Yeas and Nays — A vote in which members usually respond "aye" or "no" (despite the official title of the vote) on a question when their names are called in alphabetical order. The Constitution requires the yeas and nays when a demand for it is supported by one-fifth of the members present, and it also requires an automatic yea-and-nay vote on overriding a veto. Senate precedents require the support of at least one-fifth of a quorum, a minimum of eleven members with the present membership of 100.

Congressional Information on the Internet

A huge array of congressional information is available for free at Internet sites operated by the federal government, colleges and universities and commercial firms. The sites offer the full text of bills introduced in the House and Senate, voting records, campaign finance information, transcripts of selected congressional hearings, investigative reports and much more.

THOMAS

The most important site for congressional information is THOMAS (*http://thomas.loc.gov*), which is named for Thomas Jefferson and operated by the Library of Congress. THOMAS' highlight is its databases containing the full text of all bills introduced in Congress since 1989, the full text of the *Congressional Record* since 1989 and the status and summary information for all bills introduced since 1973.

THOMAS also offers special links to bills that have received or are expected to receive floor action during the current week and newsworthy bills that are pending or that have recently been approved. Finally, THOMAS has selected committee reports, answers to frequently asked questions about accessing congressional information, publications titled *How Our Laws Are Made* and *Enactment of a Law* and links to lots of other congressional Web sites.

HOUSE OF REPRESENTATIVES

The U.S. House of Representatives site (*http://www.house. gov*) offers the schedule of bills, resolutions and other legislative issues the House will consider in the current week. It also has updates about current proceedings on the House floor and a list of the next day's meeting of House committees. Other highlights include a database that helps users identify their representative, a directory of House members and committees, the House ethics manual, links to Web pages maintained by House members and committees, a calendar of congressional primary dates and candidate-filing deadlines for ballot access, the full text of all amendments to the Constitution that have been ratified and those that have been proposed but not ratified and lots of information about Washington, D.C., for visitors.

Another key House site is The Office of the Clerk On-line Information Center *(http://clerk.house.gov)*, which has records of all roll-call votes taken since 1990. The votes are recorded by bill, so it is a lengthy process to compile a particular representative's voting record. The site also has lists of committee assignments, a telephone directory for members and committees, mailing label templates for members and committees, rules of the current Congress, election statistics from 1920 to the present, biographies of Speakers of the House, biographies of women who have served since 1917 and a virtual tour of the House Chamber.

One of the more interesting House sites is operated by the Subcommittee on Rules and Organization of the House Committee on Rules *(http://www.house.gov/rules/ crs_reports. htm)*. Its highlight is dozens of Congressional Research Service reports about the legislative process. Some of the available titles include *Legislative Research in Congressional Offices: A Primer, How to Follow Current Federal Legislation and Regulations; Investigative Oversight: An Introduction to the Law, Practice and Procedure of Congressional Inquiry;* and *Presidential Vetoes 1789 – Present: A Summary Overview.*

SENATE

At least in the Internet world, the Senate is not as active as the House. Its main Web site *(http://www.senate.gov)* has records of all roll-call votes taken since 1989 (arranged by bill), brief descriptions of all bills and joint resolutions introduced in the Senate during the past week and a calendar of upcoming committee hearings. The site also provides the standing rules of the Senate, a directory of senators and their committee assignments, lists of nominations that the president has submitted to the Senate for approval, links to Web pages operated by senators and committees and a virtual tour of the Senate.

Information about the membership, jurisdiction and rules of each congressional committee is available at the U.S. Government Printing Office site *(http://www.access. gpo.gov/congress/ index.html)*. It also has transcripts of selected congressional hearings, the full text of selected House and Senate reports and the House and Senate rules manuals.

GENERAL REFERENCE

The Government Accountability Office, the investigative arm of Congress, operates a site *(http://www.gao. gov)* that provides the full text of its reports from 1975 to the present. The reports cover a wide range of topics: aviation safety, combating terrorism, counternarcotics efforts in Mexico, defense contracting, electronic warfare, food assistance programs, Gulf War illness, health insurance, illegal aliens, information technology, long-term care, mass transit, Medicare, military readiness, money laundering, national parks, nuclear waste, organ donation and student loan defaults, among others.

The GAO Daybook is an excellent current awareness tool. This electronic mailing list distributes a daily list of reports and testimony released by the GAO. Subscriptions are available by sending an e-mail message to *majordomo@www.gao.gov,* and in the message area typing "subscribe daybook" (without the quotation marks).

Current budget and economic projections are provided at the Congressional Budget Office Web site *(http://www.cbo.gov)*. The site also has reports about the economic and budget outlook for the next decade, the president's budget proposals, federal civilian employment, Social Security privatization, tax reform, water use conflicts in the West, marriage and the federal income tax and the role of foreign aid in development, among other topics. Other highlights include monthly budget updates, historical budget data, cost estimates for bills reported by congressional committees and transcripts of congressional testimony by CBO officials.

CAMPAIGN FINANCE

Several Internet sites provide detailed campaign finance data for congressional elections. The official site is operated by the Federal Election Commission *(http://www. fec.gov)*, which regulates political spending. The site's highlight is its database of campaign reports filed from

May 1996 to the present by House and presidential candidates, political action committees and political party committees. Senate reports are not included because they are filed with the Secretary of the Senate. The reports in the FEC's database are scanned images of paper reports filed with the commission.

The FEC site also has summary financial data for House and Senate candidates in the current election cycle, abstracts of court decisions pertaining to federal election law from 1976 to 1997, a graph showing the number of political action committees in existence each year from 1974 to the present and a directory of national and state agencies that are responsible for releasing information about campaign financing, candidates on the ballot, election results, lobbying and other issues. Another useful feature is a collection of brochures about federal election law, public funding of presidential elections, the ban on contributions by foreign nationals, independent expenditures supporting or opposing a candidate for federal office, contribution limits, filing a complaint, researching public records at the FEC and other topics. Finally, the site provides the FEC's legislative recommendations, its annual report, a report about its first twenty years in existence, the FEC's monthly newsletter, several reports about voter registration, election results for the most recent presidential and congressional elections and campaign guides for corporations and labor organizations, congressional candidates and committees, political party committees and nonconnected committees.

The best online source for campaign finance data is Political Money Line *(http://www.tray.com)*. The site's searchable databases provide extensive itemized information about receipts and expenditures by federal candidates and political action committees from 1980 to the present. The data, which are obtained from the FEC, are quite detailed. For example, for candidates contributions can be searched by Zip Code. The site also has lists of the top political action committees in various categories, lists of the top contributors from each state and much more.

Another interesting site is the American University Campaign Finance Web site *(http://www1.soc.american.edu/campfin/index.cfm)*, which is operated by the American University School of Communication. It provides electronic files from the FEC that have been reformatted in .dbf format so they can be used in database programs such as Paradox, Access and FoxPro. The files contain data on PAC, committee and individual contributions to individual congressional candidates.

More campaign finance data is available from the Center for Responsive Politics *(http://www.opensecrets.org)*, a public interest organization. The center provides a list of all "soft money" donations to political parties of $100,000 or more in the current election cycle and data about "leadership" political action committees associated with individual politicians. Other databases at the site provide information about travel expenses that House members received from private sources for attending meetings and other events, activities of registered federal lobbyists and activities of foreign agents who are registered in the United States.

Index

Boxes are indicated by "b" following the page number.